# CHILDREN'S DAILY PRAYER

## for the School Year 2010–2011

Mary Caswell Walsh

In accordance with c. 827, permission to publish is granted on January 29, 2010, by Very Reverend John F. Canary, Vicar General of the Archdiocese of Chicago. Permission to publish is an official declaration of ecclesiastical authority that the material is free from doctrinal and moral error. No legal responsibility is assumed by the grant of this permission.

The Scripture quotations are from the New Revised Standard Version Bible: Catholic Edition, copyright © 1993 and 1989 by the National Council of the Churches of Christ in the U.S.A. Used by permission. All rights reserved.

The English translation of the Conclusion for Morning and Evening Prayer from *The Liturgy of the Hours* © 1973, 1974, 1975, International Committee on English in the Liturgy, Inc. (ICEL); the English translation of Introduction and Conclusion to the Gospel, the Litany of Saints, and the Introduction to the Easter Vigil from *The Roman Missal* © 1973, ICEL; the English translation of Prayer of the Penitent from *Rite of Penance* © 1974, ICEL. All rights reserved.

Blessing prayer for birthdays adapted from *Book of Blessings,* additional blessings for use in the United States of America, © 1968, United States Conference of Catholic Bishops, Washington, DC. Used with permission.

Many of the concepts and guidelines, as well as various prayer services offered in this book, were originally conceived and developed by Dr. Sofia Cavalletti, Ms. Gianna Gobbi, and their collaborators. Theological underpinnings and many elements of these prayer services were first documented in Cavalletti's foundational books including: *The Religious Potential of the Child* and *The Religious Potential of the Child Age 6–12.*

Liturgy Training Publications acknowledges the significant contribution made by Elizabeth McMahon Jeep to the development of *Children's Daily Prayer.* Ms. Jeep worked tirelessly for more than 15 years to help this resource become the essential annual prayer resource for children and their parents, teachers, and catechists. We are indebted to her for her authorship and guidance.

CHILDREN'S DAILY PRAYER 2010–2011, copyright © 2010 Archdiocese of Chicago: Liturgy Training Publications, 3949 South Racine Avenue, Chicago IL 60609. All rights reserved.
Order phone: 1-800-933-1800
Editorial phone: 1-773-579-4900
Fax: 1-800-933-7094
E-mail: orders@ltp.org
Internet: www.LTP.org

LTP prints the text of *Children's Daily Prayer 2010–2011* with ink that contains renewable linseed oil on paper that is 100% recycled and contains a minimum of 40% postconsumer waste. ♻ Although many de-inking processes use highly toxic bleach, this paper was processed using PCF (Processed Chlorine Free) technologies. The printing process used to manufacture this book is a non-heatset process that significantly reduces emission of volatile organic compounds (VOCs) into the atmosphere.

LTP continues to work toward responsible stewardship of the environment. For more information on our efforts, please go to www.LTP.org/environment.

CHILDREN'S DAILY PRAYER was illustrated by Paula Wiggins. The book was edited by Lorie Simmons. The design is by M. Urgo. The book was typeset by Mark Hollopeter in Sabon and Kabel and printed in the United States of America.

ISBN 978-1-56854-872-2
CDP11

# INSTRUCTIONS FOR PRAYER FOR THE DAY AND WEEK

## FOR THE WHOLE GROUP

*Amen* means: "Yes! I believe it is true!" Let your "Amen," be heard by all.

The Gospel reader always begins with, "A reading from the holy Gospel according to. . ." The group responds, "Glory to you, O Lord." When the reading ends, the reader says, "The Gospel of the Lord." Everyone responds, "Praise to you, Lord Jesus Christ."

## FOR THE LEADER

1. Find the correct page and read it silently. Parts in bold black type are for everyone. All others are for you alone.

2. Practice reading your part aloud, and pronounce every syllable clearly. The parts marked with ◆ and ✛ are instructions for what to do. Follow the instructions but do not read them or the headings aloud. If you stumble over a word, repeat it until you can say it smoothly.

3. Pause after "A reading from the holy Gospel according to. . ." so the class can respond. Pause again after "The Gospel of the Lord." Remember to allow for silence when the instructions call for it, especially after the Gospel and after reading the questions "For Silent Reflection."

4. Pause after "Let us bring our hopes and needs to God . . ." so that individuals may offer their prayers aloud or in silence. After each petition, the group responds, "Lord, hear our prayer."

5. When you make the Sign of the Cross, use your right hand and do it slowly and reverently, first touching your forehead ("In the name of the Father"), next just below your chest ("and of the Son"), then your left shoulder ("and of the Holy Spirit"), and finally your right shoulder ("Amen").

6. At prayer time, stand in the front of the class straight and tall. Ask the class to use their sheet of psalm responses for reading their part. Read slowly and clearly.

## IF THERE ARE TWO LEADERS

One leader reads the Gospel while the other reads all of the other parts. Practice reading your part(s). Both leaders should stand in front of the class during the entire prayer.

Remember to read very slowly, with a loud, clear voice.

# CONTENTS

| | |
|---|---|
| Instructions | iii |
| Introduction | vi–x |
| Reproducible Psalm Responses | xi–xvi |

## ORDINARY TIME, AUTUMN

| | |
|---|---|
| About the Season | 2–3 |
| Grace before Meals and Prayer at Day's End | 4, 5 |
| Prayer Service: Beginning of School for Staff | 6–7 |
| Prayer Service: Beginning of School for Students | 8–9 |
| Prayer Service: for Peace on September 11 | 40 |
| Prayer Service: Our Lady of the Rosary, October 7 | 64–65 |
| Prayer Service: All Saints Day, November 1 | 86–87 |
| Prayer Service: Thanksgiving | 110–111 |
| Home Prayer: Morning Prayer for Families Departing for the Day | 10 |
| Home Prayer: Celebrating the Saints, Remembering the Dead | 85 |
| Home Prayer: Meal Prayer for Thanksgiving | 112 |
| Home Prayer: Gathering around an Advent Wreath for Prayer | 113 |
| Prayer for the Day and Week | 11–114 |

## ADVENT

| | |
|---|---|
| About the Season | 116–117 |
| Grace before Meals and Prayer for Day's End | 118, 119 |
| Prayer Service: Advent | 120–121 |
| Prayer Service: Solemnity of the Immaculate Conception, December 8 | 131–132 |
| Home Prayer: Gathering around a Nativity Scene for Prayer | 135 |
| Prayer for the Day and Week | 122–142 |

## CHRISTMAS

| | |
|---|---|
| About the Season | 144–145 |
| Grace before Meals and Prayer for Day's End | 146, 147 |
| Prayer Service: Epiphany | 148–149 |
| Prayer for the Day and Week | 150–156 |

## ORDINARY TIME, WINTER

| | |
|---|---|
| About the Season | 158–159 |
| Grace before Meals and Prayer for Day's End | 160, 161 |
| Prayer Service: Week of Prayer for Christian Unity | 169 |
| Prayer Service: Feast of the Presentation of the Lord | 182 |
| Home Prayer: Keeping Lent | 214 |
| Prayer for the Day and Week | 162–213 |

# CONTENTS

## LENT

| | |
|---|---|
| About the Season | 216–217 |
| Grace before Meals and Prayer at Day's End | 218, 219 |
| Prayer Service: Ash Wednesday, February 25 | 220–221 |
| Prayer Service: Lent (Any time during the season) | 227–228 |
| Prayer Service: Saint Patrick | 231–232 |
| Prayer Service: Saint Joseph | 234–235 |
| Prayer Service: Holy Week, April 6, 7, 8, or 9 | 262–263 |
| Home Prayer: Good Friday | 264 |
| Home Prayer: Holy Saturday | 265 |
| Prayer for the Day and Week | 222–270 |

## EASTER

| | |
|---|---|
| About the Season | 272–273 |
| Grace before Meals and Prayer at Day's End | 274, 275 |
| Prayer Service: Easter | 276–277 |
| Prayer Service: Honoring Mary | 286–287 |
| Prayer Service: Ascension | 314–315 |
| Prayer Service: Pentecost, May 23 (before or after) | 323–324 |
| Prayer for the Day and Week | 278–326 |

## ORDINARY TIME, SUMMER

| | |
|---|---|
| About the Season | 328–329 |
| Grace before Meals and Prayer at Day's End | 330, 331 |
| Prayer Service: Last Day of School | 343–344 |
| Prayer for the Day and Week | 332–342 |
| Psalms and Canticles | 345–351 |
| Blessing for Birthdays | 352 |

The editors appreciate your feedback.
E-mail cdp@ltp.org.

# INTRODUCTION

WELCOME to *Children's Daily Prayer* for the school year 2010–2011! In these pages you will find all the familiar elements you have come to rely on for fostering prayer in the classroom, organized for convenient use, plus elements to help you deepen and enrich your classroom prayer life.

We all want children to pray from the sincerity of their hearts. We want prayer to matter to them. We want them to grow up to be active members of the Christian community. Most of all, we want them to enter into relationship with God. How can we help children to do this? One way that works well involves encouraging children to take an active role in the prayer life of the classroom while they are still young.

Here are some tips to help you move gradually toward giving children a greater role in their own prayer life:

1. If customarily an adult reads the prayers in this book over the school public address system, consider inviting children from the upper grades to do the reading instead. Two or three children could each take a part and lead prayer together. Be sure the children rotate, so that every child gets an opportunity to grow in this way.
2. If you have already given the older children the task of reading the prayer over the public address system, consider inviting a larger group of children to prepare the readings and then send them to lead prayer in person within the various classrooms.
3. If your older students are already going out to the classrooms to lead prayer in person for the younger classes, ask the older ones to help orient the younger ones to the order of prayer. The older ones can help the younger ones to practice the readings so that the younger ones can lead prayer within their own classrooms.
4. If each class now has its own personal communal prayer time, consider allowing the children to write their own prayers to add just before the Closing Prayer. Some creative children may even write an alternate Closing Prayer.

God did not save us by announcing the Good News from the clouds. Jesus became a human being so that he could redeem us by walking beside us, eating with us, speaking to us in person, and sharing every dimension of our lives (except sin, of course!). God's method of meeting us where we are is called "incarnation." We always do best when we can follow his example and allow prayer to be "made flesh" in each of us!

## HOW THIS BOOK IS ORGANIZED

The Church year is divided into liturgical seasons and so is this book. When we begin the school year, Ordinary Time will be almost over. The first section of the book will run from the beginning of the school year until the last day of Ordinary Time that your class meets. The second section of the book corresponds to the Season of Advent running through Friday, December 17, the last day before Christmas break. The third part of the book covers that part of the Christmas Season that school is in session. The next section is Ordinary Time, Winter. Lent comes next, followed by the Easter Season, and the last section of the book is called Ordinary Time, Summer, which begins just after Pentecost. Of course Ordinary Time goes beyond June 24, but that's when most school years end.

### THE MEANING OF THE LITURGICAL SEASON

Introductions to each liturgical season help you orient the children. The first part of the introduction highlights the meaning of that Church season in language that will appeal to children. Read these guides carefully and then use the language in them to speak with the children about preparing to celebrate each liturgical season in the classroom. Alternatively, you may read the section along with the children, passing the book from child to child and allowing them to take turns reading. Make certain to pause between paragraphs to discuss the content. It is important to give the children enough time to ponder the meaning of the season.

You also will find practical suggestions for how to celebrate the particular character of that season in a classroom setting—how to arrange a special prayer area and prayer table within the classroom, which colors and objects to use on the prayer table, and which songs to sing in each liturgical season. Suggestions follow for special seasonal prayers and how best to introduce them to children. Finally, catechists who meet with their students once a week will find a note to help them adapt ideas from this book to their special circumstances.

## PRAYER FOR THE DAY AND PRAYER FOR THE WEEK

This book provides a service of prayer for each day of the school year, as well as an additional order of prayer for classes that only meet once each week. The Prayer for the Day and Prayer for the Week have several standard elements.

Date: located in the upper corner of the page, makes it easy to find your place.

Opening: prepares the children to enter into prayer, providing a brief orientation to the scripture reading, and where necessary, announcing the special feast or Saint commemorated that day.

Sign of the Cross.

Psalm: The book provides a choice. You may use either a short psalm text or a longer one. The short version of the psalm is printed on the Prayer for the Day page and also appears on the Reproducible Psalm Pages. There the short version of the psalm is followed by parts for students on Side A and Side B of your classroom. Use only the first portion (Leader/All/Leader/All) if you choose the short version, or add to it the remainder (Side A/Side B/All) if you prefer the longer version. You may make photocopies of these pages, Reproducible Psalms, for each child in your class.

Reading: The Prayer for the Week uses the Sunday Gospel reading. Each Prayer for the Day (weekday prayer) usually uses either the first or second reading from the *Lectionary for Mass, Weekdays*. However, readings may not always be from the Mass of the day; alternatives are sometimes chosen with the needs of children in mind.

Because we stand and sing alleluia only when the Gospel is read (except during Lent), everyone, except the prayer leaders, will remain seated for the scripture reading when it is not from the Gospel. After the reading, even when it is from the Gospel, all are seated for the time of silent reflection. After that time of silence, at the beginning of the closing prayer, you will find "Let us stand and bring our hopes and needs to God as we pray, **Lord, hear our prayer.**" Everyone will continue standing until after making the Sign of the Cross at the end of the prayer.

It's worth a quick call to the parish music director to discover the tune used for the Alleluia in the parish. Remember to ask whether the Gospel acclamation changes with the liturgical seasons (of course, Alleluia is not sung during Lent), so that you can change as the parish changes the melody. Practice the Alleluia until you feel comfortable. Then teach it to the class so that they can sing it well during prayer. Don't worry about your voice! If you let yourself enjoy the experience of singing, children will join in. They just need to borrow a little of your courage so that they can sing as well. Both the Psalms and the Gospels have been taken from the New Revised Standard Version of the Bible, expanding the children's experience of prayer language.

Please help leaders to practice before reading aloud to the group. Also, you will want to help the children to practice the appropriate responses. For a reading from the Gospel, when the leader announces, "A reading from the holy Gospel according to N," the class responds, **"Glory to you, Lord,"** and when the leader finishes reading and says, "The Gospel of the Lord," the group responds, **"Praise to you, Lord Jesus Christ."** The children will need to know these phrases each day that the Gospel is read, so you might even find it useful to copy these announcements and the appropriate responses on the chalkboard.

Immediately following the Gospel, you will see instructions to observe silence. The leaders should pause and allow a rich silence. How long is long enough? Suggest that the leader very slowly and silently count to ten.

For Silent Reflection: These questions have been chosen to help the children begin to *ponder* what they have heard in prayer. Some of these questions have one obvious right answer, but others may have more than one answer. Others may simply point to the mysteries and be unanswerable. These last are the most valuable questions for prayer. *Please do not ask the children to answer any of these questions.* If they do answer, simply nod to acknowledge their contribution, but don't correct them or even praise them for their answers. The reward for insight can only be given by God. Our praise leads the children to perform for our benefit. All their questions and prayers must be directed to God.

Closing Prayer: Here the children have the chance to offer their own "hopes and needs" (petitions). You may wish to jot these prayers in the margins of the page (if you gather them in advance) or simply allow the leader to invite the children to speak them at the appropriate moment. At the beginning of the school year, the children may be shy about sharing their prayers or may be uncertain how to word them. You may want to offer one as an example so that they understand the formula: "For . . . let us pray to the Lord," to which the group responds, "Lord, hear our prayer."

vii

Later in the year the children may become so enthusiastic that petitions go on very long. If this occurs, you may intervene gently with "For all of these prayers and for those unspoken prayers in our hearts, let us pray to the Lord." The leader can then move on to "Let us pray" and the Our Father.

**Also on this Day:** We pray in the midst of secular observances in society and religious observances in other faith traditions. This reference for teachers at the bottom of the page will alert you to some that you may want to share with the children. For more information about these observances, please go to http://www.ltp.org/t-productsupplements.aspx.

### GRACE BEFORE MEALS AND PRAYER AT DAY'S END

This book offers a new meal prayer and a new prayer for the end of the school day for each liturgical season so that the children's prayers can reflect the life of the Church. You may want to add singing or one of the great prayers of the Church to these prayers. You have permission to photocopy these prayers so that each child has his or her own personal copy. These sheets may be kept in folders in their desks or in the children's assignment notebooks along with their copies of the Psalm Response pages.

### PRAYER SERVICES

The book also includes Prayer Services that you can use in the classroom or for all-school assemblies. These prayer services are longer than Prayer for the Day and Prayer for the Week. They provide the opportunity to pray during the high points of the liturgical year and at important moments during the school year. All of these are listed in the table of contents. These prayer services are designed to include many leaders in order to give as many children as possible an opportunity to guide the prayer.

When you use these Prayer Services, read through them carefully first. Make certain that you have all the elements you need. In particular, gather enough Bibles for each child who will be reading scripture passages. Bookmark the Bible passages, and be sure that the students can find their readings quickly. Then help your students practice their parts several times through. You may need to teach them how to speak into a microphone, how to stand straight and tall, how to enunciate and to project their voices, and how to read slowly. Moreover, if your prayer services take place in a church building or chapel, you will need to teach the students how to reverence the altar with a profound bow before and after their contribution to the prayer service. We do not genuflect to the tabernacle *during* a liturgy, but would do so if passing the tabernacle *before or after* the liturgy.

You may make copies of these Prayer Services for each leader of the prayer. Use a highlighter to clearly mark the child's part on his or her sheet.

### HOME PRAYER PAGES

Home Prayer pages may be copied and sent home with your students, so that they may bring their experience of prayer home with them. Home Prayers are listed in the table of contents.

### PSALMS AND CANTICLES

In the back of this book, a section of psalms and canticles can be used to enrich or lengthen any prayer service in this book. They are arranged and briefly annotated so that you can easily find what you need.

## HOW CHILDREN PRAY

### THE YOUNGEST CHILDREN

Young children (up until age six) will pray simple but profound acclamations when they are given a real opportunity to hear the word of God or to experience the language of signs found in our liturgy. Their spontaneous prayers most often reflect their joy in the Word of God, their thanksgiving for God's goodness, and the pleasure they receive in relationship with Christ. Here are some examples of prayers collected by catechists: "Thank you, Lord, for the Light!" (a three-year-old); "Thank you for Everything!" (a four-year-old); "I love you!" (a three-year-old); and "I want to take a bath in your Light." (a four-year-old).

These prayers point to the young child's ability to appreciate the greatest of realities: life in relationship with God.

When praying with these "little ones," it is best to proclaim the scripture (explaining difficult words in advance to help their understanding) and then to ask one or two open-ended questions to help them to reflect on what the passage is saying to them. If you then invite them to say something to Jesus about what they've heard, you may be surprised at what comes out of the mouths of those budding little theologians!

### PRAYING WITH OLDER CHILDREN

Older children (ages 6–12) begin to appreciate the gift of prayer language. We should go slowly and use a light touch though. When they're younger, give them one beautiful phrase ("Our Father, who art in heaven.") that they can begin to appreciate and love.

As they grow you can add a second phrase, then a third. But make sure that they understand the words they are using and encourage them to pray slowly.

Older children also enjoy leading prayer and composing their own prayers. If you give them each a small prayer journal and give them time to write in it, they will produce exquisite prayers and little theological drawings (particularly if you give them time to write and draw right after reading scripture together).

## PSALMS

The psalms offer a treasure trove of prayer language! Consider praying with one or two verses at a time. You could write one or two verses onto an unlined index card and prop it on your prayer table. You can invite older children to copy them into their prayer journals. But remember to go over each word with the class, asking them to reflect on what the prayer wants to say to God. Children need time to explore the rich implications in their prayer. Also, psalms may be sung or chanted (after all, they were written as songs). There are many beautiful musical settings for the psalms. Experiment until you find the tunes that most move your students.

## MUSIC IN PRAYER

In fact, the songs we sing in church are all prayers! Include singing in your classroom prayer life; what a wonderful difference it makes! Don't be shy, and don't worry about how well you sing. Even if you don't think you have a good voice, children will happily sing with you. So go ahead and make a joyful noise! Children enjoy the chance to lift their voices to God. You may even have a few gifted singers in the class who can help you lead the singing!

The best music to use in the classroom is what your parish sings during the Sunday liturgy. Especially good to sing with the children are the Penitential Rite ("Lord Have Mercy, Christ Have Mercy, Lord Have Mercy") the Gloria, the Gospel Acclamation (Alleluia), the Sanctus ("Holy, Holy, Holy"), the Memorial Acclamations, for example, "Dying you destroyed our death," the Great Amen, the Our Father, and the Agnus Dei ("Lamb of God"). But any songs, hymns, or chants that your parish sings would be a good choice. Your parish music director or Diocesan Director of Music can be good resources.

Also, in the introductions to each liturgical season, you will find a wealth of music suggestions.

## ART AS PRAYER

Try to suggest that the children draw a picture after having heard the scripture reading. Their drawings often reveal their joy and love in ways that language can't always express. Some children are more visual than verbal. Drawing allows them a way to lengthen and deepen their enjoyment of prayer time.

For these "prayer" drawings, don't give the children assignments or themes and don't offer a lot of fancy art supplies or media. The best, most reverent drawings come from children who are simply invited to draw something to do with what they have just heard in the scripture reading, something to do with the Mass or anything to do with God. These open-ended suggestions allow the Holy Spirit room to enter into the children's work.

## PRAYER CANNOT BE EVALUATED

This book is most often used in school or religious education programs. In these settings, teachers are often required to give children a grade in religion. Teachers and catechists who have any choice in the matter should make certain *not to give the children a grade for prayer!* Prayer expresses an inner, mysterious reality and teachers can provide an environment in which prayer can flourish. Prayer is the person's conversation with God. Consider Jesus' teaching on prayer (Matthew 6:5–13) or take a close look at his parable of the Pharisee and the Tax Collector (Luke 18:9–14). We don't want the children to pray for the benefit of a grade or praise from the teacher, but rather we want them to pray to the Father "in secret."

## JOY

In all you do with the children, feel free to communicate your joy to them. Joy is a great sign of the presence of Christ. If you take pleasure in your students' company, they will understand that they are precious children of God. If you take pleasure in your work, they will understand that work is a beautiful gift. If you listen to them and take their words seriously, you will be incarnating Christ, who so valued children. While you must keep order and an atmosphere of dignity in your classrooms, don't be afraid of a little silliness at times. Both laughter and tears are signs of the presence of the Holy Spirit.

## ABOUT THE AUTHOR

Mary Caswell Walsh has worked as a family therapist, consultant and educator for over thirty years. She holds master's degrees from the University of San Francisco and the University of Michigan and a master's in theological studies from the Jesuit School of Theology in Berkeley. A Benedictine Oblate, Mary is also a spiritual director. She has authored, compiled, and contributed to numerous books on family life, healing, and prayer. Mary and Matthew, her husband of thirty-three years, have two daughters and live in California where Mary sings in one of her husband's church choirs.

## ABOUT THE ARTIST AND THE ART

Paula Wiggins, who lives and works in Cincinnati, is the artist for *Children's Daily Prayer*. With a combination of line drawing and scratchboard technique, she has given us a cover that evokes three great movements in salvation history. On the left panel is the Incarnation, when God became flesh in order to be with us. On the center panel is the Eucharist, when Jesus gave us his body and blood and, by washing the feet of his disciples, taught us that we must care for others. On the right panel we reflect on the Resurrection, the coming of the Holy Spirit at Pentecost, and Christ's Ascension to the right hand of the Father, and we remember Christ's promise to return at the end of time. On the back cover, Paula's pictures show us prayer and scripture reading and they illustrate several beloved parables: the lost coin, the sower, the good shepherd, and the vine and the branches.

Inside the book, on the top of the page for each day's prayer, you will find a special little picture that reflects on the season. During Ordinary Time in the Autumn, a sturdy mustard tree with tiny seeds blowing from it reminds us of the parable of the mustard seed. For Advent we find the familiar Advent wreath. During the short season of Christmas there is a manger scene with sheep and a dove. As we begin counting Ordinary Time, we find an oyster shell with pearls—an image for the parable of the pearl of great price. During Lent, bare branches remind us of this time of living simply, without decoration and distraction, so that we can feel God's presence. During the Easter season, we find the empty tomb in the early dawn of the first Easter. And as we return to Ordinary Time after Pentecost, a beautiful grape vine reminds us of Jesus' parable of the vine and the branches.

At the beginning of each new season, special art accompanies the Grace before Meals and Prayer at Day's End, and you will find appropriate scenes for the various prayer services throughout the year. Finally, notice the harps accompanying the psalms, reminding us that these prayers were originally sung. The incense on the pages of canticles pictures the way we want our prayers to rise to God. Thank you, Paula, for giving us visual images to accompany our prayer!

## MORE CHILDREN'S DAILY PRAYER RESOURCES ON OUR WEBSITE

For an updated list of additional resources (printed in previous edition of Children's Daily Prayer as "Reference Bibliography"), please go to http://www.ltp.org/t-productsupplements.aspx.

For more information about the holidays and observances listed under Also On This Day, please go to http://www.ltp.org/t-productsupplements.aspx.

## A NOTE ABOUT COPIES

As a purchaser of this book, you have permission to duplicate only the Reproducible Psalms pages, the Grace Before Meals and Prayer at Day's End pages, the Prayer Services, and the Home Prayer pages; these copies may be used only with your class or group; the Home Prayer pages may be used only in the students' households. You may not duplicate the psalms or prayers unless you are using them with this book. Other parts of this book may not be duplicated without the permission of Liturgy Training Publications or the copyright holders listed on the acknowledgments page.

# PSALM RESPONSES
# ORDINARY TIME, AUTUMN

## ORDINARY TIME, AUTUMN

**Psalm for Sunday, August 8–Sunday, September 26**

Psalm 95:1b, 2, 3–5, 6–7 (1a)

LEADER: O come, let us sing to the LORD.

ALL: **O come, let us sing to the LORD.**

LEADER: Let us make a joyful noise to the rock
   of our salvation!
Let us come into his presence
   with thanksgiving;
   let us make a joyful noise to him
   with songs of praise!

ALL: **O come, let us sing to the LORD.**

*Short version: use above only. Long version: use above and below.*

SIDE A: For the LORD is a great God,
   and a great King above all gods.
In his hand are the depths of the earth;
   the heights of the mountains are
   his also.
The sea is his, for he made it,
   and the dry land, which his hands
   have formed.

SIDE B: O come, let us worship and bow down,
   let us kneel before the LORD,
   our Maker!
For he is our God,
   and we are the people of his pasture,
   and the sheep of his hand.

ALL: **O come, let us sing to the LORD.**

## ORDINARY TIME, AUTUMN

**Psalm for Monday, September 27–Sunday, October 24**

Psalm 25:4, 5–6b, 8a, 9–10 (1, 2a)

LEADER: To you, O LORD, I lift up my soul.
O my God, in you I trust.

ALL: **To you, O LORD, I lift up my soul.
O my God, in you I trust.**

LEADER: Make me to know your ways, O LORD;
   teach me your paths.

ALL: **To you, O LORD, I lift up my soul.
O my God, in you I trust.**

*Short version: use above only. Long version: use above and below.*

SIDE A: Lead me in your truth, and teach me,
   for you are the God of my salvation;
   for you I wait all day long.
Be mindful of your mercy, O LORD,
   and of your steadfast love.

SIDE B: Good and upright is the LORD.
He leads the humble in what is right,
   and teaches the humble his way.
All the paths of the LORD are steadfast
   love and faithfulness
   for those who keep his covenant and
   his decrees.

ALL: **To you, O LORD, I lift up my soul.
O my God, in you I trust.**

# PSALM RESPONSES
# ORDINARY TIME, AUTUMN

## ORDINARY TIME, AUTUMN

**Psalm for Monday, October 25–Wednesday, November 24**

*Psalm 84:2a, 2b, 10, 11–12 (1)*

LEADER: How lovely is your dwelling place,
    O LORD of hosts!

ALL: **How lovely is your dwelling place,
    O LORD of hosts!**

LEADER: My soul longs, indeed it faints
    for the courts of the LORD;

ALL: **How lovely is your dwelling place,
    O LORD of hosts!**

*Short version: use above only. Long version: use above and below.*

SIDE A: My heart and my flesh sing for joy
    to the living God.
    For a day in your courts is better
    than a thousand elsewhere.
    I would rather be a doorkeeper in
    the house of my God
    than live in the tents of wickedness.

SIDE B: For the LORD God is a sun and shield;
    he bestows favor and honor.
    No good thing does the LORD withhold
    from those who walk uprightly.
    O LORD of hosts,
    happy is everyone who trusts in you.

ALL: **How lovely is your dwelling place,
    O LORD of hosts!**

## ADVENT

**Psalm for Sunday, November 28–Friday, December 17**

*Luke 1:79, 72b–75, 76–77 (78)*

LEADER: By the tender mercy of our God,
    the dawn from on high will break
    upon us.

ALL: **By the tender mercy of our God,
    the dawn from on high will break
    upon us.**

LEADER: To give light to those who sit in darkness
    and in the shadow of death,
    to guide our feet into the way
    of peace.

ALL: **By the tender mercy of our God,
    the dawn from on high will break
    upon us.**

*Short version: use above only. Long version: use above and below.*

SIDE A: He has remembered his holy covenant,
    the oath that he swore to our ancestor
    Abraham,
    to grant us that we, being rescued
    from the hands of our enemies,
    might serve him without fear, in holiness
    and righteousness
    before him all our days.

SIDE B: And you, child, will be called the prophet
    of the Most High;
    for you will go before the Lord to
    prepare his ways,
    to give knowledge of salvation to
    his people
    by forgiveness of their sins.

ALL: **By the tender mercy of our God,
    the dawn from on high will break
    upon us.**

# PSALM RESPONSES
# ADVENT AND CHRISTMAS

## CHRISTMAS

### Psalm for Sunday, January 2–Sunday, January 9

Psalm 98:4, 5–6, 7–9a (1a)

LEADER: O sing to the LORD a new song,
for he has done marvelous things.

ALL: **O sing to the LORD a new song,
for he has done marvelous things.**

LEADER: Make a joyful noise to the LORD,
all the earth;
break forth into joyous song
and sing praises.

ALL: **O sing to the LORD a new song,
for he has done marvelous things.**

Short version: use above only. Long version: use above and below.

SIDE A: Sing praises to the LORD with the lyre,
with the lyre and the sound
of melody.
With trumpets and the sound of the horn
make a joyful noise before the King,
the LORD.

SIDE B: Let the sea roar, and all that fills it;
the world and those who live in it.
Let the floods clap their hands;
let the hills sing together for joy
at the presence of the LORD.

ALL: **O sing to the LORD a new song,
for he has done marvelous things.**

## ORDINARY TIME, WINTER

### Psalm for Monday, January 10–Tuesday, March 8

Psalm 27:1b, 4, 13–14 (1a)

LEADER: The LORD is my light and my salvation;
whom shall I fear?

ALL: **The LORD is my light and my salvation;
whom shall I fear?**

LEADER: The LORD is the stronghold of my life;
of whom shall I be afraid?

ALL: **The LORD is my light and my salvation;
whom shall I fear?**

Short version: use above only. Long version: use above and below.

SIDE A: One thing I asked of the LORD,
that I will seek after:
to live in the house of the LORD
all the days of my life,
to behold the beauty of the LORD,
and to inquire in his temple.

SIDE B: I believe that I shall see the goodness of
the LORD
in the land of the living.
Wait for the LORD;
be strong, and let your heart
take courage;
wait for the LORD!

ALL: **The LORD is my light and my salvation;
whom shall I fear?**

# PSALM RESPONSES
# LENT

## LENT

**Psalm for Wednesday, March 9–Sunday, March 27**

Psalm 51:10b, 1, 2, 6, 11, 12–13, 15 (10a)

LEADER: Create in me a clean heart, O God.

ALL: **Create in me a clean heart, O God.**

LEADER: And put a new and right spirit within me.
Have mercy on me, O God,
   according to your steadfast love;
according to your abundant mercy
   blot out my transgressions.

ALL: **Create in me a clean heart, O God.**

Short version: use above only. Long version: use above and below.

SIDE A: Wash me thoroughly from my iniquity,
   and cleanse me from my sin.
You desire truth in the inward being;
   therefore teach me wisdom in
      my secret heart.
Do not cast me away from your presence,
   and do not take your holy spirit
      from me.

SIDE B: Restore to me the joy of your salvation,
   and sustain in me a willing spirit.
Then I will teach transgressors
   your ways,
   and sinners will return to you.
O Lord, open my lips,
   and my mouth will declare
      your praise.

ALL: **Create in me a clean heart, O God.**

## LENT

**Psalm for Monday, March 29–Friday, April 15**

Psalm 33:20, 4–5, 13–15 (22)

LEADER: Let your steadfast love, O Lord,
   be upon us,
even as we hope in you.

ALL: **Let your steadfast love, O Lord,
   be upon us,
even as we hope in you.**

LEADER: Our soul waits for the Lord;
   he is our help and shield.

ALL: **Let your steadfast love, O Lord,
   be upon us,
even as we hope in you.**

Short version: use above only. Long version: use above and below.

SIDE A: For the word of the Lord is upright,
   and all his work is done in
      faithfulness.
He loves righteousness and justice;
   the earth is full of the steadfast love
      of the Lord.

SIDE B: The Lord looks down from heaven;
   he sees all humankind.
From where he sits enthroned he watches
   all the inhabitants of the earth—
he who fashions the hearts of them all,
   and observes all their deeds.

ALL: **Let your steadfast love, O Lord,
   be upon us,
even as we hope in you.**

# PSALM RESPONSES
# EASTER

## HOLY WEEK

**Psalm for Sunday, April 17–Friday, April 22**

Psalm 116:2, 8–9, 12–14 (1)

LEADER: I love the Lord, because he has heard
my voice and my supplications.

ALL: **I love the Lord, because he has heard
my voice and my supplications.**

LEADER: Because he inclined his ear to me,
therefore I will call on him as long
as I live.

ALL: **I love the Lord, because he has heard
my voice and my supplications.**

Short version: use above only. Long version: use above and below.

SIDE A: For you have delivered my soul
from death,
my eyes from tears,
my feet from stumbling.
I walk before the Lord
in the land of the living.

SIDE B: What shall I return to the Lord
for all his bounty to me?
I will lift up the cup of salvation
and call on the name of the Lord,
I will pay my vows to the Lord
in the presence of all his people.

ALL: **I love the Lord, because he has heard
my voice and my supplications.**

## EASTER

**Psalm for Sunday, April 24–Friday, May 20**

Psalm 118:27a, 17, 21–22, 23, 26 (24)

LEADER: This is the day that the Lord has made;
let us rejoice and be glad in it.

ALL: **This is the day that the Lord has made;
let us rejoice and be glad in it.**

LEADER: The Lord is God,
and he has given us light.

ALL: **This is the day that the Lord has made;
let us rejoice and be glad in it.**

Short version: use above only. Long version: use above and below.

SIDE A: I shall not die, but I shall live,
and recount the deeds of the Lord.
I thank you that you have answered me
and have become my salvation.
The stone that the builders rejected
has become the chief cornerstone.

SIDE B: This is the Lord's doing;
it is marvelous in our eyes.
Blessed is the one who comes in the name
of the Lord.
We bless you from the house of the Lord.

ALL: **This is the day that the Lord has made;
let us rejoice and be glad in it.**

# PSALM RESPONSES
# EASTER

## EASTER

**Psalm for Sunday, May 22–Sunday, June 12**

Psalm 23:2, 3–4, 5–6 (1)

LEADER: The Lord is my shepherd,
I shall not want.

ALL: **The Lord is my shepherd,
I shall not want.**

LEADER: He makes me lie down
in green pastures;
he leads me beside still waters;

ALL: **The Lord is my shepherd,
I shall not want.**

Short version: use above only. Long version: use above and below.

SIDE A: He restores my soul.
He leads me in right paths
for his name's sake.
Even though I walk through
the darkest valley,
I fear no evil;
for you are with me.

SIDE B: You prepare a table before me
in the presence of my enemies;
you anoint my head with oil;
my cup overflows.
Surely goodness and mercy shall
follow me
all the days of my life.
and I shall dwell in the house of the Lord
my whole life long.

ALL: **The Lord is my shepherd,
I shall not want.**

## ORDINARY TIME, SUMMER

**Psalm for Monday, June 13–Friday, June 24**

Psalm 104:1b–2a, 2b, 3b–4, 31, 33 (1a)

LEADER: Bless the Lord, O my soul.

ALL: **Bless the Lord, O my soul.**

LEADER: O Lord my God, you are very great.
You are clothed with honor and majesty,
wrapped in light as with a garment.

ALL: **Bless the Lord, O my soul.**

Short version: use above only. Long version: use above and below.

SIDE A: You stretch out the heavens like a tent,
you make the clouds your chariot,
you ride on the wings of the wind,
you make the winds your messengers,
fire and flame your ministers.

SIDE B: May the glory of the Lord endure
forever;
may the Lord rejoice in his works.
I will sing to the Lord as long as I live;
I will sing praise to my God while
I have being.

ALL: **Bless the Lord, O my soul.**

# ORDINARY TIME AUTUMN 2010

## SUNDAY, AUGUST 8, TO WEDNESDAY, NOVEMBER 24, 2010

# AUTUMN

# ORDINARY TIME

## THE MEANING OF ORDINARY TIME

"Jesus also said, 'With what can we compare the kingdom of God, or what parable will we use for it? It is like a mustard seed, which, when sown upon the ground, is the smallest of all the seeds on earth; yet when it is sown it grows up and becomes the greatest of all shrubs, and puts forth large branches, so that the birds of the air can make nests in its shade'" (Mark 4:30–32).

Jesus told us that the kingdom of God has already arrived. We are living the mysterious reality of the kingdom of God *right now*! We need a new way of looking to see this kingdom in our world today.

Mustard seeds from the Holy Land are much smaller than the mustard seeds you buy in the grocery store. They are so small you can barely see them. The kingdom can be found in the tiny, overlooked, and forgotten. We must search for it.

What happens to the mustard seed? When it is planted in the ground, it grows into a tree, with large spreading branches. The kingdom is not only here with us; it is alive and growing. We can see the kingdom at work in our bodies, hearts, and minds. We even see the kingdom at work in our bodies and hearts. We can't tell our arms or legs to grow even one inch, but God has filled us with his life, so that we do grow, according to his amazing plan. Our hearts and minds are also full of life and made to grow in wonderful ways.

Time and seasons in the kingdom of God, in contrast to those in the secular calendar, are valued in a different, altogether new way. The Christian calendar even has a different shape! Instead of a rectangle, we draw all the days of a year in a circle. Instead of marking off seasons according to the weather, the people of the kingdom celebrate those great moments when God has revealed his love for us in marvelous and mysterious ways. There are two celebrations on the calendar that are more precious to us than any of the others: Christmas and Easter. In both, we can see the miracle of the mustard seed at work. At Christmas, we celebrate that the Son of God became flesh as a tiny, vulnerable baby. At Easter, we rejoice in the miracle that his lifeless, broken human body was buried, like a seed planted in the earth, and that he came out of the tomb alive in a risen body. Now peoples of every country and city in the world can find shelter and rest in the Church, his mystical body.

These are the seasons of the Church year: *Advent,* the season of preparation before the *season of Christmas*; and *Lent,* another season of preparation before the *Easter Season*. The fifth season of the Church year is called *Ordinary Time*.

Ordinary Time begins after Christmas (after the Baptism of the Lord), continues until Ash Wednesday when it stops for Lent and Easter, then picks up again after Pentecost Sunday and runs through the summer and autumn until the beginning of Advent. It is a season of growth and change. Sometimes that growth is hidden like that of the mustard seed when it is planted in the ground. Sometimes we are well aware of the growth taking place all around us and inside us. But to remind us that we are growing in grace and in the love of God, each Sunday in Ordinary Time has a number and the numbers increase each week.

## PREPARING TO CELEBRATE ORDINARY TIME IN THE CLASSROOM

For Ordinary Time in autumn, *Children's Daily Prayer* provides several special prayer services to use in the classroom or with larger groups: to celebrate the beginning of the school year, to pray for peace (on September 11), to honor Our Lady of the Rosary (October 7), and to celebrate All Saints (November 1) and Thanksgiving. Three Home Prayer pages can be duplicated for the students to take home and share with their families: Morning Prayer for Families Departing for the Day, Home Prayer for All Saints and All Souls, called Celebrating the Saints, Remembering the Dead, and a Meal Prayer for Thanksgiving. At the end of this season you will find a Home Prayer page for praying with an Advent Wreath. It's placed at the end of Ordinary Time so you won't

# AUTUMN ORDINARY TIME

forget to send it home with the students *before* the First Sunday of Advent.

## SACRED SPACE

With the start of the school year, you have the opportunity to make adjustments to your prayer area. Take a long look around your classroom and decide whether you would like to keep the prayer table where it is or move it to a new spot. You want it to be in a place where the children will see it often and remember to go to it in their free moments. Also, the prayer table should not be too high. A coffee table is the perfect height. You may wish to buy one or two inexpensive cushions to place before your prayer table so that children will feel invited to sit or kneel there. The most essential things for your prayer table are a cross or crucifix and a Bible with a candle. Cover the prayer table with a plain green cloth and remind the children that "green, the color of hope and life," is the color of Ordinary Time. If you can, set the Bible on a bookstand or use a beautiful cushion as a "throne" to prop it up. When you orient the children to the prayer table, point out the small candle beside the Bible, and remind them that Jesus said, "I am the Light of the world" (John 8:12). You might even light the candle, open the Bible, and read that verse to the class. Other objects you might want to include on your prayer table include: a simple statue of Christ or Mary, an image of a saint, or a small vase with a fresh flower. Try to avoid clutter! Choose objects that are beautiful, avoiding anything that looks like toys.

## SACRED MUSIC

One of the best ways to help the children enter into the special qualities of this or any liturgical season is by teaching them the music of the Church. The best music for this purpose is what your parish community sings during Sunday Mass. Teach the children how your church sings "Glory to God in the highest," the "Holy, Holy, Holy," the Great Amen, or the Memorial Acclamation, such as, "Dying you destroyed our death . . . " You may even wish to invite the music director for your parish to come one day to teach this music.

Some songs and hymns that children love to sing in Ordinary Time are *For the Beauty of the Earth, Make Me a Channel of Your Peace,* and *I Want to Walk As a Child of the Light.*

## PRAYERS FOR ORDINARY TIME

During this season, take some time to discuss the meaning of the *Our Father* with the children in your class. In particular, discuss the kingdom of God (you may wish to review the material in "The Meaning of Ordinary Time" beforehand) and what it means to ask God for his kingdom to come. Go through the prayer a few words at a time. You might even try taking a few deep breaths between each phrase. This helps children relax and listen. Pause, listen, and invite the children to tell you what they hear. Explore with them what Jesus is teaching us about how we should pray, treating God's name as blessed and holy, asking for the coming of the kingdom of God," that his name be treated as blessed and holy, for the coming of the kingdom of God, for God's will to be accomplished on earth, for our "daily bread," for forgiveness, and for strength in the face of temptation).

## A NOTE TO CATECHISTS

Because you meet with your students once a week, you may wish to use the Prayer for the Week pages. These weekly prayer pages contain an excerpt from the Sunday Gospel and will help to prepare the children for Mass. Sometimes though, you may wish to substitute the Prayer for the Day if it falls on an important solemnity, feast, or memorial of the Church (All Saints, for example).

In this introduction, you will see the suggestion to consider the best placement for your prayer table. You may have to set up a prayer table each time you meet with your group. Think in advance about where to place the prayer table and then always set it up in the same place.

# GRACE BEFORE MEALS
## FOR ORDINARY TIME • Autumn 2010

**LEADER:**
Lord, make us truly grateful for all your gifts

**ALL:** So that one day we may eat with you in the kingdom!

✠ All make the Sign of the Cross.

**In the name of the Father and of the Son and of the Holy Spirit. Amen.**

**LEADER:**
Almighty God,
how many gifts you give us!
Even if we spent our whole lives counting,
we could never number them all!
As we prepare to eat this food,
let it be a sign of all the good gifts you have
　　　given to us.
Make our hearts truly grateful.
We ask this through Jesus Christ, our Lord.

✠ All make the Sign of the Cross.

**In the name of the Father and of the Son and of the Holy Spirit. Amen.**

# PRAYER AT DAY'S END
## FOR ORDINARY TIME • Autumn 2010

**LEADER:**
Generous God, receive all that we've done today

**ALL:** As an offering from our hearts.

✛ All make the Sign of the Cross.

**In the name of the Father and of the Son and of the Holy Spirit. Amen.**

**LEADER:**
May all the work we've done today be pleasing to you.
We give all our efforts over to you
so that you may bless our work and play.
May our lives become our prayer to you
and be a help to the coming of your kingdom.
We ask this through your beloved Son,
Jesus Christ the Lord.

✛ All make the Sign of the Cross.

**In the name of the Father and of the Son and of the Holy Spirit. Amen.**

# PRAYER SERVICE
## BEGINNING OF THE YEAR FOR SCHOOL STAFF

*Seek volunteers to lead this prayer service. You may involve up to six leaders (as marked below). The fourth leader will need a Bible for the scripture passage. Choose hymns for beginning and ending if you wish.*

**FIRST LEADER:**
Our love for God helps us to hear his call to serve the educational needs of the children in our school. We have been entrusted with a most important and beautiful task. Only God can strengthen and inspire us to fulfill this responsibility with devotion and awe. Today, let us pray to the Holy Spirit to increase our love for him and for his beloved children.

◆ Gesture for all to stand.

Together we enter this time of prayer as we make the Sign of the Cross.

✚ All make the Sign of the Cross.

**In the name of the Father and of the Son and of the Holy Spirit. Amen.**

**SECOND LEADER:**
Holy Spirit, you are the breath of life that
    fills us with strength
as we face the challenges of the coming
    school year.
You are the source of all unity.
Guide us all, teachers and staff,
in our mission to educate the children
    in our school.
Encourage us to imitate the most holy Trinity
by always giving more than we receive,
and to share our burdens and joys
in trust and friendship.

# BEGINNING OF THE YEAR FOR SCHOOL STAFF

We ask all these things through Christ
 our Lord.
**Amen.**

**THIRD LEADER:**
Holy Spirit,
pour forth your seven gifts on us today.
Enlightened by your Wisdom, your holy
 Understanding, Knowledge,
 inspired Counsel,
Strength of faith, Wonder and Awe, and
 loving Reverence for Christ,
we will have all we need to do the work
 entrusted to us.
We ask this through Christ, our Savior.
**Amen.**

◆ Gesture for all to sit.

**FOURTH LEADER:** 1 Corinthians 12:4–13 and 27–31
A reading from the first letter of Saint Paul to the Corinthians.

◆ Read the passage from the Bible.

The word of the Lord.

◆ All observe silence.

**FIFTH LEADER:**

◆ Gesture for all to stand.

Let us bring our hopes and needs to God as we pray, **Lord, send forth your Spirit.**

That the Holy Spirit may come upon us, that we may pursue your Wisdom in Christ, we pray to the Lord.

For your spirit of Understanding, that we may recognize our dependence on God, we pray to the Lord.

For Knowledge of God, that we may share it with the students in our care, we pray to the Lord.

For Counsel, that we may guide others to God's truth and peace, we pray to the Lord.

For Strength, that our faith may fortify us in challenging moments, we pray to the Lord.

For Wonder and Awe before God's goodness, that our joy will be complete, we pray to the Lord.

For Piety and Reverence, that we may return the love God has given to us, we pray to the Lord.

**SIXTH LEADER:**
Let us pray as Jesus taught us: **Our Father . . .**
**Amen.**

◆ Pause and then say:

Let us offer one another the sign of Christ's peace.

**SEVENTH LEADER:**
Let us pray for God's blessing:
God, our Father,
renew us and refresh us
to do the work that has been entrusted to us.
Bless our work and send us your Holy Spirit
to lead us in the paths of peace,
now and forever.
**Amen.**

◆ All make the Sign of the Cross.

**In the name of the Father and of the Son and of the Holy Spirit. Amen.**

# PRAYER SERVICE
## BEGINNING OF THE YEAR FOR STUDENTS

*This prayer service may be led by the eighth grade students or by older students. The third and fifth leaders will each need a Bible for the passages from Luke. Take time to help the third and fifth leaders practice the readings. You may wish to sing "All Are Welcome" as an opening song and "Sing a New Song" for the closing. If the group will sing, prepare someone to lead the songs.*

**FIRST LEADER:**
We are beginning a new school year. The next months will be full of learning, new friends, joys, and pains. As we look forward to all that this school year will hold, we remember Jesus Christ, our brother and Savior, our Lord and God, who will walk with us everywhere we go, encourage us, protect us, and fascinate us.

**SONG LEADER:**
Let us begin by singing our opening song.

◆ Gesture for all to stand; lead the song.

**SECOND LEADER:**

✚ All make the Sign of the Cross.

**In the name of the Father and of the Son and of the Holy Spirit. Amen.**

Let us pray:
God of infinite power,
you made us in your image to be the light
  of the world.
You have even given us a share in the glory
  and victory of Christ,
who triumphed over evil and death.
Help us to carry your Light
into each day that lies ahead of us.

# BEGINNING OF THE YEAR FOR STUDENTS

May we wear your glorious loving kindness
    like a crown,
and grow in wisdom and understanding.
We ask this through the same Christ our Lord.

**ALL: Amen.**

◆ Remain standing and sing **Alleluia**.

**THIRD LEADER:**      Luke 2:41–52

A reading from the holy Gospel according to Luke

◆ Read the Gospel passage from the Bible.

The Gospel of the Lord.

◆ All sit and observe silence.

**FOURTH LEADER:**

◆ Gesture for all to stand.

Let us bring our hopes and needs to God as we pray, **Lord, help us to increase in wisdom.**

During this year, give us many chances to hear your teaching in your holy place, our church, we pray to the Lord.

Help us to listen well and ask questions that will help us understand, we pray to the Lord.

As we listen to the holy Gospel, may we be as amazed as those people who heard the boy Jesus speak in the temple of Jerusalem, we pray to the Lord.

When we feel lost and alone, let us remember that we will always find Jesus in his Father's house, we pray to the Lord.

Teach us to treasure all that we learn and to ponder all these things in our hearts, we pray to the Lord.

**FIFTH LEADER:**
Let us listen to the blessing given to Saint John the Baptist at his birth:

Luke 1:76–79

◆ Read the Gospel passage from the Bible.

**SIXTH LEADER:**
Let us pray:
Ever-living God,
bless us with your tender mercy,
allow your Dawn to break upon us,
give us your Light, and guide our feet in your
    way of peace,
so that all we do this year
will be according to your holy will.
We ask this through Christ our Lord.

**ALL: Amen.**

✢ All make the Sign of the Cross.

**In the name of the Father and of the Son and of the Holy Spirit. Amen.**

**SONG LEADER:**
Please join in singing our closing song.

# HOME PRAYER
## MORNING PRAYER FOR FAMILIES DEPARTING FOR THE DAY

*Gather the household in one room (breakfast is an ideal opportunity or at the door, just as everyone is ready to depart). This prayer may be led by a parent or other adult.*

**LEADER:**
Zechariah spoke these words over his newborn son, Saint John the Baptist:

Luke 1:76

"And you, child, will be called the prophet
 of the Most High;
for you will go before the Lord to prepare
 his ways."

✝ *All make the Sign of the Cross.*

**In the name of the Father and of the Son and of the Holy Spirit. Amen.**

**LEADER:**
God Most High,
we ask your protection and care
over us all as we begin our day.

◆ *Lightly touch the ears of each person present.*

May we listen to your voice
with our whole selves,
just as John the Baptist heard and answered
 your call,
and may we help to prepare the world
for your Light and Life
to fill the entire universe.
We also pray, along with your servant,
 Zechariah:

Luke 1:78–79

"By the tender mercy of our God,
 the dawn from on high will break upon us,
to give light to those who sit in darkness
and in the shadow of death,
 to guide our feet into the way of peace."
May God open our eyes to greet the dawn
 of Peace.

◆ *Lightly touch the eyes of each person present as you continue this prayer.*

We ask this through Jesus Christ, who is All Light and Peace.

**ALL: Amen.**

◆ *As each person departs for the day, exchange a kiss of peace and trace a small cross on each forehead.*

# PRAYER FOR THE WEEK

WITH A READING FROM THE GOSPEL FOR **SUNDAY, AUGUST 8, 2010**

## OPENING

In today's Gospel, Jesus tells the disciples to give alms. Alms are a gift (such as money or food) given to the poor. He also tells the disciples what God is giving them.

✢ All make the Sign of the Cross.

**In the name of the Father and of the Son and of the Holy Spirit. Amen.**

## PSALM   (For a longer psalm, see page xi.) Psalm 95:1b, 2 (1a)

O come, let us sing to the LORD.

**O come, let us sing to the LORD.**

Let us make a joyful noise to the rock
    of our salvation!
Let us come into his presence with
    thanksgiving;
let us make a joyful noise to him with
    songs of praise!

O come, let us sing to the LORD.

◆ All stand and sing **Alleluia**.

## GOSPEL   Luke 12:32–34

A reading from the holy Gospel according to Luke

Jesus said to his disciples: "Do not be afraid, little flock, for it is your Father's good pleasure to give you the kingdom. Sell your possessions and give alms. Make purses for yourselves that do not wear out, an unfailing treasure in heaven, where no thief comes near and no moth destroys. For where your treasure is, there your heart will be also.

The Gospel of the Lord.

◆ All sit and observe silence.

## FOR SILENT REFLECTION

What do you think Jesus is talking about when he says, "where your treasure is, there your heart will be also"?

## CLOSING PRAYER

Let us stand and bring our hopes and needs to God as we pray, "Lord, hear our prayer."

◆ All may add their own prayers here.

Let us pray: **Our Father . . . Amen.**

God our Father,
our hearts are happy
because you have chosen us
to be your little flock.
Knowing that you
love and protect us,
we are not afraid.
Your love is our treasure.
Help us to share
your love with others.
We ask this in the holy name of your Son,
Jesus Christ, our Lord,
**Amen.**

✢ All make the Sign of the Cross.

# PRAYER FOR MONDAY AUGUST 9, 2010

## OPENING

Today we remember Saint Teresa Benedicta of the Cross. She was born into a large Jewish family and named Edith Stein. She converted to Christianity and took the cross as part of her name when she became a Carmelite nun. During the Nazi persecution of the Jewish people, she suffered and died with them. The Church honors her as "a daughter of Israel" who remained faithful both to Christ and to the Jewish people.

✚ All make the Sign of the Cross.

**In the name of the Father and of the Son and of the Holy Spirit. Amen.**

## PSALM (For a longer psalm, see page xi.) Psalm 95:1b, 2 (1a)

O come, let us sing to the LORD.

**O come, let us sing to the LORD.**

Let us make a joyful noise to the rock
   of our salvation!
Let us come into his presence with
   thanksgiving;
let us make a joyful noise to him with
   songs of praise!

**O come, let us sing to the LORD.**

◆ All stand and sing **Alleluia**.

## GOSPEL Matthew 17:22–23

A reading from the holy Gospel according Matthew

As they were gathering in Galilee, Jesus said to them, "The Son of Man is going to be betrayed into human hands, and they will kill him, and on the third day he will be raised." And they were greatly distressed.

The Gospel of the Lord.

◆ All sit and observe silence.

## FOR SILENT REFLECTION

Why do you think the followers of Jesus were so upset? Do you think they understood what Jesus was telling them?

## CLOSING PRAYER

Let us stand and bring our hopes and needs to God as we pray, "Lord, hear our prayer."

◆ All may add their own prayers here.

Let us pray: **Our Father . . . Amen.**

Holy God,
the cross is our hope,
for by your cross we know
that your love is stronger than hate
and your life is more powerful than death.
Teach us to value your love
and grant us the gift of your peace.
We ask this in the name of Jesus Christ
   our Savior.
**Amen.**

✚ All make the Sign of the Cross.

# PRAYER FOR TUESDAY AUGUST 10, 2010

## OPENING

Today we celebrate the memorial of Saint Lawrence, a deacon who loved to help the needy and who died for his faith. Saint Lawrence believed that the poor are the Church's treasure. In today's Gospel, Jesus teaches an important lesson by talking about seeds falling into the earth. Let's listen and try to understand what he is telling us.

✢ All make the Sign of the Cross.

**In the name of the Father and of the Son and of the Holy Spirit. Amen.**

## PSALM (For a longer psalm, see page xi.) Psalm 95:1b, 2 (1a)

O come, let us sing to the LORD.

O come, let us sing to the LORD.

Let us make a joyful noise to the rock
  of our salvation!
Let us come into his presence with
  thanksgiving;
let us make a joyful noise to him with
  songs of praise!

O come, let us sing to the LORD.

◆ All stand and sing **Alleluia**.

## GOSPEL                                    John 12:24

A reading from the holy Gospel according to John

Jesus said: "Very truly, I tell you, unless a grain of wheat falls into the earth and dies, it remains just a single grain; but if it dies, it bears much fruit."

The Gospel of the Lord.

◆ All sit and observe silence.

## FOR SILENT REFLECTION

What happens to a seed when it dies in the ground? What do you think this seed is?

## CLOSING PRAYER

Let us stand and bring our hopes and needs to God as we pray, "Lord, hear our prayer."

◆ All may add their own prayers here.

Let us pray: **Our Father . . . Amen.**

God, Our Creator,
You plant the seed of faith in us.
May our fear die
so that faith can grow.
You plant the seed of love in us.
May our selfishness die
so that love can grow.
Teach us to pray,
and may our prayers bear the fruit
of good thoughts and generous actions.
We ask this through Jesus Christ our Lord.
**Amen.**

✢ All make the Sign of the Cross.

# PRAYER FOR **WEDNESDAY** **AUGUST 11, 2010**

## OPENING

Today we remember Saint Clare. Inspired by the example of Saint Francis, Saint Clare chose to live a life in which nothing, not money or fame, was more important to her than Christ. In today's Gospel, Jesus talks about the good influence we can have on each other.

✛ All make the Sign of the Cross.

**In the name of the Father and of the Son and of the Holy Spirit. Amen.**

## PSALM         (For a longer psalm, see page xi.) Psalm 95:1b, 2 (1a)

O come, let us sing to the LORD.

**O come, let us sing to the LORD.**

Let us make a joyful noise to the rock
   of our salvation!
Let us come into his presence with
   thanksgiving;
let us make a joyful noise to him with
   songs of praise!

**O come, let us sing to the LORD.**

◆ All stand and sing **Alleluia**.

## GOSPEL         Matthew 18:15–18; 19b–20

A reading from the holy Gospel according to Matthew

Jesus said: "If another member of the church sins against you, go and point out the fault when the two of you are alone. If the member listens to you, you have regained that one. But if you are not listened to, take one or two others along with you, so that every word may be confirmed by the evidence of two or three witnesses. If the member refuses to listen to them, tell it to the church; and if the offender refuses to listen even to the church, let such a one be treated as a Gentile and a tax collector. Again, truly I tell you, if two of you agree on earth about anything you ask, it will be done for you by my Father in heaven. For where two or three are gathered in my name, I am there among them."

The Gospel of the Lord.

◆ All sit and observe silence.

## FOR SILENT REFLECTION

Why does Jesus suggest being alone with someone if we want to point out a fault? Who has a good influence on your life?

## CLOSING PRAYER

Let us stand and bring our hopes and needs to God as we pray, "Lord, hear our prayer."

◆ All may add their own prayers here.

Let us pray: **Our Father . . . Amen.**

Loving God,
give us the courage to speak
and the ability to listen,
so that each day we may become
more like Jesus Christ our Lord,
in whose name we pray.
**Amen.**

✛ All make the Sign of the Cross.

**ALSO ON THIS DAY:** Ramadan (Islamic month of fasting) begins at sunset.

# PRAYER FOR **THURSDAY AUGUST 12, 2010**

## OPENING

Today we remember Saint Jane Frances de Chantal, a French woman who was a wife, mother, and later in life, the founder of a religious community. She said God's love is big, like an ocean, and we should throw all our worries and ourselves into that love. In today's Gospel, Jesus teaches Peter that forgiveness is big.

✚ All make the Sign of the Cross.

**In the name of the Father and of the Son and of the Holy Spirit. Amen.**

## PSALM  (For a longer psalm, see page xi.) Psalm 95:1b, 2 (1a)

O come, let us sing to the LORD.

**O come, let us sing to the LORD.**

Let us make a joyful noise to the rock
　　of our salvation!
Let us come into his presence with
　　thanksgiving;
let us make a joyful noise to him with
　　songs of praise!

O come, let us sing to the LORD.

◆ All stand and sing **Alleluia**.

## GOSPEL                              Matthew 18:21–22

A reading from the holy Gospel according to Matthew

Then Peter came and said to him, "Lord, if another member of the church sins against me, how often should I forgive? As many as seven times?" Jesus said to him, "Not seven times, but, I tell you, seventy-seven times."

The Gospel of the Lord.

◆ All sit and observe silence.

## FOR SILENT REFLECTION

Have you ever been forgiven? What is it like to be forgiven? Why do you think Jesus wants us to be so forgiving?

## CLOSING PRAYER

Let us stand and bring our hopes and needs to God as we pray, "Lord, hear our prayer."

◆ All may add their own prayers here.

Let us pray: **Our Father . . . Amen.**

Loving God,
we know that you are merciful
and that you forgive our sins.
Give us sorrow
when we do what is wrong
and courage to return to you,
trusting in your love.
When others ask our forgiveness,
help us to forgive them
as you forgive us.
We ask this through Jesus Christ our Lord.
**Amen.**

✚ All make the Sign of the Cross.

# PRAYER FOR FRIDAY AUGUST 13, 2010

## OPENING

In today's Gospel, Jesus talks about the love that married people should have for one another. The words "one flesh" mean "one person."

✦ All make the Sign of the Cross.

**In the name of the Father and of the Son and of the Holy Spirit. Amen.**

## PSALM (For a longer psalm, see page xi.) Psalm 95:1b, 2 (1a)

O come, let us sing to the LORD.

**O come, let us sing to the LORD.**

Let us make a joyful noise to the rock
 of our salvation!
Let us come into his presence with
 thanksgiving;
let us make a joyful noise to him with
 songs of praise!

**O come, let us sing to the LORD.**

## READING Matthew 19:3–6

A reading from the holy Gospel according to Matthew

Some Pharisees [FAIR-uh-seez] came to him, and to test him they asked, "Is it lawful for a man to divorce his wife for any cause?" He answered, "Have you not read that the one who made them at the beginning 'made them male and female,' and said, 'For this reason a man shall leave his father and mother and be joined to his wife, and the two shall become one flesh'? So they are no longer two, but one flesh. Therefore what God has joined together, let no one separate."

The Gospel of the Lord.

◆ All sit and observe silence.

## FOR SILENT REFLECTION

What do you think Jesus means when he says that a husband and wife become one? How can two people become one person?

## CLOSING PRAYER

Let us stand and bring our hopes and needs to God as we pray, "Lord, hear our prayer."

◆ All may add their own prayers here.

Let us pray: **Our Father . . . Amen.**

God, our Creator,
out of love you make
men and women,
and through love
you join them together
in marriage.
Bless all married couples.
Help them to live
in peace and unity.
May their love bring joy
to their children, friends, and neighbors.
We ask this through Jesus Christ our Lord.
**Amen.**

✦ All make the Sign of the Cross.

# PRAYER FOR THE WEEK

WITH A READING FROM THE GOSPEL FOR **SUNDAY, AUGUST 15, 2010**

## OPENING

Today we celebrate the Assumption of the Blessed Virgin Mary, when Mary was taken body and soul into heaven. In today's Gospel, Mary and her cousin, Elizabeth, rejoice that Mary will give birth to our Savior. We rejoice because, like Mary, we will be reborn into heavenly life.

✢ All make the Sign of the Cross.

**In the name of the Father and of the Son and of the Holy Spirit. Amen.**

## PSALM        (For a longer psalm, see page xi.) Psalm 95:1b, 2 (1a)

O come, let us sing to the LORD.

**O come, let us sing to the LORD.**

Let us make a joyful noise to the rock
    of our salvation!
Let us come into his presence with
    thanksgiving;
let us make a joyful noise to him with
    songs of praise!

**O come, let us sing to the LORD.**

◆ All stand and sing **Alleluia**.

## GOSPEL        Luke 1:39–42; 46–49

A reading from the holy Gospel according to Luke

In those days, Mary set out and went with haste to a Judean town in the hill country, where she entered the house of Zechariah and greeted Elizabeth. When Elizabeth heard Mary's greeting, the child leapt in her womb. And Elizabeth was filled with the Holy Spirit and exclaimed with a loud cry, "Blessed are you among women, and blessed is the fruit of your womb." And Mary said, "My soul magnifies the Lord, and my spirit rejoices in God my Savior, for he has looked with favor on the lowliness of his servant. Surely, from now on all generations will call me blessed; for the Mighty One has done great things for me, and holy is his name."

The Gospel of the Lord.

◆ All sit and observe silence.

## FOR SILENT REFLECTION

Why do you think Mary says that "all generations" will call her blessed?

## CLOSING PRAYER

Let us stand and bring our hopes and needs to God as we pray, "Lord, hear our prayer."

◆ All may add their own prayers here.

Let us pray: **Our Father . . . Amen.**

Hail Mary, full of grace,
the Lord is with you.
Blessed are you among women,
and blessed is the fruit of your womb, Jesus.
Holy Mary, mother of God,
pray for us sinners now,
and at the hour of our death.
**Amen.**

✢ All make the Sign of the Cross.

# PRAYER FOR MONDAY AUGUST 16, 2010

## OPENING

Today we remember Saint Stephen, an early king of Hungary who helped to spread the Christian faith there. He built many churches and monasteries. In today's Gospel, Jesus talks with a young man who is rich, but he thinks he lacks something. To "lack" means not to have.

✠ All make the Sign of the Cross.

**In the name of the Father and of the Son and of the Holy Spirit. Amen.**

## PSALM
(For a longer psalm, see page xi.) Psalm 95:1b, 2 (1a)

O come, let us sing to the LORD.

**O come, let us sing to the LORD.**

Let us make a joyful noise to the rock
of our salvation!
Let us come into his presence with
thanksgiving;
let us make a joyful noise to him with
songs of praise!

**O come, let us sing to the LORD.**

◆ All stand and sing **Alleluia.**

## GOSPEL
Matthew 19:16–22

A reading from the holy Gospel according to Matthew

Then someone came to him and said, "Teacher, what good deed must I do to have eternal life?" And he said to him, "Why do you ask me about what is good? There is only one who is good. If you wish to enter into life, keep the commandments." He said to him, "Which ones?" And Jesus said, "You shall not murder; you shall not commit adultery; you shall not steal; you shall not bear false witness; honor your father and mother; also, you shall love your neighbor as yourself." The young man said to him, "I have kept all these; what do I still lack?" Jesus said to him, "If you wish to be perfect, go, sell your possessions, and give the money to the poor, and you will have treasure in heaven; then come, follow me." When the young man heard this statement, he went away grieving, for he had many possessions.

The Gospel of the Lord.

◆ All sit and observe silence.

## FOR SILENT REFLECTION

What do you think the rich man really wants?
What do you really want from Jesus?

## CLOSING PRAYER

Let us stand and bring our hopes and needs to God as we pray, "Lord, hear our prayer."

◆ All may add their own prayers here.

Let us pray: **Our Father . . . Amen.**

Generous God,
everything good comes from you.
But we want more;
we want to know and love you.
May we always feel that need for you.
We ask this through Jesus Christ our Lord.
**Amen.**

✠ All make the Sign of the Cross.

# PRAYER FOR TUESDAY AUGUST 17, 2010

## OPENING

Yesterday's Gospel told the story of the rich young man who is sad because he wants to follow Jesus, but he doesn't want to give up his possessions. If you listen closely to today's Gospel, you will hear Jesus tell us how we can do the things that seem difficult, and even impossible to us.

✚ All make the Sign of the Cross.

**In the name of the Father and of the Son and of the Holy Spirit. Amen.**

## PSALM (For a longer psalm, see page xi.) Psalm 95:1b, 2 (1a)

O come, let us sing to the LORD.

**O come, let us sing to the LORD.**

Let us make a joyful noise to the rock
of our salvation!
Let us come into his presence with
thanksgiving;
let us make a joyful noise to him with
songs of praise!

**O come, let us sing to the LORD.**

◆ All stand and sing **Alleluia**.

## GOSPEL  Matthew 19:23–26

A reading from the holy Gospel according to Matthew

Then Jesus said to his disciples, "Truly I tell you, it will be hard for a rich person to enter the kingdom of heaven. Again I tell you, it is easier for a camel to go through the eye of a needle than for someone who is rich to enter the kingdom of God." When the disciples heard this, they were greatly astounded and said, "Then who can be saved?" But Jesus looked at them and said, "For mortals it is impossible, but for God all things are possible."

The Gospel of the Lord.

◆ All sit and observe silence.

## FOR SILENT REFLECTION

Can you remember a time when you needed God's help? How can we receive God's help to do things we can't do by ourselves?

## CLOSING PRAYER

Let us stand and bring our hopes and needs to God as we pray, "Lord, hear our prayer."

◆ All may add their own prayers here.

Let us pray: **Our Father . . . Amen.**

All powerful God,
we know that you can do
what is impossible for us.
Give us faith to believe in you,
and hope to trust in you
so that we will never be alone.
Be our strength in everything we do.
We ask this through Jesus Christ our Lord.
**Amen.**

✚ All make the Sign of the Cross.

# PRAYER FOR WEDNESDAY AUGUST 18, 2010

## OPENING

In today's Gospel Jesus describes a landowner with a surprising way of doing business. A "wage" is the amount of money an employer agrees to pay a worker.

✢ All make the Sign of the Cross.

**In the name of the Father and of the Son and of the Holy Spirit. Amen.**

## PSALM
(For a longer psalm, see page xi.) Psalm 95:1b, 2 (1a)

O come, let us sing to the LORD.

**O come, let us sing to the LORD.**

Let us make a joyful noise to the rock
   of our salvation!
Let us come into his presence with
   thanksgiving;
let us make a joyful noise to him with
   songs of praise!

**O come, let us sing to the LORD.**

◆ All stand and sing **Alleluia**.

## GOSPEL
Matthew 20:1–2, 6a, 7b–8, 10–13, 15

A reading from the holy Gospel according to Matthew

For the kingdom of heaven is like a landowner who went out early in the morning to hire laborers for his vineyard. After agreeing with the laborers for the usual daily wage, he sent them into his vineyard. And about five o'clock he went out and found others standing around; and he said to them, "You also go into the vineyard." When evening came, the owner of the vineyard said to his manager, "Call the laborers and give them their pay, beginning with the last and then going to the first." Now when the first came, they thought they would receive more; but each of them also received the usual daily wage. And when they received it, they grumbled against the landowner, saying, "These last worked only one hour, and you have made them equal to us who have borne the burden of the day and the scorching heat." But he replied to one of them, "Friend, I am doing you no wrong; did you not agree with me for the usual daily wage? Am I not allowed to do what I choose with what belongs to me? Or are you envious because I am generous?"

The Gospel of the Lord.

◆ All sit and observe silence.

## FOR SILENT REFLECTION

Who do you think the landowner is? Do you think the landowner is being unfair?

## CLOSING PRAYER

Let us stand and bring our hopes and needs to God as we pray, "Lord, hear our prayer."

◆ All may add their own prayers here.

Let us pray: **Our Father . . . Amen.**

God of mercy and justice,
we praise your generosity to all people.
May we also be merciful and generous!
We ask this through Christ our Lord.
**Amen.**

✢ All make the Sign of the Cross.

# PRAYER FOR **THURSDAY AUGUST 19, 2010**

## OPENING

In today's Gospel, Jesus tells a parable [PAIR-a-bl] (a story that teaches a lesson). He compares the kingdom of heaven to a king who invites people to a wedding banquet.

✚ All make the Sign of the Cross.

**In the name of the Father and of the Son and of the Holy Spirit. Amen.**

## PSALM
(For a longer psalm, see page xi.) Psalm 95:1b, 2 (1a)

O come, let us sing to the LORD.

**O come, let us sing to the LORD.**

Let us make a joyful noise to the rock
    of our salvation!
Let us come into his presence with
    thanksgiving;
let us make a joyful noise to him with
    songs of praise!

**O come, let us sing to the LORD.**

◆ All stand and sing **Alleluia**.

## GOSPEL
Matthew 22:1–4a, 5, 8–10

A reading from the holy Gospel according to Matthew

Once more Jesus spoke to them in parables [PAIR-a-bls], saying: "The kingdom of heaven may be compared to a king who gave a wedding banquet for his son. He sent his slaves to call those who had been invited to the wedding banquet, but they would not come. Again he sent other slaves, saying, 'Tell those who have been invited: "Look, I have prepared my dinner."' But they made light of it and went away, one to his farm, and another to his business. Then he said to his slaves, 'The wedding is ready but those invited were not worthy. Go therefore into the main streets, and invite everyone you find to the wedding banquet.' Those slaves went out into the streets and gathered all whom they found, both good and bad; so the wedding hall was filled with guests."

The Gospel of the Lord.

◆ All sit and observe silence.

## FOR SILENT REFLECTION

Who is the king in this story? What could this wedding banquet be?

## CLOSING PRAYER

Let us stand and bring our hopes and needs to God as we pray, "Lord, hear our prayer."

◆ All may add their own prayers here.

Let us pray: **Our Father . . . Amen.**

Holy God,
you invite us to your banquet,
so that we can share
in the joy of your presence.
May your love
rule our hearts and minds.
We ask this through Jesus Christ our Lord.
**Amen.**

✚ All make the Sign of the Cross.

# PRAYER FOR FRIDAY AUGUST 20, 2010

## OPENING

Today we remember Saint Bernard of Clairvaux, a 12th century monk and spiritual teacher. In today's Gospel, Jesus teaches a lesson on love.

✠ All make the Sign of the Cross.

**In the name of the Father and of the Son and of the Holy Spirit. Amen.**

## PSALM       (For a longer psalm, see page xi.) Psalm 95:1b, 2 (1a)

O come, let us sing to the LORD.

**O come, let us sing to the LORD.**

Let us make a joyful noise to the rock
    of our salvation!
Let us come into his presence with
    thanksgiving;
let us make a joyful noise to him with
    songs of praise!

**O come, let us sing to the LORD.**

◆ All stand and sing **Alleluia**.

## GOSPEL       Matthew 22:34–40

A reading from the holy Gospel according to Matthew

When the Pharisees [FAIR-uh-seez] heard that Jesus had silenced the Sadducees, [SAD-you-sees] they gathered together, and one of them, a lawyer, asked him a question to test him. "Teacher, which commandment in the law is the greatest?" He said to him, "You shall love the Lord your God with all your heart, and with all your soul, and with all your mind. This is the greatest and first commandment. And a second is like it: You shall love your neighbor as yourself. On these two commandments hang all the law and the prophets."

The Gospel of the Lord.

◆ All sit and observe silence.

## FOR SILENT REFLECTION

Why do you think loving God comes first, and loving your neighbor as yourself, second?

## CLOSING PRAYER

Let us stand and bring our hopes and needs to God as we pray, "Lord, hear our prayer."

◆ All may add their own prayers here.

Let us pray: **Our Father . . . Amen.**

Holy God,
all love comes from you.
We thank you for
the love our parents have for us
and the love we have for them;
for the love we share with our friends
and even our pets.
Send your Holy Spirit
to fill us with your love.
We ask this in the name of Jesus Christ,
    our Lord.
**Amen.**

✠ All make the Sign of the Cross.

# PRAYER FOR THE WEEK

WITH A READING FROM THE GOSPEL FOR **SUNDAY, AUGUST 22, 2010**

## OPENING

Yesterday, we listened to Jesus' teaching about the two great commandments: to love God and to love our neighbors as ourselves. In today's Gospel, Jesus speaks of "evildoers." An evildoer is a person who refuses to love God, himself, and others. This is not an easy reading; we need to really listen and think about what Jesus is saying.

✢ All make the Sign of the Cross.

**In the name of the Father and of the Son and of the Holy Spirit. Amen.**

## PSALM (For a longer psalm, see page xi.) Psalm 95:1b, 2 (1a)

O come, let us sing to the LORD.

**O come, let us sing to the LORD.**

Let us make a joyful noise to the rock
 of our salvation!
Let us come into his presence with
 thanksgiving;
let us make a joyful noise to him with
 songs of praise!

**O come, let us sing to the LORD.**

◆ All stand and sing **Alleluia**.

## GOSPEL Luke 13:22–25a, 27b

A reading from the holy Gospel according to Luke

Jesus went through one town and village after another, teaching as he made his way to Jerusalem. Someone asked him, "Lord, will only a few be saved?" He said to them, "Strive to enter through the narrow door; for many, I tell you, will try to enter and will not be able. When once the owner of the house has got up and shut the door, and you begin to stand outside and to knock at the door, saying, 'Lord, open to us', then in reply he will say to you, 'I do not know where you come from. Go away from me, all you evildoers!'"

The Gospel of the Lord.

◆ All sit and observe silence.

## FOR SILENT REFLECTION

Who do you think the homeowner is and why won't he let evildoers into the house?

## CLOSING PRAYER

Let us stand and bring our hopes and needs to God as we pray, "Lord, hear our prayer."

◆ All may add their own prayers here.

Let us pray: **Our Father . . . Amen.**

We praise you, God,
and we thank you
for giving us the Church,
your holy house and people.
Help us to live together
as your children,
protect us from all harm,
and grant us peace.
We ask this through Jesus Christ our Lord.
**Amen.**

✢ All make the Sign of the Cross.

# PRAYER FOR MONDAY AUGUST 23, 2010

## OPENING

Today we celebrate the memorial of Saint Rose of Lima, patroness of Latin America and the Philippines. Saint Rose had great love for God, for her family whom she helped support, and for the native people and slaves whom she cared for. In today's reading, Paul writes to the people of the church in Thessalonia [Thes-uh-LOH-nee-uh] who also had great love.

✢ All make the Sign of the Cross.

**In the name of the Father and of the Son and of the Holy Spirit. Amen.**

## PSALM
(For a longer psalm, see page xi.) Psalm 95:1b, 2 (1a)

O come, let us sing to the LORD.

**O come, let us sing to the LORD.**

Let us make a joyful noise to the rock
  of our salvation!
Let us come into his presence with
  thanksgiving;
let us make a joyful noise to him with
  songs of praise!

**O come, let us sing to the LORD.**

## READING
2 Thessalonians 1:2–4, 11–12

A reading from the Second Letter of Saint Paul to the Thessalonians [Thes-uh-LOH-nee-uhnz]

Grace to you and peace from God our Father and the Lord Jesus Christ. We must always give thanks to God for you, brothers and sisters, as is right, because your faith is growing abundantly and the love of everyone of you for one another is increasing. Therefore we ourselves boast of you among the churches of God for your steadfastness and faith during all your persecutions and the afflictions you are enduring. To this end, we always pray for you, asking that our God will make you worthy of his call and will fulfill by his power every good resolve and work of faith, so that the name of our Lord Jesus may be glorified in you, and you in him, according to the grace of our God and the Lord Jesus Christ.

The word of the Lord.

◆ All observe silence.

## FOR SILENT REFLECTION

Paul says the love of the Thessalonians is growing. What is making their love grow?

## CLOSING PRAYER

Let us stand and bring our hopes and needs to God as we pray, "Lord, hear our prayer."

◆ All may add their own prayers here.

Let us pray: **Our Father . . . Amen.**

Loving Father,
open our eyes and hearts
to the needs of others.
Let us do a little good each day, and
help us to keep growing
in faith, hope, and love.
We ask this through Jesus Christ our Lord.
**Amen.**

✢ All make the Sign of the Cross.

# PRAYER FOR TUESDAY AUGUST 24, 2010

## OPENING

Today we celebrate the memorial of the apostle, Saint Bartholomew. Some Bible experts think this apostle was called Nathanael in the Gospel according to John, which is today's reading.

✠ All make the Sign of the Cross.

**In the name of the Father and of the Son and of the Holy Spirit. Amen.**

## PSALM (For a longer psalm, see page xi.) Psalm 95:1b, 2 (1a)

O come, let us sing to the LORD.

**O come, let us sing to the LORD.**

Let us make a joyful noise to the rock
of our salvation!
Let us come into his presence with
thanksgiving;
let us make a joyful noise to him with
songs of praise!

**O come, let us sing to the LORD.**

◆ All stand and sing **Alleluia**.

## GOSPEL                John 1:45–49

A reading from the holy Gospel according to John

Philip found Nathanael and said to him, "We have found him about whom Moses in the law and also the prophets wrote, Jesus son of Joseph from Nazareth [NAH-zuh-reth]." Nathanael said to him, "Can anything good come out of Nazareth?" Philip said to him, "Come and see." When Jesus saw Nathanael coming toward him, he said of him, "Here is truly an Israelite in whom there is no deceit!" Nathanael asked him, "Where did you get to know me?" Jesus answered, "I saw you under the fig tree before Philip called you." Nathanael replied, "Rabbi, you are the Son of God! You are the King of Israel!"

The Gospel of the Lord.

◆ All sit and observe silence.

## FOR SILENT REFLECTION

How did Jesus know Nathanael so well? Do you feel that Jesus really knows you?

## CLOSING PRAYER

Let us stand and bring our hopes and needs to God as we pray, "Lord, hear our prayer."

◆ All may add their own prayers here.

Let us pray: **Our Father . . . Amen.**

Heavenly God,
you know us so well,
our needs, our desires.
You know who we truly are
and what is best in us.
We want to know you.
Help us to meet you in your Holy Word.
We ask this through Jesus Christ our Lord.
**Amen.**

✠ All make the Sign of the Cross.

# PRAYER FOR **WEDNESDAY AUGUST 25, 2010**

## OPENING

In today's reading, Saint Paul writes to the people in the Church of Thessalonia [Thes-uh-LOH-nee-uh] about how Christians ought to work. To exhort [eg-ZOHRT] means to urge or strongly encourage.

✜ All make the Sign of the Cross.

**In the name of the Father and of the Son and of the Holy Spirit. Amen.**

## PSALM     (For a longer psalm, see page xi.) Psalm 95:1b, 2 (1a)

O come, let us sing to the LORD.

**O come, let us sing to the LORD.**

Let us make a joyful noise to the rock
  of our salvation!
Let us come into his presence with
  thanksgiving;
let us make a joyful noise to him with
  songs of praise!

**O come, let us sing to the LORD.**

## READING     2 Thessalonians 3:6–8, 11–13, 16

A reading from the Second Letter of Saint Paul to the Thessalonians [Thes-uh-LOH-nee-uhnz]

Now we command you, beloved, in the name of our Lord Jesus Christ, to keep away from believers who are living in idleness [I-dulh-ness] and not according to the traditions that they received from us. For you yourselves know how you ought to imitate [IHM-ih-tayt] us; we were not idle when we were with you. For we hear that some of you are living in idleness, mere busybodies, not doing any work. Now such persons we command and exhort [eg-ZOHRT] in the Lord Jesus Christ to do their work quietly and to earn their own living. Brothers and sisters, do not be weary in doing what is right. Now may the Lord of peace himself give you peace at all times in all ways. The Lord be with all of you.

The word of the Lord.

◆ All observe silence.

## FOR SILENT REFLECTION

Why do you think Paul believes that work is important for Christians?

## CLOSING PRAYER

Let us stand and bring our hopes and needs to God as we pray, "Lord, hear our prayer."

◆ All may add their own prayers here.

Let us pray: **Our Father . . . Amen.**

Holy God,
give us enthusiasm [en-THOO-zee-az-uhm]
for doing your work in this world.
Protect us from idleness [I-duhl-ness],
    boredom,
and selfishness.
Help us to use our talents
and the many gifts you give us
to serve others.
We ask this through Jesus Christ our Lord.
**Amen.**

✜ All make the Sign of the Cross.

# PRAYER FOR **THURSDAY AUGUST 26, 2010**

## OPENING

Today we hear from Saint Paul's letter to the people of the church in Corinth [KOHR-inth]. He begins his letter by giving a blessing. All of God's work is a blessing, a gift of God's life and goodness. When we bless one another, we share this divine life and goodness.

✠ All make the Sign of the Cross.

**In the name of the Father and of the Son and of the Holy Spirit. Amen.**

## PSALM     (For a longer psalm, see page xi.) Psalm 95:1b, 2 (1a)

O come, let us sing to the LORD.

**O come, let us sing to the LORD.**

Let us make a joyful noise to the rock
    of our salvation!
Let us come into his presence with
    thanksgiving;
let us make a joyful noise to him with
    songs of praise!

**O come, let us sing to the LORD.**

## READING     1 Corinthians 1:3–9

A reading from the First Letter of Saint Paul to the Corinthians [kohr-IN-thee-uhnz]

Grace to you and peace from God our Father and the Lord Jesus Christ. I give thanks to my God always for you because of the grace of God that has been given you in Christ Jesus, for in every way you have been enriched in him, in speech and knowledge of every kind, just as the testimony of Christ has been strengthened among you, so that you are not lacking in any spiritual gift as you wait for the revealing of our Lord Jesus Christ. He will also strengthen you to the end, so that you may be blameless on the day of our Lord Jesus Christ. God is faithful; by him you were called into the fellowship of his Son, Jesus Christ our Lord.

The word of the Lord.

◆ All observe silence.

## FOR SILENT REFLECTION

What blessings are you thankful for?

## CLOSING PRAYER

Let us stand and bring our hopes and needs to God as we pray, "Lord, hear our prayer."

◆ All may add their own prayers here.

Let us pray: **Our Father . . . Amen.**

Blessed are you, Lord God,
creator of all that is good.
We thank you for your many gifts:
the gifts of faith and hope,
the gifts of speech and understanding,
the gifts of teachers and parents who
    guide us,
and friends who support us.
Help us to share with others
the blessings we receive.
We ask this through Jesus Christ our Lord.
**Amen.**

✠ All make the Sign of the Cross.

# PRAYER FOR FRIDAY AUGUST 27, 2010

## OPENING

Today we remember Saint Monica, who spent seventeen years praying that her son, Augustine [uh-GUS-tuhn], would come to know Christ. Augustine did become a Christian and a great teacher and saint. In today's Gospel, Jesus talks about waiting for the kingdom of God.

✢ All make the Sign of the Cross.

**In the name of the Father and of the Son and of the Holy Spirit. Amen.**

## PSALM
(For a longer psalm, see page xi.) Psalm 95:1b, 2 (1a)

O come, let us sing to the LORD.

**O come, let us sing to the LORD.**

Let us make a joyful noise to the rock
 of our salvation!
Let us come into his presence with
 thanksgiving;
let us make a joyful noise to him with
 songs of praise!

**O come, let us sing to the LORD.**

◆ All stand and sing **Alleluia**.

## GOSPEL
Matthew 25:1–6, 8–10, 13

A reading from the holy Gospel according to Matthew

Jesus said, "Then the kingdom of heaven will be like this. Ten bridesmaids took their lamps and went to meet the bridegroom. Five of them were foolish and five were wise. When the foolish took their lamps, they took no oil with them; but the wise took flasks of oil with their lamps. As the bridegroom was delayed, all of them became drowsy and slept. But at midnight there was a shout, 'Look! Here is the bridegroom! Come out to meet him.' The foolish said to the wise, 'Give us some of your oil, for our lamps are going out.' But the wise replied, 'No! There will not be enough for you and for us; you had better go to the dealers and buy some for yourselves.' And while they went to buy it, the bridegroom came and those who were ready went with him into the wedding banquet; and the door was shut. Keep awake therefore, for you know neither the day nor the hour."

The Gospel of the Lord.

◆ All sit and observe silence.

## FOR SILENT REFLECTION

Who do you think the bridegroom is? What is the oil?

## CLOSING PRAYER

Let us stand and bring our hopes and needs to God as we pray, "Lord, hear our prayer."

◆ All may add their own prayers here.

Let us pray: **Our Father . . . Amen.**

God of love and hope,
wake us up and give us faith to believe
that you really are coming into our lives.
We ask this in the name of Jesus Christ
 our Lord.
**Amen.**

✢ All make the Sign of the Cross.

# PRAYER FOR THE WEEK

WITH A READING FROM THE GOSPEL FOR **SUNDAY, AUGUST 29, 2010**

## OPENING

In today's Gospel we hear a parable [PAIR-a-bl] (a story that teaches a lesson). When the story tells us not to exalt [eg-ZAHLT] ourselves, it means we shouldn't praise ourselves. When we praise God instead of ourselves, we feel joy, like the joy in today's psalm.

✦ All make the Sign of the Cross.

**In the name of the Father and of the Son and of the Holy Spirit. Amen.**

## PSALM  (For a longer psalm, see page xi.) Psalm 95:1b, 2 (1a)

O come, let us sing to the LORD.

**O come, let us sing to the LORD.**

Let us make a joyful noise to the rock
    of our salvation!
Let us come into his presence with
    thanksgiving;
let us make a joyful noise to him with
    songs of praise!

O come, let us sing to the LORD.

◆ All stand and sing **Alleluia**.

## GOSPEL  Luke 14:7b–11

A reading from the holy Gospel according to Luke

Jesus told them a parable [PAIR-a-bl]. "When you are invited by someone to a wedding banquet, do not sit down at the place of honor, in case someone more distinguished than you has been invited by your host; and the host who invited both of you may come and say to you, 'Give this person your place,' and then in disgrace you would start to take the lowest place. But when you are invited, go and sit down at the lowest place so that when your host comes, he may say to you, 'Friend, move up higher.' Then you will be honored in the presence of all who sit at the table with you. For all who exalt themselves will be humbled, and those who humble themselves will be exalted."

The Gospel of the Lord.

◆ All sit and observe silence.

## FOR SILENT REFLECTION

What is Jesus telling us about what happens when we try to impress others?

## CLOSING PRAYER

Let us stand and bring our hopes and needs to God as we pray, "Lord, hear our prayer."

◆ All may add their own prayers here.

Let us pray: **Our Father . . . Amen.**

Wonderful God,
you call us "friend," and invite us
to share a holy meal with you.
Help us to not be proud and pushy.
Give us the humility to be ourselves,
that we might praise you with joy.
We ask this through Jesus Christ our Lord.
**Amen.**

✦ All make the Sign of the Cross.

# PRAYER FOR MONDAY AUGUST 30, 2010

## OPENING

In today's Gospel, Jesus reads scripture in which the prophet Isaiah (I-ZAY-uh) speaks of God's promise to send a Messiah. A synagogue (SIN-a-gog) is a Jewish house of study, where people come together to study the words of scripture.

✢ All make the Sign of the Cross.

**In the name of the Father and of the Son and of the Holy Spirit. Amen.**

## PSALM  (For a longer psalm, see page xi.) Psalm 95:1b, 2 (1a)

O come, let us sing to the LORD.

**O come, let us sing to the LORD.**

Let us make a joyful noise to the rock
of our salvation!
Let us come into his presence with
thanksgiving;
let us make a joyful noise to him with
songs of praise!

**O come, let us sing to the LORD.**

◆ All stand and sing **Alleluia**.

## GOSPEL  Luke 4:16–21

A reading from the holy Gospel according to Luke

When Jesus came to Nazareth, where he had been brought up, he went to the synagogue on the Sabbath day, as was his custom. He stood up to read, and the scroll of the prophet Isaiah [I-ZAY-uh] was given to him. He unrolled the scroll and found the place where it is written:

"The Spirit of the Lord is upon me,
 because he has anointed me
 to bring good news to the poor.
He has sent me to proclaim release
  to the captives
and recovery of sight to the blind,
 to let the oppressed go free,
 to proclaim the year of the Lord's favor."

The Gospel of the Lord.

◆ All sit and observe silence.

## FOR SILENT REFLECTION

As he is reading God's word, Jesus is telling the people about himself. Do you think Jesus helps us to know him when we study scripture?

## CLOSING PRAYER

Let us stand and bring our hopes and needs to God as we pray, "Lord, hear our prayer."

◆ All may add their own prayers here.

Let us pray: **Our Father . . . Amen.**

Word of God,
you call us by name to be your people
and you reveal yourself to us
in the words of scripture.
Teach us to listen for your voice
as we study together.
We ask this through Jesus Christ our Lord.
**Amen.**

✢ All make the Sign of the Cross.

# PRAYER FOR TUESDAY AUGUST 31, 2010

## OPENING

We often hear about angels in scripture, such as the angel who tells Mary she will give birth to the Messiah. Angels are spiritual beings who serve God. In scripture, an "unclean spirit," sometimes called a "demon," is a spiritual being who hates anything good and wants nothing to do with God. In today's Gospel, we learn about the power Jesus has over them.

✣ All make the Sign of the Cross.

**In the name of the Father and of the Son and of the Holy Spirit. Amen.**

## PSALM (For a longer psalm, see page xi.) Psalm 95:1b, 2 (1a)

O come, let us sing to the Lord.

**O come, let us sing to the Lord.**

Let us make a joyful noise to the rock
      of our salvation!
Let us come into his presence with
      thanksgiving;
let us make a joyful noise to him with
      songs of praise!

**O come, let us sing to the Lord.**

◆ All stand and sing **Alleluia**.

## GOSPEL                    Luke 4:31–32, 37

A reading from the holy Gospel according to Luke

Jesus went down to Capernaum [kuh-PER-nee-m], a city in Galilee, and was teaching them on the Sabbath [SAB-uth]. They were astounded at his teaching, because he spoke with authority [a-THOR-i-tee]. In the synagogue there was a man who had the spirit of an unclean demon, and he cried out with a loud voice, "Let us alone! What have you to do with us, Jesus of Nazareth? Have you come to destroy us? I know who you are, the Holy One of God." But Jesus rebuked him, saying, "Be silent, and come out of him!" When the demon had thrown him down before them, he came out of him without having done him any harm. They were all amazed and kept saying to one another, "What kind of utterance is this? For with authority and power he commands the unclean spirits, and out they come!"

The Gospel of the Lord.

◆ All sit and observe silence.

## FOR SILENT REFLECTION

Why is Jesus so powerful? Have you experienced his power in your life?

## CLOSING PRAYER

Let us stand and bring our hopes and needs to God as we pray, "Lord, hear our prayer."

◆ All may add their own prayers here.

Let us pray: **Our Father . . . Amen.**

All-powerful God,
we pray for all who are suffering
because of hatred, envy, and pride.
May they know your saving power.
We ask this through Jesus Christ our Lord.
**Amen.**

✣ All make the Sign of the Cross.

# PRAYER FOR **WEDNESDAY SEPTEMBER 1, 2010**

## OPENING

Today's Gospel continues to teach about Jesus' power. As you listen to this Gospel, think what this power tells us about who Jesus is.

✢ All make the Sign of the Cross.

**In the name of the Father and of the Son and of the Holy Spirit. Amen.**

## PSALM (For a longer psalm, see page xi.) Psalm 95:1b, 2 (1a)

O come, let us sing to the LORD.

**O come, let us sing to the LORD.**

Let us make a joyful noise to the rock
　　of our salvation!
Let us come into his presence with
　　thanksgiving;
let us make a joyful noise to him with
　　songs of praise!

**O come, let us sing to the LORD.**

◆ All stand and sing **Alleluia**.

## GOSPEL Luke 4:38–41

A reading from the holy Gospel according to Luke

After leaving the synagogue, he entered Simon's house. Now Simon's mother-in-law was suffering from a high fever, and they asked him about her. Then he stood over her and rebuked the fever, and it left her. Immediately she got up and began to serve them.

　As the sun was setting, all those who had any who were sick with various kinds of diseases brought them to him and he laid his hands on each of them and cured them. Demons also came out of many, shouting, "You are the Son of God!" But he rebuked them and would not allow them to speak because they knew that he was the Messiah.

The Gospel of the Lord.

◆ All sit and observe silence.

## FOR SILENT REFLECTION

What does Simon's mother-in-law do once Jesus has healed her?

## CLOSING PRAYER

Let us stand and bring our hopes and needs to God as we pray, "Lord, hear our prayer."

◆ All may add their own prayers here.

Let us pray: **Our Father . . . Amen.**

Holy God,
how great is your power!
Heal our bodies,
protect our souls,
and fill us with your love,
that we may serve you
in gratitude and joy forever.
We ask this through Jesus Christ our Lord.
**Amen.**

✢ All make the Sign of the Cross.

# PRAYER FOR **THURSDAY SEPTEMBER 2, 2010**

## OPENING

Today's Gospel tells how Simon became a follower of Jesus. Jesus later changed Simon's name to Peter.

✢ All make the Sign of the Cross.

**In the name of the Father and of the Son and of the Holy Spirit. Amen.**

## PSALM     (For a longer psalm, see page xi.) Psalm 95:1b, 2 (1a)

O come, let us sing to the LORD.

**O come, let us sing to the LORD.**

Let us make a joyful noise to the rock
  of our salvation!
Let us come into his presence with
  thanksgiving;
let us make a joyful noise to him with
  songs of praise!

**O come, let us sing to the LORD.**

◆ All stand and sing **Alleluia**.

## GOSPEL     Luke 5:1–2a, 3–6, 8–9a, 10b–11

A reading from the holy Gospel according to Luke

Once while Jesus was standing beside the lake of Gennesaret [Gen-ESS-er-et], and the crowd was pressing in on him to hear the word of God, he saw two boats there at the shore of the lake. He got into one of the boats, the one belonging to Simon, and asked him to put out a little way from the shore. Then he sat down and taught the crowds from the boat. When he had finished speaking, he said to Simon, "Put down your nets for a catch." Simon answered, "Master, we have worked all night long but have caught nothing. Yet if you say so, I will let down the nets." When they had done this, they caught so many fish that their nets were beginning to break. But when Simon Peter saw it, he fell down at Jesus' knees saying, "Go away from me, Lord, for I am a sinful man!" For he and all who were with him were amazed at the catch of fish. Then Jesus said to Simon, "Do not be afraid; from now on you will be catching people." When they had brought their boats to shore they left everything and followed him.

The Gospel of the Lord.

◆ All sit and observe silence.

## FOR SILENT REFLECTION

Why do you think they followed Jesus?

## CLOSING PRAYER

Let us stand and bring our hopes and needs to God as we pray, "Lord, hear our prayer."

◆ All may add their own prayers here.

Let us pray: **Our Father . . . Amen.**

Lord God,
give us trust to do what you ask
and courage to follow
wherever you lead.
We ask this through Jesus Christ our Lord.
**Amen.**

✢ All make the Sign of the Cross.

**ALSO ON THIS DAY:** Janmashtami (Hindu celebration of the birth of Krishna)

# PRAYER FOR FRIDAY SEPTEMBER 3, 2010

## OPENING

Today we remember Saint Gregory the Great, a monk who became Pope in the sixth century. He cared for the poor, he taught the people through his writings and sermons, and he tried to keep order and peace in a difficult time. Today's Gospel uses the word "fast" in a way that means to not eat. We often fast when we are sad or sorry about something or when we want to pay attention to the spiritual presence of God.

✚ All make the Sign of the Cross.

**In the name of the Father and of the Son and of the Holy Spirit. Amen.**

## PSALM (For a longer psalm, see page xi.) Psalm 95:1b, 2 (1a)

O come, let us sing to the LORD.

**O come, let us sing to the LORD.**

Let us make a joyful noise to the rock
 of our salvation!
Let us come into his presence with
 thanksgiving;
let us make a joyful noise to him with
 songs of praise!

**O come, let us sing to the LORD.**

◆ All stand and sing **Alleluia**.

## GOSPEL Luke 5:33–35

A reading from the holy Gospel according to Luke

Then they said to Jesus, "John's disciples, like the disciples of the Pharisees [FAIR-uh-seez], frequently fast and pray, but your disciples eat and drink." Jesus said to them, "You cannot make wedding guests fast while the bridegroom is with them, can you? The days will come when the bridegroom will be taken away from them, and then they will fast in those days."

The Gospel of the Lord.

◆ All sit and observe silence.

## FOR SILENT REFLECTION

Have you ever been to a wedding? Why don't wedding guests fast? When do Christians feast?

## CLOSING PRAYER

Let us stand and bring our hopes and needs to God as we pray, "Lord, hear our prayer."

◆ All may add their own prayers here.

Let us pray: **Our Father . . . Amen.**

Loving God,
you are with us
in your sacred word,
in your body and blood fed to us,
in the priest who leads us in prayer,
and in your people gathered together.
Open our hearts and minds
to receive you,
for when you are with us,
our hearts are full of joy.
We ask this through Jesus Christ our Lord.
**Amen.**

✚ All make the Sign of the Cross.

# PRAYER FOR THE WEEK

WITH A READING FROM THE GOSPEL FOR **SUNDAY, SEPTEMBER 5, 2010**

## OPENING

In today's Gospel, Jesus encourages us to really think about what it means to be a follower of Christ.

✣ All make the Sign of the Cross.

**In the name of the Father and of the Son and of the Holy Spirit. Amen.**

## PSALM  (For a longer psalm, see page xi.) Psalm 95:1b, 2 (1a)

O come, let us sing to the LORD.

**O come, let us sing to the LORD.**

Let us make a joyful noise to the rock
   of our salvation!
Let us come into his presence with
   thanksgiving;
let us make a joyful noise to him with
   songs of praise!

**O come, let us sing to the LORD.**

◆ All stand and sing **Alleluia**.

## GOSPEL  Luke 14:25, 27–30, 33

A reading from the holy Gospel according to Luke

Now large crowds were traveling with Jesus; and he turned and said to them, "Whoever does not carry the cross and follow me cannot be my disciple. For which of you, intending to build a tower, does not first sit down and estimate the cost, to see whether he has enough to complete it? Otherwise, when he has laid a foundation and is not able to finish, all who see it will begin to ridicule him, saying, 'This fellow began to build and was not able to finish.' So therefore, none of you can become my disciple if you do not give up all your possessions."

The Gospel of the Lord.

◆ All sit and observe silence.

## FOR SILENT REFLECTION

What do you think Jesus means when he says that we should carry the cross and follow him?

## CLOSING PRAYER

Let us stand and bring our hopes and needs to God as we pray, "Lord, hear our prayer."

◆ All may add their own prayers here.

Let us pray: **Our Father . . . Amen.**

God, our Father,
we know that we are your people
and you want us to follow you.
Give us the courage to be faithful
to your teachings;
to tell the truth,
and to be giving and loving,
even when it is not easy.
Help us to listen for your voice
guiding us, challenging us,
and reassuring us.
We ask this in the name of Jesus Christ
   our Lord.
**Amen.**

✣ All make the Sign of the Cross.

**ALSO ON THIS DAY:** Lailat Ul Qadr (Islamic Night of Decree, commemorating night the first verses of the Koran were revealed to Mohammed)

# PRAYER FOR MONDAY SEPTEMBER 6, 2010

## OPENING

In today's Gospel, the Pharisees [FAIR-uh-seez] watch Jesus to see if he will break the Jewish law that no work should be done on the Sabbath [SAB-uhth]. But Jesus understands God's law better than they do.

✙ All make the Sign of the Cross.

**In the name of the Father and of the Son and of the Holy Spirit. Amen.**

## PSALM  (For a longer psalm, see page xi.) Psalm 95:1b, 2 (1a)

O come, let us sing to the LORD.

**O come, let us sing to the LORD.**

Let us make a joyful noise to the rock
    of our salvation!
Let us come into his presence with
    thanksgiving;
let us make a joyful noise to him with
    songs of praise!

**O come, let us sing to the LORD.**

◆ All stand and sing **Alleluia**.

## GOSPEL  Luke 6:6–11

A reading from the holy Gospel according to Luke

On another sabbath he entered the synagogue and taught, and there was a man there whose right hand was withered. The scribes and the Pharisees [FAIR-uh-seez] watched him to see whether he would cure on the sabbath, so that they might find an accusation against him. Even though he knew what they were thinking, he said to the man who had the withered hand, "Come and stand here." He got up and stood there. Then Jesus said to them, "I ask you, is it lawful to do good or to do harm on the sabbath, to save life or to destroy it?" After looking around at all of them, he said to him, "Stretch out your hand." He did so, and his hand was restored. But they were filled with fury and discussed with one another what they might do to Jesus.

The Gospel of the Lord.

◆ All sit and observe silence.

## FOR SILENT REFLECTION

What do you think Jesus was teaching us by healing the man on the sabbath?

## CLOSING PRAYER

Let us stand and bring our hopes and needs to God as we pray, "Lord, hear our prayer."

◆ All may add their own prayers here.

Let us pray: **Our Father . . . Amen.**

Holy God,
if we are to follow you, we must listen.
Help us to listen
to what you have to say to us
as we study your holy word.
Give us a thirst for truth
and a hunger for justice.
We ask through Christ our Lord.
**Amen.**

✙ All make the Sign of the Cross.

---

**ALSO ON THIS DAY:** Labor Day (U.S.A., Canada)

# PRAYER FOR TUESDAY SEPTEMBER 7, 2010

## OPENING

In today's Gospel, Jesus chooses the twelve apostles [uh-POS-uhlz]. The word "apostle" means someone who is sent and has the power to act on behalf of the sender.

✝ All make the Sign of the Cross.

**In the name of the Father and of the Son and of the Holy Spirit. Amen.**

## PSALM   (For a longer psalm, see page xi.) Psalm 95:1b, 2 (1a)

O come, let us sing to the LORD.

**O come, let us sing to the LORD.**

Let us make a joyful noise to the rock
　　of our salvation!
Let us come into his presence with
　　thanksgiving;
let us make a joyful noise to him with
　　songs of praise!

**O come, let us sing to the LORD.**

◆ All stand and sing **Alleluia.**

## GOSPEL   Luke 6:12–13, 17–19

A reading from the holy Gospel according to Luke

Now during those days he went out to the mountain to pray; and he spent the night in prayer to God. And when day came, he called his disciples and chose twelve of them, whom he also named apostles. He came down with them and stood on a level place with a great crowd of his disciples and a great multitude of people from all Judea [Joo-DEE-uh], Jerusalem, and the coast of Tyre and Sidon [SI-duhn]. They had come to hear him and to be healed of their diseases; and those who were troubled with unclean spirits were cured. And all in the crowd were trying to touch him, for power came out from him and healed all of them.

The Gospel of the Lord.

◆ All sit and observe silence.

## FOR SILENT REFLECTION

Why do you think Jesus spends the night in prayer before he names the apostles?

## CLOSING PRAYER

Let us stand and bring our hopes and needs to God as we pray, "Lord, hear our prayer."

◆ All may add their own prayers here.

Let us pray: **Our Father . . . Amen.**

Lord, our God,
help us to be people of prayer,
turning first to God
when we have decisions to make.
May God's work be done through us.
We ask this through the one
who calls us to follow him,
Jesus Christ our Lord.
**Amen.**

✝ All make the Sign of the Cross.

# PRAYER FOR WEDNESDAY SEPTEMBER 8, 2010

## OPENING

Today we celebrate the birth of the Blessed Virgin Mary. We will hear how she became the mother of our Savior. Because she is so close to her son, Jesus, Mary can offer love, guidance, and support to us.

✚ All make the Sign of the Cross.

**In the name of the Father and of the Son and of the Holy Spirit. Amen.**

## PSALM   (For a longer psalm, see page xi.) Psalm 95:1b, 2 (1a)

O come, let us sing to the LORD.

**O come, let us sing to the LORD.**

Let us make a joyful noise to the rock
   of our salvation!
Let us come into his presence with
   thanksgiving;
let us make a joyful noise to him with
   songs of praise!

O come, let us sing to the LORD.

◆ All stand and sing **Alleluia**.

## GOSPEL   Matthew 1:18b–19, 20bc–23

A reading from the holy Gospel according to Matthew.

When Jesus' mother Mary had been engaged to Joseph, but before they lived together, she was found to be with child from the Holy Spirit. Her husband Joseph, being a righteous man and unwilling to expose her to public disgrace, planned to dismiss her quietly. But an angel of the Lord appeared to him in a dream and said, "Joseph, son of David, do not be afraid to take Mary as your wife, for the child conceived in her is from the Holy Spirit. She will bear a son, and you are to name him Jesus, for he will save his people from their sins." All this took place to fulfill what had been spoken by the Lord through the prophet: "Look, the virgin shall conceive and bear a son, and they shall name him Emmanuel," which means, "God is with us."

The Gospel of the Lord.

◆ All sit and observe silence.

## FOR SILENT REFLECTION

How do the words "God is with us" describe Jesus? What do these words mean to you?

## CLOSING PRAYER

Let us stand and bring our hopes and needs to God as we pray, "Lord, hear our prayer."

◆ All may add their own prayers here.

Let us pray: **Our Father . . . Amen.**

Holy God,
open our hearts,
as Mary opened her heart
to receive your grace.
Help us to say "yes"
to your love in our lives.
We ask this through Jesus Christ our Lord. **Amen.**

✚ All make the Sign of the Cross.

**ALSO ON THIS DAY:** Rosh Hashana (Jewish new year) begins at sunset.

# PRAYER FOR THURSDAY SEPTEMBER 9, 2010

## OPENING

Today we remember Saint Peter Claver [KLAY-ver], a missionary to African slaves in South America who did what Jesus tells us to do in today's Gospel. Jesus tells us to treat others as we want to be treated.

✚ All make the Sign of the Cross.

**In the name of the Father and of the Son and of the Holy Spirit. Amen.**

## PSALM  (For a longer psalm, see page xi.) Psalm 95:1b, 2 (1a)

O come, let us sing to the LORD.

**O come, let us sing to the LORD.**

Let us make a joyful noise to the rock
    of our salvation!
Let us come into his presence with
    thanksgiving;
let us make a joyful noise to him with
    songs of praise!

**O come, let us sing to the LORD.**

◆ All stand and sing **Alleluia**.

## GOSPEL  Luke 6:27–31

A reading from the holy Gospel according to Luke

Jesus said to his disciples, "But I say to you that listen, love your enemies, do good to those who hate you, bless those who curse you, pray for those who abuse you. If anyone strikes you on the cheek, offer the other also; and from anyone who takes away your coat do not withhold even your shirt. Give to everyone who begs from you; and if anyone takes away your goods, do not ask for them again. Do to others as you would have them do to you."

The Gospel of the Lord.

◆ All sit and observe silence.

## FOR SILENT REFLECTION

Think about the people in your life. Are you treating them as you would like them to treat you?

## CLOSING PRAYER

Let us stand and bring our hopes and needs to God as we pray, "Lord, hear our prayer."

◆ All may add their own prayers here.

Let us pray: **Our Father . . . Amen.**

Loving God,
sometimes it isn't easy to love people.
We get hurt and want to hurt back.
Protect and defend us from all harm,
including the harm we do ourselves
when we lash out in anger.
Be our strength when we are frightened.
Be our peace when we are angry.
May your love, not our fear,
guide us in all we do.
We ask this through Jesus Christ our Lord.
**Amen.**

✚ All make the Sign of the Cross.

---

**ALSO ON THIS DAY:** Rosh Hashana (Jewish new year)

# PRAYER SERVICE
## FOR PEACE ON SEPTEMBER 11

*Prepare six leaders for this service. The second leader will need a Bible for the scripture and may need help practicing the reading. You may begin by singing "Healer of Our Every Ill," "Song of the Body of Christ," or "This Is My Song," or perhaps begin in silence with a simple tolling of a hand bell. You may conclude by singing "Make Me a Channel of Your Peace." If the group will sing, prepare a song leader.*

**FIRST LEADER:**
May the grace and peace of our Lord Jesus Christ be with us, now and for ever.
**Amen.**

Let us pray:
Lord Jesus Christ,
after you had been killed and your followers
    deserted you out of fear and despair,
you rose from the dead.
When you appeared to these weak and
    fearful people,
you did not scold or blame them.
You said, "Peace be with you."
Today we pray for your peace,
the peace that doesn't keep score, forgives
    all weakness,
and is bigger than any wrong a person can
    do to us.
May we receive your holy peace,
which is beyond all human understanding.
We make this prayer through you,
    Christ our Lord.
**Amen.**

◆ All stand and sing **Alleluia**.

**SECOND LEADER**  Luke 24:36–43
A reading from the holy Gospel according to Luke

◆ Read the passage from the Bible.

The Gospel of the Lord.

**THIRD LEADER:**
Let us pause and pray in silence for all those who have died in wars and other conflicts around the world.

**FOURTH LEADER:**
God of all people,
help us to bear Christ, the Prince of Peace,
into all the places we will go in life.
Against all odds, may we be peacemakers
    and healers
We ask this through Christ our Lord.
**Amen.**

**FIFTH LEADER:**
Now let us offer to one another a sign of Christ's peace:

◆ All offer one another a sign of peace.

**SIXTH LEADER:**
And may the Lord bless us,

✢ All make the Sign of the Cross.

protect us from all evil
and bring us to everlasting life.
**Amen.**

# PRAYER FOR FRIDAY
# SEPTEMBER 10, 2010

## OPENING

In today's Gospel Jesus tells a parable [PAIR-a-bl] (a story that teaches a lesson) about how we should treat others. The hypocrite [HIP-uh-krit] Jesus talks about is someone who pretends to be good and faithful but is not.

✝ All make the Sign of the Cross.

**In the name of the Father and of the Son and of the Holy Spirit. Amen.**

## PSALM
(For a longer psalm, see page xi.) Psalm 95:1b, 2 (1a)

O come, let us sing to the LORD.

**O come, let us sing to the LORD.**

Let us make a joyful noise to the rock
    of our salvation!
Let us come into his presence with
    thanksgiving;
let us make a joyful noise to him with
    songs of praise!

**O come, let us sing to the LORD.**

◆ All stand and sing **Alleluia.**

## GOSPEL
Luke: 6:39–42

A reading from the holy Gospel according to Luke

Jesus also told them a parable [PAIR-a-bl]: "Can a blind person guide a blind person? Will not both fall into a pit? A disciple is not above the teacher, but everyone who is fully qualified will be like the teacher. Why do you see the speck in your neighbor's eye, but do not notice the log in your own eye? Or how can you say to your neighbor, 'Friend, let me take out the speck in your eye,' when you yourself do not see the log in our own eye? You hypocrite [HIP-uh-krit], first take the log out of your own eye, and then you will see clearly to take the speck out of your neighbor's eye."

The Gospel of the Lord.

◆ All sit and observe silence.

## FOR SILENT REFLECTION

Is it easier to see the faults of others than our own faults? What does this have to do with being blind?

## CLOSING PRAYER

Let us stand and bring our hopes and needs to God as we pray, "Lord, hear our prayer."

◆ All may add their own prayers here.

Let us pray: **Our Father . . . Amen.**

God of truth and justice,
give us the courage to look at ourselves,
the willingness to see our faults,
and the ability to accept your forgiveness
    and love.
We ask this through Jesus Christ our Lord.
**Amen.**

✝ All make the Sign of the Cross.

---

**ALSO ON THIS DAY:** Rosh Hashana (Jewish new year) ends at sunset.

Eid-al-Fitr (Islamic celebration marking the end of Ramadan, the month of fasting)

September 11, National Day of Mourning and Remembrance is tomorrow.

# PRAYER FOR THE WEEK

WITH A READING FROM THE GOSPEL FOR **SUNDAY, SEPTEMBER 12, 2010**

## OPENING

In today's Gospel, Jesus tells a parable [PAIR-a-bl] (a story that teaches a lesson) about how a good shepherd cares for his sheep. The Gospel talks about "repentance," [rih-PEN-tuhnts] which means feeling sorrow for sin and asking God's help to not sin again.

✢ All make the Sign of the Cross.

**In the name of the Father and of the Son and of the Holy Spirit. Amen.**

## PSALM
(For a longer psalm, see page xi.) Psalm 95:1b, 2 (1a)

O come, let us sing to the LORD.

**O come, let us sing to the LORD.**

Let us make a joyful noise to the rock
    of our salvation!
Let us come into his presence with
    thanksgiving;
let us make a joyful noise to him with
    songs of praise!

**O come, let us sing to the LORD.**

◆ All stand and sing **Alleluia**.

## GOSPEL
Luke 15:1–7

A reading from the holy Gospel according to Luke

Now all the tax collectors and sinners were coming near to listen to Jesus. And the Pharisees [FAIR-uh-seez] and scribes were grumbling and saying, "This fellow welcomes sinners and eats with them." So he told them this parable [PAIR-a-bl]: "Which one of you, having a hundred sheep and losing one of them, does not leave the ninety-nine in the wilderness and go after the one that is lost until he finds it? When he has found it, he lays it on his shoulders and rejoices. And when he comes home, he calls together his friends and neighbors, saying to them, 'Rejoice with me, for I have found my sheep that was lost.' Just so, I tell you, there will be more joy in heaven over one sinner who repents than over ninety-nine righteous persons who need no repentance."

The Gospel of the Lord.

◆ All sit and observe silence.

## FOR SILENT REFLECTION

Who is the shepherd in this story?

## CLOSING PRAYER

Let us stand and bring our hopes and needs to God as we pray, "Lord, hear our prayer."

◆ All may add their own prayers here.

Let us pray: **Our Father . . . Amen.**

Loving God,
help us to never think
we have wandered so far from you
that you cannot find us.
We ask this through Jesus Christ our Lord.
**Amen.**

✢ All make the Sign of the Cross.

---

**ALSO ON THIS DAY:** National Grandparents' Day (U.S.A.)

# PRAYER FOR MONDAY SEPTEMBER 13, 2010

## OPENING

Today we remember Saint John Chrysostom [krih-SAW-stum], a fourth century Greek bishop whose name means "golden mouth." He was a great teacher of the Christian faith. In today's Gospel we will hear about a centurion [sen-TOOR-ee-uhn], a Roman soldier.

✢ All make the Sign of the Cross.

**In the name of the Father and of the Son and of the Holy Spirit. Amen.**

## PSALM (For a longer psalm, see page xi.) Psalm 95:1b, 2 (1a)

O come, let us sing to the LORD.

**O come, let us sing to the LORD.**

Let us make a joyful noise to the rock
    of our salvation!
Let us come into his presence with
    thanksgiving;
let us make a joyful noise to him with
    songs of praise!

**O come, let us sing to the LORD.**

◆ All stand and sing **Alleluia.**

## GOSPEL  Luke 7:1b–3, 6, 7b, 9–10

A reading from the holy Gospel according to Luke

Jesus entered Capernaum [kuh-PER-nee-um]. A centurion [sen-TOOR-ee-uhn] there had a slave whom he valued highly, and who was ill and close to death. When he heard about Jesus, he sent some Jewish elders to him, asking him to come and heal his slave. And Jesus went with them, but when he was not far from the house, the centurion sent friends to say to him, "Lord, do not trouble yourself, for I am not worthy to have you come under my roof. But only speak the word, and let my servant be healed." When Jesus heard this he was amazed at him, and turning to the crowd that followed him, he said, "I tell you, not even in Israel have I found such faith." When those who had been sent returned to the house, they found the slave in good health.

The Gospel of the Lord.

◆ All sit and observe silence.

## FOR SILENT REFLECTION

Can you imagine having so much faith that you could say to Jesus "Only speak the word and I shall be healed?" When do we say these words?

## CLOSING PRAYER

Let us stand and bring our hopes and needs to God as we pray, "Lord, hear our prayer."

◆ All may add their own prayers here.

Let us pray: **Our Father . . . Amen.**

Our Father,
help us to grow into a faith
that is strong like the centurion's,
trusting you completely.
We ask this through Jesus Christ our Lord.
**Amen.**

✢ All make the Sign of the Cross.

# PRAYER FOR TUESDAY SEPTEMBER 14, 2010

## OPENING

Today is the feast of the Exaltation (ex-all-TAY-shun) of the Holy Cross. Exaltation means praise or thanksgiving. We give thanks for the cross. It is a sign of hope because on the cross the Father raised Jesus into new life, a life we are invited to share forever.

✚ All make the Sign of the Cross.

**In the name of the Father and of the Son and of the Holy Spirit. Amen.**

## PSALM
(For a longer psalm, see page xi.) Psalm 95:1b, 2 (1a)

O come, let us sing to the LORD.

**O come, let us sing to the LORD.**

Let us make a joyful noise to the rock
    of our salvation!
Let us come into his presence with
    thanksgiving;
let us make a joyful noise to him with
    songs of praise!

**O come, let us sing to the LORD.**

◆ All stand and sing **Alleluia**.

## GOSPEL
John 3:13, 16–17

A reading from the holy Gospel according to John

No one has ascended [a-SEND-ed] into heaven except the one who descended from heaven, the Son of Man. For God so loved the world that he gave his only Son, so that everyone who believes in him may not perish but may have eternal life. Indeed, God did not send the Son into the world to condemn the world, but in order that the world might be saved through him.

The Gospel of the Lord.

◆ All sit and observe silence.

## FOR SILENT REFLECTION

Imagine how much God must love all of us to give us eternal life through his son. What do you think it will be like to share eternal life with Jesus Christ?

## CLOSING PRAYER

Let us stand and bring our hopes and needs to God as we pray, "Lord, hear our prayer."

◆ All may add their own prayers here.

Let us pray: **Our Father . . . Amen.**

Holy God,
we praise the cross,
for by this cross we know
that you are not a God of death
but a God of life.
Through your Son, you create and renew
    all living things.
May we always rejoice in this new life.
We ask this through the same Jesus Christ
    our Lord.
**Amen.**

✚ All make the Sign of the Cross.

# PRAYER FOR WEDNESDAY SEPTEMBER 15, 2010

## OPENING

Mary is honored with many titles describing the ways in which she is an example of Christian life and a mother to all of us. Today we remember Mary as Our Lady of Sorrows, recalling her sadness at the foot of the cross, and her compassion for all who suffer.

✚ All make the Sign of the Cross.

**In the name of the Father and of the Son and of the Holy Spirit. Amen.**

## PSALM
(For a longer psalm, see page xi.) Psalm 95:1b, 2 (1a)

O come, let us sing to the LORD.

**O come, let us sing to the LORD.**

Let us make a joyful noise to the rock
    of our salvation!
Let us come into his presence with
    thanksgiving;
let us make a joyful noise to him with
    songs of praise!

**O come, let us sing to the LORD.**

## READING
1 Corinthians 13:1–8a

A reading from the first letter of Saint Paul to the Corinthians

If I speak in the tongues of mortals and of angels, but do not have love, I am a noisy gong or a clanging cymbal. And if I have prophetic powers, and understand all mysteries and all knowledge, and if I have all faith, so as to remove mountains, but do not have love, I am nothing. If I give away all my possessions, and if I hand over my body so that I may boast, but do not have love, I gain nothing. Love is patient; love is kind; love is not envious or boastful or arrogant or rude. It does not insist on its own way; it is not irritable or resentful; it does not rejoice in wrongdoing, but rejoices in the truth. It bears all things, believes all things, hopes all things, endures all things. Love never ends.

The word of the Lord.

◆ All observe silence.

## FOR SILENT REFLECTION

How does Mary show us the kind of love that Paul describes? Do you know people who are loving in this way?

## CLOSING PRAYER

Let us stand and bring our hopes and needs to God as we pray, "Lord, hear our prayer."

◆ All may add their own prayers here.

Let us pray: **Our Father . . . Amen.**

Holy God,
thank you for Mary, our mother.
Sorrow did not make her angry or resentful.
Suffering did not leave her discouraged.
Trusting in you, she lived in hope.
Give us faith and hope
to face the sorrows of our lives.
We ask this in the name of Jesus Christ
    our Lord.
**Amen.**

✚ All make the Sign of the Cross.

# PRAYER FOR **THURSDAY SEPTEMBER 16, 2010**

## OPENING

In today's Gospel, Jesus teaches a surprising lesson about sin.

✛ All make the Sign of the Cross.

**In the name of the Father and of the Son and of the Holy Spirit. Amen.**

## PSALM
(For a longer psalm, see page xi.) Psalm 95:1b, 2 (1a)

O come, let us sing to the LORD.

**O come, let us sing to the LORD.**

Let us make a joyful noise to the rock
    of our salvation!
Let us come into his presence with
    thanksgiving;
let us make a joyful noise to him with
    songs of praise!

**O come, let us sing to the LORD.**

◆ All stand and sing **Alleluia**.

## GOSPEL
Luke 7:37–39a, 39c, 44–47, 50

A reading from the holy Gospel according to Luke

A woman in the city, who was a sinner, having learned that Jesus was eating in the Pharisee's [FAIR-uh-seez] house, brought an alabaster jar of ointment. She stood behind Jesus at his feet, weeping, and began to bathe his feet with her tears and to dry them with her hair. Then she continued kissing his feet and anointing them with the ointment. Now when the Pharisee who had invited Jesus saw it, he said to himself, "If this man were a prophet, he would have known that this woman is a sinner." Then turning toward the woman, Jesus said to Simon, "Do you see this woman? I entered your house; you gave me no water for my feet, but she has bathed my feet with her tears and dried them with her hair. You gave me no kiss, but from the time I came in she has not stopped kissing my feet. You did not anoint my head with oil, but she has anointed my feet with ointment. Therefore, I tell you, her sins, which were many, have been forgiven; hence she has shown great love. But the one to whom little is forgiven, loves little." And he said to the woman, "Your faith has saved you; go in peace."

The Gospel of the Lord.

◆ All sit and observe silence.

## FOR SILENT REFLECTION

Why does Jesus defend this woman? Have you ever felt forgiven?

## CLOSING PRAYER

Let us stand and bring our hopes and needs to God as we pray, "Lord, hear our prayer."

◆ All may add their own prayers here.

Let us pray: **Our Father . . . Amen.**

Merciful God,
forgive our sins
and fill us with your abundant love.
We ask this through Jesus Christ our Lord.
**Amen.**

✛ All make the Sign of the Cross.

**ALSO ON THIS DAY:** Independence Day, Mexico

# PRAYER FOR FRIDAY
# SEPTEMBER 17, 2010

## OPENING

Today we remember Saint Robert Bellarmine [BEL-uhr-meen], a Jesuit priest and teacher of great learning who advised [ad-VIZD] Church leaders in the sixteenth century. In today's Gospel, we learn about women who traveled with Jesus and the disciples, supporting their work of spreading the Good News.

✢ All make the Sign of the Cross.

**In the name of the Father and of the Son and of the Holy Spirit. Amen.**

## PSALM
(For a longer psalm, see page xi.) Psalm 95:1b, 2 (1a)

O come, let us sing to the LORD.

**O come, let us sing to the LORD.**

Let us make a joyful noise to the rock
  of our salvation!
Let us come into his presence with
  thanksgiving;
let us make a joyful noise to him with
  songs of praise!

**O come, let us sing to the LORD.**

◆ All stand and sing **Alleluia**.

## GOSPEL
Luke 8:1–3

A reading from the holy Gospel according to Luke

Soon afterwards he went on through cities and villages, proclaiming and bringing the good news of the kingdom of God. The twelve were with him, as well as some women who had been cured of evil spirits and infirmities: Mary, called Magdalene, from whom seven demons had gone out, and Joanna, the wife of Herod's steward Chuza, and Susanna, and many others, who provided for them out of their resources.

The Gospel of the Lord.

◆ All sit and observe silence.

## FOR SILENT REFLECTION

How have you heard about the kingdom of God? Do you tell others about it?

## CLOSING PRAYER

Let us stand and bring our hopes and needs to God as we pray, "Lord, hear our prayer."

◆ All may add their own prayers here.

Let us pray: **Our Father . . . Amen.**

God our Father,
we have heard your Good News:
on the cross,
death is defeated.
By your love,
sorrow is turned into joy
and sins are forgiven.
Help us to understand this more and more
and to share it with others.
We ask this through Jesus Christ our Lord.
**Amen.**

✢ All make the Sign of the Cross.

---

**ALSO ON THIS DAY:** Yom Kippur (Jewish Day of Atonement) begins at sunset and ends tomorrow at nightfall.

# PRAYER FOR THE WEEK

WITH A READING FROM THE GOSPEL FOR **SUNDAY, SEPTEMBER 19, 2010**

## OPENING

How important are the little things we do and say each day? In today's Gospel, Jesus tells us what he thinks.

◆ All make the Sign of the Cross.

**In the name of the Father and of the Son and of the Holy Spirit. Amen.**

## PSALM  (For a longer psalm, see page xi.) Psalm 95:1b, 2 (1a)

O come, let us sing to the LORD.

O come, let us sing to the LORD.

Let us make a joyful noise to the rock
 of our salvation!
Let us come into his presence with
 thanksgiving;
let us make a joyful noise to him with
 songs of praise!

O come, let us sing to the LORD.

◆ All stand and sing **Alleluia**.

## GOSPEL  Luke 16:10–13

A reading from the holy Gospel according to Luke

Jesus said, "Whoever is faithful in a very little is faithful also in much; and whoever is dishonest in a very little is dishonest also in much. If then you have not been faithful with the dishonest wealth, who will entrust to you the true riches? And if you have not been faithful with what belongs to another, who will give you what is your own? No slave can serve two masters; for a slave will either hate the one and love the other, or be devoted to the one and despise the other. You cannot serve God and wealth."

The Gospel of the Lord.

◆ All sit and observe silence.

## FOR SILENT REFLECTION

Can you imagine a world in which everyone thought God was more important than money? What would be different?

## CLOSING PRAYER

Let us stand and bring our hopes and needs to God as we pray, "Lord, hear our prayer."

◆ All may add their own prayers here.

Let us pray: **Our Father . . . Amen.**

Blessed are you, Lord God,
ruler of the universe.
You created heaven and earth.
You order all things: planets in their orbits,
the seasons of the year,
and the rising and setting of the sun
that gives us day and night.
May your justice and love
rule our hearts and minds.
We ask this through Jesus Christ our Lord.
**Amen.**

✢ All make the Sign of the Cross.

# PRAYER FOR MONDAY
# SEPTEMBER 20, 2010

## OPENING

Today we remember Saint Andrew Kim Taegon [TAY-gon], the first Korean [kohr-EE-uhn] priest, and Saint Paul Chong Hasang [HAH-song] and his companions, Korean Christians who died for their faith. In today's Gospel, Jesus tells one of his most famous parables [PAIR-a-bls]. A parable is a story that teaches a lesson. Listen carefully and think what Jesus might be teaching us.

✢ All make the Sign of the Cross.

**In the name of the Father and of the Son and of the Holy Spirit. Amen.**

## PSALM    (For a longer psalm, see page xi.) Psalm 95:1b, 2 (1a)

O come, let us sing to the LORD.

**O come, let us sing to the LORD.**

Let us make a joyful noise to the rock
 of our salvation!
Let us come into his presence with
 thanksgiving;
let us make a joyful noise to him with
 songs of praise!

**O come, let us sing to the LORD.**

◆ All stand and sing **Alleluia.**

## GOSPEL                                       Luke 8:16–18

A reading from the holy Gospel according to Luke

Jesus said, "No one after lighting a lamp hides it under a jar, or puts it under a bed, but puts it on a lampstand, so that those who enter may see the light. For nothing is hidden that will not be disclosed, nor is anything secret that will not become known and come to light. Then pay attention to how you listen; for to those who have, more will be given; and from those who do not have, even what they seem to have will be taken away."

The Gospel of the Lord.

◆ All sit and observe silence.

## FOR SILENT REFLECTION

What is this light that shouldn't be hidden? Have you been given this light?

## CLOSING PRAYER

Let us stand and bring our hopes and needs to God as we pray, "Lord, hear our prayer."

◆ All may add their own prayers here.

Let us pray: **Our Father . . . Amen.**

Holy God,
you sent your son, Jesus
into the world
to be the light of the world.
May this Christ light
burn brightly in all we do and say,
so that your love may be known
on earth as it is in heaven.
We ask this through the same Jesus Christ
 our Lord.
**Amen.**

✢ All make the Sign of the Cross.

# PRAYER FOR TUESDAY SEPTEMBER 21, 2010

## OPENING

Today is the feast of the apostle, Saint Matthew. Today's Gospel tells how Matthew became a follower of Jesus.

✢ All make the Sign of the Cross.

**In the name of the Father and of the Son and of the Holy Spirit. Amen.**

## PSALM
(For a longer psalm, see page xi.) Psalm 95:1b, 2 (1a)

O come, let us sing to the LORD.

**O come, let us sing to the LORD.**

Let us make a joyful noise to the rock
    of our salvation!
Let us come into his presence with
    thanksgiving;
let us make a joyful noise to him with
    songs of praise!

**O come, let us sing to the LORD.**

◆ All stand and sing **Alleluia**.

## GOSPEL
Matthew 9:9–13

A reading from the holy Gospel according to Matthew

As Jesus was walking along, he saw a man called Matthew sitting at the tax booth; and he said to him, "Follow me." And he got up and followed him. And as he sat at dinner in the house, many tax-collectors and sinners came and were sitting with him and his disciples. When the Pharisees saw this, they said to his disciples, "Why does your teacher eat with tax-collectors and sinners?" But when he heard this, he said, "Those who are well have no need of a physician, but those who are sick do. Go and learn what this means, 'I desire mercy, not sacrifice.' For I have come to call not the righteous but sinners."

The Gospel of the Lord.

◆ All sit and observe silence.

## FOR SILENT REFLECTION

What do you think Jesus means when he says he has come to call sinners?

## CLOSING PRAYER

Let us stand and bring our hopes and needs to God as we pray, "Lord, hear our prayer."

◆ All may add their own prayers here.

Let us pray: **Our Father . . . Amen.**

Merciful God,
sometimes when we do something wrong
we feel ashamed and we think that
you won't want to have anything
    to do with us.
When you call our name,
help us to forget how small and ashamed
    we feel
so that we can hear
how much you love us.
Give us courage to follow you and do better.
We ask this through Jesus Christ our Lord.
**Amen.**

✢ All make the Sign of the Cross.

---

**ALSO ON THIS DAY:** International Day of Peace

# PRAYER FOR WEDNESDAY SEPTEMBER 22, 2010

## OPENING

In today's Gospel, Jesus sends his disciples out into the world to heal and to bring the Good News. Pay attention to the instructions he gives them.

✚ All make the Sign of the Cross.

**In the name of the Father and of the Son and of the Holy Spirit. Amen.**

## PSALM (For a longer psalm, see page xi.) Psalm 95:1b, 2 (1a)

O come, let us sing to the LORD.

**O come, let us sing to the LORD.**

Let us make a joyful noise to the rock
    of our salvation!
Let us come into his presence with
    thanksgiving;
let us make a joyful noise to him with
    songs of praise!

**O come, let us sing to the LORD.**

◆ All stand and sing **Alleluia**.

## GOSPEL Luke 9:1–6

A reading from the holy Gospel according to Luke

Then Jesus called the twelve together and gave them power and authority [a-THOR-i-tee] over all demons and to cure diseases, and he sent them out to proclaim the kingdom of God and to heal. He said to them, "Take nothing for your journey, no staff, nor bag, nor bread, nor money—not even an extra tunic. Whatever house you enter, stay there, and leave from there. Wherever they do not welcome you, as you are leaving that town, shake the dust off your feet as a testimony against them." They departed and went through the villages, bringing the good news and curing diseases everywhere.

The Gospel of the Lord.

◆ All sit and observe silence.

## FOR SILENT REFLECTION

What would it be like to leave on a journey without taking anything with you? Why do you think Jesus wants the disciples to do this?

## CLOSING PRAYER

Let us stand and bring our hopes and needs to God as we pray, "Lord, hear our prayer."

◆ All may add their own prayers here.

Let us pray: **Our Father . . . Amen.**

God our Father,
you walk with us on every journey.
You are with us in all we do.
Help us to trust in you
to protect and provide for us,
We ask this in the name of your Son,
    Jesus Christ our Lord.
**Amen.**

✚ All make the Sign of the Cross.

---

**ALSO ON THIS DAY:** First day of autumn
    Sukkot (Jewish Feast of Booths recalling ancient times of pilgrimage to the Jerusalem Temple) begins at sunset.

# PRAYER FOR THURSDAY SEPTEMBER 23, 2010

## OPENING

Today we remember Saint Pio [PEE-o] of Pietrelcina [pee-ay-truhl-CHEE-na], an Italian priest who trusted the power of prayer, love, and forgiveness. Today's Gospel tells about Herod, the ruler who had beheaded John the Baptist and now wonders what sort of power Jesus might have and who he might be. Herod needs to know if Jesus' power will be a threat to his power.

✠ All make the Sign of the Cross.

**In the name of the Father and of the Son and of the Holy Spirit. Amen.**

## PSALM  (For a longer psalm, see page xi.) Psalm 95:1b, 2 (1a)

O come, let us sing to the LORD.

**O come, let us sing to the LORD.**

Let us make a joyful noise to the rock
 of our salvation!
Let us come into his presence with
 thanksgiving;
let us make a joyful noise to him with
 songs of praise!

**O come, let us sing to the LORD.**

◆ All stand and sing **Alleluia.**

## GOSPEL  Luke 9:7–9

A reading from the holy Gospel according to Luke

Now Herod the ruler heard about all that had taken place, and he was perplexed, because it was said by some that John had been raised from the dead, by some that Elijah had appeared, and by others that one of the ancient prophets had arisen. Herod said, "John I beheaded; but who is this about whom I hear such things?" And he tried to see him.

The Gospel of the Lord.

◆ All sit and observe silence.

## FOR SILENT REFLECTION

Why do you think world rulers like Herod fail to understand who Jesus is and what sort of power he has?

## CLOSING PRAYER

Let us stand and bring our hopes and needs to God as we pray, "Lord, hear our prayer."

◆ All may add their own prayers here.

Let us pray: **Our Father . . . Amen.**

Almighty and all-powerful God,
yours is the creative power that made
 the universe,
the merciful power that forgives sinners,
the healing power that gives sight
 to the blind
and helps the lame to walk.
Help us to trust in your power
and follow your Son
who brings justice and love to the world.
We ask this through the same Jesus Christ
 our Lord.
**Amen.**

✠ All make the Sign of the Cross.

# PRAYER FOR FRIDAY
# SEPTEMBER 24, 2010

## OPENING

In today's Gospel, we hear Jesus asking the disciples who they think he is. The "Messiah" [meh-SI-uh], which we will hear about today, is a great leader that Jews believed God would send to save them.

✢ All make the Sign of the Cross.

**In the name of the Father and of the Son and of the Holy Spirit. Amen.**

## PSALM  (For a longer psalm, see page xi.) Psalm 95:1b, 2 (1a)

O come, let us sing to the LORD.

**O come, let us sing to the LORD.**

Let us make a joyful noise to the rock
 of our salvation!
Let us come into his presence with
 thanksgiving;
let us make a joyful noise to him with
 songs of praise!

**O come, let us sing to the LORD.**

◆ All stand and sing **Alleluia**.

## GOSPEL                              Luke 9:18–22

A reading from the holy Gospel according to Luke

Once when Jesus was praying alone, with only the disciples near him, he asked them, "Who do the crowds say that I am?" They answered, "John the Baptist; but others, Elijah; and still others, that one of the ancient prophets has arisen." He said to them, "But who do you say that I am?" Peter answered, "The Messiah [meh-SI-uh] of God." He sternly ordered and commanded them not to tell anyone, saying, "The Son of Man must undergo great suffering, and be rejected by the elders, chief priests, and scribes, and be killed, and on the third day be raised."

The Gospel of the Lord.

◆ All sit and observe silence.

## FOR SILENT REFLECTION

Who do you think Jesus is? Why would such a great leader have to suffer?

## CLOSING PRAYER

Let us stand and bring our hopes and needs to God as we pray, "Lord, hear our prayer."

◆ All may add their own prayers here.

Let us pray: **Our Father . . . Amen.**

God our Father,
the disciples knew and loved your son.
They ate with him and traveled with him
and yet only Peter suspected
that he came from you.
Open our eyes to see you
in the words of scripture,
in the sacred meal and sacrifice of the Mass,
in the example of your saints,
and in the love we have for one another.
We ask this through the same Jesus Christ
    our Lord.
**Amen.**

✢ All make the Sign of the Cross.

**ALSO ON THIS DAY:** Native American Day (U.S.A.)

# PRAYER FOR THE WEEK

WITH A READING FROM THE GOSPEL FOR **SUNDAY, SEPTEMBER 26, 2010**

## OPENING

In today's Gospel, Jesus tells a parable [PAIR-a-bl] (a story told to teach a lesson) about a rich man who fails to help a poor man.

✢ All make the Sign of the Cross.

**In the name of the Father and of the Son and of the Holy Spirit. Amen.**

## PSALM
(For a longer psalm, see page xi.) Psalm 95:1b, 2 (1a)

O come, let us sing to the LORD.

**O come, let us sing to the LORD.**

Let us make a joyful noise to the rock
    of our salvation!
Let us come into his presence with
    thanksgiving;
let us make a joyful noise to him with
    songs of praise!

**O come, let us sing to the LORD.**

◆ All stand and sing **Alleluia**.

## GOSPEL
Luke 16:19–25

A reading from the holy Gospel according to Luke

Jesus said, "There was a rich man who was dressed in purple and fine linen and who feasted sumptuously every day. And at his gate lay a poor man named Lazarus, covered with sores, who longed to satisfy his hunger with what fell from the rich man's table; even the dogs would come and lick his sores. The poor man died and was carried away by the angels to be with Abraham. The rich man also died and was buried. In Hades, where he was tormented, he looked up and saw Abraham far away with Lazarus by his side. He called out, 'Father Abraham, have mercy on me, and send Lazarus to dip the tip of his finger in water and cool my tongue; for I am in agony in these flames.' But Abraham said, 'Child, remember that during your lifetime you received your good things, and Lazarus in like manner evil things; but now he is comforted here, and you are in agony.'"

The Gospel of the Lord.

◆ All sit and observe silence.

## FOR SILENT REFLECTION

How could the rich man have helped Lazarus? Who needs your help?

## CLOSING PRAYER

Let us stand and bring our hopes and needs to God as we pray, "Lord, hear our prayer."

◆ All may add their own prayers here.

Let us pray: **Our Father . . . Amen.**

Generous God,
we thank you for all you give us.
Help us to notice the needs of others
and to willingly share with them.
We ask this through Jesus Christ our Lord.
**Amen.**

✢ All make the Sign of the Cross.

# PRAYER FOR MONDAY
# SEPTEMBER 27, 2010

## OPENING

Today we remember Saint Vincent de Paul, a French priest known for his countless acts of charity. He cared for many children in Jesus' name. In today's Gospel, the disciples are fighting over who is the greatest. Listen to what Jesus tells them.

✝ All make the Sign of the Cross.

**In the name of the Father and of the Son and of the Holy Spirit. Amen.**

## PSALM
(For a longer psalm, see page xi.) Psalm 25:4 (1, 2a)

To you, O Lord, I lift up my soul.
O my God, in you I trust.

**To you, O Lord, I lift up my soul.
O my God, in you I trust.**

Make me to know your ways, O Lord;
    teach me your paths.

**To you, O Lord, I lift up my soul.
O my God, in you I trust.**

◆ All stand and sing **Alleluia.**

## GOSPEL
Luke 9:46–48

A reading from the holy Gospel according to Luke

An argument arose among the disciples as to which one of them was the greatest. But Jesus, aware of their inner thoughts, took a little child and put it by his side, and said to them, "Whoever welcomes this child in my name welcomes me, and whoever welcomes me welcomes the one who sent me; for the least among all of you is the greatest."

The Gospel of the Lord.

◆ All sit and observe silence.

## FOR SILENT REFLECTION

Imagine that you were the little child whom Jesus puts by his side. What would it be like, being so close to Jesus? What do you think Jesus mean when he says "the least among all of you is the greatest"?

## CLOSING PRAYER

Let us stand and bring our hopes and needs to God as we pray, "Lord, hear our prayer."

◆ All may add their own prayers here.

Let us pray: **Our Father . . . Amen.**

God our Father,
you are great, yet you care for
the smallest of your creatures.
You are powerful,
yet you remember the weak.
Keep us from quarrelling,
teach us humility,
and draw us to your side.
May all children be welcomed in your name
and treated with loving kindness.
We ask this through Jesus Christ our Lord.
**Amen.**

✝ All make the Sign of the Cross.

# PRAYER FOR TUESDAY SEPTEMBER 28, 2010

## OPENING

Today we remember Saint Wenceslaus [WEN-suhs-lahs], a tenth century Christian king and patron saint of the Czech [chek] Republic. You may recognize his name from the Christmas carol, "Good King Wenceslas." In today's Gospel Jesus doesn't agree with the disciples' idea about how to use his divine power.

✢ All make the Sign of the Cross.

**In the name of the Father and of the Son and of the Holy Spirit. Amen.**

## PSALM  (For a longer psalm, see page xi.) Psalm 25:4 (1, 2a)

To you, O Lord, I lift up my soul.
O my God, in you I trust.

**To you, O Lord, I lift up my soul.
O my God, in you I trust.**

Make me to know your ways, O Lord;
   teach me your paths.

**To you, O Lord, I lift up my soul.
O my God, in you I trust.**

◆ All stand and sing **Alleluia**.

## GOSPEL  Luke 9:51–56

A reading from the holy Gospel according to Luke

When the days drew near for him to be taken up, he set his face to go to Jerusalem. And he sent messengers ahead of him. On their way they entered a village of the Samaritans to make ready for him; but they did not receive him, because his face was set towards Jerusalem. When his disciples James and John saw it, they said, "Lord, do you want us to command fire to come down from heaven and consume them?" But he turned and rebuked them. Then they went on to another village.

The Gospel of the Lord.

◆ All sit and observe silence.

## FOR SILENT REFLECTION

Have you ever wished you had the power to hurt someone? What do you think Jesus might say to you?

## CLOSING PRAYER

Let us stand and bring our hopes and needs to God as we pray, "Lord, hear our prayer."

◆ All may add their own prayers here.

Let us pray: **Our Father . . . Amen.**

Holy God,
help us to seek your power:
a power that forgives
rather than destroys;
a power that seeks peace
rather than revenge.
Open our hearts to the power of life,
of goodness, and healing.
We ask this through Jesus Christ our Lord.
**Amen.**

✢ All make the Sign of the Cross.

# PRAYER FOR **WEDNESDAY** **SEPTEMBER 29, 2010**

## OPENING

Today we celebrate the feast of the archangels, Michael, Gabriel, and Raphael. Angels are servants and messengers of God. God also communicated through the visions of saints and prophets. Today's reading, from the Old Testament, is important to Christians. See if you can guess why.

✚ All make the Sign of the Cross.

**In the name of the Father and of the Son and of the Holy Spirit. Amen.**

## PSALM   (For a longer psalm, see page xi.) Psalm 25:4 (1, 2a)

To you, O Lord, I lift up my soul.
O my God, in you I trust.

**To you, O Lord, I lift up my soul.
O my God, in you I trust.**

Make me to know your ways, O Lord;
   teach me your paths.

**To you, O Lord, I lift up my soul.
O my God, in you I trust.**

## READING   Daniel 7:13–14

A reading from the Book of the Prophet Daniel

As I watched in the night visions,
I saw one like a human being
coming with the clouds of heaven.
And he came to the Ancient One
and was presented before him.
To him was given dominion
and glory and kingship,
that all peoples, nations, and languages
should serve him.
His dominion is an everlasting dominion
that shall not pass away,
and his kingship is one
that shall never be destroyed.

The word of the Lord.

◆ All observe silence.

## FOR SILENT REFLECTION

Who do you think the Ancient One is, and who is "the one like a human being"?

## CLOSING PRAYER

Let us stand and bring our hopes and needs to God as we pray, "Lord, hear our prayer."

◆ All may add their own prayers here.

Let us pray: **Our Father . . . Amen.**

Holy God,
you are ever seeking us and speaking to us
through angel messages and the visions
      of prophets;
in the dreams of saints, and the words
      of scriptures.
Help us to hear you and know you.
We ask this through Jesus Christ our Lord.
**Amen.**

✚ All make the Sign of the Cross.

---

**ALSO ON THIS DAY:** Sukkot (Jewish Feast of Booths recalling ancient times of pilgrimage to the Jerusalem Temple) ends at nightfall.

# PRAYER FOR THURSDAY SEPTEMBER 30, 2010

### OPENING

Today is the memorial of Saint Jerome, a fourth century priest and scholar of the Bible. In today's Gospel, we learn about followers who helped Jesus spread the news of the kingdom of God.

✝ All make the Sign of the Cross.

**In the name of the Father and of the Son and of the Holy Spirit. Amen.**

### PSALM     (For a longer psalm, see page xi.) Psalm 25:4 (1, 2a)

To you, O Lord, I lift up my soul.
O my God, in you I trust.

To you, O Lord, I lift up my soul.
O my God, in you I trust.

Make me to know your ways, O Lord;
   teach me your paths.

To you, O Lord, I lift up my soul.
O my God, in you I trust.

◆ All stand and sing **Alleluia**.

### GOSPEL     Luke 10:1–3, 5–9

A reading from the holy Gospel according to Luke

After this the Lord appointed seventy others and sent them on ahead of him in pairs to every town and place where he himself intended to go. He said to them, "The harvest is plentiful, but the laborers are few; therefore ask the Lord of the harvest to send out laborers into his harvest. Go on your way. See, I am sending you out like lambs into the midst of wolves. Whatever house you enter, first say, 'Peace to this house!' And if anyone is there who shares in peace, your peace will rest on that person; but if not, it will return to you. Remain in the same house, eating and drinking whatever they provide, for the laborer deserves to be paid. Do not move about from house to house. Whenever you enter a town and its people welcome you, eat what is set before you; cure the sick who are there, and say to them, 'The kingdom of God has come near to you.'"

The Gospel of the Lord.

◆ All sit and observe silence.

### FOR SILENT REFLECTION

Who are the laborers and what is the harvest that Jesus speaks of?

### CLOSING PRAYER

Let us stand and bring our hopes and needs to God as we pray, "Lord, hear our prayer."

◆ All may add their own prayers here.

Let us pray: **Our Father . . . Amen.**

Holy God,
you send us into the world
to make your love known.
Bless all who do your work on earth.
We ask this through Jesus Christ Our Lord.
**Amen.**

✝ All make the Sign of the Cross.

**ALSO ON THIS DAY:** Simchat Torah (Jewish Rejoicing in the Torah) begins today at sunset.

# PRAYER FOR FRIDAY
# OCTOBER 1, 2010

## OPENING

In the reading we will hear, Job [johb] realizes how small he is compared to the great power of God. Today we remember Saint Thérèse [tair-EZ] of the Child Jesus, who understood that to be small is good. She found a "little way" to God by loving God in everything, even the smallest experiences of daily life.

✢ All make the Sign of the Cross.

**In the name of the Father and of the Son and of the Holy Spirit. Amen.**

## PSALM  (For a longer psalm, see page xi.) Psalm 25:4 (1, 2a)

To you, O Lord, I lift up my soul.
O my God, in you I trust.

**To you, O Lord, I lift up my soul.
O my God, in you I trust.**

Make me to know your ways, O Lord;
　teach me your paths.

**To you, O Lord, I lift up my soul.
O my God, in you I trust.**

## READING  Job 38:1, 12–13, 16–18; 40:3–4a

A reading from the Book of Job

Then the Lord answered Job out of the whirlwind:
"Have you commanded the morning since
　　your days began,
and caused the dawn to know its place,
so that it might take hold of the skirts
　　of the earth,
and the wicked be shaken out of it?
Have you entered into the springs of the sea,
or walked in the recesses of the deep?
Have the gates of death been revealed to you,
or have you seen the gates of deep darkness?
Have you comprehended the expanse
　　of the earth?
Declare, if you know all this."
Then Job answered the Lord:
"See, I am of small account; what shall
　　I answer you?"

The word of the Lord.

◆ All observe silence.

## FOR SILENT REFLECTION

What little things can you do with love this week?

## CLOSING PRAYER

Let us stand and bring our hopes and needs to God as we pray, "Lord, hear our prayer."

◆ All may add their own prayers here.

Let us pray: **Our Father . . . Amen.**

Loving God,
you showed Saint Thérèse [tair-EZ]
how to know you more deeply
by doing everything with love.
Although we are small,
give us big hearts.
We ask this through Jesus Christ our Lord.
**Amen.**

✢ All make the Sign of the Cross.

---

**ALSO ON THIS DAY:** Simchat Torah (Jewish Rejoicing in the Torah) ends today at nightfall.

# PRAYER FOR THE WEEK

WITH A READING FROM THE GOSPEL FOR **SUNDAY, OCTOBER 3, 2010**

## OPENING

In today's Gospel, Jesus tells us that a person with a little faith can do big things. The mustard seeds Jesus talks about in this reading are the kind grown in the Holy Land, which are even smaller than the ones we have seen here in North America. The faith that Jesus talks about today means believing what a person says because you trust that person. Faith in God means believing what God tells us.

✝ All make the Sign of the Cross.

**In the name of the Father and of the Son and of the Holy Spirit. Amen.**

## PSALM
(For a longer psalm, see page xi.) Psalm 25:4 (1, 2a)

To you, O Lord, I lift up my soul.
O my God, in you I trust.

**To you, O Lord, I lift up my soul.
O my God, in you I trust.**

Make me to know your ways, O Lord;
 teach me your paths.

**To you, O Lord, I lift up my soul.
O my God, in you I trust.**

◆ All stand and sing **Alleluia.**

## GOSPEL
Luke 17:5–6

A reading from the holy Gospel according to Luke

The apostles said to the Lord, "Increase our faith!" The Lord replied, "If you had faith the size of a mustard seed, you could say to this mulberry tree, 'Be uprooted and planted in the sea', and it would obey you."

The Gospel of the Lord.

◆ All sit and observe silence.

## FOR SILENT REFLECTION

Why do you think Jesus wants the disciples to know how powerful faith is? Can you think of something God has told you in scripture that you really firmly believe?

## CLOSING PRAYER

Let us stand and bring our hopes and needs to God as we pray, "Lord, hear our prayer."

◆ All may add their own prayers here.

Let us pray: **Our Father . . . Amen.**

God our Father,
increase our faith.
Let it grow
a little more every day.
Help us to accept and trust you
when you say you love us;
to believe you
when you tell us not to be afraid;
to give easily when you ask us to be generous,
and to listen when you invite us to learn.
We ask this through your son,
 our Lord Jesus Christ.
**Amen.**

✝ All make the Sign of the Cross.

**ALSO ON THIS DAY:** Respect Life Sunday (U.S.A.)

# PRAYER FOR MONDAY OCTOBER 4, 2010

## OPENING

Today we remember Saint Francis of Assisi. Saint Francis took the words of today's Gospel to heart. He treated people who were sick, poor, and rejected by society, with the love one gives to a neighbor and friend.

✢ All make the Sign of the Cross.

**In the name of the Father and of the Son and of the Holy Spirit. Amen.**

## PSALM
(For a longer psalm, see page xi.) Psalm 25:4 (1, 2a)

To you, O Lord, I lift up my soul.
O my God, in you I trust.

To you, O Lord, I lift up my soul.
O my God, in you I trust.

Make me to know your ways, O Lord;
  teach me your paths.

To you, O Lord, I lift up my soul.
O my God, in you I trust.

◆ All stand and sing **Alleluia**.

## GOSPEL
Luke 10:29–34, 36–37

A reading from the holy Gospel according to Luke

Wanting to justify himself, the lawyer asked Jesus, "And who is my neighbor?" Jesus replied, "A man was going down from Jerusalem to Jericho, and fell into the hands of robbers, who stripped him, beat him, and went away, leaving him half dead. Now by chance a priest was going down that road; and when he saw him he passed by on the other side. So likewise a Levite, when he came to the place and saw him, passed by on the other side. But a Samaritan [suh-MAYR-ih-tuhn] while traveling came near him; and when he saw him, he was moved with pity. He went to him and bandaged his wounds, having poured oil and wine on them. Then he put him on his own animal, brought him to an inn, and took care of him. Which of these three, do you think, was a neighbor to the man who fell into the hands of the robbers?" He said, "The one who showed him mercy." Jesus said to him, "Go and do likewise."

The Gospel of the Lord.

◆ All sit and observe silence.

## FOR SILENT REFLECTION

How might you be a good neighbor to someone who is hurting and needs a friend?

## CLOSING PRAYER

Let us stand and bring our hopes and needs to God as we pray, "Lord, hear our prayer."

◆ All may add their own prayers here.

Let us pray: **Our Father . . . Amen.**

Loving God,
open our eyes to see
the people who need our love.
Open our hearts to share
your love with them.
We ask this through Jesus Christ our Lord.
**Amen.**

✢ All make the Sign of the Cross.

# PRAYER FOR TUESDAY OCTOBER 5, 2010

## OPENING

Today's Gospel reminds us that even when we are doing good work, we need to take time to be with Jesus.

✢ All make the Sign of the Cross.

**In the name of the Father and of the Son and of the Holy Spirit. Amen.**

## PSALM  (For a longer psalm, see page xi.) Psalm 25:4 (1, 2a)

To you, O Lord, I lift up my soul.
O my God, in you I trust.

To you, O Lord, I lift up my soul.
O my God, in you I trust.

Make me to know your ways, O Lord;
  teach me your paths.

To you, O Lord, I lift up my soul.
O my God, in you I trust.

◆ All stand and sing **Alleluia**.

## GOSPEL  Luke 10:38–42

A reading from the holy Gospel according to Luke

Now as they went on their way, he entered a certain village, where a woman named Martha welcomed him into her home. She had a sister named Mary, who sat at the Lord's feet and listened to what he was saying. But Martha was distracted by her many tasks; so she came to him and asked, "Lord, do you not care that my sister has left me to do all the work by myself? Tell her then to help me." But the Lord answered her, "Martha, Martha, you are worried and distracted by many things; there is need of only one thing. Mary has chosen the better part, which will not be taken away from her."

The Gospel of the Lord.

◆ All sit and observe silence.

## FOR SILENT REFLECTION

What do you think Jesus wants Martha to do? Do you think it is important to take time for prayer each day?

## CLOSING PRAYER

Let us stand and bring our hopes and needs to God as we pray, "Lord, hear our prayer."

◆ All may add their own prayers here.

Let us pray: **Our Father . . . Amen.**

Loving God,
you teach us
that the little things we do
are important when they are done with love.
But it is easy for us
to get distracted
and forget to love.
Teach us to pray.
Help us to pay attention
to your presence in our lives.
We ask this through Jesus Christ our Lord.
**Amen.**

✢ All make the Sign of the Cross.

---

**ALSO ON THIS DAY:** World Teachers' Day

# PRAYER FOR WEDNESDAY OCTOBER 6, 2010

## OPENING

Today we remember Saint Bruno, who founded the Carthusian [car-THU-shun] order of monks and nuns in the eleventh century. These devoted people spend their lives in remote monasteries [mon-a-STAIR-ees] in silence and prayer. Today's Gospel contains Jesus' famous teaching to his followers about how to pray. Since we are Jesus' followers, we need to pay special attention to this reading.

✢ All make the Sign of the Cross.

**In the name of the Father and of the Son and of the Holy Spirit. Amen.**

## PSALM (For a longer psalm, see page xi.) Psalm 25:4 (1, 2a)

To you, O Lord, I lift up my soul.
O my God, in you I trust.

**To you, O Lord, I lift up my soul.
O my God, in you I trust.**

Make me to know your ways, O Lord;
    teach me your paths.

**To you, O Lord, I lift up my soul.
O my God, in you I trust.**

◆ All stand and sing **Alleluia**.

## GOSPEL                               Luke 11:1–4

A reading from the holy Gospel according to Luke

He was praying in a certain place, and after he had finished, one of his disciples said to him, "Lord, teach us to pray, as John taught his disciples." He said to them, "When you pray, say:
Father, hallowed be your name.
Your kingdom come.
Give us each day our daily bread.
And forgive us our sins,
    for we ourselves forgive everyone indebted
        to us.
And do not bring us to the time of trial."

The Gospel of the Lord.

◆ All sit and observe silence.

## FOR SILENT REFLECTION

What does this prayer teach us about how we should talk to God?

## CLOSING PRAYER

Let us stand and bring our hopes and needs to God as we pray, "Lord, hear our prayer."

◆ All may add their own prayers here.

Let us pray: **Our Father . . . Amen.**

Heavenly Father,
you are holy,
and your name is holy.
You are powerful
and creation shows us your power.
Who but you could make
the wonders of heaven and earth?
Help us to pray
as your Son has taught us,
trusting in your mercy
and confident of your loving care.
We ask this in the name of Jesus Christ
    our Lord.
**Amen.**

✢ All make the Sign of the Cross.

# PRAYER SERVICE
## MEMORIAL OF OUR LADY OF THE ROSARY

*Prepare eight leaders for this service. The Second and Fourth leaders will need Bibles to read the passages from Luke and may need help practicing the reading. You may wish to begin by singing "Hail Mary, Gentle Woman" and end with "Immaculate Mary." If the group will sing, prepare a song leader. All are seated as you begin.*

**FIRST LEADER:**
The rosary is a prayer that we pray with a circle of beads. Each bead helps us to keep track of where we are in our prayer. In the circle there is also a cross, where we begin, holding it as we make the Sign of the Cross and pray the Apostles' Creed. The Creed contains the most essential things that we believe. At the long spaces between the beads, we pray the Glory Be. At the single large beads, we pray the Our Father, and on each of the 53 small beads we pray the Hail Mary.

When we pick up a rosary, it is as if Mary holds us by the hand and takes us to the throne of her Son in heaven, where we can see, through her eyes, his amazing light.

Because the Hail Mary is the prayer that we repeat most often as we pray the rosary, let us turn to the Bible to discover where this beloved prayer comes from.

✢ All make the Sign of the Cross.

**In the name of the Father and of the Son and of the Holy Spirit. Amen.**

◆ All stand and sing **Alleluia**.

**SECOND LEADER:** Luke 1:26–28
A reading from the holy Gospel according to Luke

◆ Read the Luke passage from a Bible.

The Gospel of the Lord.

# MEMORIAL OF OUR LADY OF THE ROSARY

**THIRD LEADER:**
The angel was the first person ever to say "Hail! The Lord is with you." When we say the Hail Mary, we are echoing the words of an angel!

The words of this beautiful prayer are ancient, and they came from holy people. When we pray them, we are joining our prayer to theirs. Let us pray one Hail Mary together, and while we pray, we can think about the Angel Gabriel as he announced his startling news to Mary.

**Hail Mary, full of grace . . .**

**FOURTH LEADER:** Luke 1:41–42
A reading from the holy Gospel according to Luke

◆ Read the Luke passage from a Bible.

**The Gospel of the Lord.**

**FIFTH LEADER:**
When the Holy Spirit inspired Elizabeth to know that Mary was pregnant with the Lord Jesus, she said, "Blessed are you among women, and blessed is the fruit of your womb." When we pray the Hail Mary, we also can experience the Holy Spirit as we declare how blessed Mary is for bearing Jesus, our Lord and Savior, in her body.

**SIXTH LEADER:**
Let us pray the Hail Mary once more, but this time, let's remember Saint Elizabeth, Mary's cousin, who was able to recognize that Mary was pregnant with the Son of God before anyone told her. As we pray, let's hope that we, like Elizabeth, will be able to see the hidden presence of Jesus in the world around us.

**Hail Mary, full of grace . . .**

**SEVENTH LEADER:**
Now let us pray the words that Jesus gave us.

**Our Father . . . Amen.**

**SEVENTH LEADER:**
Let us pray:
Lord God,
we thank you for giving us the desire
to come closer to you in prayer.
Help us to pray the rosary with all our hearts,
so that Mary's loving care will lead us
    to your Son.
**Amen.**

**EIGHTH LEADER:**
May the Lord bless us,

✢ All make the Sign of the Cross.

protect us from all evil
and bring us to everlasting life.
**Amen.**

# PRAYER FOR THURSDAY OCTOBER 7, 2010

## OPENING

Today we remember Mary as Our Lady of the Rosary. When we pray the rosary, we ponder moments, called "mysteries," in Jesus' life as Mary did. Today's Gospel encourages us to pray as Mary did, without giving up.

✢ All make the Sign of the Cross.

**In the name of the Father and of the Son and of the Holy Spirit. Amen.**

## PSALM
(For a longer psalm, see page xi.) Psalm 25:4 (1, 2a)

To you, O Lord, I lift up my soul.
O my God, in you I trust.

To you, O Lord, I lift up my soul.
O my God, in you I trust.

Make me to know your ways, O Lord;
  teach me your paths.

To you, O Lord, I lift up my soul.
O my God, in you I trust.

◆ All stand and sing **Alleluia**.

## GOSPEL
Luke 11:9–13

A reading from the holy Gospel according to Luke

Jesus said, "So I say to you, ask, and it will be given to you; search, and you will find; knock, and the door will be opened for you. For everyone who asks receives, and everyone who searches finds, and for everyone who knocks, the door will be opened. Is there anyone among you who, if your child asks for a fish, will give a snake instead of a fish? Or if the child asks for an egg, will give a scorpion? If you then, who are evil, know how to give good gifts to your children, how much more will the heavenly Father give the Holy Spirit to those who ask him!"

The Gospel of the Lord.

◆ All sit and observe silence.

## FOR SILENT REFLECTION

What do you think Jesus means when he says, "Knock and the door will be opened"? What door opens when we pray?

## CLOSING PRAYER

Let us stand and bring our hopes and needs to God as we pray, "Lord, hear our prayer."

◆ All may add their own prayers here.

Let us pray: **Our Father . . . Amen.**

Holy God,
help us to follow the example of Mary.
Grant this through Jesus Christ our Lord.
Amen.
And today, in honor of Our Lady of the
  Rosary, we also pray:
**Hail Mary, full of grace,
the Lord is with you.
Blessed are you among women,
and blessed is the fruit of your womb, Jesus.
Holy Mary, mother of God,
pray for us sinners now,
and at the hour of our death. Amen.**

✢ All make the Sign of the Cross.

# PRAYER FOR FRIDAY OCTOBER 8, 2010

## OPENING

In today's Gospel, Jesus has just cured a person who could not speak by casting out a demon from him. In ancient times people often believed that illnesses or disabilities were caused by demons. Some in the crowd accuse Jesus of using evil powers to cast out the demon—of using the power of the ruler of demons, called Beelzebul [bee-EL-zeh-bull]. But Jesus says this cannot be. You cannot fight evil with more evil; Satan cannot fight against himself. Let's listen to the answer Jesus gives.

✚ All make the Sign of the Cross.

**In the name of the Father and of the Son and of the Holy Spirit. Amen.**

## PSALM (For a longer psalm, see page xi.) Psalm 25:4 (1, 2a)

To you, O Lord, I lift up my soul.
O my God, in you I trust.

**To you, O Lord, I lift up my soul.
O my God, in you I trust.**

Make me to know your ways, O Lord;
 teach me your paths.

**To you, O Lord, I lift up my soul.
O my God, in you I trust.**

## READING                    Luke 11:17–18, 20

A reading from the holy Gospel according to Luke

Jesus knew what the crowd was thinking and said to them, "Every kingdom divided against itself becomes a desert, and house falls on house. If Satan also is divided against himself, how will his kingdom stand? For you say that I cast out the demons by Beelzebul. But if it is by the finger of God that I cast out the demons, then the kingdom of God has come to you."

The Gospel of the Lord.

◆ All sit and observe silence.

## FOR SILENT REFLECTION

What do you think Jesus means when he says "the kingdom of God has come to you"?

## CLOSING PRAYER

Let us stand and bring our hopes and needs to God as we pray, "Lord, hear our prayer."

◆ All may add their own prayers here.

Let us pray: **Our Father . . . Amen.**

All-powerful and loving God,
we thank you for sending your Son
to teach us about your kingdom
in which the sick are healed
and goodness overpowers evil.
Show us how each of us
can help to bring your kingdom into the world.
We ask this through our Lord Jesus Christ,
 your Son, who lives and reigns with
 you and the Holy Spirit, one God, for
 ever and ever.
**Amen.**

✚ All make the Sign of the Cross.

**ALSO ON THIS DAY:** Navaratri (Hindu 9 day festival) begins.

# PRAYER FOR THE WEEK

WITH A READING FROM THE GOSPEL FOR **SUNDAY OCTOBER 10, 2010**

## OPENING

In today's Gospel, Jesus cures ten lepers. Leprosy is a skin disease. At the time of Jesus, lepers had to live far apart from other people. To "prostate" oneself means to lie face down on the ground as a sign of humility.

✢ All make the Sign of the Cross.

**In the name of the Father and of the Son and of the Holy Spirit. Amen.**

## PSALM
(For a longer psalm, see page xi.) Psalm 25:4 (1, 2a)

To you, O LORD, I lift up my soul.
O my God, in you I trust.

**To you, O LORD, I lift up my soul.
O my God, in you I trust.**

Make me to know your ways, O LORD;
   teach me your paths.

**To you, O LORD, I lift up my soul.
O my God, in you I trust.**

◆ All stand and sing **Alleluia**.

## GOSPEL
Luke 17:11–19

A reading from the holy Gospel according to Luke

On the way to Jerusalem Jesus was going through the region between Samaria [Suh-MAYR-ee-uh] and Galilee [GAL-ih-lee]. As he entered a village, ten lepers approached him. Keeping their distance, they called out, saying, "Jesus, Master, have mercy on us!" When he saw them, he said to them, "Go and show yourselves to the priests." And as they went, they were made clean. Then one of them, when he saw that he was healed, turned back, praising God with a loud voice. He prostrated himself at Jesus' feet and thanked him. And he was a Samaritan. Then Jesus asked, "Were not ten made clean? But the other nine, where are they? Was none of them found to return and give praise to God except this foreigner?" Then he said to him, "Get up and go on your way; your faith has made you well."

The Gospel of the Lord.

◆ All sit and observe silence.

## FOR SILENT REFLECTION

Can you think why this leper wanted to thank Jesus when the others did not?

## CLOSING PRAYER

Let us stand and bring our hopes and needs to God as we pray, "Lord, hear our prayer."

◆ All may add their own prayers here.

Let us pray: **Our Father . . . Amen.**

Holy God,
give the joy of your presence
to all who are sick and suffering.
Teach us to be grateful
for all the blessings we receive.
We ask this through our Lord Jesus Christ.
**Amen.**

✢ All make the Sign of the Cross.

# PRAYER FOR MONDAY
# OCTOBER 11, 2010

## OPENING

As Jesus traveled around the country, teaching, there were often people in the crowd who wanted to see miracles and signs, but would not listen to his teachings, change their lives, and grow closer to God. In today's Gospel, Jesus challenges them to think more deeply. He reminds them of Jonah, who was the prophet God sent to the people of Nineveh [NIN-uh-vuh] to warn them that they must repent and change their ways. When Jesus speaks of the "Son of Man," he is speaking about himself.

✚ All make the Sign of the Cross.

**In the name of the Father and of the Son and of the Holy Spirit. Amen.**

## PSALM  (For a longer psalm, see page xi.) Psalm 25:4 (1, 2a)

To you, O Lord, I lift up my soul.
O my God, in you I trust.

**To you, O Lord, I lift up my soul.
O my God, in you I trust.**

Make me to know your ways, O Lord;
    teach me your paths.

**To you, O Lord, I lift up my soul.
O my God, in you I trust.**

◆ All stand and sing **Alleluia**.

## GOSPEL  Luke 11:29–30

A reading from the holy Gospel according to Luke

When the crowds were increasing, he began to say, "This generation is an evil generation; it asks for a sign, but no sign will be given to it except the sign of Jonah. For just as Jonah became a sign to the people of Nineveh, so the Son of Man will be to this generation."

The Gospel of the Lord.

◆ All sit and observe silence.

## FOR SILENT REFLECTION

How is Jesus helping you to grow closer to him and his Father?

## CLOSING PRAYER

Let us stand and bring our hopes and needs to God as we pray, "Lord, hear our prayer."

◆ All may add their own prayers here.

Let us pray: **Our Father . . . Amen.**

God our Father,
you sent your Son
to teach us your ways
and bring us closer to you.
Open our hearts to his teachings
so that we can be a sign of your kingdom
    to others.
We ask this through the same Jesus Christ
    our Lord.
**Amen.**

✚ All make the Sign of the Cross.

---

**ALSO ON THIS DAY:** Columbus Day (U.S.A.); Thanksgiving (Canada)

# PRAYER FOR TUESDAY OCTOBER 12, 2010

## OPENING

In Jesus' time, the Pharisees [FAIR-uh-seez] were Jewish teachers who were very rigid about the details of the law, often without understanding the spirit of the law. In today's Gospel, Jesus challenges them to pay attention to what is most important. Alms are a loving donation given to the poor

✚ All make the Sign of the Cross.

**In the name of the Father and of the Son and of the Holy Spirit. Amen.**

## PSALM
(For a longer psalm, see page xi.) Psalm 25:4 (1, 2a)

To you, O Lord, I lift up my soul.
O my God, in you I trust.

**To you, O Lord, I lift up my soul.
O my God, in you I trust.**

Make me to know your ways, O Lord;
 teach me your paths.

**To you, O Lord, I lift up my soul.
O my God, in you I trust.**

◆ All stand and sing **Alleluia**.

## GOSPEL
Luke 11:37–41

A reading from the holy Gospel according to Luke

While [Jesus] was speaking, a Pharisee [FAIR-uh-see] invited him to dine with him; so he went in and took his place at the table. The Pharisee was amazed to see that he did not first wash before dinner. Then the Lord said to him, "Now you Pharisees clean the outside of the cup and of the dish, but inside you are full of greed and wickedness. You fools! Did not the one who made the outside make the inside also? So give for alms those things that are within; and see, everything will be clean for you."

The Gospel of the Lord.

◆ All sit and observe silence.

## FOR SILENT REFLECTION

Is Jesus saying we shouldn't wash our hands before dinner? What do we have within us that we can give to the poor and needy?

## CLOSING PRAYER

Let us stand and bring our hopes and needs to God as we pray, "Lord, hear our prayer."

◆ All may add their own prayers here.

Let us pray: **Our Father . . . Amen.**

Holy God,
when you invite us to the Eucharist
you welcome us.
Even though we are not worthy of your love
you welcome us.
You see who we truly are,
and, calling each of us by name,
you welcome us.
Help us to welcome others in your name.
We ask this through Jesus Christ our Lord.
**Amen.**

✚ All make the Sign of the Cross.

# PRAYER FOR **WEDNESDAY OCTOBER 13, 2010**

## OPENING

Today we hear Jesus criticize the Pharisees [FAIR-uh-seez] for the way they perform charity. Jews were required to tithe [tyth] which means to give a tenth of one's income to the temple. In today's passage Jesus speaks about them giving herbs.

✚ All make the Sign of the Cross.

**In the name of the Father and of the Son and of the Holy Spirit. Amen.**

## PSALM    (For a longer psalm, see page xi.) Psalm 25:4 (1, 2a)

To you, O Lord, I lift up my soul.
O my God, in you I trust.

**To you, O Lord, I lift up my soul.
O my God, in you I trust.**

Make me to know your ways, O Lord;
   teach me your paths.

**To you, O Lord, I lift up my soul.
O my God, in you I trust.**

◆ All stand and sing **Alleluia**.

## GOSPEL                                       Luke 11:42–44

A reading from the holy Gospel according to Luke

Jesus said, "But woe to you Pharisees [FAIR-uh-seez]! For you tithe [tyth] mint and rue and herbs of all kinds, and neglect justice and the love of God; it is these you ought to have practiced, without neglecting the others. Woe to you Pharisees [FAIR-uh-seez]! For you love to have the seat of honor in the synagogues [SIN-uh-gogs] and to be greeted with respect in the marketplaces. Woe to you! For you are like unmarked graves, and people walk over them without realizing it."

The Gospel of the Lord.

◆ All sit and observe silence.

## FOR SILENT REFLECTION

What do you think Jesus doesn't like about the way the Pharisees make their donations?

## CLOSING PRAYER

Let us stand and bring our hopes and needs to God as we pray, "Lord, hear our prayer."

◆ All may add their own prayers here.

Let us pray: **Our Father . . . Amen.**

God of justice,
help us to love others as ourselves,
to give from our hearts,
out of love, not pride.
Help us to desire justice
more than praise,
and your will more than our own.
We ask this through Jesus Christ our Lord.
**Amen.**

✚ All make the Sign of the Cross.

# PRAYER FOR **THURSDAY** OCTOBER 14, 2010

## OPENING

In today's reading, Paul writes about the wealth of blessings God gives us.

✚ All make the Sign of the Cross.

**In the name of the Father and of the Son and of the Holy Spirit. Amen.**

## PSALM
(For a longer psalm, see page xi.) Psalm 25:4 (1, 2a)

To you, O LORD, I lift up my soul.
O my God, in you I trust.

**To you, O LORD, I lift up my soul.
O my God, in you I trust.**

Make me to know your ways, O LORD;
 teach me your paths.

**To you, O LORD, I lift up my soul.
O my God, in you I trust.**

## READING
Ephesians 1:3–10

A reading from the Letter of Saint Paul to the Ephesians [ee-FEE-zhuhnz]

Blessed be the God and Father of our Lord Jesus Christ, who has blessed us in Christ with every spiritual blessing in the heavenly places, just as he chose us in Christ before the foundation of the world to be holy and blameless before him in love. He destined us for adoption as his children through Jesus Christ, according to the good pleasure of his will, to the praise of his glorious grace that he freely bestowed on us in the Beloved. In him we have redemption through his blood, the forgiveness of our trespasses, according to the riches of his grace that he lavished on us. With all wisdom and insight he has made known to us the mystery of his will, according to his good pleasure that he set forth in Christ, as a plan for the fullness of time, to gather up all things in him, things in heaven and things on earth.

The Gospel of the Lord.

◆ All observe silence.

## FOR SILENT REFLECTION

In this list of spiritual blessings, what things were familiar? What things were new to you?

## CLOSING PRAYER

Let us stand and bring our hopes and needs to God as we pray, "Lord, hear our prayer."

◆ All may add their own prayers here.

Let us pray: **Our Father . . . Amen.**

Gracious God,
you give us so much.
You give us minds eager to learn,
and hearts ready to love.
You give us a world
full of wonders and mysteries.
And you bless us with longing
for your beauty and truth.
Help us to enjoy the gifts you give us
and to use them in the service of others.
We ask this through your Son, Jesus Christ
 our Lord.
**Amen.**

✚ All make the Sign of the Cross.

# PRAYER FOR FRIDAY
# OCTOBER 15, 2009

## OPENING

Today we remember Saint Teresa of Jesus, also known as Teresa of Avila. She was a sixteenth century Carmelite nun whose life of prayer helped her understand how to know Christ more deeply and trust God more completely. Unlike the Pharisees [FAIR-uh-seez] in today's Gospel, Saint Teresa believed it is important for us to know ourselves so that we can be our true selves with God.

✦ All make the Sign of the Cross.

**In the name of the Father and of the Son and of the Holy Spirit. Amen.**

## PSALM (For a longer psalm, see page xi.) Psalm 25:4 (1, 2a)

To you, O Lord, I lift up my soul.
O my God, in you I trust.

**To you, O Lord, I lift up my soul.
O my God, in you I trust.**

Make me to know your ways, O Lord;
  teach me your paths.

**To you, O Lord, I lift up my soul.
O my God, in you I trust.**

◆ All stand and sing **Alleluia**.

## GOSPEL    Luke 12:1ac–3, 6–7

A reading from the holy Gospel according to Luke

When the crowd gathered by the thousands, Jesus began to speak first to his disciples, "Beware of the yeast of the Pharisees [FAIR-uh-seez], that is their hypocrisy [hih-PAWK-rih-see]. Nothing is covered up that will not be uncovered, and nothing secret that will not become known. Therefore, whatever you have said in the dark will be heard in the light, and what you have whispered behind closed doors will be proclaimed from the housetop.

Are not five sparrows sold for two pennies? Yet not one of them is forgotten in God's sight. But even the hairs on your head are all counted. Do not be afraid; you are of more value than many sparrows."

The Gospel of the Lord.

◆ All sit and observe silence.

## FOR SILENT REFLECTION

Do you believe that God loves you just as you are? Do you ever want to hide part of yourself from God?

## CLOSING PRAYER

Let us stand and bring our hopes and needs to God as we pray, "Lord, hear our prayer."

◆ All may add their own prayers here.

Let us pray: **Our Father . . . Amen.**

Merciful and loving God,
even the smallest sparrow
is precious to you.
Help us not to be afraid
to be ourselves when we pray to you.
Give us faith in your love for us.
We ask this through Jesus Christ our Lord,
**Amen.**

✦ All make the Sign of the Cross.

# PRAYER FOR THE WEEK

WITH A READING FROM THE GOSPEL FOR **SUNDAY, OCTOBER 17, 2010**

## OPENING

To do justice is to do what is right and fair. Today Jesus tells about a woman who wanted justice so much that she wouldn't give up.

✢ All make the Sign of the Cross.

**In the name of the Father and of the Son and of the Holy Spirit. Amen.**

## PSALM  (For a longer psalm, see page xi.) Psalm 25:4 (1, 2a)

To you, O Lord, I lift up my soul.
O my God, in you I trust.

**To you, O Lord, I lift up my soul.
O my God, in you I trust.**

Make me to know your ways, O Lord;
   teach me your paths.

**To you, O Lord, I lift up my soul.
O my God, in you I trust.**

◆ All stand and sing **Alleluia**.

## GOSPEL                                    Luke 18:1–8

A reading from the holy Gospel according to Luke

Then Jesus told them a parable about their need to pray always and not to lose heart. He said, "In a certain city there was a judge who neither feared God nor had respect for people. In that city there was a widow who kept coming to him and saying, 'Grant me justice against my opponent.' For awhile he refused; but later he said to himself, 'Though I have no fear of God and no respect for anyone, yet because this widow keeps bothering me, I will grant her justice, so that she may not wear me out by continually coming.'" And the Lord said, "Listen to what the unjust judge says. And will not God grant justice to his chosen ones who cry to him day and night? Will he delay long in helping them? I tell you, he will quickly grant justice to them. And yet, when the Son of Man comes, will he find faith on earth?"

The Gospel of the Lord.

◆ All sit and observe silence.

## FOR SILENT REFLECTION

How do you think Jesus wants us to pray? What should we pray for today?

## CLOSING PRAYER

Let us stand and bring our hopes and needs to God as we pray, "Lord, hear our prayer."

◆ All may add their own prayers here.

Let us pray: **Our Father . . . Amen.**

Dear God,
bless and protect
all who suffer from injustice.
May your goodness, mercy, and love
be known everywhere on earth.
We ask this through Jesus Christ our Lord.
**Amen.**

✢ All make the Sign of the Cross.

---

**ALSO ON THIS DAY:** Vijaya Dasami (Hindu closing of Navaratri and celebration of Lord Rama's victory over an evil demon.)

# PRAYER FOR MONDAY OCTOBER 18, 2010

## OPENING

Today is the feast of Saint Luke, a doctor who became a Christian and traveled with Saint Paul on his missionary journeys. Luke wrote the Gospel account we read from today.

✠ All make the Sign of the Cross.

**In the name of the Father and of the Son and of the Holy Spirit. Amen.**

## PSALM (For a longer psalm, see page xi.) Psalm 25:4 (1, 2a)

To you, O Lord, I lift up my soul.
O my God, in you I trust.

**To you, O Lord, I lift up my soul.
O my God, in you I trust.**

Make me to know your ways, O Lord;
    teach me your paths.

**To you, O Lord, I lift up my soul.
O my God, in you I trust.**

◆ All stand and sing **Alleluia**.

## GOSPEL                              Luke 10:1–3, 5–9

A reading from the holy Gospel according to Luke

After this the Lord appointed seventy others and sent them on ahead of him in pairs to every town and place where he himself intended to go. He said to them, "The harvest is plentiful, but the laborers are few; therefore ask the Lord of the harvest to send out laborers into his harvest. Go on your way. See, I am sending you out like lambs into the midst of wolves. Whatever house you enter, first say, 'Peace to this house!' And if anyone is there who shares in peace, your peace will rest on that person; but if not, it will return to you. Remain in the same house, eating and drinking whatever they provide, for the laborer deserves to be paid. Do not move about from house to house. Whenever you enter a town and its people welcome you, eat what is set before you; cure the sick who are there, and say to them, 'The kingdom of God has come near to you.'"

The Gospel of the Lord.

◆ All sit and observe silence.

## FOR SILENT REFLECTION

Do you know any missionaries working today? What work are they doing? How can we help them in this work?

## CLOSING PRAYER

Let us stand and bring our hopes and needs to God as we pray, "Lord, hear our prayer."

◆ All may add their own prayers here.

Let us pray: **Our Father . . . Amen.**

Lord God,
we pray for missionaries
who bring your word, your love,
    and your justice
to people throughout the world.
Be their strength.
Give them courage and willing hearts.
We ask this through Jesus Christ our Lord.
**Amen.**

✠ All make the Sign of the Cross.

# PRAYER FOR TUESDAY OCTOBER 19, 2010

## OPENING

Today we remember two Jesuit missionaries, Saint John de Brebeuf [BRAY-buf] and Saint Isaac Jogues, who came from France to Quebec, [kwe-BECK] in Canada, to bring the good news of the Gospel to the Huron [HYUR-on] Indians. These saints were ready to do God's work. In today's Gospel, Jesus tells his followers to be ready for action.

✢ All make the Sign of the Cross.

**In the name of the Father and of the Son and of the Holy Spirit. Amen.**

## PSALM
(For a longer psalm, see page xi.) Psalm 25:4 (1, 2a)

To you, O Lord, I lift up my soul.
O my God, in you I trust.

**To you, O Lord, I lift up my soul.
O my God, in you I trust.**

Make me to know your ways, O Lord;
  teach me your paths.

**To you, O Lord, I lift up my soul.
O my God, in you I trust.**

◆ All stand and sing **Alleluia**.

## GOSPEL
Luke 12:35–38

A reading from the holy Gospel according to Luke

Jesus said to the crowd, "Be dressed for action and have your lamps lit; be like those who are waiting for their master to return from the wedding banquet, so that they may open the door for him as soon as he comes and knocks. Blessed are those slaves whom the master finds alert when he comes; truly I tell you, he will fasten his belt and have them sit down to eat, and he will come and serve them. If he comes during the middle of the night, or near dawn, and finds them so, blessed are those slaves."

The Gospel of the Lord.

◆ All sit and observe silence.

## FOR SILENT REFLECTION

What kind of action does a Christian need to be ready for? What are the lamps we are to keep lit?

## CLOSING PRAYER

Let us stand and bring our hopes and needs to God as we pray, "Lord, hear our prayer."

◆ All may add their own prayers here.

Let us pray: **Our Father . . . Amen.**

Lord God,
as we study your word,
enlighten our hearts and minds
so that we will be ready
to do your will.
We ask this through your Son, Jesus Christ
  our Lord.
**Amen.**

✢ All make the Sign of the Cross.

# PRAYER FOR WEDNESDAY OCTOBER 20, 2010

## OPENING

Like yesterday's reading, today's Gospel talks about being awake and ready. Throughout history, those who are awake to God's presence in their lives have led the people of God into freedom. Notice that Jesus refers to himself as the Son of Man.

✚ All make the Sign of the Cross.

**In the name of the Father and of the Son and of the Holy Spirit. Amen.**

## PSALM          (For a longer psalm, see page xi.) Psalm 25:4 (1, 2a)

To you, O Lord, I lift up my soul.
O my God, in you I trust.

**To you, O Lord, I lift up my soul.
O my God, in you I trust.**

Make me to know your ways, O Lord;
   teach me your paths.

**To you, O Lord, I lift up my soul.
O my God, in you I trust.**

◆ All stand and sing **Alleluia**.

## GOSPEL                                         Luke 12:39–43

A reading from the holy Gospel according to Luke

Jesus said to the crowd, "But know this: if the owner of the house had known at what hour the thief was coming, he would not have let his house be broken into. You also must be ready, for the Son of Man is coming at an unexpected hour."

   Peter said, "Lord, are you telling this parable for us or for everyone?" And the Lord said, "Who then is the faithful and prudent manager whom his master will put in charge of his slaves, to give them their allowance of food at the proper time? Blessed is that slave whom his master will find at work, when he arrives."

The Gospel of the Lord.

◆ All sit and observe silence.

## FOR SILENT REFLECTION

If you knew Jesus were coming to see you, how would you get ready to meet him?

## CLOSING PRAYER

Let us stand and bring our hopes and needs to God as we pray, "Lord, hear our prayer."

◆ All may add their own prayers here.

Let us pray: **Our Father . . . Amen.**

Wonderful God,
how can we be ready to receive you?
Was Abraham ready to receive your promise?
Was Moses ready to lead your people
   into freedom?
Was Mary ready to become the Mother
   of God?
Was Peter ready to lead your Church?
How can we be ready to receive your glory
   and power?
It is you who prepare us to receive you.
Then send your Spirit
to prepare a place for you in our hearts.
We ask this through our Lord Jesus Christ.
      **Amen.**

✚ All make the Sign of the Cross.

# PRAYER FOR THURSDAY OCTOBER 21, 2010

## OPENING

Today we read part of a letter written by Saint Paul to the Christians he had taught and led in the city of Ephesus [EF-uh-suhs]. These people were known as Ephesians [ee-FEE-zhuhnz]. In this part of the letter, Paul writes about the Holy Spirit.

✚ All make the Sign of the Cross.

**In the name of the Father and of the Son and of the Holy Spirit. Amen.**

## PSALM
(For a longer psalm, see page xi.) Psalm 25:4 (1, 2a)

To you, O LORD, I lift up my soul.
O my God, in you I trust.

To you, O LORD, I lift up my soul.
O my God, in you I trust.

Make me to know your ways, O LORD;
 teach me your paths.

To you, O LORD, I lift up my soul.
O my God, in you I trust.

## READING
Ephesians 3:16–21

A reading from the Letter of Saint Paul to the Ephesians [ee-FEE-zhuhnz]

I pray that, according to the riches of his glory, the Father may grant that you may be strengthened in your inner being with power through his Spirit, and that Christ may dwell in your hearts through faith, as you are being rooted and grounded in love. I pray that you may have the power to comprehend, with all the saints, what is the breadth and length and height and depth, and to know the love of Christ that surpasses knowledge, so that you may be filled with all the fullness of God. Now to him who by the power at work within us is able to accomplish abundantly far more than all we can ask or imagine, to him be glory in the church and in Christ Jesus to all generations, for ever and ever. Amen.

The word of the Lord.

◆ All observe silence.

## FOR SILENT REFLECTION

How do you want the Holy Spirit to make you stronger?

## CLOSING PRAYER

Let us stand and bring our hopes and needs to God as we pray, "Lord, hear our prayer."

◆ All may add their own prayers here.

Let us pray: **Our Father . . . Amen.**

God our Father,
send your Holy Spirit to us.
Make us strong in faith, hope, and love.
Do for us what we cannot do for ourselves.
We ask this through Jesus Christ our Lord.
**Amen.**

✚ All make the Sign of the Cross.

# PRAYER FOR FRIDAY OCTOBER 22, 2010

### OPENING

Today we continue to read from Paul's letter to the Ephesians [ee-FEE-zhuhnz]. He reminds Christians that we are called to work for unity and harmony.

✚ All make the Sign of the Cross.

**In the name of the Father and of the Son and of the Holy Spirit. Amen.**

### PSALM   (For a longer psalm, see page xi.) Psalm 25:4 (1, 2a)

To you, O Lord, I lift up my soul.
O my God, in you I trust.

**To you, O Lord, I lift up my soul.
O my God, in you I trust.**

Make me to know your ways, O Lord;
　teach me your paths.

**To you, O Lord, I lift up my soul.
O my God, in you I trust.**

### READING   Ephesians 4:1–6

A reading from the Letter of Saint Paul to the Ephesians [ee-FEE-zhuhnz]

I therefore, the prisoner in the Lord, beg you to lead a life worthy of the calling to which you have been called, with all humility and gentleness, with patience, bearing with one another in love, making every effort to maintain the unity of the Spirit in the bond of peace. There is one body and one Spirit, just as you were called to the one hope of your calling, one Lord, one faith, one baptism, one God and Father of all, who is above all and through all and in all.

The word of the Lord.

◆ All observe silence.

### FOR SILENT REFLECTION

What do you think Paul means when he says "There is one body and one Spirit"? What efforts can you make to live in unity with others?

### CLOSING PRAYER

Let us stand and bring our hopes and needs to God as we pray, "Lord, hear our prayer."

◆ All may add their own prayers here.

Let us pray: **Our Father . . . Amen.**

Loving God,
we pray that all people
may live together in unity and peace.
Help us to be patient with one another,
and free us from envy and selfishness.
Grant us the precious gift of your peace.
We ask this through our Lord Jesus Christ,
　your Son, who lives and reigns with
　you in the unity of the Holy Spirit,
　one God, for ever and ever.
**Amen.**

✚ All make the Sign of the Cross.

# PRAYER FOR THE WEEK

WITH A READING FROM THE GOSPEL FOR **SUNDAY, OCTOBER 24, 2010**

## OPENING

In today's Gospel Jesus teaches us how to pray by telling us about two people who pray in very different ways. One prays by exalting himself. This means he praises himself. The other admits he is a sinner.

✚ All make the Sign of the Cross.

**In the name of the Father and of the Son and of the Holy Spirit. Amen.**

## PSALM (For a longer psalm, see page xi.) Psalm 25:4 (1, 2a)

To you, O Lord, I lift up my soul.
O my God, in you I trust.

**To you, O Lord, I lift up my soul.
O my God, in you I trust.**

Make me to know your ways, O Lord;
   teach me your paths.

**To you, O Lord, I lift up my soul.
O my God, in you I trust.**

◆ All stand and sing **Alleluia**.

## GOSPEL                                   Luke 18:9–14

A reading from the holy Gospel according to Luke

Jesus then addressed this parable to those who were convinced of their own righteousness and despised everyone else. "Two people went up to the temple area to pray; one was a Pharisee [FAIR-uh-see] and the other was a tax collector. The Pharisee took up his position and spoke this prayer to himself, 'O God, I thank you that I am not like the rest of humanity—greedy, dishonest, adulterous—or even like this tax collector. I fast twice a week, and I pay tithes on my whole income.' But the tax collector stood off at a distance and would not even raise his eyes to heaven but beat his breast and prayed, 'O God, be merciful to me a sinner.' I tell you, the latter went home justified, not the former; for everyone who exalts himself will be humbled, and the one who humbles himself will be exalted."

The Gospel of the Lord.

◆ All sit and observe silence.

## FOR SILENT REFLECTION

Is the Pharisee [FAIR-uh-see] right when he says he is not a sinner? How did prayer help the tax collector?

## CLOSING PRAYER

Let us stand and bring our hopes and needs to God as we pray, "Lord, hear our prayer."

◆ All may add their own prayers here.

Let us pray: **Our Father . . . Amen.**
Merciful God,
only you are perfectly fair and just.
Help us not to pretend
we are better than others.
Give us faith to believe you love us
even when we do something wrong.
We ask this through your Son, our Lord Jesus Christ.
**Amen.**

✚ All make the Sign of the Cross.

# PRAYER FOR MONDAY OCTOBER 25, 2010

## OPENING

In today's Gospel, Jesus shows his knowledge of the sabbath laws given by God to the Jewish people. He challenges leaders who are more interested in their power than in God's law.

✢ All make the Sign of the Cross.

**In the name of the Father and of the Son and of the Holy Spirit. Amen.**

## PSALM
(For a longer psalm, see page xii.) Psalm 84:2a(1)

How lovely is your dwelling place,
O Lord of hosts!

**How lovely is your dwelling place,
O Lord of hosts!**

My soul longs, indeed it faints
for the courts of the Lord.

**How lovely is your dwelling place,
O Lord of hosts!**

◆ All stand and sing **Alleluia**.

## GOSPEL
Luke 13:10–17

A reading from the holy Gospel according to Luke

Now Jesus was teaching in one of the synagogues [SIN-uh-gogs] on the sabbath. And just then there appeared a woman with a spirit that had crippled her for eighteen years. She was bent over and was quite unable to stand up straight. When Jesus saw her, he called her over and said, "Woman, you are set free from your ailment." When he laid his hands on her, immediately she stood up straight and began praising God. But the leader of the synagogue, indignant because Jesus had cured on the sabbath, kept saying to the crowd, "There are six days on which work ought to be done: come on those days and be cured, and not on the sabbath day." But the Lord answered him and said, "You hypocrites [HIP-uh-kritz]! Does not each of you on the sabbath untie his ox or his donkey from the manger, and lead it away to give it water? And ought not this woman, a daughter of Abraham whom Satan bound for eighteen long years, be set free from this bondage on the sabbath day?" When he said this, all his opponents were put to shame; and the entire crowd was rejoicing at all the wonderful things that he was doing.

The Gospel of the Lord.

◆ All sit and observe silence.

## FOR SILENT REFLECTION

Why do you think Jesus always heals the sick?

## CLOSING PRAYER

Let us stand and bring our hopes and needs to God as we pray, "Lord, hear our prayer."

◆ All may add their own prayers here.

Let us pray: **Our Father . . . Amen.**

God, our healer,
we pray for all who are sick and suffering;
may they know your healing love.
We ask this through Jesus Christ our Lord.
**Amen.**

✢ All make the Sign of the Cross.

# PRAYER FOR TUESDAY OCTOBER 26, 2010

## OPENING

In today's Gospel, Jesus compares the kingdom of God to things that grow, even though they start out small. A mustard seed is very small but grows up into a big bush. Yeast is an ingredient cooks put into bread to make it rise. Bread made without yeast is flat.

✠ All make the Sign of the Cross.

**In the name of the Father and of the Son and of the Holy Spirit. Amen.**

## PSALM
(For a longer psalm, see page xii.) Psalm 84:2a (1)

How lovely is your dwelling place,
O Lord of hosts!

**How lovely is your dwelling place,
O Lord of hosts!**

My soul longs, indeed it faints
for the courts of the Lord.

**How lovely is your dwelling place,
O Lord of hosts!**

◆ All stand and sing **Alleluia**.

## GOSPEL
Luke 13:18–21

A reading from the holy Gospel according to Luke

Jesus said therefore: "What is the kingdom of God like? And to what should I compare it? It is like a mustard seed that someone took and sowed in the garden; it grew and became a tree, and the birds of the air made nests in its branches." And again he said, "To what should I compare the kingdom of God? It is like yeast that a woman took and mixed in with three measures of flour until all of it was leavened."

The Gospel of the Lord.

◆ All sit and observe silence.

## FOR SILENT REFLECTION

What do you think the yeast and the mustard seed stand for? What makes the kingdom of God grow?

## CLOSING PRAYER

Let us stand and bring our hopes and needs to God as we pray, "Lord, hear our prayer."

◆ All may add their own prayers here.

Let us pray: **Our Father . . . Amen.**

Blessed are you, Lord God,
ruler of the universe.
Plant in us the seed of faith
so that we may know the power of
   your truth.
Knead the yeast of love into our lives
so that we may know love's power.
We ask this through our Lord Jesus Christ,
   your Son, who lives and reigns with
   you in the unity of the Holy Spirit,
   one God, for ever and ever.

**Amen.**

✠ All make the Sign of the Cross.

# PRAYER FOR **WEDNESDAY** OCTOBER 27, 2010

## OPENING

Paul is always trying to encourage people to live together in love and peace because that is what God wants for us. In today's reading, Paul talks about how children and parents should treat one another.

✢ All make the Sign of the Cross.

**In the name of the Father and of the Son and of the Holy Spirit. Amen.**

## PSALM
(For a longer psalm, see page xii.) Psalm 84:2a (1)

How lovely is your dwelling place,
O Lord of hosts!

**How lovely is your dwelling place,
O Lord of hosts!**

My soul longs, indeed it faints
for the courts of the Lord.

**How lovely is your dwelling place,
O Lord of hosts!**

## READING
Ephesians 6:1–4

A reading from the Letter of Saint Paul to the Ephesians [ee-FEE-zhuhnz]

Children, obey your parents in the Lord, for this is right. "Honor your father and mother." This is the first commandment with a promise: "so that it may be well with you and you may live long on the earth." And, fathers, do not provoke your children to anger, but bring them up in the discipline and instruction of the Lord.

The word of the Lord.

◆ All observe silence.

## FOR SILENT REFLECTION

How do you honor your parents? How do they care for you?

## CLOSING PRAYER

Let us stand and bring our hopes and needs to God as we pray, "Lord, hear our prayer."

◆ All may add their own prayers here.

Let us pray: **Our Father . . . Amen.**

Loving God,
we thank you for our parents,
grand-parents, god-parents,
and all who teach us
through words and by example
how to live as children of God.
We pray that you will bless all families.
Help parents to raise their children
to know and love you.
Help children to respect their parents
and learn from them how to live
good and holy lives.
We ask this through Jesus Christ the Lord.
**Amen.**

✢ All make the Sign of the Cross.

# PRAYER FOR **THURSDAY OCTOBER 28, 2010**

### OPENING

Today we celebrate the feast of the apostles, Saint Simon and Saint Jude. Both traveled to teach others about Christ and both were martyred for their faith. Christians in great need often ask Saint Jude to pray for them.

✣ All make the Sign of the Cross.

**In the name of the Father and of the Son and of the Holy Spirit. Amen.**

### PSALM (For a longer psalm, see page xii.) Psalm 84:2a (1)

How lovely is your dwelling place,
O Lord of hosts!

**How lovely is your dwelling place,
O Lord of hosts!**

My soul longs, indeed it faints
for the courts of the Lord.

**How lovely is your dwelling place,
O Lord of hosts!**

### READING Ephesians 2:19–22

A reading from the Letter of Saint Paul to the Ephesians

So then you are no longer strangers and aliens, but you are citizens with the saints and also members of the household of God, built upon the foundation of the apostles and prophets, with Christ Jesus himself as the cornerstone. In him the whole structure is joined together and grows into a holy temple in the Lord; in whom you also are built together spiritually into a dwelling place for God.

The word of the Lord.

◆ All observe silence.

### FOR SILENT REFLECTION

What do you think Paul is talking about when he says we are members of the "household of God"?

### CLOSING PRAYER

Let us stand and bring our hopes and needs to God as we pray, "Lord, hear our prayer."

◆ All may add their own prayers here.

Let us pray: **Our Father . . . Amen.**

God our Father,
your Son came as a child
into a family
to make your home with us.
You sent the Holy Spirit
so that your church could become
a household of faith.
Help us to live as your family,
welcoming others
into this holy household.
We ask this through our Lord Jesus Christ,
  your Son, who lives and reigns with
  you in the unity of the Holy Spirit,
  one God, for ever and ever.
**Amen.**

✣ All make the Sign of the Cross.

# HOME PRAYER
## CELEBRATING THE SAINTS, REMEMBERING THE DEAD

*Find the reading (1 John 3:1–3) in your Bible, ask for a volunteer to read it, and encourage the reader to practice reading it twice. Then gather the household in one room. If you have a candle, bring it out for prayer time and light it. You may wish to begin with a simple song, such as "Holy, Holy, Holy Lord." Then an older child or adult reads the leader parts:*

**LEADER:**
The saints are living people who spend their eternity walking next to us and praying for us, while at the same time they bask in the marvelous Light of God's presence. Truly they are with us, urging us to goodness. In this life, each saint had special interests and strengths. We use their names when we turn to them for help, and we can draw strength from their special talents.

◆ All make the Sign of the Cross.

**ALL: In the name of the Father and of the Son and of the Holy Spirit. Amen.**

**LEADER:** *Psalm 24:1, 5a*
Let us pray the psalm response:
They will receive blessing from the LORD.

**ALL: They will receive blessing from the LORD.**

**LEADER:**
The earth is the LORD's, as is all that is in it and those who live in it.

**ALL: They will receive blessing from the LORD.**

◆ All stand and sing **Alleluia**

*1 John 3:1–3*

**LEADER:**
A reading from the First Letter of John

◆ Read the Scripture passage from the Bible.

The word of the Lord.

◆ All observe a brief silence.

**LEADER:**
And now let us remember family members and friends who have died:

◆ The leader begins, then pauses so others may add names too.

**LEADER:**
O Lord God, almighty,
we ask you to bring these
and all your departed children
into the glorious Light of your presence.

◆ Leader pauses, then continues:

Lord, what tender care you have for all
    your creatures!
You are higher than our minds can wonder,
deeper than we can imagine,
but you care for each of us as your own
    dear children!
Help us to see one another through
    your eyes
so that one day, with all the saints in heaven,
we, and all those we love, may see your face.
We ask this through Jesus Christ, our Lord.

**ALL: Amen.**

◆ All make the Sign of the Cross.

# PRAYER SERVICE
## FOR ALL SAINTS DAY

*Prepare nine leaders for this service. The third, fourth, and fifth leaders will need Bibles for the scripture passages and may need help practicing the readings. You may wish to begin by singing "Sing with All the Saints in Glory" and end with "Blest Are They." If the group will sing, prepare a song leader.*

**FIRST LEADER:**
May the grace and peace of our Lord Jesus Christ be with us, now and for ever.
**Amen.**

**SECOND LEADER:**
Let us pray:
Each of the saints is precious in your sight!
Their love for you shone out so clear and
    bright in the love they showered on
    those around them.
May we love you as they did,
and may we express our love for you
in the gentleness and mercy we show to those
    around us.
We ask this through Christ our Lord.
**Amen.**

◆ All stand and sing **Alleluia.**

**THIRD LEADER:**                               Matthew 5:1–2
A reading from the holy Gospel according to Matthew

◆ The third, fourth, and fifth leaders read the Gospel passages from a Bible.

**FOURTH LEADER:**                         Matthew 5:3–6

# FOR ALL SAINTS DAY

**FIFTH LEADER:**          Matthew 5:7–10
The Gospel of the Lord.

◆ All sit and observe silence.

**SIXTH LEADER:**
Let us pray a very ancient prayer called the Litany of the Saints, responding "Pray for us" after each name.

Holy Mary, Mother of God,

**ALL: Pray for us.**

Saint Michael,

**ALL: Pray for us.**

Holy angels of God,

**ALL: Pray for us.**

Saint John the Baptist,

**ALL: Pray for us.**

Saint Joseph,

**ALL: Pray for us.**

Saint Peter and Saint Paul,

**ALL: Pray for us.**

**SEVENTH LEADER:**
Saint Andrew and Saint John,

**ALL: Pray for us.**

Saint Mary Magdalene,

**ALL: Pray for us.**

Saint Stephen and Saint Ignatius

**ALL: Pray for us.**

Saint Perpetua and Saint Felicity,

**ALL: Pray for us.**

Saint Francis and Saint Dominic,

**ALL: Pray for us.**

◆ Add other saints if you wish. Then end with:

All you holy men and women,

**ALL: Pray for us.**

**EIGHTH LEADER:**
Let us pray:
God, you are the source of all holiness.
May all the prayers we have asked for today
help us to grow in your love,
and may the beautiful examples of your saints
draw our hearts and souls ever closer to you.
We offer this prayer through Christ our Lord.

**ALL: Amen.**

**NINTH LEADER:**
May the love of God,

✝ All make the Sign of the Cross.

Father, Son, and Holy Spirit,
draw us together in faith, hope, and love
now and for ever.

**ALL: Amen.**

# PRAYER FOR **FRIDAY OCTOBER 29, 2010**

## OPENING

In today's reading, Paul expresses the joy and thanksgiving he feels for people of the church in Philippi [fih-LIP-ī], a church he had helped to start some years earlier.

✚ All make the Sign of the Cross.

**In the name of the Father and of the Son and of the Holy Spirit. Amen.**

## PSALM
(For a longer psalm, see page xii.) Psalm 84:2a (1)

How lovely is your dwelling place,
O Lord of hosts!

**How lovely is your dwelling place,
O Lord of hosts!**

My soul longs, indeed it faints
for the courts of the Lord.

**How lovely is your dwelling place,
O Lord of hosts!**

## READING
Philippians 1:3–11

A reading from the letter of Saint Paul to the Philippians [fih-LIP-ee-uhnz]

I thank my God every time I remember you, constantly praying with joy in every one of my prayers for all of you, because of your sharing in the gospel from the first day until now. I am confident of this, that the one who began a good work among you will bring it to completion by the day of Jesus Christ. It is right for me to think this way about all of you, because you hold me in your heart, for all of you share in God's grace with me, both in my imprisonment and in the defense and confirmation of the gospel. For God is my witness, how I long for all of you with the compassion of Christ Jesus. And this is my prayer, that your love may overflow more and more with knowledge and full insight to help you to determine what is best, so that on the day of Christ you may be pure and blameless, having produced the harvest of righteousness that comes through Jesus Christ for the glory and praise of God.

The word of the Lord.

◆ All observe silence.

## FOR SILENT REFLECTION

Why do you think Paul is so grateful for the people of this church? What people in your church are you grateful for?

## CLOSING PRAYER

Let us stand and bring our hopes and needs to God as we pray, "Lord, hear our prayer."

◆ All may add their own prayers here.

Let us pray: **Our Father . . . Amen.**

Holy God,
we ask you to bless our parish family.
Guide and protect us
as we try to serve each other.
Grant this through Jesus Christ our Lord.
**Amen.**

✚ All make the Sign of the Cross.

---

**ALSO ON THIS DAY:** Halloween is on Sunday but may be celebrated in some communities on Saturday.

# PRAYER FOR THE WEEK

WITH A READING FROM THE GOSPEL FOR **SUNDAY, OCTOBER 31, 2010**

## OPENING

Today Jesus comes to the home of Zacchaeus (zuh-KEE-us). The word "stature" means height and the word "defraud" means to cheat.

✢ All make the Sign of the Cross.

**In the name of the Father and of the Son and of the Holy Spirit. Amen.**

## PSALM
(For a longer psalm, see page xii.) Psalm 84:2a (1)

How lovely is your dwelling place,
O Lord of hosts!

**How lovely is your dwelling place,
O Lord of hosts!**

My soul longs, indeed it faints
for the courts of the Lord.

**How lovely is your dwelling place,
O Lord of hosts!**

◆ All stand and sing **Alleluia**.

## GOSPEL
Luke 19:1–10

A reading from the holy Gospel according to Luke

Jesus entered Jericho and was passing through it. A man was there named Zacchaeus; he was a chief tax collector and was rich. He was trying to see who Jesus was, but on account of the crowd he could not, because he was short in stature. So he ran ahead and climbed a sycamore tree to see him, because he was going to pass that way. When Jesus came to the place, he looked up and said to him, "Zacchaeus, hurry and come down; for I must stay at your house today." So he hurried down and was happy to welcome him. All who saw it began to grumble and said, "He has gone to be the guest of one who is a sinner." Zacchaeus stood there and said to the Lord, "Look, half of my possessions, Lord, I will give to the poor; and if I have defrauded anyone of anything, I will pay back four times as much." Then Jesus said to him, "Today salvation has come to this house, because he too is a son of Abraham. For the Son of Man came to seek out and save the lost."

The Gospel of the Lord.

◆ All sit and observe silence.

## FOR SILENT REFLECTION

Imagine that Jesus comes to your home. What do you want to show him? To tell him?

## CLOSING PRAYER

Let us stand and bring our hopes and needs to God as we pray, "Lord, hear our prayer."

◆ All may add their own prayers here.

Let us pray: **Our Father . . . Amen.**

Wonderful God,
help us to make our home your home,
open to your divine presence.
We ask this through Jesus Christ our Lord.
**Amen.**

✢ All make the Sign of the Cross.

**ALSO ON THIS DAY:** Reformation Day (Lutheran and Reformed communities' commemoration of Martin Luther's Ninety-five Theses.)

# PRAYER FOR MONDAY NOVEMBER 1, 2010

## OPENING

On the solemnity of All Saints, we celebrate all the saints, living in the fullness of life in Christ. The Gospel tells us how to become saints.

✚ All make the Sign of the Cross.

**In the name of the Father and of the Son and of the Holy Spirit. Amen.**

## PSALM
(For a longer psalm, see page xii.) Psalm 84:2a (1)

How lovely is your dwelling place,
O Lord of hosts!

**How lovely is your dwelling place,
O Lord of hosts!**

My soul longs, indeed it faints
for the courts of the Lord.

**How lovely is your dwelling place,
O Lord of hosts!**

◆ All stand and sing **Alleluia**.

## GOSPEL
Matthew 5:1a, 2–12a

A reading from the holy Gospel according to Matthew

When Jesus saw the crowds, he went up the mountain. Then he began to speak, and taught them, saying:

"Blessed are the poor in spirit, for theirs is the kingdom of heaven.
Blessed are those who mourn, for they will be comforted.
Blessed are the meek, for they will inherit the earth.
Blessed are those who hunger and thirst for righteousness, for they will be filled.
Blessed are the merciful, for they will receive mercy.
Blessed are the pure in heart, for they will see God.
Blessed are the peacemakers, for they will be called children of God.
Blessed are those who are persecuted for righteousness' sake, for theirs is the kingdom of heaven.
Blessed are you when people revile you and persecute you and utter all kinds of evil against you falsely on my account. Rejoice and be glad, for your reward is great in heaven."

The Gospel of the Lord.

◆ All sit and observe silence.

## FOR SILENT REFLECTION

Which of these many blessings do you most desire?

## CLOSING PRAYER

Let us stand and bring our hopes and needs to God as we pray, "Lord, hear our prayer."

◆ All may add their own prayers here.

Let us pray: **Our Father . . . Amen.**

Holy God,
may the example and prayers of the saints
help us to live holy lives.
Grant this through Christ our Lord.
**Amen.**

✚ All make the Sign of the Cross.

# PRAYER FOR TUESDAY NOVEMBER 2, 2010

## OPENING

Today is the Commemoration [kuh-mem-or-AY-shun] of all the Faithful Departed. To commemorate someone is to remember them. Today we remember and pray for all the faithful who have died. In today's Gospel, Jesus assures us that all who come to him will enjoy eternal life.

✢ All make the Sign of the Cross.

**In the name of the Father and of the Son and of the Holy Spirit. Amen.**

## PSALM  (For a longer psalm, see page xii.) Psalm 84:2a (1)

How lovely is your dwelling place,
O Lord of hosts!

**How lovely is your dwelling place,
O Lord of hosts!**

My soul longs, indeed it faints
for the courts of the Lord.

**How lovely is your dwelling place,
O Lord of hosts!**

◆ All stand and sing **Alleluia.**

## GOSPEL    John 6:37–40

A reading from the holy Gospel according to John

Jesus said, "Everything that the Father gives me will come to me, and anyone who comes to me I will never drive away; for I have come down from heaven, not to do my own will, but the will of him who sent me. And this is the will of him who sent me, that I should lose nothing of all that he has given me, but raise it up on the last day. This is indeed the will of my Father, that all who see the Son and believe in him may have eternal life; and I will raise them up on the last day."

The Gospel of the Lord.

◆ All sit and observe silence.

## FOR SILENT REFLECTION

Who are some of the people who have died that you want to pray for today?

## CLOSING PRAYER

Let us stand and bring our hopes and needs to God as we pray, "Lord, hear our prayer."

◆ All may add their own prayers here.

Let us pray: **Our Father . . . Amen.**

God of life,
you desire eternal life
for all who come to you.
Today we pray for our loved ones who
    have died.
May they be healed of all sin and suffering.
Grant them the peace and joy of
    your presence for all eternity.
We ask this through Jesus Christ our Lord.
**Amen.**

✢ All make the Sign of the Cross.

---

**ALSO ON THIS DAY:** Election Day (U.S.A)

# PRAYER FOR WEDNESDAY NOVEMBER 3, 2010

## OPENING

Today we remember Saint Martin de Porres [day-POHRS], who lived in Lima, Peru. He was a Dominican brother and devoted his life to caring for the sick and the poor. He was also known for his love of animals and had a hospital for cats and dogs. In today's reading, Saint Paul is writing to the people in the town of Phillipi [fih-LIP-ī], encouraging them as they try to live the Christian life without his daily guidance.

✚ All make the Sign of the Cross.

**In the name of the Father and of the Son and of the Holy Spirit. Amen.**

## PSALM (For a longer psalm, see page xii.) Psalm 84:2a (1)

How lovely is your dwelling place,
O Lord of hosts!

**How lovely is your dwelling place,
O Lord of hosts!**

My soul longs, indeed it faints
for the courts of the Lord.

**How lovely is your dwelling place,
O Lord of hosts!**

## READING Philippians 2:12–16

A reading from the Letter of Saint Paul to the Philippians [fih-LIP-ee-uhnz]

Therefore, my beloved, just as you have always obeyed me, not only in my presence, but much more now in my absence, work out your own salvation with fear and trembling; for it is God who is at work in you, enabling you both to will and to work for his good pleasure. Do all things without murmuring and arguing, so that you may be blameless and innocent, children of God without blemish in the midst of a crooked and perverse generation, in which you shine like stars in the world. It is by your holding fast to the word of life that I can boast on the day of Christ that I did not run in vain or labor in vain.

The word of the Lord.

◆ All observe silence.

## FOR SILENT REFLECTION

What do you think Paul means when he says the Philippians shine like stars?

## CLOSING PRAYER

Let us stand and bring our hopes and needs to God as we pray, "Lord, hear our prayer."

◆ All may add their own prayers here.

Let us pray: **Our Father . . . Amen.**

God our Father,
this week as we remember all the saints
and pray for our loved ones who have died,
we thank you for the heavenly light
that shines through the lives of holy people.
Help us to live good and holy lives
so that your light may shine through us.
We ask this through Christ our Lord.
**Amen.**

✚ All make the Sign of the Cross.

# PRAYER FOR THURSDAY NOVEMBER 4, 2010

## OPENING

Today we remember Saint Charles Borromeo, who followed the example of the good shepherd we read about in today's Gospel. He cared for the needy and supported education, including religious education for children.

✛ All make the Sign of the Cross.

**In the name of the Father and of the Son and of the Holy Spirit. Amen.**

## PSALM   (For a longer psalm, see page xii.) Psalm 84:2a (1)

How lovely is your dwelling place,
O Lord of hosts!

**How lovely is your dwelling place,
O Lord of hosts!**

My soul longs, indeed it faints
for the courts of the Lord.

**How lovely is your dwelling place,
O Lord of hosts!**

◆ All stand and sing **Alleluia**.

## GOSPEL   Luke 15:1–10

A reading from the holy Gospel according to Luke

Now all the tax collectors and sinners were coming near to listen to Jesus. And the Pharisees (FAIR-uh-seez) and the scribes were grumbling and saying, "This fellow welcomes sinners and eats with them."

So he told them this parable: "Which one of you, having a hundred sheep and losing one of them, does not leave the ninety-nine in the wilderness and go after the one that is lost until he finds it? When he has found it, he lays it on his shoulders and rejoices. And when he comes home, he calls together his friends and neighbors, saying to them, 'Rejoice with me, for I have found my sheep that was lost.' Just so, I tell you, there will be more joy in heaven over one sinner who repents than over ninety-nine righteous persons who need no repentance."

The Gospel of the Lord.

◆ All sit and observe silence.

## FOR SILENT REFLECTION

Why do you think Jesus chose this story to tell the Pharisees?

## CLOSING PRAYER

Let us stand and bring our hopes and needs to God as we pray, "Lord, hear our prayer."

◆ All may add their own prayers here.

Let us pray: **Our Father . . . Amen.**

Lord our God,
help us to listen to your voice calling us.
May we never stray from your loving care.
Help our Church leaders to be
    good shepherds,
serving those in need
and guiding the lost sheep back to you.
We ask this through Jesus Christ our Lord.
**Amen.**

✛ All make the Sign of the Cross.

# PRAYER FOR FRIDAY NOVEMBER 5, 2010

### OPENING

In today's reading, Paul reminds the Philippians [fih-LIP-ee-uhnz] that they are citizens of heaven. They must not set their minds on earthly things.

✠ All make the Sign of the Cross.

**In the name of the Father and of the Son and of the Holy Spirit. Amen.**

### PSALM  (For a longer psalm, see page xii.) Psalm 84:2a (1)

How lovely is your dwelling place,
O Lord of hosts!

**How lovely is your dwelling place,
O Lord of hosts!**

My soul longs, indeed it faints
for the courts of the Lord.

**How lovely is your dwelling place,
O Lord of hosts!**

### READING  Philippians 3:17–21

A reading from the Letter of Saint Paul to the Philippians [fih-LIP-ee-uhnz]

Brothers and sisters, join in imitating me, and observe those who live according to the example you have in us. For many live as enemies of the cross of Christ; I have often told you of them, and now I tell you even with tears. Their end is destruction; their god is the belly; and their glory is in their shame; their minds are set on earthly things. But our citizenship is in heaven, and it is from there that we are expecting a Savior, the Lord Jesus Christ. He will transform the body of our humiliation that it may be conformed to the body of his glory, by the power that also enables him to make all things subject to himself.

The word of the Lord.

◆ All observe silence.

### FOR SILENT REFLECTION

What do you think Paul means when he says "their god is the belly"?

### CLOSING PRAYER

Let us stand and bring our hopes and needs to God as we pray, "Lord, hear our prayer."

◆ All may add their own prayers here.

Let us pray: **Our Father . . . Amen.**

Heavenly Father,
you invite us to dine with you in heaven,
to share in your glory forever.
But sometimes we pay more attention
to our stomachs and to material things
than to you.
Give us a taste for the heavenly food
of faith, hope, and love.
We ask this through Jesus Christ our Lord.
**Amen.**

✠ All make the Sign of the Cross.

---

**ALSO ON THIS DAY:** Diwali (Hindu festival of lights)
Daylight saving time ends on Sunday. (Turn clocks back.)

# PRAYER FOR THE WEEK

WITH A READING FROM THE GOSPEL FOR **SUNDAY, NOVEMBER 7, 2010**

## OPENING

In today's Gospel, Jesus talks with people who don't believe in the Resurrection. "Resurrection" means to rise from the dead and share in the eternal life of God. Jesus helps us begin to understand what this is like.

✝ All make the Sign of the Cross.

**In the name of the Father and of the Son and of the Holy Spirit. Amen.**

## PSALM   (For a longer psalm, see page xii.) Psalm 84:2a (1)

How lovely is your dwelling place,
O Lord of hosts!

**How lovely is your dwelling place,
O Lord of hosts!**

My soul longs, indeed it faints
for the courts of the Lord.

**How lovely is your dwelling place,
O Lord of hosts!**

◆ All stand and sing **Alleluia**.

## GOSPEL   Luke 20:27, 34–38

A reading from the holy Gospel according to Luke

Some Sadducees, those who say there is no resurrection, came to him. Jesus said to them, "Those who belong to this age marry and are given in marriage; but those who are considered worthy of a place in that age and in the resurrection from the dead neither marry nor are given in marriage. Indeed they cannot die any more, because they are like angels and are children of God, being children of the resurrection. And the fact that the dead are raised Moses himself showed, in the story about the bush, where he speaks of the Lord as the God of Abraham, the God of Isaac, and the God of Jacob. Now he is God not of the dead, but of the living; for to him all of them are alive."

The Gospel of the Lord.

◆ All sit and observe silence.

## FOR SILENT REFLECTION

What does it mean to you to believe in the Resurrection?

## CLOSING PRAYER

Let us stand and bring our hopes and needs to God as we pray, "Lord, hear our prayer."

◆ All may add their own prayers here.

Let us pray: **Our Father . . . Amen.**

Generous God,
you have promised to share
your eternal life with us.
It is a wonderful mystery.
Open our minds to your glory,
and our hearts to your beauty.
Help us to move closer to you every day
and to this gift of eternal life.
Grant this through Jesus Christ,
    our Risen Lord.
**Amen.**

✝ All make the Sign of the Cross.

**ALSO ON THIS DAY:** Daylight saving time ends.

# PRAYER FOR MONDAY NOVEMBER 8, 2010

### OPENING

In today's Gospel, Jesus speaks out strongly against anyone who encourages another person to sin and tells us how forgiving we must be with one another. Christians are to help one another live holy lives.

✢ All make the Sign of the Cross.

**In the name of the Father and of the Son and of the Holy Spirit. Amen.**

### PSALM      (For a longer psalm, see page xii.) Psalm 84:2a (1)

How lovely is your dwelling place,
O Lord of hosts!

**How lovely is your dwelling place,
O Lord of hosts!**

My soul longs, indeed it faints
for the courts of the Lord.

**How lovely is your dwelling place,
O Lord of hosts!**

◆ All stand and sing **Alleluia.**

### GOSPEL      Luke 17:1–4

A reading from the holy Gospel according to Luke

Jesus said to his disciples, "Occasions for stumbling are bound to come, but woe to anyone by whom they come! It would be better for you if a millstone were hung around your neck and you were thrown into the sea than for you to cause one of these little ones to stumble. Be on your guard! If another disciple sins, you must rebuke the offender, and if there is repentance, you must forgive. And if the same person sins against you seven times a day, and turns back to you seven times and says, 'I repent,' you must forgive."

The Gospel of the Lord.

◆ All sit and observe silence.

### FOR SILENT REFLECTION

Is there someone you need to forgive? How can we help each other be better Christians?

### CLOSING PRAYER

Let us stand and bring our hopes and needs to God as we pray, "Lord, hear our prayer."

◆ All may add their own prayers here.

Let us pray: **Our Father . . . Amen.**

Holy God,
we are not meant to live the Christian life
all by ourselves.
You send your Holy Spirit to be our
 companion
and your angels to watch over us.
We pray for our sisters and brothers
 in the faith
who teach us, guide us, pray with us,
work, play, and sing with us.
Help us to grow together in love.
We ask this through Jesus Christ our Lord.
**Amen.**

✢ All make the Sign of the Cross.

# PRAYER FOR TUESDAY NOVEMBER 9, 2010

## OPENING

Today is the feast of the Basilica [buh-SIL-i-cuh] of Saint John Lateran [LAA-ter-un]. We honor this cathedral of the city of Rome because it is the Pope's parish church, a spiritual home for all Catholics. In today's Gospel, Jesus drives out those who dishonor his Father's house.

✚ All make the Sign of the Cross.

**In the name of the Father and of the Son and of the Holy Spirit. Amen.**

## PSALM  (For a longer psalm, see page xii.) Psalm 84:2a (1)

How lovely is your dwelling place,
O Lord of hosts!

**How lovely is your dwelling place,
O Lord of hosts!**

My soul longs, indeed it faints
for the courts of the Lord.

**How lovely is your dwelling place,
O Lord of hosts!**

◆ All stand and sing **Alleluia**.

## GOSPEL  John 2:13–21

A reading from the holy Gospel according to John

The Passover of the Jews was near, and Jesus went up to Jerusalem. In the temple he found people selling cattle, sheep, and doves, and the money-changers seated at their tables. Making a whip of cords, he drove all of them out of the temple, both the sheep and the cattle. He also poured out the coins of the money-changers and overturned their tables. He told those who were selling the doves, "Take these things out of here! Stop making my Father's house a market-place!" His disciples remembered that it was written, "Zeal for your house will consume me." The Jews then said to him, "What sign can you show us for doing this?" Jesus answered them, "Destroy this temple, and in three days I will raise it up." The Jews then said, "This temple has been under construction for forty-six years, and will you raise it up in three days?" But he was speaking of the temple of his body.

The Gospel of the Lord.

◆ All sit and observe silence.

## FOR SILENT REFLECTION

Why do you think Jesus cares so much for the temple?

## CLOSING PRAYER

Let us stand and bring our hopes and needs to God as we pray, "Lord, hear our prayer."

◆ All may add their own prayers here.

Let us pray: **Our Father . . . Amen.**

Lord God,
help us to honor the sacred places
where we come together to worship you.
Help us to respect and care for our bodies
which are the temples of your Holy Spirit.
We ask this through Jesus Christ our Lord.
**Amen.**

✚ All make the Sign of the Cross.

# PRAYER FOR **WEDNESDAY NOVEMBER 10, 2010**

## OPENING

Today we remember Saint Leo the Great, a fifth century Pope, who kept order in the Church at a time of great confusion and danger, including the threat of Rome's invasion by Attila the Hun. Today's Gospel offers a lesson on gratitude.

✢ All make the Sign of the Cross.

**In the name of the Father and of the Son and of the Holy Spirit. Amen.**

## PSALM  (For a longer psalm, see page xii.) Psalm 84:2a (1)

How lovely is your dwelling place,
O Lord of hosts!

**How lovely is your dwelling place,
O Lord of hosts!**

My soul longs, indeed it faints
for the courts of the Lord.

**How lovely is your dwelling place,
O Lord of hosts!**

◆ All stand and sing **Alleluia.**

## GOSPEL   Luke 17:11–19

A reading from the holy Gospel according to Luke

On the way to Jerusalem Jesus was going through the region between Samaria (Suh-MAIR-ee-uh) and Galilee (GAL-ih-lee). As he entered a village, ten lepers approached him. Keeping their distance, they called out, saying, "Jesus, Master, have mercy on us!" When he saw them, he said to them, "Go and show yourselves to the priests." And as they went, they were made clean. Then one of them, when he saw that he was healed, turned back, praising God with a loud voice. He prostrated himself at Jesus' feet and thanked him. And he was a Samaritan. Then Jesus asked, "Were not ten made clean? But the other nine, where are they? Was none of them found to return and give praise to God except this foreigner?" Then he said to him, "Get up and go on your way; your faith has made you well."

The Gospel of the Lord.

◆ All sit and observe silence.

## FOR SILENT REFLECTION

Which of the ten lepers do you think got to know Jesus the best? Do you think you grow closer to Jesus when you give thanks?

## CLOSING PRAYER

Let us stand and bring our hopes and needs to God as we pray, "Lord, hear our prayer."

◆ All may add their own prayers here.

Let us pray: **Our Father . . . Amen.**

Merciful God,
to those who receive your gifts
with thanksgiving, more is given.
Open our hearts to receive
all that you desire to give us.
We ask this through Christ our Lord.
**Amen.**

✢ All make the Sign of the Cross.

# PRAYER FOR THURSDAY NOVEMBER 11, 2010

## OPENING

Today we remember Saint Martin of Tours [toor], the patron saint of soldiers. In his youth he served as a soldier, and once tore his cloak in half to clothe a naked beggar. He became a monk, and then, the Bishop of Tours. He was also an active missionary. Today's Gospel teaches us about the mystery of the kingdom of God.

✠ All make the Sign of the Cross.

**In the name of the Father and of the Son and of the Holy Spirit. Amen.**

## PSALM         (For a longer psalm, see page xii.) Psalm 84:2a (1)

How lovely is your dwelling place,
O Lord of hosts!

**How lovely is your dwelling place,
O Lord of hosts!**

My soul longs, indeed it faints
for the courts of the Lord.

**How lovely is your dwelling place,
O Lord of hosts!**

◆ All stand and sing **Alleluia**.

## GOSPEL         Luke 17:20–21

A reading from the holy Gospel according to Luke

Once Jesus was asked by the Pharisees [FAIR-uh-seez] when the kingdom of God was coming, and he answered, "The kingdom of God is not coming with things that can be observed; nor will they say, 'Look, here it is!' or 'There it is!' For, in fact, the kingdom of God is among you."

The Gospel of the Lord.

◆ All sit and observe silence.

## FOR SILENT REFLECTION

How do we know that the kingdom of God is among us?

## CLOSING PRAYER

Let us stand and bring our hopes and needs to God as we pray, "Lord, hear our prayer."

◆ All may add their own prayers here.

Let us pray: **Our Father . . . Amen.**

Our Father,
may your kingdom come
and your will be done on earth.
Give us eyes, we pray,
to see that your kingdom is already coming
and wisdom to know how to do your will.
May all creation be ruled
by your peace and love.
We ask this through your beloved Son,
    Jesus Christ our Lord.
**Amen.**

✠ All make the Sign of the Cross.

---

**ALSO ON THIS DAY:** Veterans Day (U.S.A.)
Remembrance Day (Canada)

# PRAYER FOR FRIDAY NOVEMBER 12, 2010

## OPENING

Today we remember Saint Josaphat [JAW-suh-fat], a Polish [POH-lish] bishop of the Eastern Church who worked for Church unity in a time of conflict in the seventeenth century. The reading we hear today is from the letter of John written to a church community that he refers to as "dear lady," a custom of that time. In the letter, John encourages the people, and us, to live by the commandment of love.

✜ All make the Sign of the Cross.

**In the name of the Father and of the Son and of the Holy Spirit. Amen.**

## PSALM
(For a longer psalm, see page xii.) Psalm 84:2a (1)

How lovely is your dwelling place,
O Lord of hosts!

**How lovely is your dwelling place,
O Lord of hosts!**

My soul longs, indeed it faints
for the courts of the Lord.

**How lovely is your dwelling place,
O Lord of hosts!**

## READING
2 John 4–6, 8–9

A reading from the Second Letter of John

I was overjoyed to find some of your children walking in the truth, just as we have been commanded by the Father. But now, dear lady, I ask you, not as though I were writing you a new commandment, but one we have had from the beginning, let us love one another. And this is love, that we walk according to his commandments; this is the commandment just as you have heard it from the beginning—you must walk in it. Be on your guard, so that you do not lose what we have worked for, but may receive a full reward. Everyone who does not abide in the teaching of Christ, but goes beyond it, does not have God; whoever abides in the teaching has both the Father and the Son.

The word of the Lord.

◆ All observe silence.

## FOR SILENT REFLECTION

How are you living God's commandment to love one another?

## CLOSING PRAYER

Let us stand and bring our hopes and needs to God as we pray, "Lord, hear our prayer."

◆ All may add their own prayers here.

Let us pray: **Our Father . . . Amen.**

Loving God,
you command us to love one another
as you have loved us.
We pray that you will help everyone in your Church
to live this commandment of love
in peace and unity.
We ask this through Christ our Lord.
**Amen.**

✜ All make the Sign of the Cross.

# PRAYER FOR THE WEEK

WITH A READING FROM THE GOSPEL FOR **SUNDAY, NOVEMBER 14, 2010**

## OPENING

In today's Gospel, Jesus seems to be looking into the future to a time when the temple of Jerusalem [juh-ROO-suh-lem] will be destroyed and his followers will be treated badly. Knowing that they will suffer, he reassures them of God's love and protection.

✝ All make the Sign of the Cross.

**In the name of the Father and of the Son and of the Holy Spirit. Amen.**

## PSALM  (For a longer psalm, see page xii.) Psalm 84:2a (1)

How lovely is your dwelling place,
O Lord of hosts!

**How lovely is your dwelling place,
O Lord of hosts!**

My soul longs, indeed it faints
for the courts of the Lord.

**How lovely is your dwelling place,
O Lord of hosts!**

◆ All stand and sing **Alleluia.**

## GOSPEL  Luke 21:5–10a, 17–19

A reading from the holy Gospel according to Luke

When some were speaking about the temple, how it was adorned with beautiful stones and gifts dedicated to God, he said, "As for these things that you see, the days will come when not one stone will be left upon another; all will be thrown down."

They asked him, "Teacher, when will this be, and what will be the sign that this is about to take place?" And he said, "Beware that you are not led astray; for many will come in my name and say, 'I am he!' and, 'The time is near!' Do not go after them. When you hear of wars and insurrections, do not be terrified; for these things must take place first, but the end will not follow immediately." Then he said to them, "You will be hated by all because of my name. But not a hair of your head will perish. By your endurance you will gain your souls."

The Gospel of the Lord.

◆ All sit and observe silence.

## FOR SILENT REFLECTION

How can we keep our faith in God's love even when we are suffering?

## CLOSING PRAYER

Let us stand and bring our hopes and needs to God as we pray, "Lord, hear our prayer."

◆ All may add their own prayers here.

Let us pray: **Our Father . . . Amen.**

God our Father,
protect us from all evil.
Give us strength in the face of suffering.
Help us to keep our faith and hope
even when bad things happen.
We ask this through our Lord Jesus Christ.
**Amen.**

✝ All make the Sign of the Cross.

# PRAYER FOR MONDAY NOVEMBER 15, 2010

## OPENING

In today's Gospel, Jesus cures a blind man who seems to know who Jesus is: the "Son of David," the long-awaited Messiah [meh-SI-uh] and Savior. Not only his physical eyesight is healed, but his way of life is changed.

✚ All make the Sign of the Cross.

**In the name of the Father and of the Son and of the Holy Spirit. Amen.**

## PSALM  (For a longer psalm, see page xii.) Psalm 84:2a (1)

How lovely is your dwelling place,
O Lord of hosts!

**How lovely is your dwelling place,
O Lord of hosts!**

My soul longs, indeed it faints
for the courts of the Lord.

**How lovely is your dwelling place,
O Lord of hosts!**

◆ All stand and sing **Alleluia**.

## GOSPEL  Luke 18:35–43

A reading from the holy Gospel according to Luke

As he approached Jericho [JAYR-ih-koh], a blind man was sitting by the roadside begging. When he heard a crowd going by, he asked what was happening. They told him, "Jesus of Nazareth is passing by." Then he shouted, "Jesus, Son of David, have mercy on me!" Those who were in front of him sternly ordered him to be quiet; but he shouted even more loudly, "Son of David, have mercy on me!" Jesus stood still and ordered the man to be brought to him; and when he came near, he asked him, "What do you want me to do for you?" He said, "Lord, let me see again." Jesus said to him, "Receive your sight; your faith has saved you." Immediately he regained his sight and followed him, glorifying God; and all the people, when they saw it, praised God.

The Gospel of the Lord.

◆ All sit and observe silence.

## FOR SILENT REFLECTION

How do you think the blind man is able to see who Jesus really is?

## CLOSING PRAYER

Let us stand and bring our hopes and needs to God as we pray, "Lord, hear our prayer."

◆ All may add their own prayers here.

Let us pray: **Our Father . . . Amen.**

Holy God,
help us to see you in our midst,
to hear your voice in the words of scripture,
to know your presence in the Eucharist
    [YEW-kuh-rist],
and in the love we have for one another.
Let us see that you are always with us.
We ask this through Jesus Christ,
    our Savior and Lord.
**Amen.**

✚ All make the Sign of the Cross.

# PRAYER FOR TUESDAY NOVEMBER 16, 2010

## OPENING

Today's reading comes from the Book of Revelation and describes a vision of the risen Christ who calls us to repent [ree-PENT]. To repent means to feel sorrow for our sins and desire not to sin again. To reprove [ree-PROOV] is to scold or correct. Jesus promises that he will come to those who hear his voice and "open the door" to them.

✦ All make the Sign of the Cross.

**In the name of the Father and of the Son and of the Holy Spirit. Amen.**

## PSALM  (For a longer psalm, see page xii.) Psalm 84:2a (1)

How lovely is your dwelling place,
O Lord of hosts!

**How lovely is your dwelling place,
O Lord of hosts!**

My soul longs, indeed it faints
for the courts of the Lord.

**How lovely is your dwelling place,
O Lord of hosts!**

## READING  Revelation 3:19–22

A reading from the book of Revelation to John

I reprove and discipline those whom I love. Be earnest, therefore, and repent. Listen! I am standing at the door, knocking; if you hear my voice and open the door, I will come in to you and eat with you, and you with me. To the one who conquers I will give a place with me on my throne, just as I myself conquered and sat down with my Father on his throne. Let anyone who has an ear listen to what the Spirit is saying to the churches.

The word of the Lord.

◆ All observe silence.

## FOR SILENT REFLECTION

What is the door that we need to open if Jesus is to come in and eat with us?

## CLOSING PRAYER

Let us stand and bring our hopes and needs to God as we pray, "Lord, hear our prayer."

◆ All may add their own prayers here.

Let us pray: **Our Father . . . Amen.**

Almighty God,
your Son, our risen Lord,
calls each of us by name
to open the door of our hearts.
Help us to open ourselves to him.
Your Son, our risen Lord,
invites us to share in his eternal life.
Make us worthy, we pray,
through the same Jesus Christ our Lord.
**Amen.**

✦ All make the Sign of the Cross.

**ALSO ON THIS DAY:** Eid Al-Adha (Islamic Feast of Sacrifice)

# PRAYER FOR WEDNESDAY NOVEMBER 17, 2010

## OPENING

Today's Gospel reminds us that the gifts and talents God gives us are not for us alone, but are to be used for the sake of God's kingdom.

✦ All make the Sign of the Cross.

**In the name of the Father and of the Son and of the Holy Spirit. Amen.**

## PSALM
*(For a longer psalm, see page xii.) Psalm 84:2a (1)*

How lovely is your dwelling place,
O Lord of hosts!

**How lovely is your dwelling place,
O Lord of hosts!**

My soul longs, indeed it faints
for the courts of the Lord.

**How lovely is your dwelling place,
O Lord of hosts!**

◆ All stand and sing **Alleluia**.

## GOSPEL
*Luke 19:11b, 12–13, 15a, 16–21a, 22a, 23*

A reading from the holy Gospel according to Luke

Jesus went on to tell a parable, "A nobleman went to a distant country to get royal power for himself and then return. He summoned ten of his slaves, and gave them ten pounds, and said to them, 'Do business with these until I come back.' When he returned, the first came forward and said, 'Lord, your pound has made ten more pounds.' He said to him, 'Well done, good slave! Because you have been trustworthy in a very small thing, take charge of ten cities.' Then the second came, saying, 'Lord your pound has made five pounds.' He said to him, 'And you, rule over five cities.' Then the other came, saying, 'Lord, here is your pound. I wrapped it up in a piece of cloth, for I was afraid of you.' He said to him, 'Why then did you not put my money into the bank? Then when I returned, I could have collected it with interest.'"

The Gospel of the Lord.

◆ All sit and observe silence.

## FOR SILENT REFLECTION

What gifts has God given you? How can you use these gifts to do God's work on earth?

## CLOSING PRAYER

Let us stand and bring our hopes and needs to God as we pray, "Lord, hear our prayer."

◆ All may add their own prayers here.

Let us pray: **Our Father . . . Amen.**

Generous God,
we thank you for the many
gifts you have given us.
Free us from all fear, selfishness, and pride
that would keep us from using these gifts
for the well-being of others.
We ask this through Jesus Christ our Lord.
**Amen.**

✦ All make the Sign of the Cross.

# PRAYER FOR THURSDAY NOVEMBER 18, 2010

## OPENING

In today's Gospel, Jesus weeps for Jerusalem (Juh-ROO-suh-lem), the city he loves, and for his people whom he loves. He knows that soon he will suffer and die at their hands, for the people were unable to recognize their Savior.

✠ All make the Sign of the Cross.

**In the name of the Father and of the Son and of the Holy Spirit. Amen.**

## PSALM  (For a longer psalm, see page xii.) Psalm 84:2a (1)

How lovely is your dwelling place,
O Lord of hosts!

**How lovely is your dwelling place,
O Lord of hosts!**

My soul longs, indeed it faints
for the courts of the Lord.

**How lovely is your dwelling place,
O Lord of hosts!**

◆ All stand and sing **Alleluia**.

## GOSPEL  Luke 19:41–44

A reading from the holy Gospel according to Luke

As Jesus came near and saw the city, he wept over it, saying, "If you, even you, had only recognized on this day the things that make for peace! But now they are hidden from your eyes. Indeed, the days will come upon you, when your enemies will set up ramparts around you and surround you, and hem you in on every side. They will crush you to the ground, you and your children within you, and they will not leave within you one stone upon another; because you did not recognize the time of your visitation from God."

The Gospel of the Lord.

◆ All sit and observe silence.

## FOR SILENT REFLECTION

How can we recognize those moments when God visits us?

## CLOSING PRAYER

Let us stand and bring our hopes and needs to God as we pray, "Lord, hear our prayer."

◆ All may add their own prayers here.

Let us pray: **Our Father . . . Amen.**

Almighty God,
we pray for the peace of Jerusalem,
and for peace throughout the Middle East.
Help Christians, Jews, and the people
    of Islam [is-LAHM]
to live together as children of the one God.
We ask this through our Lord Jesus Christ,
    your Son, who lives and reigns with
    you and the Holy Spirit, one God
    forever and ever.
**Amen.**

✠ All make the Sign of the Cross.

# PRAYER FOR FRIDAY NOVEMBER 19, 2010

## OPENING

In today's Gospel reading, we learn about the love and reverence Jesus felt for the temple. The Jerusalem temple was a holy place and house of prayer where God dwelt with his people.

✝ All make the Sign of the Cross.

**In the name of the Father and of the Son and of the Holy Spirit. Amen.**

## PSALM  (For a longer psalm, see page xii.) Psalm 84:2a (1)

How lovely is your dwelling place,
O Lord of hosts!

**How lovely is your dwelling place,
O Lord of hosts!**

My soul longs, indeed it faints
for the courts of the Lord.

**How lovely is your dwelling place,
O Lord of hosts!**

◆ All stand and sing **Alleluia**.

## GOSPEL   Luke 19:45–48

A reading from the holy Gospel according to Luke

Then Jesus entered the temple and began to drive out those who were selling things there; and he said, "It is written,
   'My house shall be a house of prayer,
    but you have made it a den of robbers.'"
Every day he was teaching in the temple. The chief priests, the scribes, and the leaders of the people kept looking for a way to kill him; but they did not find anything they could do, for all the people were spellbound by what they heard.

The Gospel of the Lord.

◆ All sit and observe silence.

## FOR SILENT REFLECTION

Would it be strange for people to sell things in your church? How do we care for our churches?

## CLOSING PRAYER

Let us stand and bring our hopes and needs to God as we pray, "Lord, hear our prayer."

◆ All may add their own prayers here.

Let us pray: **Our Father . . . Amen.**

Lord God,
when your people wandered in the wilderness,
you went with them in the ark of
    the covenant.
You had King Solomon build the temple
so your people could be near you.
You sent your Son into the world
that we might know you through him
and you sent your Holy Spirit,
to be your presence in our hearts.
Open our eyes to your love for us.
We ask this through Jesus Christ our Lord.
**Amen.**

✝ All make the Sign of the Cross.

# PRAYER FOR THE WEEK

WITH A READING FROM THE GOSPEL FOR **SUNDAY, NOVEMBER 21, 2010**

## OPENING

Today is the Solemnity of our Lord Jesus Christ the King. The people in today's Gospel are watching as Jesus dies on the cross. They were expecting an earthly Messiah, someone who would begin an earthly kingdom of God; but they don't understand the kind of king Jesus is. "Scoffed" means to be made fun of.

✠ All make the Sign of the Cross.

**In the name of the Father and of the Son and of the Holy Spirit. Amen.**

## PSALM     (For a longer psalm, see page xii.) Psalm 84:2a (1)

How lovely is your dwelling place,
O Lord of hosts!

**How lovely is your dwelling place,
O Lord of hosts!**

My soul longs, indeed it faints
for the courts of the Lord.

**How lovely is your dwelling place,
O Lord of hosts!**

◆ All stand and sing **Alleluia**.

## GOSPEL     Luke 23:35–38

A reading from the holy Gospel according to Luke

The people stood by, watching; but the leaders scoffed at him, saying, "He saved others; let him save himself if he is the Messiah of God, his chosen one!" The soldiers also mocked him, coming up and offering him sour wine, and saying, "If you are the King of the Jews, save yourself." There was also an inscription over him, "This is the King of the Jews."

The Gospel of the Lord.

◆ All sit and observe silence.

## FOR SILENT REFLECTION

Why do we call Jesus king? What sort of king is he and how can we serve him?

## CLOSING PRAYER

Let us stand and bring our hopes and needs to God as we pray, "Lord, hear our prayer."

◆ All may add their own prayers here.

Let us pray: **Our Father . . . Amen.**

Almighty God,
you rule the universe,
yet you sent your Son to be a servant to all.
You have power over life and death,
yet you let him die that we might live.
Help us to serve you
this day and every day
with humility and love.
We ask this through the same Jesus Christ
  our Lord.
**Amen.**

✠ All make the Sign of the Cross.

# PRAYER FOR MONDAY NOVEMBER 22, 2010

In today's Gospel Jesus teaches us a lesson about giving, showing that the poorest people can sometimes be the most generous.

✦ All make the Sign of the Cross.

**In the name of the Father and of the Son and of the Holy Spirit. Amen.**

## PSALM
(For a longer psalm, see page xii.) Psalm 84:2a (1)

How lovely is your dwelling place,
O Lord of hosts!

**How lovely is your dwelling place,
O Lord of hosts!**

My soul longs, indeed it faints
for the courts of the Lord.

**How lovely is your dwelling place,
O Lord of hosts!**

◆ All stand and sing **Alleluia**.

## GOSPEL
Luke 21:1–4

A reading from the holy Gospel according to Luke

Jesus looked up and saw rich people putting their gifts into the treasury; he also a saw a poor widow put in two small copper coins. He said, "Truly I tell you, this poor widow has put in more than all of them; for all of them have contributed out of their abundance, but she out of her poverty has put in all she had to live on."

The Gospel of the Lord.

◆ All sit and observe silence.

## FOR SILENT REFLECTION

Why does Jesus say that the widow has given more when she put in only two coins? What can you give?

## CLOSING PRAYER

Let us stand and bring our hopes and needs to God as we pray, "Lord, hear our prayer."

◆ All may add their own prayers here.

Let us pray: **Our Father . . . Amen.**

Generous God,
you gave us the gift of yourself.
You gave your very life for us.
Help us not to be stingy
with the gifts you have given us.
Make us generous with our talents,
our money, and our time.
Give us courage to share the precious gifts
of faith, hope, and love with others.
We ask this through our Lord Jesus Christ,
   your Son, who lives and reigns with
   you in the unity of the Holy Spirit,
   one God, for ever and ever.
**Amen.**

✦ All make the Sign of the Cross.

# PRAYER FOR TUESDAY NOVEMBER 23, 2010

## OPENING

Today we remember Saint Clement [KLEH-ment], a disciple of Saint Peter, who became bishop of Rome after Peter. Today's reading comes from the Book of Revelation and describes a vision of Christ the King. Farmers harvest their crops when they are fully grown. For example, a fruit farmer picks his fruit when it is ripe. In this vision, the work of Jesus has borne fruit; it is now ripe and ready to be harvested. To reap is to cut and gather in the fully grown crop.

✚ All make the Sign of the Cross.

**In the name of the Father and of the Son and of the Holy Spirit. Amen.**

## PSALM
(For a longer psalm, see page xii.) Psalm 84:2a (1)

How lovely is your dwelling place,
O Lord of hosts!

**How lovely is your dwelling place,
O Lord of hosts!**

My soul longs, indeed it faints
for the courts of the Lord.

**How lovely is your dwelling place,
O Lord of hosts!**

## READING
Revelation 14:14–16

A reading from the Book of Revelation [rev-uh-LAY-shuhn]

Then I looked, and there was a white cloud, and seated on the cloud was one like the Son of Man, with a golden crown on his head, and a sharp sickle in his hand! Another angel came out of the temple, calling with a loud voice to the one who sat on the cloud, "Use your sickle and reap, for the hour to reap has come, because the harvest of the earth is fully ripe." So the one who sat on the cloud swung his sickle over the earth, and the earth was reaped.

The word of the Lord.

◆ All observe silence.

## FOR SILENT REFLECTION

What is the harvest that is being gathered in?

## CLOSING PRAYER

Let us stand and bring our hopes and needs to God as we pray, "Lord, hear our prayer."

◆ All may add their own prayers here.

Let us pray: **Our Father . . . Amen.**

Holy God,
we thank you for planting
the seed of eternal life within us
and for sending your Spirit
to help us grow in faith.
Complete the good work you have begun
    in us
and gather us into your kingdom.
We ask this through our Lord Jesus Christ,
    our Lord and King.
**Amen.**

✚ All make the Sign of the Cross.

# PRAYER SERVICE
## FOR THANKSGIVING

*Prepare nine leaders for this service. The sixth and seventh leaders will need a Bible to read the Gospel passage and may need help finding and practicing the reading. You may want to begin by singing "For the Beauty of the Earth" and end with "Now Thank We All Our God." If the group will sing, prepare a song leader.*

**FIRST LEADER:**

✚ All make the Sign of the Cross.

**In the name of the Father and of the Son and of the Holy Spirit. Amen.**

Let us pray:
God, Creator of heaven and earth,
we thank you for the priceless gifts
you have given us: our bodies, our talents,
our hopes, and even what we offer to you
came first from your generous hands!
We think of the foods we will soon eat,
and we are filled with excitement and joy,
knowing that they all came from this earth
which you have given to us for a home.

**SECOND LEADER:**
We lift our grateful hearts to you
as we remember all the good things you have
    given to us.
How can we ever thank you for loving us?
In the fullness of time, you even
    gave yourself,
in the person of your Son, Jesus.
He taught us, walked beside us,
    and sacrificed himself on the cross.
We are truly overwhelmed by his goodness
as we offer this prayer through him.

**ALL: Amen.**

# FOR THANKSGIVING

**THIRD LEADER:**                               Psalm 104:35cd
Bless the Lord, O my soul.
Praise the Lord!

**ALL:** Bless the Lord, O my soul.
Praise the Lord!

**FOURTH LEADER:**                Psalm 104:24ab, 14–15
O Lord, how manifold are your works!
   In wisdom you have made them all.
You cause the grass to grow for the cattle,
   and plants for people to use,
to bring forth food from the earth
   and wine to gladden the human heart,
oil to make the face shine,
   and bread to strengthen the human heart.

**THIRD LEADER:**                             Psalm 104:35cd
Bless the Lord, O my soul.
Praise the Lord!

**ALL:** Bless the Lord, O my soul.
Praise the Lord!

**FIFTH LEADER:**                         Psalm 104: 31, 33–34
May the glory of the Lord endure forever;
may the Lord rejoice in his works—
I will sing to the Lord as long as I live
   I will sing praise to my God while
      I have being.
May my meditation be pleasing to him,
   for I rejoice in the Lord.

**THIRD LEADER:**                             Psalm 104:35cd
Bless the Lord, O my soul.
Praise the Lord!

**ALL:** Bless the Lord, O my soul.
Praise the Lord!

◆ All stand and sing **Alleluia**.

**SIXTH LEADER:**                               Luke 17:11–14
A reading from the holy Gospel according to Luke

◆ The sixth leader reads the Gospel passage from a Bible.

**SEVENTH LEADER:**                          Luke 17:15–19

◆ The seventh leader reads the Gospel passage from a Bible.

The Gospel of the Lord.

**EIGHTH LEADER:**
Generous and loving God,
our hearts overflow with gratitude
as we celebrate your unending goodness to us.
May we always remember who has given us
everything we can see or touch or hold,
      including our lives!
We ask this through Christ our Lord.

**ALL:** Amen.

**NINTH LEADER:**
May the love of God,

✢ All make the Sign of the Cross.

Father, Son and Holy Spirit,
draw us together in faith and hope,
now and for ever.

**ALL:** Amen.

# HOME PRAYER
## MEAL PRAYER FOR THANKSGIVING

*Find the reading (John 15:12–17) in your Bible, ask for a volunteer to read the scripture passage, and encourage the reader to practice reading it twice. If practical, light candles for your Thanksgiving table. You may wish to begin with a simple song of thanksgiving or a favorite "Alleluia." Then an older child or an adult reads the leader parts.*

**LEADER:**
How good it is to be here! We can smell the delicious food, and as we look around the table, we see the people we love so much! Let us begin our prayer with the Sign of the Cross:

✢ All make the Sign of the Cross.

**ALL: In the name of the Father and of the Son and of the Holy Spirit. Amen.**

**LEADER:** *Psalm 138:1a and 2a*
Let us pray the psalm response:
I give you thanks, O Lord, with my
    whole heart.

**ALL: I give you thanks, O Lord, with my
    whole heart.**

**LEADER:**
I bow down toward your holy temple
   and give thanks to your name for your
      steadfast love and your faithfulness.

**ALL: I give you thanks, O Lord, with my
    whole heart.**

◆ All stand and sing **Alleluia**.

**LEADER:** *John 15:12–17*
A reading from the holy Gospel according to John

◆ Read the Scripture passage from the Bible.

The Gospel of the Lord.

◆ All sit and observe silence.

**LEADER:**
We come together at this table to thank God
for sending us his Son and for loving us
as his own sons and daughters.
Let us pray:
Heavenly Father,
send your blessing on us
and on the food before us.
We thank you for feeding our hungers
and giving us peace beyond all understanding.
We thank you especially for the love
    around this table today.
May your love continue to grow in our hearts,
making us generous to all who are in need.
We ask this through our Lord Jesus Christ,
    your Son, who lives and reigns with
    you and the Holy Spirit, one God,
    for ever and ever.

**ALL: Amen.**

✢ All make the Sign of the Cross.

# HOME PRAYER

## GATHERING AROUND AN ADVENT WREATH FOR PRAYER

*Saturday evening before the First Sunday of Advent, gather the household around the wreath. Point out that the wreath is circular, with no beginning or end, like God's love. Explain that there are four candles, one for each Sunday of Advent. The third candle is rose because on the third Sunday we celebrate the joy of waiting for Christmas.*

*Use this service the first time you light your wreath and then on the following three Sundays when you light each new candle after the psalm response.*

*During the first week of Advent, light the first purple candle. During the second week of Advent, light two purple candles. For the third week, light two purple candles and one rose candle. During the final week of Advent, light all four candles! For your weekday celebration, simply light the candle(s), read one verse from Isaiah 40:1–5 and 9–11 (choose a different verse each time) and then say grace.*

*Before you begin, find the reading (Luke 1:39–45) in your Bible, ask a volunteer to read it, and encourage the reader to practice reading it twice.*

*You may wish to begin with a simple Advent song, such as "Soon and Very Soon." Then an older child or adult reads the leader parts.*

**LEADER:**
In this holy season of Advent, let us turn our hearts to God, who showers blessings on all those who hope and wait for him to come again in glory.

For thousands of years, people had been waiting for a Great Light to dawn. God promised that one day that Light would be ours. Soon, we will celebrate Christmas, that wonderful day when the Great Light was born in Bethlehem and shed his peaceful joy on all humanity. God keeps his promises! We begin our prayer with the Sign of the Cross:

✚ All make the Sign of the Cross.

**ALL: In the name of the Father and of the Son and of the Holy Spirit. Amen.**

**LEADER:** *Psalm 25:1, 21*
Let us pray the psalm response:
To you, O Lord, I lift up my soul.

**ALL: To you, O Lord, I lift up my soul.**

**LEADER:**
May integrity and uprightness preserve me,
 for I wait for you.

**ALL: To you, O Lord, I lift up my soul.**

◆ Light candles. Then all stand and sing **Alleluia**.

**LEADER:** *Luke 1:39–45*
A reading from the holy Gospel according to Luke

◆ Read the scripture passage from the Bible.

The Gospel of the Lord.

◆ All sit and observe silence.

**LEADER:**
Lord God, as we gather around this Advent wreath to celebrate the coming of your Son, fill our hearts with your light. We ask for this blessing through Jesus Christ, our Lord.

**ALL: Amen.**

✚ All make the Sign of the Cross.

# PRAYER FOR **WEDNESDAY** NOVEMBER 24, 2010

## OPENING

We read again today from the Book of Revelation [rev-uh-LAY-shuhn]. This reading describes a beast. It is an image of evil. Holy people who love God are able to conquer evil by trusting in God's power. The reading reminds us that nothing is more powerful than God. If we love God with all our hearts, we too will sing God's praises with all the saints in heaven.

✙ All make the Sign of the Cross.

**In the name of the Father and of the Son and of the Holy Spirit. Amen.**

## PSALM
(For a longer psalm, see page xii.) Psalm 84:2a (1)

How lovely is your dwelling place,
O LORD of hosts!

**How lovely is your dwelling place,
O LORD of hosts!**

My soul longs, indeed it faints
for the courts of the LORD.

**How lovely is your dwelling place,
O LORD of hosts!**

## READING
Revelation 15: 2–4

A reading from the Book of Revelation [rev-uh-LAY-shuhn]

And I saw what appeared to be a sea of glass mixed with fire, and those who had conquered the beast and its image and the number of its name standing beside the sea of glass with harps of God in their hands. And they sing the song of Moses, the servant of God, and the song of the Lamb:

"Great and amazing are your deeds,
  Lord God the Almighty!
Just and true are your ways,
  King of the nations!
Lord, who will not fear
  and glorify your name?
For you alone are holy.
  All nations will come
  and worship before you,
for your judgments have been revealed."

The word of the Lord.

◆ All observe silence.

## FOR SILENT REFLECTION

Imagine the joy you would feel, knowing that there is no more evil in the world, and you are singing with all the saints in heaven.

## CLOSING PRAYER

Let us stand and bring our hopes and needs to God as we pray, "Lord, hear our prayer."

◆ All may add their own prayers here.

Let us pray: **Our Father . . . Amen.**

Holy are you, Lord,
God all-powerful and mighty.
Your glory fills all of heaven and earth.
Let us praise you forever.
We ask this through Christ our Lord.
**Amen.**

✙ All make the Sign of the Cross.

# ADVENT

## SUNDAY, NOVEMBER 28 TO FRIDAY, DECEMBER 17

# ADVENT 2010

## THE MEANING OF ADVENT

"A shoot shall come out from the stump of Jesse, and a branch shall grow out of his roots" (Isaiah 11:1).

Jesse was the father of King David, a great leader of the Jewish people. His family tree gave rise to the greatest kings the world had ever known. But then Jesse's family became weak and scattered. The Jewish people no longer had a strong ruler and they suffered many periods of darkness, misery, and despair. The people of Israel had become like a great tree cut down to its stump. Yet God did not forsake his people.

God, Israel's faithful protector, promises to make a new plant sprout. The people waited and prayed and hoped for many years. They knew that God would keep his promise, just as he had kept his promise to Abraham to give him children and a land—and just as he had brought the Israelites out of slavery into the freedom of living God's holy commandments.

We, too, are a people to whom God has made a solemn promise. During Advent, we read in the Bible about God's promise to send a great Light in the darkness, to give sight to the blind, to fill us with comfort and hope, to put an end to sin and death, to give us more than we could ever hope for or imagine, and to fill us with his joy and peace.

We believe that God's plan of promise took flesh when his Son was born in Bethlehem. We believe that Christ is a light for the world. When all people share in this light, which is the fullness of God's life and love, then the ancient promises will come to fulfillment. Then the wolf will be the guest of the lamb, the lion will lie down with the calf, and there will be no more death or suffering on all God's holy mountain.

Advent is a time of quiet, joyful preparation for the celebration of Jesus' birth and also a time to remember that we wait for Christ to come again at the end of time. It is a season to enjoy the hope that Christ's Resurrection points to. The first Sunday of Advent is also a time of new beginnings—it is the official start of the Church's calendar. Happy New Year!

## PREPARING TO CELEBRATE ADVENT IN THE CLASSROOM

Consider organizing an Advent procession. Children of all ages love solemn processions. Take some time to speak with the children about the season of Advent, sharing the material in "The Meaning of Advent" with them. Explain that Advent has a new color, purple. Then suggest to the children that you have a procession to change the color of your prayer table cloth.

You will want to speak with the children about processions they have participated in or have seen in church. Explain that a procession is a prayerful way to walk, and stress the importance of silence (or singing along if you plan to sing in the procession). You may want to demonstrate a slow, careful walk. Then give each child an object from the prayer table to carry in the procession, and remember to include an Advent wreath with three purple candles and one rose-colored candle (if you need more objects, have some spare candles handy so that everyone has something to hold). The child at the head of the procession should carry the purple cloth. You may simply process in a circle around your classroom, or you may lead your procession through the school. Be bold! Other classes will benefit from witnessing your procession. Just make certain to discuss your plans with your principal or Religious Education Director first. If you wish to sing, you might try the first verse of "Creator of the Stars of Night," or the Taizé canon "Prepare the Way of the Lord."

In this book you will find special prayer services that may be used in the classroom or with a larger group. One is a service for Advent, pages 120–121, which could be used at any time during the season; the other is for the solemnity of the Immaculate Conception of Mary on December 8, pages 130–131. Three "Home Prayer" pages have been created for Advent and Christmas. These can be photocopied and sent home with the students so that their households can pray together at special times: Gathering around an Advent Wreath for Prayer appeared at the end of Ordinary Time in Autumn on page 113 so that

# 2010 ADVENT

you would send it home before the First Sunday of Advent. Gathering around a Nativity Scene for Prayer, page 135, may be sent home before school breaks for the Christmas holiday.

## SACRED SPACE

During Advent there are several ways you can create a mood of anticipation in the classroom. You can place the empty manger from a Christmas nativity scene on your classroom prayer table. Set a large white pillar candle in a prominent place and explain to the children that you are waiting for Christmas to light it. You can also use an Advent wreath.

The Advent wreath is a circular candleholder, usually decorated with pine branches. It contains four candles: three purple and one rose-colored. When you first introduce the wreath to your class, wonder together with the children about its circular shape, why we use pine boughs, and the significance of the four candles. Children will often come up with beautiful answers to these questions: the wreath is round because God's love has no beginning and no end; the pine branches never lose their leaves just as God cannot die; and the four candles represent the four Sundays of Advent, the four points of the compass, the four branches of the Cross, the four Gospels, the four rivers in Eden, and so on. Explain that you will light one candle for each week in Advent; when all the candles are lit, then Christmas will be right around the corner! The children may be curious about the rose-colored candle. Explain that it is the third one that we light, for the third Sunday in Advent, which is called Gaudete (Gow-DAY-tay) Sunday, on which we celebrate the joy of waiting on the Lord. Here is a prayer to use before lighting your Advent wreath:

"The people who walked in darkness have seen a great light" (Isaiah 9:2a).

*Lord God, you promise to send us joy beyond all telling. Let your blessing come upon us as we wait for your promised Light to dispel the darkness of our minds and hearts. Send your peace into the world, and may the fire of your love fill our hearts and make us one with you and with each other. We ask this through the Great Light, Jesus Christ, who enlightens and encourages us always.* **Amen.**

Please consider saving your celebration of Christmas until the Christmas Season. The season of Advent is a great spiritual gift that helps us grow in the beautiful theological virtue of hope. Also, if you wait until you return from Christmas break to celebrate Christmas in the classroom, the children will have settled down and may be more able to listen to the glad tidings of great joy that you have to share with them.

## SACRED MUSIC

Discover which songs your parish will be singing during Advent. Sometimes the setting for the sung parts of the Mass will change with the liturgical season. Other Advent songs that children love include: "The King of Glory Comes," "People Look East," "O Come, O Come Emmanuel," and "Savior of the Nations Come."

## PRAYERS FOR ADVENT

A wonderful prayer to learn during Advent is the *Magnificat* of Mary (Luke 1:46–55). All those who faithfully pray the Liturgy of the Hours recite this beautiful prayer each evening, to remember and to relive Mary's joy as she prayed to God, the Mighty One. It has been set to various tunes and may be sung. Two lovely settings are the Taizé canon, "Magnificat," and "And Holy Is Your Name."

## A NOTE TO CATECHISTS

Make arrangements with your Religious Education Director to store your Advent wreath somewhere in the classroom during the week so that you don't need to carry it back and forth between school and home.

# GRACE BEFORE MEALS
## ADVENT

**LEADER:**
Wait on the Lord with hearts full of hope

**ALL: O, wait on the Lord!**

✢ All make the Sign of the Cross.

**In the name of the Father and of the Son and of the Holy Spirit. Amen.**

**LEADER:**
Lord God,
you give us the rivers and forests and fields,
filled with clean water, grain, and fruits
that help us to live.
This food we are about to eat
is a sign of all your loving care for us.
May it remind us of your Son's promise
to return to us at the end of time
when all the earth will be filled
    with your presence.
We ask this through the same Jesus Christ
    our Lord.
**Amen.**

✢ All make the Sign of the Cross.

**In the name of the Father and of the Son and of the Holy Spirit. Amen.**

# PRAYER AT DAY'S END
## ADVENT

**LEADER:**
The Lord gives Light to those who wait
   in darkness

**ALL:** To guide our feet into the way of peace.

✤ All make the Sign of the Cross.

> **In the name of the Father and of the Son and of the Holy Spirit. Amen.**

**LEADER:**
Holy Lord,
this day that you have given us
has been filled with the gift of our work,
which you invite us to do in partnership
   with you.
We now offer it all to you with grateful hearts.
May all our work and play be colored
by the memory of your goodness to us.
We ask this through your beloved Son,
   Jesus Christ our Lord.

**ALL: Amen.**

✤ All make the Sign of the Cross.

> **In the name of the Father and of the Son and of the Holy Spirit. Amen.**

# PRAYER SERVICE
## FOR ADVENT

*Prepare six leaders for this service. The third leader will need a Bible for the scripture passage (Isaiah 40:1–4) and may need help finding it and practicing.*

*Help the class write the petitions to be read by the fourth reader.*

*Gather near your classroom Advent wreath or, if you will be in a different space, be sure an Advent wreath is prominent. You may begin by singing "O Come, O Come Emmanuel" and end with "Soon and Very Soon."*

*If the group will sing, prepare a song leader.*

**FIRST LEADER:**

◆ Gesture for all to stand.

✚ All make the Sign of the Cross.

> **In the name of the Father and of the Son and of the Holy Spirit. Amen.**

May the grace and light of our Lord Jesus Christ be with us.

**ALL: Amen.**

**FIRST LEADER:**
Lord, you are the Light of all nations.
You are our Hope and our Peace.
As we wait for the bright promise
    of Christmas,
may we remember all the great promises
that you have made to your chosen people.
You have fed us and clothed us in your Light,
and you have taught us to expect the miracle
of your love to fill the universe.
May we never forget your promises
and may we always trust in you.
We ask this through Christ, our Lord.
**Amen.**

# FOR ADVENT

- Gesture for all to sit. An adult lights the appropriate number of candles on the Advent wreath. Allow a moment of silence to enjoy the beauty of the lighted wreath. (For a discussion of the significance of the Advent wreath and a prayer for blessing it, see Preparing to Celebrate Advent in the Classroom, the section on Sacred Space on page 113.).

**SECOND LEADER:** *Psalm 80:3a, 7, 18*
Let us pray the psalm response:
Restore us, O God

- Gesture for group to respond.

**ALL: Restore us, O God**

**SECOND LEADER:**
Restore us, O God of hosts;
let your face shine, that we may be saved.
Then we will never turn back from you;
give us life, and we will call on your name.

- Gesture for group to respond.

**ALL: Restore us, O God**

- Brief pause.

**THIRD LEADER:** *Isaiah 40:1–4*
A reading from the book of the prophet Isaiah

- Read the scripture passage from a Bible.

The word of the Lord.

- All observe silence.

**FOURTH LEADER:**
Let us bring our hopes and needs to God as we pray, **Lord, hear our prayer.**

- Read the petitions prepared by the class, pausing after each for the response.

**FIFTH LEADER:**
Come Lord Jesus!
Fill our hearts with love for you,
and let your wisdom and love fill all the earth
so that your peace will rule over all the world.
Let our celebration of Christmas
keep you at the center, this year and
  every year,
until you come to set us free!
**Amen.**

**SIXTH LEADER:**
May the Lord bless us,

✠ All make the Sign of the Cross.

protect us from all evil
and bring us to everlasting life.

**ALL: Amen.**

- After the service, an adult extinguishes the candles on the Advent wreath.

# PRAYER FOR THE WEEK

WITH A READING FOR **SUNDAY, NOVEMBER 28, 2010**

## OPENING

Today is the first Sunday of Advent, the beginning of the Church year. This is the time when we prepare for the coming of the Messiah [meh-SI-uh], the one who is anointed with the Holy Spirit of God. In today's reading, the prophet Isaiah [ī-ZAY-uh] describes what it will be like when the Messiah comes.

✦ All make the Sign of the Cross.

> **In the name of the Father and of the Son and of the Holy Spirit. Amen.**

## PSALM
(For a longer psalm, see page xii.) Luke 1:79 (78)

By the tender mercy of our God,
 the dawn from on high will break upon us.

**By the tender mercy of our God,
 the dawn from on high will break upon us.**

To give light to those who sit in darkness
 and in the shadow of death,
 to guide our feet into the way of peace.

**By the tender mercy of our God,
 the dawn from on high will break upon us.**

## READING
Isaiah 2:2–3c, 4

A reading from the Book of the Prophet Isaiah [ī-ZAY-uh]

In days to come
 the mountain of the LORD's house
shall be established as the highest
  of the mountains,
 and shall be raised above the hills;
all the nations shall stream to it.
Many peoples shall come and say,
"Come, let us go up to the mountain
  of the LORD,
 to the house of the God of Jacob;
that he may teach us his ways
 and that we may walk in his paths."
He shall judge between the nations,
 and shall arbitrate for many peoples;
they shall beat their swords into plowshares,
 and their spears into pruning-hooks;
nation shall not lift up sword against nation,
 neither shall they learn war any more.

The word of the Lord.

◆ All observe silence.

## FOR SILENT REFLECTION

What do you think Isaiah is talking about when he refers to the "mountain of the Lord"?

## CLOSING PRAYER

Let us stand and bring our hopes and needs to God as we pray, "Lord, hear our prayer."

◆ All may add their own prayers here.

Let us pray: **Our Father . . . Amen.**

God of hope,
help us to prepare a place
for you in our lives.
Open our hearts to receive you
and teach us to walk in your ways.
We ask this in the name of Jesus Christ
  our Lord.
**Amen.**

✦ All make the Sign of the Cross.

# PRAYER FOR MONDAY
# NOVEMBER 29, 2010

## OPENING

In today's reading, the prophet Isaiah [ī-ZAY-uh] continues to describe what it will be like when the Messiah comes. The followers of Jesus believed that these words foretold his coming. The word canopy [KAN-oh-pee] means a shelter. Here it describes a holy place where people gather to enjoy God's loving presence and protection.

✛ All make the Sign of the Cross.

**In the name of the Father and of the Son and of the Holy Spirit. Amen.**

## PSALM
(For a longer psalm, see page xii.) Luke 1:79 (78)

By the tender mercy of our God,
   the dawn from on high will break upon us.

**By the tender mercy of our God,
the dawn from on high will break upon us.**

To give light to those who sit in darkness
   and in the shadow of death,
     to guide our feet into the way of peace.

**By the tender mercy of our God,
the dawn from on high will break upon us.**

## READING
Isaiah 4:2–3; 5–6

A reading from the Book of the Prophet Isaiah [ī-ZAY-uh]

On that day, the branch of the LORD shall be beautiful and glorious, and the fruit of the land shall be the pride and glory of the survivors of Israel. Whoever is left in Zion and remains in Jerusalem will be called holy: everyone who has been recorded for life in Jerusalem. Then the LORD will create over the whole site of Mount Zion and over its places of assembly, a cloud by day and smoke and the shining of a flaming fire by night. Indeed, over all the glory there will be a canopy [KAN-oh-pee]. It will serve as a pavilion [puh-VIL-yun], a shade by day from the heat, and a refuge and a shelter from the storm and rain.

The word of the Lord.

◆ All observe silence.

## FOR SILENT REFLECTION

Can you think of a holy place where you can experience God's love and protection?

## CLOSING PRAYER

Let us stand and bring our hopes and needs to God as we pray, "Lord, hear our prayer."

◆ All may add their own prayers here.

Let us pray: **Our Father . . . Amen.**

God our Father,
in this Advent season,
show us holy places where we can pray
and holy people to teach us
so that we may grow each day
in faith, hope, and love.
We ask this through Jesus Christ our Lord.
**Amen.**

✛ All make the Sign of the Cross.

# PRAYER FOR TUESDAY NOVEMBER 30, 2010

### OPENING

Today we celebrate the feast of Saint Andrew, one of the first persons Jesus called to be an apostle.

✚ All make the Sign of the Cross.

**In the name of the Father and of the Son and of the Holy Spirit. Amen.**

### PSALM
(For a longer psalm, see page xii.) Luke 1:79 (78)

By the tender mercy of our God,
   the dawn from on high will break upon us.

**By the tender mercy of our God,
   the dawn from on high will break upon us.**

To give light to those who sit in darkness
   and in the shadow of death,
   to guide our feet into the way of peace.

**By the tender mercy of our God,
   the dawn from on high will break upon us.**

◆ All stand and sing **Alleluia.**

### GOSPEL
Matthew 4:18–22

A reading from the holy Gospel according to Matthew

As he walked by the Sea of Galilee, he saw two brothers, Simon, who is called Peter, and Andrew his brother, casting a net into the sea—for they were fishermen. And he said to them, "Follow me, and I will make you fish for people." Immediately they left their nets and followed him. As he went from there, he saw two other brothers, James son of Zebedee and his brother John, in the boat with their father Zebedee, mending their nets, and he called them. Immediately they left the boat and their father, and followed him.

The Gospel of the Lord.

◆ All sit and observe silence.

### FOR SILENT REFLECTION

Why do you think these men knew so quickly that they wanted to follow Jesus?

### CLOSING PRAYER

Let us stand and bring our hopes and needs to God as we pray, "Lord, hear our prayer."

◆ All may add their own prayers here.

Let us pray: **Our Father . . . Amen.**

Holy and all powerful God,
you sent your Son
to call followers, to teach them,
and to die for them.
Through the intercession of Saint Andrew,
help us to be trusting followers
and to share our love of you with everyone.
We ask this through the same Jesus Christ
   our Lord.
**Amen.**

✚ All make the Sign of the Cross.

# PRAYER FOR **WEDNESDAY DECEMBER 1, 2010**

### OPENING

Today we listen again to the prophet Isaiah [ī-ZAY-uh]. In the reading, the word shroud means a sheet used to wrap the body of a person who dies. Isaiah says that God will destroy this sheet, meaning that God will destroy death.

✢ All make the Sign of the Cross.

**In the name of the Father and of the Son and of the Holy Spirit. Amen.**

Amen.

### PSALM
*(For a longer psalm, see page xii.) Luke 1:79 (78)*

By the tender mercy of our God,
    the dawn from on high will break upon us.

**By the tender mercy of our God,
    the dawn from on high will break upon us.**

To give light to those who sit in darkness
    and in the shadow of death,
    to guide our feet into the way of peace.

**By the tender mercy of our God,
    the dawn from on high will break upon us.**

### READING
*Isaiah 25:6–8a*

A reading from the book of the prophet Isaiah [ī-ZAY-uh]

On this mountain the LORD of hosts will
        make for all peoples
    a feast of rich food, a feast of
        well-matured wines,
    of rich food filled with marrow,
        of well-matured wines strained clear.
And he will destroy on this mountain
    the shroud that is cast over all peoples,
    the sheet that is spread over all nations;
    he will swallow up death forever.
Then the LORD GOD will wipe away
        the tears from all faces,
    and the disgrace of his people he will
        take away from all the earth,
    for the Lord has spoken.

The word of the Lord.

◆ All observe silence.

### FOR SILENT REFLECTION

Isaiah describes a feast, where people come together to celebrate the happiness of eternal life. What does this remind you of?

### CLOSING PRAYER

Let us stand and bring our hopes and needs to God as we pray, "Lord, hear our prayer."

◆ All may add their own prayers here.

Let us pray: **Our Father . . . Amen.**

God of life,
during these days of Advent,
fill us with hope and enthusiasm.
Help us to live as people
who truly believe in your promise of life.
We ask this through Christ our Lord.
**Amen.**

✢ All make the Sign of the Cross.

**ALSO ON THIS DAY:** Chanukah (Jewish festival of lights) begins at sunset.

# PRAYER FOR THURSDAY DECEMBER 2, 2010

## OPENING

In today's Gospel, Jesus tells a story that shows us how to enter God's kingdom. To be God's people, we must do God's will.

✛ All make the Sign of the Cross.

**In the name of the Father and of the Son and of the Holy Spirit. Amen.**

## PSALM (For a longer psalm, see page xii.) Luke 1:79 (78)

By the tender mercy of our God,
   the dawn from on high will break upon us.

**By the tender mercy of our God,
   the dawn from on high will break upon us.**

To give light to those who sit in darkness
   and in the shadow of death,
   to guide our feet into the way of peace.

**By the tender mercy of our God,
   the dawn from on high will break upon us.**

◆ All stand and sing **Alleluia.**

## GOSPEL                                Matthew 7:21, 24–27

A reading from the holy Gospel according to Matthew

Jesus said, "Not everyone who says to me, 'Lord, Lord', will enter the kingdom of heaven, but only the one who does the will of my Father in heaven. Everyone then who hears these words of mine and acts on them will be like a wise man who built his house on rock. The rain fell, the floods came, and the winds blew and beat on that house, but it did not fall, because it had been founded on rock. And everyone who hears these words of mine and does not act on them will be like a foolish man who built his house on sand. The rain fell, and the floods came, and the winds blew and beat against that house, and it fell; and great was its fall!"

The Gospel of the Lord.

◆ All sit and observe silence.

## FOR SILENT REFLECTION

What is the house we are building when we listen to God's word and act on it?

## CLOSING PRAYER

Let us stand and bring our hopes and needs to God as we pray, "Lord, hear our prayer."

◆ All may add their own prayers here.

Let us pray: **Our Father . . . Amen.**

Heavenly Father,
you invite us to be your people
and live with you forever in your kingdom.
Help us to listen and act
according to your words.
Grant us the wisdom to build our lives
on your love and truth.
We ask this through Christ our Lord.
**Amen.**

✛ All make the Sign of the Cross.

# PRAYER FOR FRIDAY
# DECEMBER 3, 2010

## OPENING

Today we remember Saint Francis Xavier [ZAY-vee-uhr], one of the first Jesuit [JEZH-oo-it] priests and a missionary in India and Japan as well as parts of Southeast Asia. He is the patron saint of missionaries. The Gospel today tells of Jesus healing two men who are blind.

✚ All make the Sign of the Cross.

**In the name of the Father and of the Son and of the Holy Spirit. Amen.**

## PSALM
*(For a longer psalm, see page xii.) Luke 1:79 (78)*

By the tender mercy of our God,
   the dawn from on high will break upon us.

**By the tender mercy of our God,
   the dawn from on high will break upon us.**

To give light to those who sit in darkness
   and in the shadow of death,
   to guide our feet into the way of peace.

**By the tender mercy of our God,
   the dawn from on high will break upon us.**

◆ All stand and sing **Alleluia**.

## GOSPEL
Matthew 9:27–31

A reading from the holy Gospel according to Matthew

As Jesus went on from there, two blind men followed him, crying loudly, "Have mercy on us, Son of David!" When he entered the house, the blind men came to him; and Jesus said to them, "Do you believe that I am able to do this?" They said to him, "Yes, Lord." Then he touched their eyes and said, "According to your faith let it be done to you." And their eyes were opened. Then Jesus sternly ordered them, "See that no one knows of this." But they went away and spread the news about him throughout that district.

The Gospel of the Lord.

◆ All sit and observe silence.

## FOR SILENT REFLECTION

Why do you think Jesus asks if they believe in him? What do you want Jesus to do for you? Do you believe he can do it?

## CLOSING PRAYER

Let us stand and bring our hopes and needs to God as we pray, "Lord, hear our prayer."

◆ All may add their own prayers here.

Let us pray: **Our Father . . . Amen.**

Mighty God,
in this season of waiting,
give us faith to believe
that you are coming into our lives.
Give us confidence
in your power to heal us,
to guide and strengthen us,
to protect and care for us.
We ask this through Jesus Christ our Lord.
**Amen.**

✚ All make the Sign of the Cross.

# PRAYER FOR THE WEEK

WITH A READING FROM THE GOSPEL FOR **SUNDAY, DECEMBER 5, 2010**

## OPENING

This week, as we continue to prepare for the coming of Christ's light into the world, we light the second candle on our Advent wreath. The four candles on the wreath help us count the four Sundays in Advent as we wait for Christmas. Each week the light increases. Today's Gospel tells how John the Baptist helped to prepare the way for Jesus.

✚ All make the Sign of the Cross.

**In the name of the Father and of the Son and of the Holy Spirit. Amen.**

## PSALM   (For a longer psalm, see page xii.) Luke 1:79 (78)

By the tender mercy of our God,
   the dawn from on high will break upon us.

**By the tender mercy of our God,
   the dawn from on high will break upon us.**

To give light to those who sit in darkness
   and in the shadow of death,
   to guide our feet into the way of peace.

**By the tender mercy of our God,
   the dawn from on high will break upon us.**

◆ All stand and sing **Alleluia**.

## GOSPEL   Matthew 3:1–6

A reading from the holy Gospel according to Matthew

In those days John the Baptist appeared in the wilderness of Judea, proclaiming, "Repent, for the kingdom of heaven has come near." This is the one of whom the prophet Isaiah spoke when he said,

"The voice of one crying out in the wilderness:
   'Prepare the way of the Lord,
   make his paths straight.'"

Now John wore clothing of camel's hair with a leather belt around his waist, and his food was locusts and wild honey. Then the people of Jerusalem and all Judea were going out to him, and all the region along the Jordan, and they were baptized by him in the river Jordan, confessing their sins.

The Gospel of the Lord.

◆ All sit and observe silence.

## FOR SILENT REFLECTION

What are some ways that we prepare for the coming of the Lord during Advent?

## CLOSING PRAYER

Let us stand and bring our hopes and needs to God as we pray, "Lord, hear our prayer."

◆ All may add their own prayers here.

Let us pray: **Our Father . . . Amen.**

God of mercy,
John the Baptist called people
to prepare for the coming of the Messiah
by turning away from sin
and toward God's love.
Help us to turn away from selfishness
and toward kindness, mercy, and love.
We ask this through Christ our Lord.
**Amen.**

✚ All make the Sign of the Cross.

# PRAYER FOR MONDAY DECEMBER 6, 2010

## OPENING

There are different kinds of waiting. We can wait with dread, fearful of what is coming, or we can wait with joy, expecting something wonderful. Advent is a time of joyful waiting. How does the prophet Isaiah [ī-ZAY-uh] await God's coming in today's reading?

✦ All make the Sign of the Cross.

**In the name of the Father and of the Son and of the Holy Spirit. Amen.**

## PSALM  (For a longer psalm, see page xii.) Luke 1:79 (78)

By the tender mercy of our God,
  the dawn from on high will break upon us.

**By the tender mercy of our God,
  the dawn from on high will break upon us.**

To give light to those who sit in darkness
  and in the shadow of death,
  to guide our feet into the way of peace.

**By the tender mercy of our God,
  the dawn from on high will break upon us.**

## READING  Isaiah 35:1–2, 5–6, 8a

A reading from the Book of the Prophet Isaiah [ī-ZAY-uh]

The wilderness and the dry land shall be glad,
  the desert shall rejoice and blossom;
like the crocus it shall blossom abundantly,
  and rejoice with joy and singing.
The glory of Lebanon shall be given to it,
  the majesty of Carmel [KAHR-ml] and
    Sharon [SHAYR-uhn].
They shall see the glory of the LORD,
  the majesty of our God.
Then the eyes of the blind shall be opened,
  and the ears of the deaf unstopped;
then the lame shall leap like a deer,
  and the tongue of the speechless sing for joy.
For waters shall break forth in the wilderness,
  and streams in the desert.

A highway shall be there,
  and it shall be called the Holy Way.

The word of the Lord

◆ All observe silence.

## FOR SILENT REFLECTION

What wonderful things do you imagine God doing in the world and in your life? What are you waiting for this Advent?

## CLOSING PRAYER

Let us stand and bring our hopes and needs to God as we pray, "Lord, hear our prayer."

◆ All may add their own prayers here.

Let us pray: **Our Father . . . Amen.**

God of hope,
as we await your coming,
we remember your care for us
and for all of creation.
Help us to trust in your goodness and love.
We ask this through our Lord Jesus Christ,
    your Son, who lives and reigns with
    you in the unity of the Holy Spirit,
    one God, for ever and ever.
**Amen.**

✦ All make the Sign of the Cross.

# PRAYER FOR TUESDAY DECEMBER 7, 2010

## OPENING

Today we remember Saint Ambrose [AM-brohz], a bishop of Milan, and one of the great teachers of the Church. Saint Ambrose is famous for writing beautiful hymns that praise God and inspire faith. Today's reading is again from the prophet Isaiah [i-ZAY-uh].

✢ All make the Sign of the Cross.

**In the name of the Father and of the Son and of the Holy Spirit. Amen.**

## PSALM
(For a longer psalm, see page xii.) Luke 1:79 (78)

By the tender mercy of our God,
  the dawn from on high will break upon us.

**By the tender mercy of our God,
  the dawn from on high will break upon us.**

To give light to those who sit in darkness
  and in the shadow of death,
  to guide our feet into the way of peace.

**By the tender mercy of our God,
  the dawn from on high will break upon us.**

## READING
Isaiah 40:3–5, 10a, 11

A reading from the Book of the Prophet Isaiah [ī-ZAY-uh]

A voice cries out:
"In the wilderness prepare the way
    of the LORD,
  make straight in the desert a highway
    for our God.
Every valley shall be lifted up,
  and every mountain and hill be made low;
the uneven ground shall become level,
  and the rough places a plain.
Then the glory of the Lord shall be revealed,
  and all people shall see it together,
  for the mouth of the Lord has spoken."

See, the Lord GOD comes with might,

He will feed his flock like a shepherd;
  he will gather the lambs in his arms,
and carry them in his bosom,
  and gently lead the mother sheep.

The word of the Lord.

◆ All observe silence.

## FOR SILENT REFLECTION

God is all-powerful. What does this reading tell us about how God uses this power?

## CLOSING PRAYER

Let us bring our hopes and needs to God as we pray, "Lord, hear our prayer."

◆ All may add their own prayers here.

Let us pray: **Our Father . . . Amen.**

Lord God,
you are mighty and you are also gentle.
Show us how to do our part
to prepare for the coming of your Son.
We ask this through the same Jesus Christ
    our Lord.
**Amen.**

✢ All make the Sign of the Cross.

# PRAYER SERVICE

## SOLEMNITY OF THE IMMACULATE CONCEPTION OF MARY

*Prepare six leaders for this service. The third leader will need a Bible from which to read the scripture passage and may need help finding it and practicing. You may wish to begin by singing "Immaculate Mary." If the group will sing, prepare a song leader.*

**FIRST LEADER:**
Today we celebrate the great solemnity of the Immaculate Conception of the Blessed Virgin Mary. People all over the world go to church today to worship God for giving us Mary, who was pure, holy, and worthy of becoming the mother of Jesus Christ. When Mary was still inside her own mother's body, she was chosen to be different from all other people. God gave Mary the special grace to be completely pure—free from any stain of original sin. This is what we mean when we call her Mary of the "Immaculate Conception." "Immaculate" means free from the stain of all sin. Under this title, Mary is the patroness of the United States, and so this day is particularly wonderful for all of us here in the United States of America. Let us stand and sing our opening song.

**SECOND LEADER:**

✢ All make the Sign of the Cross.

> **In the name of the Father and of the Son and of the Holy Spirit. Amen.**

*continued on next page*

# SOLEMNITY OF THE IMMACULATE CONCEPTION OF MARY
## CONTINUED

Let us pray:
Father,
You gifted Mary with Immaculate Conception
and she followed you with a pure heart,
trusting in your promises.
Because she said "yes" and held nothing back,
you gave her the greatest grace.
The Lord lived inside her body and grew up
    in her care.
Through her prayers,
make us holy and true,
    so that we may one day share her joy
    in eternity.
We ask this through Christ our Lord.

**ALL: Amen.**

◆ All stand and sing **Alleluia**.

**THIRD LEADER:**     Luke 1:26–38
A reading from the holy Gospel according to Luke

◆ Read the Gospel passage from the Bible.

The Gospel of the Lord.

◆ All sit and observe silence.

**FOURTH LEADER:**
Let us stand and bring our bring our hopes and needs to God as we pray, **Lord, hear our prayer.**

For the courage to follow Mary's example and always say "yes" to God and his will, we pray to the Lord.

For all who are hungry, sad, tired, or in pain, that Mary's loving and immaculate heart may give comfort and peace, we pray to the Lord.

For all mothers, may Mary's example of gentle motherhood help them to share God's love and peace in their families, we pray to the Lord.

For those who are sick and for those who have died, we pray to the Lord.

For people everywhere, that we may learn to respect and to protect all life, from the moment of conception until natural death, we pray to the Lord.

**FIFTH LEADER:**
Let us pray the Hail Mary:

**ALL: Hail Mary, full of grace . . .**

◆ Pause and then say:

Let us offer one another the sign of Christ's peace.

**SIXTH LEADER:**     Luke 1:46–49
Let us pray Mary's special prayer,
    the Magnificat:
"My soul magnifies the Lord,
    and my spirit rejoices in God my Savior,
for he has looked with favor on the lowliness
    of his servant.
    Surely, from now on all generations will
    call me blessed;
for the Mighty One has done great things
    for me,
and holy is his name."

✢ All make the Sign of the Cross.

**In the name of the Father and of the Son and of the Holy Spirit. Amen.**

# PRAYER FOR WEDNESDAY DECEMBER 8, 2010

## OPENING

Today we celebrate the solemnity of the Immaculate Conception of the Blessed Virgin Mary. God gave Mary, Jesus' mother, the special grace of having no stain of sin, even from the time she was in her mother's womb.

✤ All make the Sign of the Cross.

**In the name of the Father and of the Son and of the Holy Spirit. Amen.**

## PSALM
(For a longer psalm, see page xii.) Luke 1:79 (78)

By the tender mercy of our God,
 the dawn from on high will break upon us.

**By the tender mercy of our God,
 the dawn from on high will break upon us.**

To give light to those who sit in darkness
 and in the shadow of death,
 to guide our feet into the way of peace.

**By the tender mercy of our God,
 the dawn from on high will break upon us.**

◆ All stand and sing **Alleluia.**

## GOSPEL
Luke 1:26–33, 38

A reading from the holy Gospel according to Luke

In the sixth month the angel Gabriel was sent by God to a town in Galilee called Nazareth, to a virgin engaged to a man whose name was Joseph, of the house of David. The virgin's name was Mary. And he came to her and said, "Greetings, favored one! The Lord is with you." But she was much perplexed by his words and pondered what sort of greeting this might be. The angel said to her, "Do not be afraid, Mary, for you have found favor with God. And now, you will conceive in your womb and bear a son, and you will name him Jesus. He will be great, and will be called the Son of the Most High, and the Lord God will give to him the throne of his ancestor David. He will reign over the house of Jacob forever, and of his kingdom there will be no end."

Then Mary said, "Here am I, the servant of the Lord; let it be with me according to your word." Then the angel departed from her.

The Gospel of the Lord.

◆ All sit and observe silence.

## FOR SILENT REFLECTION

How can we also be God's servants?

## CLOSING PRAYER

Let us stand and bring our hopes and needs to God as we pray, "Lord, hear our prayer."

◆ All may add their own prayers here.

Let us pray: **Our Father . . . Amen.**

Loving God,
Help us to learn from Mary
how to serve you well.
We ask this through Christ our Lord.
**Amen.**

✤ All make the Sign of the Cross.

---

**ALSO ON THIS DAY:** Muharramn (Islamic New Year)
Bodhi Day (Buddhist celebration of the day the Buddha attained enlightenment under the bodhi tree.)

# PRAYER FOR **THURSDAY DECEMBER 9, 2010**

## OPENING

Today we remember a native Mexican saint, Juan Diego [hwan dee-AY-goh]. Mary appeared to him, speaking in his native tongue, expressing her compassion for the suffering people of Mexico. At her request a shrine was built, which is now the Basilica of Our Lady of Guadalupe [gwa-da-LOO-pay]. The feast of Our Lady of Guadalupe does not appear on the calendar this year as it falls on a Sunday, but she will be honored in songs and prayers.

✢ All make the Sign of the Cross.

**In the name of the Father and of the Son and of the Holy Spirit. Amen.**

## PSALM     (For a longer psalm, see page xii.) Luke 1:79 (78)

By the tender mercy of our God,
   the dawn from on high will break upon us.

**By the tender mercy of our God,
   the dawn from on high will break upon us.**

To give light to those who sit in darkness
   and in the shadow of death,
      to guide our feet into the way of peace.

**By the tender mercy of our God,
   the dawn from on high will break upon us.**

## READING                    Isaiah 41:17–20

A reading from the Book of the Prophet Isaiah [i-ZAY-uh]

   When the poor and needy seek water,
      and there is none,
         and their tongue is parched with thirst,
   I the Lord will answer them,
   I the God of Israel will not forsake them.
   I will open rivers on the bare heights,
      and fountains in the midst of the valleys;
   I will make the wilderness a pool of water,
      and the dry land springs of water.
   I will put in the wilderness the cedar,
      the acacia, the myrtle, and the olive;
   I will set in the desert the cypress,
      the plane and the pine together,
   so that all may see and know,
      all may consider and understand,
   that the hand of the Lord has done this,
      the Holy One of Israel has created it.

The word of the Lord.

◆ All sit and observe silence.

## FOR SILENT REFLECTION

Who do you know who needs God's love?

## CLOSING PRAYER

Let us stand and bring our hopes and needs to God as we pray, "Lord, hear our prayer."

◆ All may add their own prayers here.

Let us pray: **Our Father . . . Amen.**

God of hope,
keep us mindful of the needs of others.
Through our actions may they know
   your love.
We ask this through Christ our Lord.
**Amen.**

✢ All make the Sign of the Cross.

**ALSO ON THIS DAY:** Chanukah (Jewish festival of lights) ends at nightfall.

# HOME PRAYER
## GATHERING AROUND A NATIVITY SCENE FOR PRAYER

Throughout Advent, keep a votive candle beside your Christmas Nativity scene. Place the figures of Mary and Joseph inside the stable, but leave the manger empty (if you can't separate the infant Jesus from the manger, then remove them both). Leave the Nativity scene like that throughout Advent; keep it near your Advent wreath, if possible. Use this prayer service on Christmas Eve. You may want to use it again on Christmas Day, but at that time begin with the baby Jesus in the stable; then replace the Gospel reading with Luke 2:8–20 and, at the end of verse 16, pause and add the figures of the shepherds to your stable. Conclude as before. You might be wondering what to do with those wise men! Place them on a shelf a good distance from the stable. Each day of the Christmas season, have the children move them a little closer to your little "Bethlehem" so that they will arrive on January 4, the Solemnity of Epiphany of the Lord, when we celebrate their discovery of the baby Jesus.

Before you begin, locate the reading (Luke 2:1–7) in your Bible; ask for a volunteer to read the scripture, and encourage the reader to practice reading it twice.

Light the candle. You may wish to begin with a simple Christmas song like "Silent Night." Then an older child or an adult reads the leader parts.

**LEADER:**
Throughout Advent, we have waited for this moment to celebrate the glorious Good News that God gave us the greatest gift imaginable—himself! Jesus Christ is born, and now the world will never be the same! Let us begin our prayer with the Sign of the Cross:

✦ All make the Sign of the Cross.

In the name of the Father and of the Son and of the Holy Spirit. Amen.

**LEADER:** *Psalm 96:1a, 10ab*
Please repeat the psalm response:
O sing to the LORD a new song.

**ALL:** O sing to the LORD a new song.

**LEADER:**
Say among the nations, "The LORD is king! The world is firmly established; it shall never be moved.

**ALL:** O sing to the LORD a new song.

◆ All stand and sing **Alleluia**.

**READER:** *Luke 2:1–7*
A reading from the holy Gospel according to Luke

◆ Read the scripture passage from the Bible.

The Gospel of the Lord.

◆ All sit and observe silence. Keep the silence as you place the infant Jesus figure in the Nativity scene.

**LEADER:**
Let us stand and pray: **Our Father . . . Amen.**

Heavenly Father,
we rejoice in the gift of your only Son,
made flesh in this child
and offered to all peoples.
Open our eyes to see
your power and glory in your Son
and may the wonder of his saving peace
be on us and on all those we love.
We ask this through Jesus Christ, our Lord.

**ALL:** Amen.

# PRAYER FOR FRIDAY DECEMBER 10, 2010

## OPENING

In today's reading, the prophet Isaiah [ī-ZAY-uh] describes God lamenting when people will not listen to him. God wants to give us all that is good, but to receive these blessings, we need to do God's will, not our own will.

✢ All make the Sign of the Cross.

**In the name of the Father and of the Son and of the Holy Spirit. Amen.**

## PSALM          (For a longer psalm, see page xii.) Luke 1:79 (78)

By the tender mercy of our God,
   the dawn from on high will break upon us.

**By the tender mercy of our God,
   the dawn from on high will break upon us.**

To give light to those who sit in darkness
   and in the shadow of death,
      to guide our feet into the way of peace.

**By the tender mercy of our God,
   the dawn from on high will break upon us.**

## READING                                          Isaiah 48:17–19

A reading from the Book of the Prophet Isaiah [ī-ZAY-uh]

Thus says the LORD,
   your Redeemer, the Holy One of Israel:
I am the LORD your God,
   who teaches you for your own good,
   who leads you in the way you should go.
O that you had paid attention to
   my commandments!
Then your prosperity would have been
   like a river,
   and your success like the waves of the sea;
your offspring would have been like
   the sand,
   and your descendants like its grains;
their name would never be cut off
   or destroyed from before me.

The word of the Lord.

◆ All observe silence.

## FOR SILENT REFLECTION

How do we feel when we are doing God's will?

## CLOSING PRAYER

Let us stand and bring our hopes and needs to God as we pray, "Lord, hear our prayer."

◆ All may add their own prayers here.

Let us pray: **Our Father . . . Amen.**

Gracious God,
too often we think
that getting our own way will make us happy
and we are disappointed when it doesn't.
You long to bless us in so many ways.
Open our hearts and minds
to receive your many blessings.
We ask this through the same Jesus Christ,
   our Lord.

✢ All make the Sign of the Cross.

# PRAYER FOR THE WEEK

WITH A READING FROM THE GOSPEL FOR **SUNDAY, DECEMBER 12, 2010**

## OPENING

Be joyful, for today is *Gaudete* (gow-DAY-tay) Sunday. *Gaudete* is a Latin word that means "rejoice!" Today, we light the rose-colored candle on our Advent wreath. In today's Gospel we hear Jesus speaking about John the Baptist, who had been preaching and baptizing people in the desert, urging them to change their lives.

✚ All make the Sign of the Cross.

**In the name of the Father and of the Son and of the Holy Spirit. Amen.**

## PSALM
(For a longer psalm, see page xii.) Luke 1:79 (78)

By the tender mercy of our God,
   the dawn from on high will break upon us.

**By the tender mercy of our God,
   the dawn from on high will break upon us.**

To give light to those who sit in darkness
   and in the shadow of death,
   to guide our feet into the way of peace.

**By the tender mercy of our God,
   the dawn from on high will break upon us.**

◆ All stand and sing **Alleluia**.

## GOSPEL
Matthew 11:7b–11

A reading from the holy Gospel according to Matthew

Jesus began to speak to the crowds about John: "What did you go out into the wilderness to look at? A reed shaken by the wind? What then did you go out to see? Someone dressed in soft robes? Look, those who wear soft robes are in royal palaces. What then did you go out to see? A prophet? Yes, I tell you, and more than a prophet. This is the one about whom it is written, 'See, I am sending my messenger ahead of you, who will prepare your way before you.' Truly I tell you, among those born of women no one has arisen greater than John the Baptist; yet the least in the kingdom of heaven is greater than he."

The Gospel of the Lord.

◆ All sit and observe silence.

## FOR SILENT REFLECTION

Why do you think that Jesus says the least in the kingdom of heaven are greater than John the Baptist?

## CLOSING PRAYER

Let us stand and bring our hopes and needs to God as we pray, "Lord, hear our prayer."

◆ All may add their own prayers here.

Let us pray: **Our Father . . . Amen.**

Holy God,
give us patience as we wait for you to come,
as we await the fulfillment of your kingdom,
in which even the least is very great.
We ask this through our Lord Jesus Christ,
   your Son, who lives and reigns with
   you in the unity of the Holy Spirit,
   one God, for ever and ever.
**Amen.**

✚ All make the Sign of the Cross.

# PRAYER FOR **MONDAY DECEMBER 13, 2010**

## OPENING

Today we remember Saint Lucy, a young woman who died for her faith in the fourth century. Her name means light. In today's Gospel, Jesus is asked where his authority [a-THOR-i-tee] comes from. Authority is the power to do or say something.

✣ All make the Sign of the Cross.

**In the name of the Father and of the Son and of the Holy Spirit. Amen.**

## PSALM
(For a longer psalm, see page xii.) Luke 1:79 (78)

By the tender mercy of our God,
 the dawn from on high will break upon us.

**By the tender mercy of our God,
 the dawn from on high will break upon us.**

To give light to those who sit in darkness
 and in the shadow of death,
 to guide our feet into the way of peace.

**By the tender mercy of our God,
 the dawn from on high will break upon us.**

◆ All stand and sing **Alleluia**.

## GOSPEL
Matthew 21:23–27

A reading from the holy Gospel according to Matthew

When Jesus entered the temple, the chief priests and the elders of the people came to him as he was teaching, and said, "By what authority [a-THOR-i-tee] are you doing these things, and who gave you this authority?" Jesus said to them, "I will also ask you one question; if you tell me the answer, then I will also tell you by what authority I do these things. Did the baptism of John come from heaven, or was it of human origin?" And they argued with one another, "If we say, 'From heaven,' he will say to us, 'Why then did you not believe him?' But if we say, 'Of human origin,' we are afraid of the crowd; for all regard John as a prophet." So they answered Jesus, "We do not know." And he said to them, "Neither will I tell you by what authority I am doing these things."

The Gospel of the Lord.

◆ All sit and observe silence.

## FOR SILENT REFLECTION

Where does the power of Jesus come from?
How does Jesus use this power?

## CLOSING PRAYER

Let us stand and bring our hopes and needs to God as we pray, "Lord, hear our prayer."

◆ All may add their own prayers here.

Let us pray: **Our Father . . . Amen.**

God of power and might,
open our hearts to understand
how Jesus used your power
to heal and forgive,
to strengthen and guide,
and how he is working in our lives.
We ask this through the same Jesus Christ
 our Lord.
**Amen.**

✣ All make the Sign of the Cross.

# PRAYER FOR TUESDAY DECEMBER 14, 2010

## OPENING

Today we remember Saint John of the Cross, a Spanish theologian [thee-o-LOW-jn] and poet who wrote about prayer and the spiritual life. In today's reading, the prophet Zephaniah [zef-uh-NI-uh] describes what it will be like when God's will is done on earth.

✛ All make the Sign of the Cross.

**In the name of the Father and of the Son and of the Holy Spirit. Amen.**

## PSALM
(For a longer psalm, see page xii.) Luke 1:79 (78)

By the tender mercy of our God,
  the dawn from on high will break upon us.

**By the tender mercy of our God,
  the dawn from on high will break upon us.**

To give light to those who sit in darkness
  and in the shadow of death,
    to guide our feet into the way of peace.

**By the tender mercy of our God,
  the dawn from on high will break upon us.**

## READING
Zephaniah 3:11–13

A reading from the Book of the Prophet Zephaniah [zef-uh-NI-uh]

On that day you shall not be put to shame
    because of all the deeds by which you
        have rebelled against me;
for then I will remove from
    your midst your proudly exultant ones,
and you shall no longer be haughty
    in my holy mountain.
For I will leave in the midst of you
    a people humble and lowly.
They shall seek refuge in the name
        of the LORD—
    the remnant of Israel;
they shall do no wrong
    and utter no lies,
nor shall a deceitful tongue
    be found in their mouths.
Then they will pasture and lie down,
    and no one shall make them afraid.

The word of the Lord.

◆ All observe silence.

## FOR SILENT REFLECTION

How should God's people speak and behave towards one another?

## CLOSING PRAYER

Let us stand and bring our hopes and needs to God as we pray, "Lord, hear our prayer."

◆ All may add their own prayers here.

Let us pray: **Our Father . . . Amen.**

God of peace,
give us loving words
to bring your peace
into the lives of all we meet.
Teach us to be humble, not proud,
so that we may know your peace in
    our hearts.
We ask this through Christ our Lord.
**Amen.**

✛ All make the Sign of the Cross.

# PRAYER FOR **WEDNESDAY DECEMBER 15, 2010**

## OPENING

In today's reading, the prophet Isaiah [ī-ZAY-uh] talks about God's great power. During Advent, we await the coming of the powerful love of Christ into our lives.

✝ All make the Sign of the Cross.

**In the name of the Father and of the Son and of the Holy Spirit. Amen.**

## PSALM  (For a longer psalm, see page xii.) Luke 1:79 (78)

By the tender mercy of our God,
　the dawn from on high will break upon us.

**By the tender mercy of our God,
　the dawn from on high will break upon us.**

To give light to those who sit in darkness
　and in the shadow of death,
　to guide our feet into the way of peace.

**By the tender mercy of our God,
　the dawn from on high will break upon us.**

## READING  Isaiah 45:8, 22–23

A reading from the Book of the Prophet Isaiah [ī-ZAY-uh]

Shower, O heavens, from above,
　and let the skies rain down
　　righteousness;
let the earth open, that salvation may
　　spring up,
　and let it cause righteousness to sprout
　　up also;
　I the LORD have created it.

Turn to me and be saved,
　all the ends of the earth!
For I am God, and there is no other.
By myself I have sworn,
　from my mouth has gone forth
　　in righteousness
　a word that shall not return:
"To me every knee shall bow,
　every tongue shall swear."

The word of the Lord.

◆ All observe silence.

## FOR SILENT REFLECTION

What does the beauty of creation tell us about God, our Creator?

## CLOSING PRAYER

Let us stand and bring our hopes and needs to God as we pray, "Lord, hear our prayer."

◆ All may add their own prayers here.

Let us pray: **Our Father . . . Amen.**

God, our Creator,
how wonderfully you use
your infinite power
to make this world beautiful,
renewing its beauty each day.
How wonderfully you use your power
to forgive sinners, to heal the sick,
and to restore justice.
Help us to trust in your saving power.
We ask this through Jesus Christ our Lord.
**Amen.**

✝ All make the Sign of the Cross.

**ALSO ON THIS DAY:** Day of Ashura (Islamic commemoration of martyrdom of Husayn ibn Ali) begins at sunset.

# PRAYER FOR THURSDAY DECEMBER 16, 2010

## OPENING

In today's reading, the prophet Isaiah [ī-ZAY-uh] talks about God's steadfast love for us. "Steadfast" means enduring and unchanging. God never stops loving us.

✢ All make the Sign of the Cross.

**In the name of the Father and of the Son and of the Holy Spirit. Amen.**

## PSALM    (For a longer psalm, see page xii.) Luke 1:79 (78)

**By the tender mercy of our God,
the dawn from on high will break upon us.**

**By the tender mercy of our God,
the dawn from on high will break upon us.**

To give light to those who sit in darkness
and in the shadow of death,
to guide our feet into the way of peace.

**By the tender mercy of our God,
the dawn from on high will break upon us.**

## READING    Isaiah 54:9–10

A reading from the Book of the Prophet Isaiah [ī-ZAY-uh]

This is like the days of Noah to me:
Just as I swore that the waters of Noah
would never again go over the earth,
so I have sworn that I will not be angry
with you
and will not rebuke you.
For the mountains may depart
and the hills be removed,
but my steadfast love shall not depart
from you,
and my covenant of peace shall not
be removed,
says the LORD, who has compassion
on you.

The word of the Lord.

◆ All observe silence.

## FOR SILENT REFLECTION

Do you ever think God is angry with you? How do you know that God always loves you?

## CLOSING PRAYER

Let us stand and bring our hopes and needs to God as we pray, "Lord, hear our prayer."

◆ All may add their own prayers here.

Let us pray: **Our Father . . . Amen.**

God of love,
from the first moment of creation
to this very moment,
you have never ceased to love us.
You long to protect and guide us always
and to give us every blessing.
May your love teach us to love.
We ask this through Christ our Lord.
**Amen.**

✢ All make the Sign of the Cross.

---

**ALSO ON HIS DAY:** The Advent Novena, Las Posadas ("Lodgings"), begins.

Day of Ashura (Islamic commemoration of martyrdom of Husayn ibn Ali) ends at nightfall.

# PRAYER FOR **FRIDAY DECEMBER 17, 2010**

## OPENING

Today the Church begins praying the O Antiphons [AN-tih-fonz), an ancient [AYN-chent] prayer that we will continue to pray until Christmas Eve. Today's closing prayer is the O Antiphon that names Jesus as wisdom.

✢ All make the Sign of the Cross.

**In the name of the Father and of the Son and of the Holy Spirit. Amen.**

## PSALM
(For a longer psalm, see page xii.) Luke 1:79 (78)

By the tender mercy of our God,
   the dawn from on high will break upon us.

**By the tender mercy of our God,
   the dawn from on high will break upon us.**

To give light to those who sit in darkness
   and in the shadow of death,
   to guide our feet into the way of peace.

**By the tender mercy of our God,
   the dawn from on high will break upon us.**

◆ All stand and sing **Alleluia.**

## GOSPEL
Matthew 1:18–19, 20bc–23

A reading from the holy Gospel according to Matthew

Now the birth of Jesus the Messiah [meh-SI-uh] took place in this way. When his mother Mary had been engaged to Joseph, but before they lived together, she was found to be with child from the Holy Spirit. Her husband Joseph, being a righteous man and unwilling to expose her to public disgrace, planned to dismiss her quietly. But an angel of the Lord appeared to him in a dream and said, "Joseph, son of David, do not be afraid to take Mary as your wife, for the child conceived in her is from the Holy Spirit. She will bear a son, and you are to name him Jesus, for he will save his people from their sins." All this took place to fulfill what had been spoken by the Lord through the prophet:
   "Look, the virgin shall conceive and bear
      a son,
   and they shall name him Emmanuel
      [ee-MAN-yoo-el],"
which means, "God is with us."

The Gospel of the Lord.

◆ All sit and observe silence.

## FOR SILENT REFLECTION

What do the names Emmanuel [ee-MAN-yoo-el], "God with us" and Wisdom tell us about who Jesus is and what he is like?

## CLOSING PRAYER

Let us stand and bring our hopes and needs to God as we pray, "Lord, hear our prayer."

◆ All may add their own prayers here.

Let us pray: **Our Father . . . Amen.**

"O come, O Wisdom from on high,
Who orders all things mightily;
To us the paths of knowledge show,
And teach us in her ways to go."
**Amen.**

✢ All make the Sign of the Cross.

**ALSO ON THIS DAY:** Muharram (Islamic New Year)

# CHRISTMAS

## SUNDAY, JANUARY 2, TO SUNDAY, JANUARY 9

# CHRISTMAS 2010

## THE MEANING OF CHRISTMAS

"For a child has been born for us,
  a son given to us;
authority rests upon his shoulders;
  and he is named
Wonderful Counselor, Mighty God,
  Everlasting Father, Prince of Peace."
(Isaiah 9:6)

God keeps his promises! He amazes us with gifts we never could have imagined or asked for.

The earth is filled with God's gifts. Think of the solid ground that supports us, gravity that keeps us from floating away, the atmosphere that provides oxygen for breathing and a shield to protect us from the heat of the sun, and water that keeps our cells healthy. We need so many things just to stay alive. And yet the earth contains much more than is necessary to keep us going. Within the earth, precious metals and gems delight us with their shine. Seashells and pinecones amaze us with their geometry. Roses and lilacs fill the air with perfume. Peacocks and panthers and pecans add to the world's great fascination. And every day our friends and family share new thoughts and fresh ways to love. What a world we have been given!

But God wants to give us something even more precious than all these wonders. He wants to share his life with us. One day, in Bethlehem, he placed himself in our hands. He, who was there from the beginning of the universe, who was the Word that spoke every one of us into this world, gave himself to us as a small child who could do nothing for himself.

This gift has changed everything. He has opened his heart for us. He has shown us how to live according to his way. Out of the tree stump of despair, God has brought a flowering branch. Now we can bloom with the love of Christ if we follow his example and give our whole selves.

Let us stand in front of the manger in Bethlehem and gaze with wonder on Mary and Joseph, the shepherds and angels, and the holy child, Jesus, our Lord.

As we listen to the Gospel readings for the Christmas season, we can follow the thread of Mary's story: how she listened to God and trusted in his promises, how the Holy Spirit worked in her life and filled Elizabeth and later Simeon, how Mary rejoiced in God's mighty power, how her prayers became prayers of the Church, and how she said "yes" to God's plan. If we walk with Mary through these sacred days, we will deepen our understanding and enjoyment of this holy season.

## PREPARING TO CELEBRATE CHRISTMAS IN THE CLASSROOM

It's time to exchange the purple cloth on your prayer table for a white one! If your students enjoyed the Advent procession, you can have another procession to celebrate Christmas (see Preparing to Celebrate Advent in the Classroom on page 116). The last child in the procession can carry a figure of the infant Jesus and place it in the manger that has been waiting empty on your prayer table during Advent.

This book provides a prayer service to celebrate the solemnity of the Epiphany of the Lord in the classroom or with a larger group (see pages 148–149). The Home Prayer page, Gathering around a Nativity Scene for Prayer, was intended to accompany the students home during the Christmas break.

### SACRED SPACE

If, during Advent, you kept a big, unlit white pillar candle in your classroom in anticipation of the remembrance of Christ's birth, now is the time to light it! You may wish to sing the joyful hymn, "Let all Things now Living," the beautiful "O Radiant Light," or "Many are the Light Beams."

If you set up a Christmas Nativity scene in your classroom, consider placing the three Magi figures at a distance from the Holy Family. Each day the children can help you bring the Magi closer to Christ until the Epiphany of the Lord, when they arrive. Each time you handle the figures, you can sing "We Three Kings." The prayer service for Epiphany on page 146–147 provides a beautiful and prayerful way to celebrate the eventual arrival of the Magi in Bethlehem.

Here is a prayer you can use to bless all who pray with your Christmas nativity scene:

"To you is born this day in the city of David a Savior, who is the Messiah, the Lord" (Luke 2:11).

Loving Father, as we look at this scene, may we remember Mary, the holy Mother of God who said "yes" to your plan of salvation, may we imitate Saint Joseph, who protected and loved your Son and his blessed mother, and may we adore Jesus forever and ever. We ask this through the same Jesus Christ, our Light and our Life. Amen.

"Silent Night" and "Away in a Manger" are perfect to sing at the conclusion of this prayer.

### SACRED MUSIC

Christmas is the season of music! There are so many beautiful carols you can sing with the children. Don't forget "Joy to the World," "Angels We Have Heard On High," or "O Come, All Ye Faithful." You may even wish to organize a caroling party and go door to door through your school.

### PRAYERS FOR CHRISTMAS

The opening verses of the Gospel according to Saint John contain some of the most beautiful poetry in the world:

"In the beginning was the Word, and the Word was with God, and the Word was God. He was in the beginning with God. All things came into being through him, and without him not one thing came into being. What has come into being in him was life, and the life was the light of all people. The light shines in the darkness, and the darkness did not overcome it" (John 1:1–5).

These verses beautifully express the mystery of the Incarnation. You might want to spend some time during religion class reading this beautiful hymn line by line. Ask the children who Saint John means when he speaks about the "Word of God." See what they say when you ask them how "all things came into being" through Christ when we know he was born after the creation of the world. How can one person be the "light of all people"? What do the children think Saint John means when he says, "the darkness did not overcome" the Light of the Word?

### A NOTE TO CATECHISTS

See whether you can share a Christmas Nativity scene with the teacher who shares your classroom. If not, perhaps the Religious Education Director can help you find a place to keep a Nativity scene. Or bring your students on a "field trip" to the church and let them pray in front of the parish Nativity scene!

# GRACE BEFORE MEALS
## CHRISTMAS

**LEADER:**
The Light of Christ

**ALL:** Has come into the world!

✚ All make the Sign of the Cross.

**In the name of the Father and of the Son and of the Holy Spirit. Amen.**

**LEADER:**
Heavenly Father,
may the food we are about to eat
remind us of your Son,
who ate and drank as we did
when he walked the earth.
Just as he humbled himself to share
 in our humanity,
may we one day come to share in his divinity.
We ask this through Christ our Lord.

✚ All make the Sign of the Cross.

**In the name of the Father and of the Son and of the Holy Spirit. Amen.**

# PRAYER AT DAY'S END
## CHRISTMAS

**LEADER:**
This is the day the Lord has made!

**ALL: Let us rejoice and be glad.**

✠ All make the Sign of the Cross.

**In the name of the Father and of the Son and of the Holy Spirit. Amen.**

**LEADER:**
Lord God,
what can we offer to you,
when you have given us all that we have
and all that we are?
As we get ready to leave school today,
help us to remember your greatest gift of all,
sending your Son to walk with us
and share his life with us.
May we always be mindful of his life in ours.
Grant this through Christ our Lord.

✠ All make the Sign of the Cross.

**In the name of the Father and of the Son and of the Holy Spirit. Amen.**

# PRAYER SERVICE
## EPIPHANY

Prepare six leaders and a song leader for this service. The second and fourth leaders will need Bibles to read the scripture passages and may need help practicing the reading. Before you begin, remove the figures of shepherds and the Three Kings from your Nativity scene. Put the shepherds away until next year. Place the kings a short distance from the Nativity scene. Then gather the class near it. (For an explanation and description of the Christmas Nativity scene and a prayer for blessing it, please turn to Preparing to Celebrate Christmas in the Classroom on page 142.) This service calls for two songs. Help the song leader prepare to lead the singing.

**SONG LEADER:**
Please stand and join in singing our opening song, "We Three Kings."

**FIRST LEADER:**

✠ All make the Sign of the Cross.

May the Light of Christ lead us to worship you in holiness.

**ALL: Amen.**

**FIRST LEADER:**
Let us pray: Father of Light,
may we worship your Son as the Magi did when they arrived in Bethlehem,
and may we return to our lives
with that love and delight in our hearts.
Help us to give your Son all our best gifts
and to bring your gifts of holiness and peace back to those we love.
We ask this through Christ our Lord.

**ALL: Amen.**

◆ Gesture for all to sit.

# EPIPHANY

**SECOND LEADER:**                           Isaiah 60:1–3, 6

A reading from the book of the prophet Isaiah

- ◆ Read the scripture passage from a Bible.

**The word of the Lord.**

- ◆ All observe silence.

**THIRD LEADER:**                            Psalm 72:11, 7

Please repeat the psalm response:
May all kings fall down before him,
   all nations give him service.

**ALL: May all kings fall down before him,
   all nations give him service.**

**THIRD LEADER:**

In his days may righteousness flourish
   and peace abound, until the moon is
      no more.

**ALL: May all kings fall down before him,
   all nations give him service.**

- ◆ All stand and sing **Alleluia**.

**FOURTH LEADER:**                      Matthew 2:9b–12

A reading from the holy Gospel according to Matthew

- ◆ Read the Gospel passage from a Bible.

**The Gospel of the Lord.**

- ◆ All sit and observe silence.
- ◆ In silence, an adult slowly moves the three figures of the wise men, one at a time, into the stable.

**SONG LEADER:**

Please stand and sing, "Joy to the World."

**FIFTH LEADER:**

Let us pray: **Our Father . . . Amen.**

Loving God,
you bless the earth and give us new life.
Just as you inspired the wise men
to follow the star with great joy,
keep our eyes open to the wonders
      in the world around us.
May our hearts overflow with gladness
for the love and friendship we share
and may we always live in your Light.
Grant this through Christ our Lord.

**ALL: Amen.**

**SIXTH LEADER:**

May Jesus, the Light of the World,
shine on our paths and in our hearts forever.
And may the Lord bless us:
the Father who made the star,
the Son for whom it shone,
and the Spirit who calls us to holiness.

**ALL: Amen.**

- ✛ All make the Sign of the Cross.

# PRAYER FOR THE WEEK

WITH A READING FROM THE GOSPEL FOR **SUNDAY, JANUARY 2, 2011**

## OPENING

Today is the solemnity of the Epiphany [ih-PIF-uh-nee] (or "showing") of Christ. God showed the wise men the way to Jesus, the light of the world, by the light of a star.

✢ All make the Sign of the Cross.

**In the name of the Father and of the Son and of the Holy Spirit. Amen.**

## PSALM  (For a longer psalm, see page xiii.) Psalm 98:4 (1a)

O sing to the LORD a new song,
 for he has done marvelous things.

**O sing to the LORD a new song,
 for he has done marvelous things.**

Make a joyful noise to the LORD, all the earth;
 break forth into joyous song and
  sing praises.

**O sing to the LORD a new song,
 for he has done marvelous things.**

◆ All stand and sing **Alleluia**.

## GOSPEL  Matthew 2:1–2, 5b, 9b–11

A reading from the holy Gospel according to Matthew

In the time of King Herod, after Jesus was born in Bethlehem of Judea, wise men from the East came to Jerusalem, asking, "Where is the child who has been born king of the Jews? For we observed his star at its rising, and have come to pay him homage." The chief priests and scribes said, "In Bethlehem of Judea; for so it has been written by the prophet."

The wise men set out; and there, ahead of them, went the star that they had seen at its rising, until it stopped over the place where the child was. When they saw that the star had stopped, they were overwhelmed with joy. On entering the house, they saw the child with Mary his mother; and they knelt down and paid him homage. Then, opening their treasure chests, they offered him gifts of gold, frankincense, and myrrh.

The Gospel of the Lord.

◆ All sit and observe silence.

## FOR SILENT REFLECTION

How does God show you the way to Jesus?

## CLOSING PRAYER

Let us stand and bring our hopes and needs to God as we pray, "Lord, hear our prayer."

◆ All may add their own prayers here.

Let us pray: **Our Father . . . Amen.**

Heavenly Father,
show us the way to Jesus, your Son.
Help us to see the signs
of your divine presence in our lives.
Give us the courage and wisdom to seek you,
and the faith to find you.
We ask this through the same Jesus Christ
  our Lord.
**Amen.**

✢ All make the Sign of the Cross.

# PRAYER FOR MONDAY JANUARY 3, 2011

## OPENING

In today's Gospel, Jesus, the light which the prophets foretold, begins to teach and heal, bringing God's light into the world.

✠ All make the Sign of the Cross.

**In the name of the Father and of the Son and of the Holy Spirit. Amen.**

## PSALM (For a longer psalm, see page xiii.) Psalm 98:4 (1a)

O sing to the LORD a new song,
   for he has done marvelous things.

**O sing to the LORD a new song,
   for he has done marvelous things.**

Make a joyful noise to the LORD, all the earth;
   break forth into joyous song and
      sing praises.

**O sing to the LORD a new song,
   for he has done marvelous things.**

◆ All stand and sing **Alleluia**.

## GOSPEL Matthew 4:13–17, 23–24ab, 24d–25a

A reading from the holy Gospel according to Matthew

Jesus left Nazareth and made his home in Capernaum by the sea, in the territory of Zebulun (ZEB-yoo-luhn) and Naphtali (NAF-tuh-lee), so that what had been spoken through the prophet Isaiah might be fulfilled:
   "Land of Zebulun, land of Naphtali,
      on the road by the sea, across the Jordan,
         Galilee of the Gentiles,
   the people who sat in darkness
      have seen a great light,
   and for those who sat in the region and
         shadow of death
      light has dawned."
From that time Jesus began to proclaim, "Repent, for the kingdom of heaven has come near."

Jesus went throughout Galilee, teaching in their synagogues and proclaiming the good news of the kingdom and curing every disease and every sickness among the people. So his fame spread throughout all Syria, and they brought to him all the sick, those who were afflicted with various diseases and pains, and he cured them. And great crowds followed him.

The Gospel of the Lord.

◆ All sit and observe silence.

## FOR SILENT REFLECTION

In this reading, how do the people respond to Jesus?

## CLOSING PRAYER

Let us stand and bring our hopes and needs to God as we pray, "Lord, hear our prayer."

◆ All may add their own prayers here.

Let us pray: **Our Father . . . Amen.**

Holy God,
help us to follow you,
rejoicing in the Good News
that has come into our lives.
Make your light shine on us.
We ask this through Christ our Lord.
**Amen.**

✠ All make the Sign of the Cross.

# PRAYER FOR TUESDAY JANUARY 4, 2011

## OPENING

Today we remember the American-born saint, Elizabeth Ann Seton [SEE-tuhn]. After her husband died and her five children were grown, Mother Seton founded an order of sisters, and devoted her life to the care of the poor and sick.

✦ All make the Sign of the Cross.

**In the name of the Father and of the Son and of the Holy Spirit. Amen.**

## PSALM  (For a longer psalm, see page xiii.) Psalm 98:4 (1a)

O sing to the LORD a new song,
 for he has done marvelous things.

**O sing to the LORD a new song,
 for he has done marvelous things.**

Make a joyful noise to the LORD, all the earth;
 break forth into joyous song and
  sing praises.

O sing to the LORD a new song,
 for he has done marvelous things.

◆ All stand and sing **Alleluia**.

## GOSPEL  Mark 6:34–35a, 36–37b, 38b–39, 41–44

A reading from the holy Gospel according to Mark

As he went ashore, he saw a great crowd; and he had compassion for them, because they were like sheep without a shepherd; and he began to teach them many things. When it grew late, his disciples came to him and said, "Send them away so that they may go into the surrounding country and villages and buy something for themselves to eat." But he answered them, "You give them something to eat. How many loaves have you? Go and see." When they had found out, they said, "Five, and two fish." Then he ordered them to get all the people to sit down in groups on the green grass. Taking the five loaves and the two fish, he looked up to heaven, and blessed and broke the loaves, and gave them to his disciples to set before the people; and he divided the two fish among them all. And all ate and were filled; and they took up twelve baskets full of broken pieces and of the fish. Those who had eaten the loaves numbered five thousand men.

The Gospel of the Lord.

◆ All sit and observe silence.

## FOR SILENT REFLECTION

Imagine you are one of the crowd who shares this meal. What do you want to say to Jesus?

## CLOSING PRAYER

Let us stand and bring our hopes and needs to God as we pray, "Lord, hear our prayer."

◆ All may add their own prayers here.

Let us pray: **Our Father . . . Amen.**

Gracious God,
feed us with your words of wisdom.
Fill us with gratitude for your love.
We ask this through Jesus Christ, our Lord,
**Amen.**

✦ All make the Sign of the Cross.

# PRAYER FOR WEDNESDAY JANUARY 5, 2011

## OPENING

Today we remember another American saint, John Neumann [NOO-muhn], a teacher who became the bishop of Philadelphia. He opened new parishes and started several Catholic schools. Today's reading, tells us to abide (to dwell, or live) in God's love.

✚ All make the Sign of the Cross.

**In the name of the Father and of the Son and of the Holy Spirit. Amen.**

## PSALM
(For a longer psalm, see page xiii.) Psalm 98:4 (1a)

O sing to the LORD a new song,
   for he has done marvelous things.

**O sing to the LORD a new song,
for he has done marvelous things.**

Make a joyful noise to the LORD, all the earth;
   break forth into joyous song and
      sing praises.

**O sing to the LORD a new song,
for he has done marvelous things.**

## READING
1 John 4:11–16

A reading from the First Letter of Saint John

Beloved, since God loved us so much, we also ought to love one another. No one has ever seen God; if we love one another, God lives in us, and his love is perfected in us.

By this we know that we abide in him and he in us, because he has given us of his Spirit. And we have seen and do testify that the Father has sent his Son as the Savior of the world. God abides in those who confess that Jesus is the Son of God, and they abide in God. So we have known and believe the love that God has for us.

God is love, and those who abide in love abide in God, and God abides in them.

The word of the Lord.

◆ All observe silence.

## FOR SILENT REFLECTION

Can you think of places where God abides?

## CLOSING PRAYER

Let us stand and bring our hopes and needs to God as we pray, "Lord, hear our prayer."

◆ All may add their own prayers here.

Let us pray: **Our Father . . . Amen.**

Holy God,
come and make your home with us.
Bless your Church, your holy house
   and family.
Enter our hearts and homes.
and fill us with your love.
We ask this through Jesus Christ our Lord.
**Amen.**

✚ All make the Sign of the Cross.

# PRAYER FOR THURSDAY JANUARY 6, 2011

## OPENING

Today's reading shows us that loving each other, loving God, and keeping God's commandments are all tied together.

✢ All make the Sign of the Cross.

**In the name of the Father, and of the Son and of the Holy Spirit. Amen.**

## PSALM
(For a longer psalm, see page xiii.) Psalm 98:4 (1a)

O sing to the LORD a new song,
  for he has done marvelous things.

**O sing to the LORD a new song,
  for he has done marvelous things.**

Make a joyful noise to the LORD, all the earth;
  break forth into joyous song and
    sing praises.

**O sing to the LORD a new song,
  for he has done marvelous things.**

## READING
1 John 4:19—5:4

A reading from the First Letter of Saint John

We love because God first loved us. Those who say, "I love God," and hate their brothers or sisters, are liars; for those who do not love a brother or sister whom they have seen, cannot love God whom they have not seen. The commandment we have from him is this; those who love God must love their brothers and sisters also.

Everyone who believes that Jesus is the Christ has been born of God, and everyone who loves the parent loves the child. By this we know that we love the children of God, when we love God and obey his commandments. For the love of God is this, that we obey his commandments. And his commandments are not burdensome, for whatever is born of God conquers [KONG-ker] the world. And this is the victory that conquers the world, our faith.

The word of the Lord.

◆ All observe silence.

## FOR SILENT REFLECTION

What are some of God's commandments?

## CLOSING PRAYER

Let us stand and bring our hopes and needs to God as we pray, "Lord, hear our prayer."

◆ All may add their own prayers here.

Let us pray: **Our Father . . . Amen.**

God of love,
all love comes from you.
Help us to obey your commandments
and do your will
so that we can learn to love others
with the love you have given to us.
We ask this through Jesus Christ our Lord.
**Amen.**

✢ All make the Sign of the Cross.

# PRAYER FOR FRIDAY JANUARY 7, 2011

## OPENING

In today's reading from the Gospel, Jesus heals a man who was suffering from the disease of leprosy (LEP-ruh-see). At the time of Jesus, people with leprosy lived apart from others due to fear of infection.

✢ All make the Sign of the Cross.

**In the name of the Father and of the Son and of the Holy Spirit. Amen.**

## PSALM     (For a longer psalm, see page xiii.) Psalm 98:4 (1a)

O sing to the LORD a new song,
    for he has done marvelous things.

O sing to the LORD a new song,
    for he has done marvelous things.

Make a joyful noise to the LORD, all the earth;
    break forth into joyous song and
        sing praises.

O sing to the LORD a new song,
    for he has done marvelous things.

◆ All stand and sing **Alleluia**.

## GOSPEL     Luke 5:12–13, 14b–16

A reading from the holy Gospel according to Luke

Once, when Jesus was in one of the cities, there was a man covered with leprosy. When he saw Jesus, he bowed with his face to the ground and begged him, "Lord, if you choose, you can make me clean." Then Jesus stretched out his hand, touched him, and said, "I do choose. Be made clean." Immediately the leprosy left him. "Go," he said, "and show yourself to the priest, and, as Moses commanded, make an offering for your cleansing, for a testimony to them." But now more than ever the word about Jesus spread abroad; many crowds would gather to hear him and to be cured of their diseases. But he would withdraw to deserted places and pray.

The Gospel of the Lord.

◆ All sit and observe silence.

## FOR SILENT REFLECTION

Why do you think Jesus doesn't hesitate to touch the leper? How does the leper approach Jesus?

## CLOSING PRAYER

Let us stand and bring our hopes and needs to God as we pray, "Lord, hear our prayer."

◆ All may add their own prayers here.

Let us pray: **Our Father . . . Amen.**

God, our healer,
give us confidence
in your loving power.
Help us to come to you,
without embarrassment or shame,
    in every need.
Touch us with your healing grace
and make us whole.
We ask this through Jesus Christ our Lord.
**Amen.**

✢ All make the Sign of the Cross.

# PRAYER FOR THE WEEK

WITH A READING FROM THE GOSPEL FOR **SUNDAY, JANUARY 9, 2011**

## OPENING

Today is the feast of the Baptism of the Lord. Today's Gospel tells of how the heavens opened, the Spirit descended, and the voice of God was heard. This is another epiphany [ih-PIF-uh-nee], or showing, when God shows who this person, Jesus, really is.

✦ All make the Sign of the Cross.

**In the name of the Father and of the Son and of the Holy Spirit. Amen.**

## PSALM (For a longer psalm, see page xiii.) Psalm 98:4(1a)

O sing to the LORD a new song,
　for he has done marvelous things.

**O sing to the LORD a new song,
　for he has done marvelous things.**

Make a joyful noise to the LORD, all the earth;
　break forth into joyous song and
　　sing praises.

**O sing to the LORD a new song,
　for he has done marvelous things.**

◆ All stand and sing **Alleluia.**

## GOSPEL    Matthew 3:13–17

A reading from the holy Gospel according to Matthew

Then Jesus came from Galilee to John at the Jordan, to be baptized by him. John would have prevented him, saying, "I need to be baptized by you, and do you come to me?" But Jesus answered him, "Let it be so now; for it is proper for us in this way to fulfill all righteousness." Then he consented. And when Jesus had been baptized, just as he came up from the water, suddenly the heavens were opened to him and he saw the Spirit of God descending like a dove and alighting on him. And a voice from heaven said, "This is my Son, the Beloved, with whom I am well pleased."

The Gospel of the Lord.

◆ All sit and observe silence.

## FOR SILENT REFLECTION

God wants us to see Jesus, and to know that Jesus is God's Son. How does God help you to see Jesus?

## CLOSING PRAYER

Let us stand and bring our hopes and needs to God as we pray, "Lord, hear our prayer."

◆ All may add their own prayers here.

Let us pray: **Our Father . . . Amen.**

Loving God,
you guided your people through
　the wilderness
to the promised land.
You guided the wise men to your Son
by the light of a star.
And in a wonderful way
you show us your Son at his baptism.
Grant us faith to believe
that you will show us the way to you.
We ask this through Jesus Christ the Lord.
**Amen.**

✦ All make the Sign of the Cross.

# ORDINARY TIME
# WINTER 2011

## MONDAY, JANUARY 10, TO TUESDAY, MARCH 8

# WINTER ORDINARY TIME

## THE MEANING OF ORDINARY TIME

Jesus said, "Again, the kingdom of heaven is like a merchant in search of fine pearls; on finding the one pearl of great value, he went and sold all that he had and bought it" (Matthew 13:45–46).

Advent filled our hearts with quiet hope and Christmas brought us warmth and light and joy. Now it is Ordinary Time again, but we are not the same people we were during the last Ordinary Time. Our bodies have been growing and changing, we have learned new things, and our friendships have deepened. But even more important than all these things, we are not the same as we were before because we have opened our hearts and minds to God's love.

Remember, everyone who looks for the kingdom of God and lives its promise will change and grow in hidden but miraculous ways. The grace of Advent and the holiness of Christmas are like water and sun for the mustard seed kingdom in our hearts. They cause God's Life in us to sprout and grow.

Jesus tells us that the kingdom also has another quality. Not only does it grow in a miraculous way, the kingdom is like a pearl, precious beyond everything else.

Imagine spending your whole life searching for the most precious pearl. When you finally find it, how would you recognize it? Would searching for pearls help you to learn something about them? What if we were to search in every situation, every moment of our lives, for the precious pearl that is the kingdom of God here on earth? Then, when we finally have eyes to see, what must we "sell" before we can "buy" it? What can selling and buying even mean when we're speaking about the kingdom of God? Surely Jesus doesn't mean that we need money in order to "buy" the kingdom? If that were so, only rich people could be saved! In the parable of the precious pearl, "selling" means to give up other, lesser pearls. But why would the merchant need to give up something that brings him happiness? Is it possible that spending our attention and love on things that won't last cannot make us truly and deeply happy? How do we then "buy" the kingdom? Can we keep back any little part of ourselves and still enter the kingdom of our God, the One who gives us all?

During Ordinary Time this winter, we will see how the Gospels reflect on the question "When and how did the world first come to see that Jesus Christ is the Son of the Living God?" It seems that God willed that the truth would dawn on us slowly and that different people would have many different ways of coming to believe in Jesus. Elizabeth felt her baby leap in her womb, angels announced the Good News to the Jewish shepherds, the Magi followed a new star, Simeon somehow "just knew," God spoke from a cloud to those at Jesus' Baptism, and the servants at the wedding in Cana knew when they saw the wine that came from the water jars. Even for us today, our faith in Christ is constantly deepening and strengthening as we recognize his gifts and power with ever-greater understanding.

## PREPARING TO CELEBRATE ORDINARY TIME IN THE CLASSROOM

You will need to replace your white cloth with a green one now that it is Ordinary Time again. Plan another procession with your students if they respond well to them. Otherwise, you might ask them if they have any ideas about how to change the cloths with care and dignity. You might be surprised at the depth of their suggestions.

From January 18 through 29, the Church joins with our Protestant brothers and sisters in the Week of Prayer for Christian Unity. A special prayer service, which may be used anytime during the week, is provided on page 169.

On February 2 we celebrate the Feast of the Presentation of the Lord, also known as "Candlemas." A special prayer service is provided on page 182. This is a beautiful feast to celebrate with children! Before you begin prayer

# WINTER ORDINARY TIME

that day, dim the classroom lights and light a candle. Help the student proclaiming the scripture to practice so that it can be done well and allow time for the class to ponder the story together. (See more below, under Prayers for Ordinary Time and A Note to Catechists.)

## SACRED SPACE

Now would be a good time to bring a potted plant to place on your prayer table. A spider plant or an ivy will withstand long weekends without attention. Give the care and watering over to your students. Make a job chart and allow them to take turns fetching water in a watering can for the plant. Watching the plant grow will provide a concrete sign of the growth that takes place in our hearts during this liturgical season.

## SACRED MUSIC

This would be the perfect time to learn how to sing one of the psalms. Psalm 27 ("The Lord Is My Light and My Salvation") and Psalm 23 ("The Lord Is My Shepherd") are two beautiful psalms that have many different musical settings.

Children also love to learn spirituals ("This Little Light of Mine," "Lord I Want to Be a Christian," and "There Is a Balm in Gilead"). Invite children to share favorite spiritual songs from their ethnic backgrounds and try singing songs from other countries ("We are Marching in the Light," "Pan de Vida," the round "Shalom Chevarim,").

Also, don't forget to sing Alleluia often during these days. When Lent arrives, we will have to wait a long time before Easter, when we can sing it again. The best Alleluia to sing is the one your parish uses before the Sunday Gospel.

## PRAYERS FOR ORDINARY TIME

Each night before going to bed, Catholic men and women around the world pray the "Canticle of Simeon," the prayer of the elderly man who met the Holy Family in the temple of Jerusalem when Mary and Joseph brought Jesus there as a baby. God had promised Simeon that he would not die before he saw the Messiah. So when Simeon saw the child Jesus, he took him in his arms and said this prayer:

"Master, now you are dismissing your servant
    in peace,
according to your word;
for my eyes have seen your salvation,
    which you have prepared in the presence
        of all peoples,
    a light for revelation to the Gentiles
        and for glory to your people Israel"
        (Luke 2:29–32).

Introduce this prayer on February 2, the feast of the Presentation of the Lord. You may want to ask the children about certain key words in the prayer. Possible "wondering" questions could include: Why does Simeon call himself God's "servant"? Does the word "servant" recall anything that Mary once said? How did Simeon know that Jesus was a special baby? How is this small baby a "light" and a "glory"?

## A NOTE TO CATECHISTS

Sometimes building codes will not allow school teachers or catechists to burn matches or light candles in the classroom. If possible, for February 2, plan a visit to a room where fire is permitted so that your celebration of the feast of the Presentation of the Lord will be set apart from the days surrounding it.

# GRACE BEFORE MEALS
## ORDINARY TIME • Winter

**LEADER:**
I will proclaim the goodness of God

**ALL: In the land of the living.**

✝ All make the Sign of the Cross.

**In the name of the Father and of the Son and of the Holy Spirit. Amen.**

**LEADER:**
Lord God Almighty,
you fill the hungry with good things.
May we see, in this food we are about to eat,
the wonder of your loving care for us,
in every part of our lives.
We ask this through your Son, our Lord
  Jesus Christ.

**ALL: Amen.**

✝ All make the Sign of the Cross.

**In the name of the Father and of the Son and of the Holy Spirit. Amen.**

# PRAYER AT DAY'S END
## ORDINARY TIME • Winter

**LEADER:**
May the peace of Christ reign in our hearts

**ALL: Now and forever.**

✢ All make the Sign of the Cross.

**In the name of the Father and of the Son and of the Holy Spirit. Amen.**

**LEADER:**
Dear God,
in this moment of quiet
at the end of our busy day,
may we turn to you with all our hearts.
Give us a safe journey home
and keep our hearts full of love for you.
Grant this through our Lord Jesus Christ,
    your Son, who lives and reigns with
    you in the unity of the Holy Spirit,
    one God, for ever and ever.
**Amen.**

✢ All make the Sign of the Cross.

**In the name of the Father and of the Son and of the Holy Spirit. Amen.**

# PRAYER FOR **MONDAY JANUARY 10, 2011**

## OPENING

Today we begin Ordinary Time—that part of the Church year that is outside the seasons of Advent, Christmas, Lent, Triduum [TRID-oo-uhm], and Easter. Each of the weeks of Ordinary Time is counted and we begin now with week one. Today's Gospel tells us how Jesus began his ministry by calling others to join him.

✢ All make the Sign of the Cross.

**In the name of the Father and of the Son and of the Holy Spirit. Amen.**

## PSALM (For a longer psalm, see page xiii.) Psalm 27:1b (1a)

The LORD is my light and my salvation;
  whom shall I fear?

**The LORD is my light and my salvation;
  whom shall I fear?**

The LORD is the stronghold of my life;
  of whom shall I be afraid?

**The LORD is my light and my salvation;
  whom shall I fear?**

◆ All stand and sing **Alleluia**.

## GOSPEL Mark 1:16–20

A reading from the holy Gospel according to Mark

As Jesus passed along the Sea of Galilee, he saw Simon and his brother Andrew casting a net into the sea; for they were fishermen. And Jesus said to them, "Follow me and I will make you fish for people." And immediately they left their nets and followed him. As he went a little farther, he saw James son of Zebedee and his brother John, who were in their boat mending the nets. Immediately he called them; and they left their father Zebedee in the boat with the hired men, and followed him.

The Gospel of the Lord.

◆ All sit and observe silence.

## FOR SILENT REFLECTION

Jesus is the Son of God, who has the power of God. Why do you think he calls ordinary people to help him in his ministry?

## CLOSING PRAYER

Let us stand and bring our hopes and needs to God as we pray, "Lord, hear our prayer."

◆ All may add their own prayers here.

Let us pray: **Our Father . . . Amen.**

Lord God,
on an ordinary day
Simon, Andrew, James and John,
were called to follow Jesus.
They could not have known
the wonders they would see,
the sorrows they would feel,
or the great work you were doing.
Yet they left everything and followed.
Help us to recognize our Savior's voice,
and give us hearts to respond without
    hesitation.
Grant this through the same Christ our Lord.
**Amen.**

✢ All make the Sign of the Cross.

# PRAYER FOR TUESDAY JANUARY 11, 2011

### OPENING

In today's Gospel, Jesus teaches as someone with authority [a-THOR-i-tee], which means power. He has the power to heal us, not only physically but also spiritually.

✢ All make the Sign of the Cross.

**In the name of the Father and of the Son and of the Holy Spirit. Amen.**

### PSALM  (For a longer psalm, see page xiii.) Psalm 27:1b (1a)

The LORD is my light and my salvation; whom shall I fear?

**The LORD is my light and my salvation; whom shall I fear?**

The LORD is the stronghold of my life; of whom shall I be afraid?

**The LORD is my light and my salvation; whom shall I fear?**

◆ All stand and sing **Alleluia**.

### GOSPEL  Mark 1:21–28

A reading from the holy Gospel according to Mark

Jesus and the disciples went to Capernaum; and when the sabbath came, he entered the synagogue and taught. They were astounded at his teaching, for he taught them as one having authority, and not as the scribes. Just then there was in their synagogue a man with an unclean spirit, and he cried out, "What have you to do with us, Jesus of Nazareth? Have you come to destroy us? I know who you are, the Holy One of God." But Jesus rebuked him, saying, "Be silent, and come out of him!" And the unclean spirit, throwing him into convulsions and crying with a loud voice, came out of him. They were all amazed, and they kept on asking one another, "What is this? A new teaching—with authority! He commands even the unclean spirits, and they obey him." At once his fame began to spread throughout the surrounding region of Galilee.

The Gospel of the Lord.

◆ All sit and observe silence.

### FOR SILENT REFLECTION

Does it ever feel like your spirit needs a healing from Jesus? How have you experienced his healing power?

### CLOSING PRAYER

Let us stand and bring our hopes and needs to God as we pray, "Lord, hear our prayer."

◆ All may add their own prayers here.

Let us pray: **Our Father . . . Amen.**

Almighty God,
come into our lives and make a difference.
Heal us of anger, impatience, and selfishness.
Fill us with your love and peace.
We ask this through Jesus Christ our Lord,
**Amen.**

✢ All make the Sign of the Cross.

**ALSO ON THIS DAY:** Vocation Awareness Week begins.

# PRAYER FOR **WEDNESDAY JANUARY 12, 2011**

## OPENING

Today's reading tells of the call of Samuel [SAM-yoo-uhl], who became a great prophet.

✚ All make the Sign of the Cross.

**In the name of the Father and of the Son and of the Holy Spirit. Amen.**

## PSALM  (For a longer psalm, see page xiii.) Psalm 27:1b (1a)

The LORD is my light and my salvation; whom shall I fear?

**The LORD is my light and my salvation; whom shall I fear?**

The LORD is the stronghold of my life; of whom shall I be afraid?

**The LORD is my light and my salvation; whom shall I fear?**

## READING  1 Samuel 3:1, 2a, 2c–9b

A reading from the First Book of Samuel [SAM-yoo-uhl]

Now the boy Samuel [SAM-yoo-uhl] was ministering to the LORD under Eli. The word of the LORD was rare in those days; visions were not widespread.

At that time Eli [EE-lī] was lying down in his room; the lamp of God had not yet gone out, and Samuel was lying down in the temple of the LORD, where the ark of God was. Then the LORD called, "Samuel! Samuel!" and he said, "Here I am!" and ran to Eli, and said, "Here I am, for you called me." But he said, "I did not call; lie down again." So he went and lay down. The LORD called again, "Samuel!" Samuel got up and went to Eli, and said, "Here I am, for you called me." But he said, "I did not call, my son; lie down again." Now Samuel did not yet know the LORD, and the word of the LORD had not yet been revealed to him. The LORD called Samuel again, a third time. And he got up and went to Eli, and said, "Here I am for you called me." Then Eli perceived [per-SEEVD] that the LORD was calling the boy. Therefore Eli said to Samuel, "Go, lie down; and if he calls you, you shall say, 'Speak, LORD, for your servant is listening.'"

The word of the Lord.

◆ All observe silence.

## FOR SILENT REFLECTION

Why do you think Samuel needs Eli to recognize that it is God calling? Who helps you hear God's voice in your life?

## CLOSING PRAYER

Let us stand and bring our hopes and needs to God as we pray, "Lord, hear our prayer."

◆ All may add their own prayers here.

Let us pray: **Our Father . . . Amen.**

Holy God,
help us to listen for your call.
May we find our joy in serving you.
We ask this through Christ our Lord.
**Amen.**

✚ All make the Sign of the Cross.

# PRAYER FOR THURSDAY JANUARY 13, 2011

## OPENING

We have heard how the disciples [dih-SI-puhlz] and the prophet Samuel [SAM-yoo-uhl] responded to God's call. In today's reading, Paul talks about how Christians should respond to God's call.

✛ All make the Sign of the Cross.

**In the name of the Father and of the Son and of the Holy Spirit. Amen.**

## PSALM     (For a longer psalm, see page xiii.) Psalm 27:1b (1a)

The LORD is my light and my salvation;
  whom shall I fear?

**The LORD is my light and my salvation;
  whom shall I fear?**

The LORD is the stronghold of my life;
  of whom shall I be afraid?

**The LORD is my light and my salvation;
  whom shall I fear?**

## READING     Hebrews 3:7–9; 12–14

A reading from the Letter to the Hebrews

Therefore, as the Holy Spirit says,
  "Today, if you hear his voice,
  do not harden your hearts as in
      the rebellion,
    as on the day of testing in the wilderness,
    where your ancestors put me to the test,
      though they had seen my works."
Take care, brothers and sisters, that none of you may have an evil, unbelieving heart that turns away from the living God. But exhort one another every day, as long as it is called "today", so that none of you may be hardened by the deceitfulness [dih-SEET-ful-ness] of sin. For we have become partners of Christ, if only we hold our first confidence firm to the end.

The word of the Lord.

◆ All observe silence.

## FOR SILENT REFLECTION

What does it mean to harden our hearts?

## CLOSING PRAYER

Let us stand and bring our hopes and needs to God as we pray, "Lord, hear our prayer."

◆ All may add their own prayers here.

Let us pray: **Our Father . . . Amen.**

Loving God,
the seed of eternal life
does not grow well in hard ground.
Give us the friendship of your saints
and our brothers and sisters in Christ
to soften our hearts with their love.
May these spiritual friendships help us
to live in your peace,
to recognize your voice when you call us
      to service,
and to respond to your call with confidence.
We ask this through your son, Jesus Christ
      our Lord.
**Amen.**

✛ All make the Sign of the Cross.

# PRAYER FOR **FRIDAY JANUARY 14, 2011**

## OPENING

In today's Gospel, a paralytic [PAYR-uh-lit-ik] is someone who cannot move.

✚ All make the Sign of the Cross.

**In the name of the Father and of the Son and of the Holy Spirit. Amen.**

## PSALM (For a longer psalm, see page xiii.) Psalm 27:1b (1a)

The LORD is my light and my salvation; whom shall I fear?

**The LORD is my light and my salvation; whom shall I fear?**

The LORD is the stronghold of my life; of whom shall I be afraid?

**The LORD is my light and my salvation; whom shall I fear?**

◆ All stand and sing **Alleluia**.

## GOSPEL  Mark 2:1b–2a, 2c–4b, 4d–12b

A reading from the holy Gospel according to Mark

It was reported that Jesus was at home. So many gathered around that there was no longer room for them, not even in front of the door; and he was speaking the word to them. Then some people came, bringing to him a paralyzed man, carried by four of them. And when they could not bring him to Jesus because of the crowd, they removed the roof above him; and they let down the mat on which the paralytic lay. When Jesus saw their faith, he said to the paralytic, "Son, your sins are forgiven." Now some of the scribes were sitting there, questioning in their hearts, "Why does this fellow speak in this way? It is blasphemy [BLAS-fuh-mee]! Who can forgive sins but God alone?" At once Jesus perceived [pur-SEEVD] in his spirit that they were discussing these questions among themselves; and he said to them, "Why do you raise such questions in your hearts? Which is easier, to say to the paralytic, 'Your sins are forgiven', or to say, 'Stand up and take your mat and walk'? But so that you may know that the Son of Man has authority on earth to forgive sins"—he said to the paralytic, "I say to you, stand up, take your mat and go to your home." And he stood up, and immediately took the mat and went out before all of them.

The Gospel of the Lord.

◆ All sit and observe silence.

## FOR SILENT REFLECTION

Who has helped you to come to Jesus?

## CLOSING PRAYER

Let us stand and bring our hopes and needs to God as we pray, "Lord, hear our prayer."

◆ All may add their own prayers here.

Let us pray: **Our Father . . . Amen.**

God, our Healer,
give us friends who will help us come to you.
We ask this through Jesus Christ our Lord.
**Amen.**

✚ All make the Sign of the Cross.

# PRAYER FOR THE WEEK

WITH A READING FROM THE GOSPEL FOR **SUNDAY, JANUARY 16, 2011**

## OPENING

In today's Gospel we hear the words of John the Baptist when he meets Jesus. John sees in Jesus the one whom God promised to send to heal the people of Israel and to bring light to all people.

**In the name of the Father and of the Son and of the Holy Spirit. Amen.**

## PSALM     (For a longer psalm, see page xiii.) Psalm 27:1b (1a)

The LORD is my light and my salvation;
  whom shall I fear?

**The LORD is my light and my salvation;
  whom shall I fear?**

The LORD is the stronghold of my life;
  of whom shall I be afraid?

**The LORD is my light and my salvation;
  whom shall I fear?**

◆ All stand and sing **Alleluia**.

## GOSPEL                              John 1:29–34

A reading from the holy Gospel according to John

The next day John the Baptist saw Jesus coming towards him and declared, "Here is the Lamb of God who takes away the sin of the world! This is he of whom I said, 'After me comes a man who ranks ahead of me because he was before me.' I myself did not know him; but I came baptizing with water for this reason, that he might be revealed to Israel." And John testified, "I saw the Spirit descending from heaven like a dove, and it remained on him. I myself did not know him, but the one who sent me to baptize with water said to me, 'He on whom you see the Spirit descend and remain is the one who baptizes with the Holy Spirit.' And I myself have seen and have testified that this is the Son of God."

The Gospel of the Lord.

◆ All sit and observe silence.

## FOR SILENT REFLECTION

When you meet Jesus in the words of scripture, whom do you see?

## CLOSING PRAYER

Let us stand and bring our hopes and needs to God as we pray, "Lord, hear our prayer."

◆ All may add their own prayers here.

Let us pray: **Our Father . . . Amen.**

Holy God,
you come to meet us through your Son.
You heal our wounds and give us light
to live with you in peace and joy.
Help us to listen when you speak to us
in the words of scripture,
the worship of the Church,
and in the silence of our own hearts.
Be our light, showing us the way to you.
We ask this through Jesus Christ our Lord.
**Amen.**

✢ All make the Sign of the Cross.

# PRAYER FOR MONDAY JANUARY 17, 2011

## OPENING

Today we remember Saint Anthony [AN-thuh-nee], a holy man of the fourth century. He taught us the importance of fasting (eating very little), prayer, gentleness, humility, love of the poor, and devotion to Christ. We will hear more about fasting in today's Gospel.

✚ All make the Sign of the Cross.

**In the name of the Father and of the Son and of the Holy Spirit. Amen.**

## PSALM   (For a longer psalm, see page xiii.) Psalm 27:1b (1a)

The LORD is my light and my salvation;
  whom shall I fear?

**The LORD is my light and my salvation;
  whom shall I fear?**

The LORD is the stronghold of my life;
  of whom shall I be afraid?

**The LORD is my light and my salvation;
  whom shall I fear?**

◆ All stand and sing **Alleluia**.

## GOSPEL   Mark 2:18–20

A reading from the holy Gospel according to Mark

Now John's disciples and the Pharisees were fasting; and people came and said to him, "Why do John's disciples and the disciples of the Pharisees fast, but your disciples do not fast?" Jesus said to them, "The wedding guests cannot fast while the bridegroom is with them, can they? As long as they have the bridegroom with them, they cannot fast. The days will come when the bridegroom is taken away from them, and then they will fast on that day."

The Gospel of the Lord.

◆ All sit and observe silence.

## FOR SILENT REFLECTION

Why do Christians fast?

## CLOSING PRAYER

Let us stand and bring our hopes and needs to God as we pray, "Lord, hear our prayer."

◆ All may add their own prayers here.

Let us pray: **Our Father . . . Amen.**

Lord God,
we know that you are never far from us
yet there are times when you seem distant.
Grant us patience when we feel far from you
and joy when we know you are near.
Teach us to desire you
more than anything else.
We ask this through Christ our Lord.
Amen.

✚ All make the Sign of the Cross.

---

**ALSO ON THIS DAY:** The Week of Prayer for Christian Unity begins.
Martin Luther King, Jr. Day (U.S.A.)

# PRAYER SERVICE
# FOR CHRISTIAN UNITY

*Prepare six leaders for this service. The second leader will need a Bible for the scripture and may need help finding it and practicing. You may begin by singing "We Are Many Parts" or "They'll Know We Are Christians By Our Love." You may conclude by singing "In Christ There Is No East or West." If the group will sing, prepare a song leader.*

**FIRST LEADER:**
The grace and peace of our Lord Jesus Christ be with us, now and for ever.
**Amen.**

✜ All make the Sign of the Cross.

**FIRST LEADER:**
Let us pray:
God of all the Nations,
through our Baptism,
you have joined us to you in Christ,
who is the source of our unity and peace.
Send your Spirit upon all Christians,
that we may live as one
in the perfect unity of the Holy Trinity.
We ask this through our Lord Jesus Christ,
your Son, who lives and reigns with you in
the unity of the Holy Spirit, one God,
forever and ever.
**Amen.**

◆ All stand and sing **Alleluia**.

**SECOND LEADER:** John 15:1–11
A reading from the holy Gospel according to John

◆ Read the passage from the Bible.

The Gospel of the Lord.

**THIRD LEADER:**
Let us pause and pray in silence for peace and unity among all Christians.

**FOURTH LEADER:**
Lord God,
grant that we may remain in your love
and always seek unity with all the branches
of the True Vine.
May we respect our brothers and sisters
   in Christ
and work tirelessly for reconciliation.
We ask this through Christ our Lord.
**Amen.**

**FIFTH LEADER:**
Now let us offer to one another a sign of Christ's peace:

◆ All offer one another a sign of peace.

**SIXTH LEADER:**
And may the Lord bless us,

✜ All make the Sign of the Cross.

protect us from all evil
and bring us to everlasting life.
**Amen.**

# PRAYER FOR TUESDAY JANUARY 18, 2011

## OPENING

Today's reading from the letter to the Hebrews encourages us to trust in God's promises. It speaks of God's promise to Abraham [AY-bruh-ham] that, even though Abraham was old and childless, God would provide many generations of descendants—as many as the stars in the sky. Abraham trusted in God and became the founding father of the Israelites.

✢ All make the Sign of the Cross.

**In the name of the Father and of the Son and of the Holy Spirit. Amen.**

## PSALM (For a longer psalm, see page xiii.) Psalm 27:1b (1a)

The LORD is my light and my salvation; whom shall I fear?

**The LORD is my light and my salvation; whom shall I fear?**

The LORD is the stronghold of my life; of whom shall I be afraid?

**The LORD is my light and my salvation; whom shall I fear?**

## READING    Hebrews 6:10–15

A reading from the letter to the Hebrews

For God is not unjust; he will not overlook your work and the love that you showed for his sake in serving the saints, as you still do. And we want each one of you to show the same diligence, so as to realize the full assurance of hope to the very end, so that you may not become sluggish, but imitators of those who, through faith and patience, inherit the promises. When God made a promise to Abraham, because he had no one greater by whom to swear, he swore by himself, saying, "I will surely bless you and multiply you." And thus Abraham, having patiently endured, obtained the promise.

The word of the Lord.

◆ All observe silence.

## FOR SILENT REFLECTION

What does God promise us?

## CLOSING PRAYER

Let us stand and bring our hopes and needs to God as we pray, "Lord, hear our prayer."

◆ All may add their own prayers here.

Let us pray: **Our Father . . . Amen.**

Faithful God,
how patiently you guide and care for us.
Give us faith in your word,
and hope in your steadfast love,
so that we will never lose heart.
Keep us mindful of your many blessings,
and help us to be a blessing to others.
We ask this through Jesus Christ, our Lord.
**Amen.**

✢ All make the Sign of the Cross.

# PRAYER FOR WEDNESDAY JANUARY 19, 2011

## OPENING

In today's Gospel, the Pharisees [FAIR-uh-seez] criticize Jesus for healing on the sabbath. According to Jewish law, one could heal on the sabbath if a person's life was in danger.

✢ All make the Sign of the Cross.

**In the name of the Father and of the Son and of the Holy Spirit. Amen.**

## PSALM
(For a longer psalm, see page xiii.) Psalm 27:1b (1a)

The LORD is my light and my salvation; whom shall I fear?

**The LORD is my light and my salvation; whom shall I fear?**

The LORD is the stronghold of my life; of whom shall I be afraid?

**The LORD is my light and my salvation; whom shall I fear?**

◆ All stand and sing **Alleluia**.

## GOSPEL
Mark 3:1–6

A reading from the holy Gospel according to Mark

Again he entered the synagogue, and a man was there who had a withered hand. They watched him to see whether he would cure him on the sabbath, so that they might accuse him. And he said to the man who had the withered hand, "Come forward." Then he said to them, "Is it lawful to do good or to do harm on the sabbath, to save life or to kill?" But they were silent. He looked around at them with anger; he was grieved at their hardness of heart and said to the man, "Stretch out your hand." He stretched it out, and his hand was restored. The Pharisees [FAIR-uh-seez] went out and immediately conspired with the Herodians [her-OH-dee-uhns] against him, how to destroy him.

The Gospel of the Lord.

◆ All sit and observe silence.

## FOR SILENT REFLECTION

Do you ever act in a hard-hearted way? What helps you to be more loving?

## CLOSING PRAYER

Let us stand and bring our hopes and needs to God as we pray, "Lord, hear our prayer."

◆ All may add their own prayers here.

Let us pray: **Our Father . . . Amen.**

God our Father,
may we never sadden you
by being selfish and uncaring.
Heal us from all unkindness and pride.
Let us rejoice not only in the gifts we receive
but also when others are blessed,
knowing that your great love
is given for the healing of all people.
We ask this through your Son, our Lord,
    Jesus Christ.
**Amen.**

✢ All make the Sign of the Cross.

# PRAYER FOR **THURSDAY JANUARY 20, 2011**

### OPENING

Today's Gospel tells of how many people come to Jesus because they have heard about his power to heal.

✠ All make the Sign of the Cross.

**In the name of the Father and of the Son and of the Holy Spirit. Amen.**

### PSALM  (For a longer psalm, see page xiii.) Psalm 27:1b (1a)

The LORD is my light and my salvation;
  whom shall I fear?

**The LORD is my light and my salvation;
  whom shall I fear?**

The LORD is the stronghold of my life;
  of whom shall I be afraid?

**The LORD is my light and my salvation;
  whom shall I fear?**

◆ All stand and sing **Alleluia.**

### GOSPEL                                    Mark 3:7–12

A reading from the holy Gospel according to Mark

Jesus departed with his disciples to the sea, and a great multitude from Galilee followed him; hearing all that he was doing, they came to him in great numbers from Judea, Jerusalem, Idumea, beyond the Jordan, and the region around Tyre and Sidon. He told his disciples to have a boat ready for him because of the crowd, so that they would not crush him; for he had cured many, so that all who had diseases pressed upon him to touch him. Whenever the unclean spirits saw him, they fell down before him and shouted, "You are the Son of God!" But he sternly ordered them not to make him known.

The Gospel of the Lord.

◆ All sit and observe silence.

### FOR SILENT REFLECTION

What draws you to Jesus?

### CLOSING PRAYER

Let us stand and bring our hopes and needs to God as we pray, "Lord, hear our prayer."

◆ All may add their own prayers here.

Let us pray: **Our Father . . . Amen.**

Loving God,
you come to make a difference
in our lives.
Touch us with your healing power.
Strengthen our bodies,
renew our minds,
and cleanse [klenz] our souls.
We ask this through Jesus Christ our Lord.
**Amen.**

✠ All make the Sign of the Cross.

---

**ALSO ON THIS DAY:** Tu B'Shvat (Jewish arbor day)

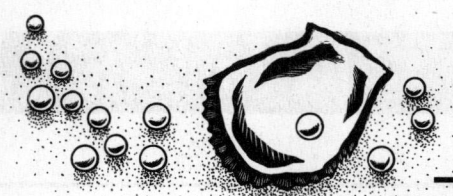

# PRAYER FOR FRIDAY JANUARY 21, 2011

## OPENING

Today we remember Saint Agnes [AG-nuhs], a young girl who died for her faith in fourth century Rome. Her name means lamb.

✢ All make the Sign of the Cross.

**In the name of the Father and of the Son and of the Holy Spirit. Amen.**

## PSALM
(For a longer psalm, see page xiii.) Psalm 27:1b (1a)

The LORD is my light and my salvation; whom shall I fear?

**The LORD is my light and my salvation; whom shall I fear?**

The LORD is the stronghold of my life; of whom shall I be afraid?

**The LORD is my light and my salvation; whom shall I fear?**

◆ All stand and sing **Alleluia.**

## GOSPEL
Mark 3:13–19

A reading from the holy Gospel according to Mark

Jesus went up the mountain and called to him those whom he wanted, and they came to him. And he appointed twelve, whom he also named apostles, to be with him, and to be sent out to proclaim the message, and to have authority to cast out demons. So he appointed the twelve: Simon (to whom he gave the name Peter); James son of Zebedee [ZEB-uh-dee] and John the brother of James (to whom he gave the name Boanerges [boh-uh-NUHR-jeez], that is, Sons of Thunder); and Andrew, and Philip [FIL-ip], and Bartholomew [bahr-THAL-uh-myoo], and Matthew, and Thomas [TOM-uhs], and James son of Alphaeus [AL-fee-uhs], and Thaddaeus [THAD-ee-uhs], and Simon the Cananaean [kay-nuh-NEE-uhn], and Judas Iscariot [is-KAYR-ee-uht], who betrayed him.

The Gospel of the Lord.

◆ All sit and observe silence.

## FOR SILENT REFLECTION

Why do you think Jesus went up the mountain when he called the apostles?

## CLOSING PRAYER

Let us stand and bring our hopes and needs to God as we pray, "Lord, hear our prayer."

◆ All may add their own prayers here.

Let us pray: **Our Father . . . Amen.**

Lord God,
grant your Church every grace.
Bless her ministers, guide her leaders,
and strengthen all who do the work of Christ.
We ask this through the same Jesus Christ our Lord.
**Amen.**

✢ All make the Sign of the Cross.

# PRAYER FOR THE WEEK

WITH A READING FROM THE GOSPEL FOR **SUNDAY, JANUARY 23, 2011**

## OPENING

Today's Gospel gives an example of how the life of Jesus fulfills the promises spoken by the prophets of Israel. A prophet is a person who carries God's messages to the people.

✚ All make the Sign of the Cross.

**In the name of the Father and of the Son and of the Holy Spirit. Amen.**

## PSALM  (For a longer psalm, see page xiii.) Psalm 27:1b (1a)

The LORD is my light and my salvation;
  whom shall I fear?

**The LORD is my light and my salvation;
  whom shall I fear?**

The LORD is the stronghold of my life;
  of whom shall I be afraid?

**The LORD is my light and my salvation;
  whom shall I fear?**

◆ All stand and sing **Alleluia**.

## GOSPEL  Matthew 4:12–17

A reading from the holy Gospel according to Matthew

Now when Jesus heard that John had been arrested, he withdrew to Galilee [GAL-ih-lee]. He left Nazareth [NAZ-uh-reth] and made his home in Capernaum [kuh-PER-nee-uhm] by the sea, in the territory of Zebulun [ZEB-yoo-luhn] and Naphtali [NAF-tuh-lee], so that what had been spoken through the prophet Isaiah might be fulfilled:

"Land of Zebulun, land of Naphtali,
  on the road by the sea, across the
    Jordan, Galilee of the Gentiles,
the people who sat in darkness
  have seen a great light,
and for those who sat in the region and
    shadow of death
light has dawned."

From that time Jesus began to proclaim, "Repent, for the kingdom of heaven has come near."

The Gospel of the Lord.

◆ All sit and observe silence.

## FOR SILENT REFLECTION

What do you think Jesus means when he says, "the kingdom of heaven has come near"?

## CLOSING PRAYER

Let us stand and bring our hopes and needs to God as we pray, "Lord, hear our prayer."

◆ All may add their own prayers here.

Let us pray: **Our Father . . . Amen.**

Holy God,
through Jesus you come near to us.
Help us to know just how near you are.
Touch our hearts and minds
when we study your holy words
and when we come together to pray.
We ask this through Christ our Lord.
**Amen.**

✚ All make the Sign of the Cross.

# PRAYER FOR MONDAY JANUARY 24, 2011

## OPENING

Today we remember Saint Francis de Sales, a bishop, preacher, and writer who believed that ordinary lives could and should be holy. Today's reading says that the priests in the temple of Jerusalem [juh-ROO-suh-lem] had made many sacrifices of animals, but Jesus made one sacrifice—of himself—on the cross. A sacrifice is an offering made to honor God, to atone for the people's sin, and to express relationship between God and humankind.

✚ All make the Sign of the Cross.

**In the name of the Father and of the Son and of the Holy Spirit. Amen.**

## PSALM  (For a longer psalm, see page xiii.) Psalm 27:1b (1a)

The LORD is my light and my salvation;
  whom shall I fear?

**The LORD is my light and my salvation;
  whom shall I fear?**

The LORD is the stronghold of my life;
  of whom shall I be afraid?

**The LORD is my light and my salvation;
  whom shall I fear?**

## READING  Hebrews 9:24–28

A reading from the Letter to the Hebrews [HEE-brooz]

For Christ did not enter a sanctuary made by human hands, a mere copy of the true one, but he entered into heaven itself, now to appear in the presence of God on our behalf. Nor was it to offer himself again and again, as the high priest enters the Holy Place year after year with blood that is not his own; for then he would have had to suffer again and again since the foundation of the world. But as it is, he has appeared once for all at the end of the age to remove sin by the sacrifice of himself. And just as it is appointed for mortals to die once, and after that the judgment, so Christ, having been offered once to bear the sins of many, will appear a second time, not to deal with sin, but to save those who are eagerly waiting for him.

The word of the Lord.

◆ All observe silence.

## FOR SILENT REFLECTION

What do you think the letter means when it says Jesus removes sin by the sacrifice of himself?

## CLOSING PRAYER

Let us stand and bring our hopes and needs to God as we pray, "Lord, hear our prayer."

◆ All may add their own prayers here.

Let us pray: **Our Father . . . Amen.**

Merciful God,
we thank you for the great sacrifice
Jesus made for us on the cross.
Help us to joyfully await his coming.
To you be all glory, for ever and ever.
**Amen.**

✚ All make the Sign of the Cross.

# PRAYER FOR **TUESDAY JANUARY 25, 2011**

## OPENING

Today we remember the Conversion [kuhn-VER-zuhn] of Saint Paul and we hear Paul telling the story of his experience on the road to Damascus [dum-MAS-kuhs]. Paul had persecuted Christians and now suddenly he would hear the voice of Christ and begin to change his life.

✚ All make the Sign of the Cross.

**In the name of the Father and of the Son and of the Holy Spirit. Amen.**

## PSALM  (For a longer psalm, see page xiii.) Psalm 27:1b (1a)

The LORD is my light and my salvation;
  whom shall I fear?

**The LORD is my light and my salvation;
  whom shall I fear?**

The LORD is the stronghold of my life;
  of whom shall I be afraid?

**The LORD is my light and my salvation;
  whom shall I fear?**

## READING  Acts 22:6–11

A reading from the Acts of the Apostles [uh-POS-lz]

Paul said, "While I was on my way and approaching Damascus, about noon a great light from heaven suddenly shone about me. I fell to the ground and heard a voice saying to me, 'Saul, Saul, why are you persecuting me?' I answered, 'Who are you, Lord?' Then he said to me, 'I am Jesus of Nazareth whom you are persecuting.' Now those who were with me saw the light but did not hear the voice of the one who was speaking to me. I asked, 'What am I to do, Lord?' The Lord said to me, 'Get up and go to Damascus; there you will be told everything that has been assigned to you to do.' Since I could not see because of the brightness of that light, those who were with me took my hand and led me to Damascus."

The word of the Lord.

◆ All observe silence.

## FOR SILENT REFLECTION

Most of us don't have big experiences of Jesus like Paul's. But even little experiences can change us. How has Jesus helped you to change and grow?

## CLOSING PRAYER

Let us stand and bring our hopes and needs to God as we pray, "Lord, hear our prayer."

◆ All may add their own prayers here.

Let us pray: **Our Father . . . Amen.**

Loving God,
we pray for our Christian family—
for everyone who is praying to be changed
and for those who do not even know
they need to change.
Help each of us to grow in your ways.
We ask this through Jesus Christ our Lord.
**Amen.**

✚ All make the Sign of the Cross.

**ALSO ON THIS DAY:** Week of Prayer for Christian Unity ends.

# PRAYER FOR WEDNESDAY JANUARY 26, 2011

## OPENING

Today we remember Saint Timothy [TIM-uh-thee and Saint Titus [TĪ-tuhs, both converts who worked with Saint Paul to spread the Good News. In today's Gospel, Jesus teaches about the kingdom of God.

+ All make the Sign of the Cross.

**In the name of the Father and of the Son and of the Holy Spirit. Amen.**

## PSALM (For a longer psalm, see page xiii.) Psalm 27:1b (1a)

The Lord is my light and my salvation;
 whom shall I fear?

**The Lord is my light and my salvation;
 whom shall I fear?**

The Lord is the stronghold of my life;
 of whom shall I be afraid?

**The Lord is my light and my salvation;
 whom shall I fear?**

◆ All stand and sing **Alleluia**.

## GOSPEL Mark 4:1–9

A reading from the holy Gospel according to Mark

Again Jesus began to teach beside the sea. Such a very large crowd gathered around him that he got into a boat on the sea and sat there, while the whole crowd was beside the sea on the land. He began to teach them many things in parables, and in his teaching he said to them: "Listen! A sower went out to sow. And as he sowed, some seed fell on the path, and the birds came and ate it up. Other seed fell on rocky ground, where it did not have much soil, and it sprang up quickly, since it had no depth of soil. And when the sun rose, it was scorched; and since it had no root, it withered away. Other seed fell among thorns, and the thorns grew up and choked it, and it yielded no grain. Other seed fell into good soil and brought forth grain, growing up and increasing and yielding thirty and sixty and a hundredfold." And he said, "Let anyone with ears to hear listen!"

The Gospel of the Lord.

◆ All sit and observe silence.

## FOR SILENT REFLECTION

How did Saint Paul, Saint Timothy, and Saint Titus help sow the seed?

## CLOSING PRAYER

Let us stand and bring our hopes and needs to God as we pray, "Lord, hear our prayer."

◆ All may add their own prayers here.

Let us pray: **Our Father . . . Amen.**

Lord God,
prepare our hearts and minds
to receive your holy word.
May faith, hope, and love planted in us
bear fruit in good works so that others may
 come to know you through us.
We ask this through Jesus Christ, our Lord.
**Amen.**

+ All make the Sign of the Cross.

# PRAYER FOR THURSDAY JANUARY 27, 2011

## OPENING

In today's Gospel, Jesus continues to teach us about the kingdom of God.

✠ All make the Sign of the Cross.

**In the name of the Father and of the Son and of the Holy Spirit. Amen.**

## PSALM (For a longer psalm, see page xiii.) Psalm 27:1b (1a)

The LORD is my light and my salvation;
   whom shall I fear?

**The LORD is my light and my salvation;
   whom shall I fear?**

The LORD is the stronghold of my life;
   of whom shall I be afraid?

**The LORD is my light and my salvation;
   whom shall I fear?**

◆ All stand and sing **Alleluia**.

## GOSPEL    Mark 4:21–25

A reading from the holy Gospel according to Mark

Jesus said to them, "Is a lamp brought in to be put under the bushel basket, or under the bed, and not on the lampstand? For there is nothing hidden, except to be disclosed; nor is anything secret, except to come to light. Let anyone with ears to hear listen!" And he said to them, "Pay attention to what you hear; the measure you give will be the measure you get, and still more will be given you. For to those who have, more will be given; and from those who have nothing, even what they have will be taken away."

The Gospel of the Lord.

◆ All sit and observe silence.

## FOR SILENT REFLECTION

What is the light of the lamp Jesus is talking about? Why can't it be hidden?

## CLOSING PRAYER

Let us stand and bring our hopes and needs to God as we pray, "Lord, hear our prayer."

◆ All may add their own prayers here.

Let us pray: **Our Father . . . Amen.**

God of light,
we long to give others your joy and peace;
but we cannot give what we have not received.
Open our hearts and minds
to receive your light.
Then we will live in that light
and our lives will praise you.
We ask this through Jesus Christ our Lord.
**Amen.**

✠ All make the Sign of the Cross.

**ALSO ON THIS DAY:** Holocaust Memorial Day

# PRAYER FOR FRIDAY JANUARY 28, 2011

## OPENING

Today we remember Saint Thomas Aquinas [uh-KWĪ-nuhs], a medieval scholar [SKAW-ler] who was one of the great teachers and writers of the Church. His wisdom was grounded in his lifelong study of scripture and a life of prayer. In the Gospel reading, Jesus uses the idea of a farmer's field of wheat to talk about what the kingdom of God is like.

✚ All make the Sign of the Cross.

**In the name of the Father and of the Son and of the Holy Spirit. Amen.**

## PSALM    (For a longer psalm, see page xiii.) Psalm 27:1b (1a)

The LORD is my light and my salvation;
    whom shall I fear?

**The LORD is my light and my salvation;
    whom shall I fear?**

The LORD is the stronghold of my life;
    of whom shall I be afraid?

**The LORD is my light and my salvation;
    whom shall I fear?**

◆ All stand and sing **Alleluia.**

## GOSPEL    Mark 4:26–29

A reading from the holy Gospel according to Mark

Jesus also said, "The kingdom of God is as if someone would scatter seed on the ground, and would sleep and rise night and day, and the seed would sprout and grow, he does not know how. The earth produces of itself, first the stalk, then the head, then the full grain in the head. But when the grain is ripe, at once he goes in with his sickle, because the harvest has come."

The Gospel of the Lord.

◆ All sit and observe silence.

## FOR SILENT REFLECTION

Do you see signs that God's kingdom is growing in your Church, in your family, in yourself? What are these signs?

## CLOSING PRAYER

Let us stand and bring our hopes and needs to God as we pray, "Lord, hear our prayer."

◆ All may add their own prayers here.

Let us pray: **Our Father . . . Amen.**

God our Creator,
your kingdom is always sprouting and
        budding,
even in places where we do not notice it.
Give us eyes to see it growing
and wisdom to help it increase.
We ask this through our Lord Jesus Christ,
        your Son, who lives and reigns with
        you in the unity of the Holy Spirit,
        one God, for ever and ever.
**Amen.**

✚ All make the Sign of the Cross.

# PRAYER FOR THE WEEK

WITH A READING FROM THE GOSPEL FOR **SUNDAY, JANUARY 30, 2011**

## OPENING

In today's Gospel we will hear six of the nine short teachings that Jesus offers just before giving his famous Sermon on the Mount. These teachings are called the Beatitudes [bee-AT-ih-toodz], because each begins with the words, "Blessed are."

✚ All make the Sign of the Cross.

**In the name of the Father and of the Son and of the Holy Spirit. Amen.**

## PSALM
(For a longer psalm, see page xiii.) Psalm 27:1b (1a)

The LORD is my light and my salvation;
  whom shall I fear?

**The LORD is my light and my salvation;
  whom shall I fear?**

The LORD is the stronghold of my life;
  of whom shall I be afraid?

**The LORD is my light and my salvation;
  whom shall I fear?**

◆ All stand and sing **Alleluia**.

## GOSPEL
Matthew 5:1–8

A reading from the holy Gospel according to Matthew

When Jesus saw the crowds, he went up the mountain; and after he had sat down, his disciples came to him. Then he began to speak and taught them, saying:
  "Blessed are the poor in spirit, for theirs is the kingdom of heaven.
  Blessed are those who mourn, for they will be comforted.
  Blessed are the meek, for they will inherit the earth.
  Blessed are those who hunger and thirst for righteousness,
    for they will be filled.
  Blessed are the merciful, for they will receive mercy.
  Blessed are the pure in heart, for they will see God."

The Gospel of the Lord.

◆ All sit and observe silence.

## FOR SILENT REFLECTION

What do you think it means to be blessed?
What blessings have you received?

## CLOSING PRAYER

Let us stand and bring our hopes and needs to God as we pray, "Lord, hear our prayer."

◆ All may add their own prayers here.

Let us pray: **Our Father . . . Amen.**

Loving God.
you bless us with such great love!
You remember the poor and the lonely.
May we never forget them either.
Help us to live as blessed people
with humility and holiness.
We ask this through Christ our Lord.
**Amen.**

✚ All make the Sign of the Cross.

**ALSO ON THIS DAY:** Catholic Schools Week begins.

# PRAYER FOR MONDAY
# JANUARY 31, 2011

## OPENING

Today we remember Saint John Bosco [BAW-skoh], who was devoted to educating poor children. The Gospel today shows Jesus' power to heal physical, mental, and spiritual illness.

✣ All make the Sign of the Cross.

**In the name of the Father and of the Son and of the Holy Spirit. Amen.**

## PSALM  (For a longer psalm, see page xiii.) Psalm 27:1b (1a)

The LORD is my light and my salvation;
  whom shall I fear?

**The LORD is my light and my salvation;
  whom shall I fear?**

The LORD is the stronghold of my life;
  of whom shall I be afraid?

**The LORD is my light and my salvation;
  whom shall I fear?**

◆ All stand and sing **Alleluia**.

## GOSPEL  Mark 5:1–3, 6–13a, 15ab

A reading from the holy Gospel according to Mark

They came to the other side of the sea, to the country of the Gerasenes [JEHR-uh-seenz]. And when Jesus had stepped out of the boat, immediately a man out of the tombs with an unclean spirit met him. He lived among the tombs; and no one could restrain him anymore, even with a chain. When he saw Jesus from a distance, he ran and bowed down before him; and he shouted at the top of his voice, "What have you to do with me, Jesus Son of the Most High God? I adjure you by God, do not torment me." For he had said to him, "Come out of the man, you unclean spirit." Then Jesus asked him, "What is your name?" He replied, "My name is Legion [LEE-juhn]; for we are many." He begged him earnestly not to send them out of the country. Now there on the hillside a great herd of swine was feeding; and the unclean spirits begged him, "Send us into the swine; let us enter them." So he gave them permission.

People came to Jesus and saw the demoniac [duh-MAH-nee-ak] sitting there, clothed and in his right mind.

The Gospel of the Lord.

◆ All sit and observe silence.

## FOR SILENT REFLECTION

Why do you think the unclean spirits know who Jesus is?

## CLOSING PRAYER

Let us stand and bring our hopes and needs to God as we pray, "Lord, hear our prayer."

◆ All may add their own prayers here.

Let us pray: **Our Father . . . Amen.**

Compassionate [com-PASH-uh-net] God,
we pray for all
who feel hopeless and abandoned.
May they know your healing love.
Grant this through Christ our Lord.
**Amen.**

✣ All make the Sign of the Cross.

**ALSO ON THIS DAY:** Catholic Schools Week continues.

# PRAYER SERVICE
## FEAST OF THE PRESENTATION OF THE LORD

*Prepare six leaders for this service. The third and fourth leaders will need a Bible for the scripture passage and may need help finding it and practicing. You may wish to begin by singing "I Want to Walk as a Child of the Light" and conclude with "The Light of Christ Has Come into the World." If there will be singing, prepare a song leader.*

**FIRST LEADER:**
May the light of Christ surround us.

**ALL: Amen.**

**FIRST LEADER:**
Today we celebrate the feast of the Presentation of the Lord. When Jesus was still a newborn, his parents, Mary and Joseph, brought him to the temple in Jerusalem. The word "presentation" means showing. All parents would bring their firstborn sons to the temple to show them to God. While Mary and Joseph were in the temple, two elderly people came up to them and recognized who their baby, Jesus, really was!

**SECOND LEADER:**

✚ All make the Sign of the Cross.

> **In the name of the Father and of the Son and of the Holy Spirit. Amen.**

Let us pray:
Loving God, give us the eyes of Mary and Joseph to see your marvelous work alive in our own lives. We ask this through Christ our Lord.

**ALL: Amen.**

◆ All stand and sing **Alleluia**.

**THIRD LEADER:** Luke 2:22–32
A reading from the holy Gospel according to Luke

◆ Read the Gospel passage from the Bible.

**FOURTH LEADER:** Luke 2:33–38

◆ Read the Gospel passage from the Bible.

The Gospel of the Lord.

◆ All sit and observe silence.

**FIFTH LEADER:**
Let us bring our hopes and needs to God as we pray, **Lord, hear our prayer.**

• For all of us, that we may see the world as Simeon and Anna did and be mindful of your Light, we pray to the Lord.

• For newborn babies, may they receive your Light in Baptism, we pray to the Lord.

• For the elderly, the sick, and for those who have died, we pray to the Lord.

• That through the intercession of the Holy Family, all people may come to respect and protect life from the moment of conception until natural death, we pray to the Lord.

**SIXTH LEADER:**
Let us pray: **Our Father . . . Amen.**

Lord God, like Simeon we thank you for showing us your salvation in the light of Christ Jesus. Keep us ever mindful of this grace. Grant this through Jesus Christ, our Lord.

**ALL: Amen.**

✚ All make the Sign of the Cross.

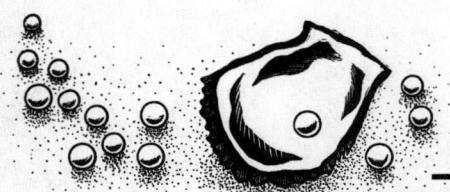

# PRAYER FOR **TUESDAY FEBRUARY 1, 2011**

## OPENING

In today's Gospel, Jesus heals a young girl who was believed to be dead.

✝ All make the Sign of the Cross.

**In the name of the Father and of the Son and of the Holy Spirit. Amen.**

## PSALM  (For a longer psalm, see page xiii.) Psalm 27:1b (1a)

The LORD is my light and my salvation; whom shall I fear?

**The LORD is my light and my salvation; whom shall I fear?**

The LORD is the stronghold of my life; of whom shall I be afraid?

**The LORD is my light and my salvation; whom shall I fear?**

◆ All stand and sing **Alleluia.**

## GOSPEL  Mark 5:35–43

A reading from the holy Gospel according to Mark

While he was still speaking, some people came from the leader's house to say, "Your daughter is dead. Why trouble the teacher any further?" But overhearing what they said, Jesus said to the leader of the synagogue, "Do not fear, only believe." He allowed no one to follow him except Peter, James, and John, the brother of James. When they came to the house of the leader of the synagogue, he saw a commotion, people weeping and wailing loudly. When he had entered, he said to them, "Why do you make a commotion and weep? The child is not dead but sleeping." And they laughed at him. Then he put them all outside, and took the child's father and mother and those who were with him, and went in where the child was. He took her by the hand and said to her, "Talitha cum" [TAH-lee-thah-KOOM], which means, "Little girl, get up!" And immediately the girl got up and began to walk about (she was twelve years of age). At this they were overcome with amazement. He strictly ordered them that no one should know this, and told them to give her something to eat.

The Gospel of the Lord.

◆ All sit and observe silence.

## FOR SILENT REFLECTION

What does this story tell us about Jesus?

## CLOSING PRAYER

Let us stand and bring our hopes and needs to God as we pray, "Lord, hear our prayer."

◆ All may add their own prayers here.

Let us pray: **Our Father . . . Amen.**

God of power and life,
you had compassion on a young child.
Give us faith in your great power
and trust in your love for us.
Grant this through Jesus Christ our Lord.
**Amen.**

✝ All make the Sign of the Cross.

**ALSO ON THIS DAY:** Groundhog Day (U.S.A.) (Canada) Catholic Schools Week continues.

# PRAYER FOR **WEDNESDAY** **FEBRUARY 2, 2011**

### OPENING

Today is the feast of the Presentation of the Lord. When today's Gospel reading begins, Mary and Joseph have brought the baby Jesus to the temple in Jerusalem to fulfill the commandment to present their firstborn son to the Lord. They have just met the old prophet Simeon [SIM-ee-uhn]. Listen to what Simeon says and see if you can figure out why it is customary to bless candles on this day. The Messiah [meh-SĪ-uh] was the great leader, promised by the prophets in the Old Testament, who would be sent by God to rescue the people of Israel.

✚ All make the Sign of the Cross.

**In the name of the Father and of the Son and of the Holy Spirit. Amen.**

### PSALM   (For a longer psalm, see page xiii.) Psalm 27:1b (1a)

The LORD is my light and my salvation;
  whom shall I fear?

**The LORD is my light and my salvation;
  whom shall I fear?**

The LORD is the stronghold of my life;
  of whom shall I be afraid?

**The LORD is my light and my salvation;
  whom shall I fear?**

◆ All stand and sing **Alleluia**.

### GOSPEL   Luke 2:27–33

A reading from the holy Gospel according to Luke

Guided by the Spirit, Simeon came into the temple; and when the parents brought in the child Jesus, to do for him what was customary under the law, Simeon took him in his arms and praised God, saying,
  "Master, now you are dismissing your
    servant in peace,
    according to your word;
  for my eyes have seen your salvation,
    which you have prepared in the presence
      of all peoples,
  a light for revelation to the Gentiles
    and for glory to your people Israel."
And the child's father and mother were amazed at what was being said about him.

The Gospel of the Lord.

◆ All sit and observe silence.

### FOR SILENT REFLECTION

How could Simeon know these things?

### CLOSING PRAYER

Let us stand and bring our hopes and needs to God as we pray, "Lord, hear our prayer."

◆ All may add their own prayers here.

Let us pray: **Our Father . . . Amen.**

Eternal God,
you sent your Son to save all people.
Help us to spread his light.
We ask this through the same Jesus Christ
  our Lord.
**Amen.**

✚ All make the Sign of the Cross.

---

**ALSO ON THIS DAY:** Catholic Schools Week continues.

# PRAYER FOR THURSDAY FEBRUARY 3, 2011

## OPENING

Today we remember Saint Blaise [blayz], a doctor and bishop who is patron saint of the sick, especially those with illnesses of the throat. According to tradition, the saint once saved the life of a young boy who was choking on a fishbone. In many churches today, people will have their throats blessed. Today's Gospel tells of the disciples going out to teach and to heal.

✢ All make the Sign of the Cross.

**In the name of the Father and of the Son and of the Holy Spirit. Amen.**

## PSALM  (For a longer psalm, see page xiii.) Psalm 27:1b (1a)

The LORD is my light and my salvation;
  whom shall I fear?

**The LORD is my light and my salvation;
  whom shall I fear?**

The LORD is the stronghold of my life;
  of whom shall I be afraid?

**The LORD is my light and my salvation;
  whom shall I fear?**

◆ All stand and sing **Alleluia.**

## GOSPEL  Mark 6:7–13

A reading from the holy Gospel according to Mark

He called the twelve and began to send them out two by two, and gave them authority over the unclean spirits. He ordered them to take nothing for their journey except a staff; no bread, no bag, no money in their belts; but to wear sandals and not to put on two tunics. He said to them, "Whenever you enter a house, stay there until you leave the place. If any place will not welcome you and they refuse to hear you, as you leave, shake off the dust that is on your feet as a testimony against them." So they went out and proclaimed that all should repent. They cast out many demons, and anointed with oil many who were sick and cured them.

The Gospel of the Lord.

◆ All sit and observe silence.

## FOR SILENT REFLECTION

Why do you think Jesus sent his disciples two by two? Does this remind you of another story in scripture?

## CLOSING PRAYER

Let us stand and bring our hopes and needs to God as we pray, "Lord, hear our prayer."

◆ All may add their own prayers here.

Let us pray: **Our Father . . . Amen.**

Lord God,
we pray for those called to ministry.
May they hear your voice
and have the courage to answer your call.
We ask this through Jesus Christ our Lord.
**Amen.**

✢ All make the Sign of the Cross.

**ALSO ON THIS DAY:** Lunar New Year (Chinese, Vietnamese, Year of the Rabbit)
Catholic Schools Week continues.

# PRAYER FOR FRIDAY FEBRUARY 4, 2011

## OPENING

In today's reading, we learn how Christians are to live. To be undefiled [un-dee-FILD] means to be pure.

✦ All make the Sign of the Cross.

**In the name of the Father and of the Son and of the Holy Spirit. Amen.**

## PSALM
(For a longer psalm, see page xiii.) Psalm 27:1b (1a)

The Lord is my light and my salvation;
 whom shall I fear?

**The Lord is my light and my salvation;
 whom shall I fear?**

The Lord is the stronghold of my life;
 of whom shall I be afraid?

**The Lord is my light and my salvation;
 whom shall I fear?**

## READING
Hebrews 13:1–6

A reading from the Letter to the Hebrews [HEE-brooz]

Let mutual love continue. Do not neglect to show hospitality to strangers, for by doing that some have entertained angels without knowing it. Remember those who are in prison, as though you were in prison with them; those who are being tortured, as though you yourselves were being tortured. Let marriage be held in honor by all, and let the marriage bed be kept undefiled [un-dee-FYLD]; for God will judge fornicators and adulterers. Keep your lives free from the love of money, and be content with what you have; for he has said, "I will never leave you or forsake you." So we can say with confidence:
 "The Lord is my helper;
  I will not be afraid.
 What can anyone do to me?"

The word of the Lord.

◆ All observe silence.

## FOR SILENT REFLECTION

How are you showing God's love to others in your life?

## CLOSING PRAYER

Let us stand and bring our hopes and needs to God as we pray, "Lord, hear our prayer."

◆ All may add their own prayers here.

Let us pray: **Our Father . . . Amen.**

Loving God,
open our hearts
to befriend the friendless
and to help those in need.
Make us content with what we have,
knowing that you generously give us
whatever we need.
We ask this through Jesus Christ our Lord.
**Amen.**

✦ All make the Sign of the Cross.

---

**ALSO ON THIS DAY:** Catholic Schools Week ends.

# PRAYER FOR THE WEEK

WITH A READING FROM THE GOSPEL FOR **SUNDAY, FEBRUARY 6, 2011**

## OPENING

In today's Gospel, Jesus compares Christians to salt and light. These are ordinary things that we encounter every day. Listen to how Jesus uses these common things to talk about being a Christian.

✚ All make the Sign of the Cross.

**In the name of the Father and of the Son and of the Holy Spirit. Amen.**

## PSALM (For a longer psalm, see page xiii.) Psalm 27:1b (1a)

The Lord is my light and my salvation; whom shall I fear?

**The Lord is my light and my salvation; whom shall I fear?**

The Lord is the stronghold of my life; of whom shall I be afraid?

**The Lord is my light and my salvation; whom shall I fear?**

◆ All stand and sing **Alleluia**.

## GOSPEL                Matthew 5:13–16

A reading from the holy Gospel according to Matthew

Jesus said: "You are the salt of the earth; but if salt has lost its taste, how can its saltiness be restored? It is no longer good for anything, but is thrown out and trampled under foot.

You are the light of the world. A city built on a hill cannot be hidden. No one after lighting a lamp puts it under the bushel basket, but on the lampstand, and it gives light to all in the house. In the same way, let your light shine before others, so that they may see your good works and give glory to your Father in heaven."

The Gospel of the Lord.

◆ All sit and observe silence.

## FOR SILENT REFLECTION

Salt is used in cooking because it draws out the flavors of food. What does the Christian draw out in the world? What does Christ bring out in you?

## CLOSING PRAYER

Let us stand and bring our hopes and needs to God as we pray, "Lord, hear our prayer."

◆ All may add their own prayers here.

Let us pray: **Our Father . . . Amen.**

Holy God,
fill us with your love
and help us to live in your peace.
May we be a blessing to others
so that all may taste and see
the goodness of the Lord.
We ask this through Jesus Christ our Lord.
**Amen.**

✚ All make the Sign of the Cross.

---

**ALSO ON THIS DAY:** World Day for Consecrated Life
Boy Scout Sunday (U.S.A.),(Canada)

# PRAYER FOR MONDAY FEBRUARY 7, 2011

### OPENING

Today's Gospel tells of the great healing power Jesus has. He and the disciples have been traveling by boat around the Sea of Galilee [GAL-ih-lee], visiting villages so that Jesus can teach and heal.

✢ All make the Sign of the Cross.

**In the name of the Father and of the Son and of the Holy Spirit. Amen.**

### PSALM (For a longer psalm, see page xiii.) Psalm 27:1b (1a)

The LORD is my light and my salvation; whom shall I fear?

**The LORD is my light and my salvation; whom shall I fear?**

The LORD is the stronghold of my life; of whom shall I be afraid?

**The LORD is my light and my salvation; whom shall I fear?**

◆ All stand and sing **Alleluia**.

### GOSPEL                                Mark 6:53–56

A reading from the holy Gospel according to Mark

When Jesus and the disciples had crossed over, they came to land at Gennesaret [geh-NES-uh-ret] and moored the boat. When they got out of the boat, people at once recognized him and rushed about that whole region and began to bring the sick on mats to wherever they heard he was. And wherever he went, into villages or cities or farms, they laid the sick in the marketplaces, and begged him that they might touch even the fringe of his cloak; and all who touched it were healed.

The Gospel of the Lord.

◆ All sit and observe silence.

### FOR SILENT REFLECTION

How can we "touch" Jesus when we need healing?

### CLOSING PRAYER

Let us stand and bring our hopes and needs to God as we pray, "Lord, hear our prayer."

◆ All may add their own prayers here.

Let us pray: **Our Father . . . Amen.**

God, our Healer,
we thank you
for the healing words of scripture;
the sacraments of healing;
the gifts of healing you have given
to doctors, nurses, therapists and ministers;
and for the healing love
of family and friends.
Help us to know that you, in so many ways,
are always close to us.
We ask this through your Son, our Lord,
    Jesus Christ.
**Amen.**

✢ All make the Sign of the Cross.

# PRAYER FOR TUESDAY FEBRUARY 8, 2011

## OPENING

Today we remember Saint Josephine Bakhita [JOH-suh-feen buh-KEE-tuh]. She was born in Darfur, [dar-FUR] Sudan [soo-DAN] in 1869, and she was captured and sold into slavery when she was a young girl and taken to Italy. When she became an adult, she fought for her freedom in an Italian court and won. She became a nun, and was much loved by the children at the sisters' school. The reading today tells part of the wonderful story of creation.

✚ All make the Sign of the Cross.

**In the name of the Father and of the Son and of the Holy Spirit. Amen.**

## PSALM  (For a longer psalm, see page xiii.) Psalm 27:1b (1a)

The LORD is my light and my salvation;
 whom shall I fear?

**The LORD is my light and my salvation;
 whom shall I fear?**

The LORD is the stronghold of my life;
 of whom shall I be afraid?

**The LORD is my light and my salvation;
 whom shall I fear?**

## READING  Genesis 1:26–28, 30b, 31

A reading from the Book of Genesis [JEN-uh-sis]

Then God said, "Let us make humankind in our image, according to our likeness; and let them have dominion over the fish of the sea, and over the birds of the air, and over the cattle, and over all the wild animals of the earth, and over every creeping thing that creeps upon the earth."
 So God created humankind in his image,
  in the image of God he created them;
  male and female he created them.
God blessed them, and God said to them, "Be fruitful and multiply, and fill the earth and subdue it; and have dominion over the fish of the sea and over the birds of the air and over every living thing that moves upon the earth." And it was so. God saw everything that he had made, and indeed, it was very good. And there was evening and there was morning, the sixth day.

The word of the Lord.

◆ All observe silence.

## FOR SILENT REFLECTION

According to the story, how are we like God?

## CLOSING PRAYER

Let us stand and bring our hopes and needs to God as we pray, "Lord, hear our prayer."

◆ All may add their own prayers here.

Let us pray: **Our Father . . . Amen.**

God of Creation,
you made us in your image.
Help us to grow in your likeness.
We ask this through Christ our Lord.
**Amen.**

✚ All make the Sign of the Cross.

# PRAYER FOR **WEDNESDAY FEBRUARY 9, 2011**

## OPENING

Today's reading tells a second story of how God created humankind. Listen for what is similar to and what is different from the story we heard yesterday.

✤ All make the Sign of the Cross.

**In the name of the Father and of the Son and of the Holy Spirit. Amen.**

## PSALM
(For a longer psalm, see page xiii.) Psalm 27:1b (1a)

The LORD is my light and my salvation;
  whom shall I fear?

**The LORD is my light and my salvation;
  whom shall I fear?**

The LORD is the stronghold of my life;
  of whom shall I be afraid?

**The LORD is my light and my salvation;
  whom shall I fear?**

## READING
Genesis 2:4b–9

A reading from the Book of Genesis [JEN-uh-sis]

In the day that the LORD God made the earth and the heavens, when no plant of the field was yet in the earth and no herb of the field had yet sprung up—for the LORD God had not caused it to rain upon the earth, and there was no one to till the ground; but a stream would rise from the earth, and water the whole face of the ground—then the LORD God formed man from the dust of the ground, and breathed into his nostrils the breath of life; and the man became a living being. And the LORD God planted a garden in Eden, in the east; and there he put the man whom he had formed. Out of the ground the LORD God made to grow every tree that is pleasant to the sight and good for food, the tree of life also in the midst of the garden, and the tree of the knowledge of good and evil.

The word of the Lord.

◆ All observe silence.

## FOR SILENT REFLECTION

What does this story tell us about the relationship between human beings and the rest of creation?

## CLOSING PRAYER

Let us stand and bring our hopes and needs to God as we pray, "Lord, hear our prayer."

◆ All may add their own prayers here.

Let us pray: **Our Father . . . Amen.**

God, our Creator
you have given us a place to live,
that gives us food for our bodies
and beauty for the joy of our souls.
Help us to take care
of this wonderful creation.
We ask this through our Lord Jesus Christ,
  your Son, who lives and reigns with
  you in the unity of the Holy Spirit,
  one God, for ever and ever.
**Amen.**

✤ All make the Sign of the Cross.

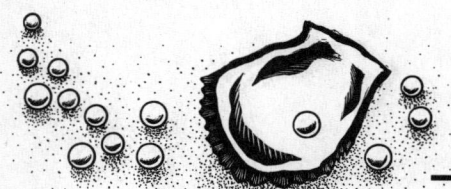

# PRAYER FOR THURSDAY FEBRUARY 10, 2011

## OPENING

Listen to what today's reading tells us about the creation of men and women.

✚ All make the Sign of the Cross.

**In the name of the Father and of the Son and of the Holy Spirit. Amen.**

## PSALM
(For a longer psalm, see page xiii.) Psalm 27:1b (1a)

The LORD is my light and my salvation;
    whom shall I fear?

**The LORD is my light and my salvation;
    whom shall I fear?**

The LORD is the stronghold of my life;
    of whom shall I be afraid?

**The LORD is my light and my salvation;
    whom shall I fear?**

## READING
Genesis 2:18–25

A reading from the Book of Genesis [JEN-uh-sis]

Then the LORD God said, "It is not good that the man should be alone; I will make him a helper as his partner." So out of the ground the LORD God formed every animal of the field and every bird of the air, and brought them to the man to see what he would call them; and whatever the man called each living creature, that was its name. The man gave names to all cattle, and to the birds of the air, and to every animal of the field; but for the man there was not found a helper as his partner. So the LORD God caused a deep sleep to fall upon the man, and he slept; then he took one of his ribs and closed up its place with flesh. And the rib that the LORD God had taken from the man he made into a woman and brought her to the man. Then the man said, "This at last is bone of my bones and flesh of my flesh; this one shall be called 'Woman,' for out of 'Man' this one was taken." Therefore a man leaves his father and his mother and clings to his wife, and they become one flesh. And the man and his wife were both naked, and were not ashamed.

The word of the Lord.

◆ All observe silence.

## FOR SILENT REFLECTION

How are men and women partners?

## CLOSING PRAYER

Let us stand and bring our hopes and needs to God as we pray, "Lord, hear our prayer."

◆ All may add their own prayers here.

Let us pray: **Our Father . . . Amen.**

Loving God,
we pray for all married people.
Give them the grace to work together
for peace in their homes,
the health and holiness of their children,
and the companionship of one another.
We ask this in the name of Jesus, our Lord.
**Amen.**

✚ All make the Sign of the Cross.

# PRAYER FOR FRIDAY FEBRUARY 11, 2011

### OPENING

Today's reading from Genesis [JEN-uh-sis] tells of how Adam and Eve disobeyed God.

✚ All make the Sign of the Cross.

**In the name of the Father and of the Son and of the Holy Spirit. Amen.**

### PSALM
(For a longer psalm, see page xiii.) Psalm 27:1b (1a)

The LORD is my light and my salvation;
 whom shall I fear?

**The LORD is my light and my salvation;
 whom shall I fear?**

The LORD is the stronghold of my life;
 of whom shall I be afraid?

**The LORD is my light and my salvation;
 whom shall I fear?**

### READING
Genesis 3:1–8

A reading from the book of Genesis [JEN-uh-sis]

Now the serpent was more crafty than any other wild animal that the LORD God had made. He said to the woman, "Did God say, 'You shall not eat from any tree in the garden'?" The woman said to the serpent, "We may eat of the fruit of the trees in the garden; but God said, 'You shall not eat of the fruit of the tree that is in the middle of the garden, nor shall you touch it, or you shall die.'" But the serpent said to the woman, "You will not die; for God knows that when you eat of it your eyes will be opened, and you will be like God, knowing good and evil." So when the woman saw that the tree was good for food, and that it was a delight to the eyes, and that the tree was to be desired to make one wise, she took of its fruit and ate; and she also gave some to her husband, who was with her, and he ate. Then the eyes of both were opened, and they knew that they were naked; and they sewed fig leaves together and made loincloths for themselves. They heard the sound of the LORD God walking in the garden at the time of the evening breeze, and the man and his wife hid themselves from the presence of the LORD God among the trees of the garden.

The word of the Lord.

◆ All observe silence.

### FOR SILENT REFLECTION

How do Adam and Eve feel after they disobey God? How would you feel?

### CLOSING PRAYER

Let us stand and bring our hopes and needs to God as we pray, "Lord, hear our prayer."

◆ All may add their own prayers here.

Let us pray: **Our Father . . . Amen.**

God, our Creator,
give us friends who will help us do good.
Then we will feel joy, not shame,
 in your presence.
We ask this through Jesus Christ our Lord.
**Amen.**

✚ All make the Sign of the Cross.

**ALSO ON THIS DAY:** World Day of Prayer for the Sick

# PRAYER FOR THE WEEK

WITH A READING FROM THE GOSPEL FOR **SUNDAY, FEBRUARY 13, 2011**

## OPENING

God gave the Jewish people the commandments so that, following these commandments, they could be close to God. Listen to what Jesus says in today's Gospel about the commandments and what he has come to do.

✚ All make the Sign of the Cross.

**In the name of the Father and of the Son and of the Holy Spirit. Amen.**

## PSALM  (For a longer psalm, see page xiii.) Psalm 27:1b (1a)

The LORD is my light and my salvation; whom shall I fear?

**The LORD is my light and my salvation; whom shall I fear?**

The LORD is the stronghold of my life; of whom shall I be afraid?

**The LORD is my light and my salvation; whom shall I fear?**

◆ All stand and sing **Alleluia**.

## GOSPEL  Matthew 5:17–20

A reading from the holy Gospel according to Matthew

Jesus said, "Do not think that I have come to abolish the law or the prophets; I have come not to abolish but to fulfill. For truly I tell you, until heaven and earth pass away, not one letter, not one stroke of a letter, will pass from the law until all is accomplished. Therefore, whoever breaks one of the least of these commandments, and teaches others to do the same, will be called least in the kingdom of heaven; but whoever does them and teaches them will be called great in the kingdom of heaven. For I tell you, unless your righteousness exceeds that of the scribes and Pharisees, you will never enter the kingdom of heaven."

The Gospel of the Lord.

◆ All sit and observe silence.

## FOR SILENT REFLECTION

What are some of the commandments Jesus is talking about?

## CLOSING PRAYER

Let us stand and bring our hopes and needs to God as we pray, "Lord, hear our prayer."

◆ All may add their own prayers here.

Let us pray: **Our Father . . . Amen.**

Loving God,
you show us the way to you
by giving us your commandments,
and giving us Jesus as an example to follow.
Help us to walk in your way of love.
And, should we lose our way,
turn our hearts back to you.
We ask this through the same Jesus Christ
    our Lord.
**Amen.**

✚ All make the Sign of the Cross.

---

**ALSO ON THIS DAY:** World Marriage Day

# PRAYER FOR MONDAY FEBRUARY 14, 2011

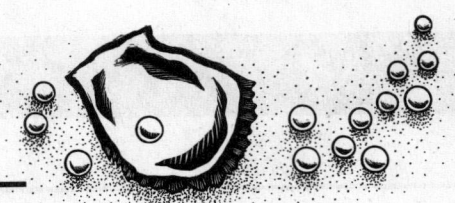

### OPENING

Today we continue reading from the book of Genesis [JEN-uh-sis]. Notice what God says to Cain about his feelings of resentment.

+ All make the Sign of the Cross.

**In the name of the Father and of the Son and of the Holy Spirit. Amen.**

### PSALM
(For a longer psalm, see page xiii.) Psalm 27:1b (1a)

The LORD is my light and my salvation;
  whom shall I fear?

**The LORD is my light and my salvation;
  whom shall I fear?**

The LORD is the stronghold of my life;
  of whom shall I be afraid?

**The LORD is my light and my salvation;
  whom shall I fear?**

### READING
Genesis 4:1–7

A reading from the Book of Genesis [JEN-uh-sis]

Now the man knew his wife Eve, and she conceived and bore Cain, saying, "I have produced a man with the help of the Lord." Next she bore his brother Abel. Now Abel was a keeper of sheep, and Cain a tiller of the ground. In the course of time Cain brought to the LORD an offering of the fruit of the ground, and Abel for his part brought of the firstlings of his flock, their fat portions. And the LORD had regard for Abel and his offering, but for Cain and his offering he had no regard. So Cain was very angry, and his countenance fell. The LORD said to Cain, "Why are you angry, and why has your countenance fallen? If you do well, will you not be accepted? And if you do not do well, sin is lurking at the door; its desire is for you, but you must master it."

The word of the Lord.

◆ All observe silence.

### FOR SILENT REFLECTION

Do you ever feel angry? What can you do to get over your anger?

### CLOSING PRAYER

Let us stand and bring our hopes and needs to God as we pray, "Lord, hear our prayer."

◆ All may add their own prayers here.

Let us pray: **Our Father . . . Amen.**

God our Father,
rid us of all our resentment.
Help us to believe that you love us,
and to trust that with your grace
we can do well in life.
Protect us from sin
and give us holy and loving thoughts.
We ask this through Jesus Christ our Lord.
**Amen.**

+ All make the Sign of the Cross.

---

**ALSO ON THIS DAY:** Valentine's Day

# PRAYER FOR TUESDAY FEBRUARY 15, 2011

## OPENING

Today's reading tells how God decided to rid the world of evil while protecting Noah [NOH-uh], his family, and two of every creature.

✚ All make the Sign of the Cross.

**In the name of the Father and of the Son and of the Holy Spirit. Amen.**

## PSALM
(For a longer psalm, see page xiii.) Psalm 27:1b (1a)

The LORD is my light and my salvation;
  whom shall I fear?

**The LORD is my light and my salvation;
  whom shall I fear?**

The LORD is the stronghold of my life;
  of whom shall I be afraid?

**The LORD is my light and my salvation;
  whom shall I fear?**

## READING
Genesis 6:5a, 6–8; 7:1–5

A reading from the Book of Genesis [JEN-uh-sis]

The LORD saw that the wickedness of humankind was great in the earth. And the LORD was sorry that he had made humankind on the earth, and it grieved him to his heart. So the LORD said, "I will blot out from the earth the human beings I have created—people together with animals and creeping things and birds of the air, for I am sorry that I have made them." But Noah found favor in the sight of the LORD.

Then the LORD said to Noah, "Go into the ark, you and all your household, for I have seen that you alone are righteous before me in this generation. Take with you seven pairs of all clean animals, the male and its mate; and a pair of the animals that are not clean, the male and its mate; and seven pairs of the birds of the air also, male and female, to keep their kind alive on the face of all the earth. For in seven days I will send rain on the earth for forty days and forty nights; and every living thing that I have made I will blot out from the face of the ground." And Noah did all that the LORD had commanded him.

The word of the Lord.

◆ All observe silence.

## FOR SILENT REFLECTION

Why does God protect Noah and his family?

## CLOSING PRAYER

Let us stand and bring our hopes and needs to God as we pray, "Lord, hear our prayer."

◆ All may add their own prayers here.

Let us pray: **Our Father . . . Amen.**

God, our Creator,
you want humans to live in harmony.
Re-create us in your saving love.
We ask this through Jesus Christ our Lord.
**Amen.**

✚ All make the Sign of the Cross.

**ALSO ON THIS DAY:** National Flag of Canada Day (Canada)
Mawlid An-Nabi (Islamic Observance of the Birth of the Prophet)
Nirvana Day (Buddhist anniversary of the death and enlightenment of the Buddha)

# PRAYER FOR **WEDNESDAY FEBRUARY 16, 2011**

### OPENING

We continue reading from the book of Genesis [JEN-uh-sis]. In today's reading, the flood has finally come to an end.

✢ All make the Sign of the Cross.

**In the name of the Father and of the Son and of the Holy Spirit. Amen.**

### PSALM
(For a longer psalm, see page xiii.) Psalm 27:1b (1a)

The LORD is my light and my salvation; whom shall I fear?

**The LORD is my light and my salvation; whom shall I fear?**

The LORD is the stronghold of my life; of whom shall I be afraid?

**The LORD is my light and my salvation; whom shall I fear?**

### READING
Genesis 8:6–11

A reading from the Book of Genesis [JEN-uh-sis]

At the end of forty days Noah [NOH-uh] opened the window of the ark that he had made and sent out the raven; and it went to and fro until the waters were dried up from the earth. Then he sent out the dove from him, to see if the waters had subsided from the face of the ground; but the dove found no place to set its foot, and it returned to him in the ark, for the waters were still on the face of the whole earth. He waited another seven days, and again he sent out the dove from the ark; and the dove came back to him in the evening, and there in its beak was a freshly plucked olive leaf; so Noah knew that the waters had subsided from the earth.

The word of the Lord.

◆ All observe silence.

### FOR SILENT REFLECTION

There are many symbols in this story (the dove, forty days, the olive branch). Do any of these symbols remind you of other stories in scripture?

### CLOSING PRAYER

Let us stand and bring our hopes and needs to God as we pray, "Lord, hear our prayer."

◆ All may add their own prayers here.

Let us pray: **Our Father . . . Amen.**

God, our Creator,
your power is great
and your love for us is strong.
When we do what is wrong,
help us to return to you.
Restore in us the peace of your presence.
We ask this through our Lord Jesus Christ,
your Son, who lives and reigns with
you in the unity of the Holy Spirit,
one God, for ever and ever.
**Amen.**

✢ All make the Sign of the Cross.

# PRAYER FOR **THURSDAY FEBRUARY 17, 2011**

## OPENING

Today we continue reading the story of Noah [NOH-uh] from the Book of Genesis [JEN-uh-sis]. A covenant is a solemn agreement that binds two parties together.

✛ All make the Sign of the Cross.

**In the name of the Father and of the Son and of the Holy Spirit. Amen.**

## PSALM (For a longer psalm, see page xiii.) Psalm 27:1b (1a)

The Lord is my light and my salvation; whom shall I fear?

**The Lord is my light and my salvation; whom shall I fear?**

The Lord is the stronghold of my life; of whom shall I be afraid?

**The Lord is my light and my salvation; whom shall I fear?**

## READING Genesis 9:8–13, 16–17

A reading from the Book of Genesis [JEN-uh-sis]

Then God said to Noah and to his sons with him, "As for me, I am establishing my covenant with you and your descendants after you, and with every living creature that is with you, the birds, the domestic animals, and every animal of the earth with you, as many as came out of the ark. I establish my covenant [KUV-uh-nunt] with you, that never again shall all flesh be cut off by the waters of a flood, and never again shall there be a flood to destroy the earth." God said, "This is the sign of the covenant that I make between me and you and every living creature that is with you, for all future generations: I have set my bow in the clouds, and it shall be a sign of the covenant between me and the earth. When the bow is in the clouds, I will see it and remember the everlasting covenant between God and every living creature of all flesh that is on the earth." God said to Noah, "This is the sign of the covenant that I have established between me and all flesh that is on the earth."

The word of the Lord.

◆ All observe silence.

## FOR SILENT REFLECTION

What is the bow in the clouds? Have you ever seen it?

## CLOSING PRAYER

Let us stand and bring our hopes and needs to God as we pray, "Lord, hear our prayer."

◆ All may add their own prayers here.

Let us pray: **Our Father . . . Amen.**

Merciful God,
may we always remember your promise
    to forgive
and return to you,
confident of your love for us
and for all of your creation.
We ask this through Jesus Christ our Lord.
**Amen.**

✛ All make the Sign of the Cross.

# PRAYER FOR **FRIDAY FEBRUARY 18, 2011**

### OPENING

Our reading from Genesis [JEN-uh-sis] today suggests that people originally spoke the same language and could understand each other.

✙ All make the Sign of the Cross.

**In the name of the Father and of the Son and of the Holy Spirit. Amen.**

### PSALM
(For a longer psalm, see page xiii.) Psalm 27:1b (1a)

The LORD is my light and my salvation;
   whom shall I fear?

**The LORD is my light and my salvation;
   whom shall I fear?**

The LORD is the stronghold of my life;
   of whom shall I be afraid?

**The LORD is my light and my salvation;
   whom shall I fear?**

### READING
Genesis 11:1, 4–9

A reading from the Book of Genesis [JEN-uh-sis]

Now the whole earth had one language and the same words. Then they said, "Come, let us build ourselves a city, and a tower with its top in the heavens, and let us make a name for ourselves; otherwise we shall be scattered abroad upon the face of the whole earth." The LORD came down to see the city and the tower, which mortals had built. And the LORD said, "Look, they are one people, and they have all one language; and this is only the beginning of what they will do; nothing that they propose to do will now be impossible for them. Come, let us go down, and confuse their language there, so that they will not understand one another's speech." So the LORD scattered them abroad from there over the face of all the earth, and they left off building the city. Therefore it was called Babel [BAB-uhl], because there the LORD confused the language of all the earth; and from there the LORD scattered them abroad over the face of all the earth.

The word of the Lord.

◆ All observe silence.

### FOR SILENT REFLECTION

Why does God confuse the peoples' language?

### CLOSING PRAYER

Let us stand and bring our hopes and needs to God as we pray, "Lord, hear our prayer."

◆ All may add their own prayers here.

Let us pray: **Our Father . . . Amen.**

All-powerful God,
when we rely on our own power
and get puffed up with pride,
we hurt ourselves and others.
Teach us humility and grant us your grace.
We ask this through Jesus Christ our Lord.
**Amen.**

✙ All make the Sign of the Cross.

---

**ALSO ON THIS DAY:** Magha Puja (Buddhist celebration of teachings of the Buddha)

# PRAYER FOR THE WEEK

WITH A READING FROM GOSPEL FOR SUNDAY, **FEBRUARY 20, 2011**

## OPENING

In today's Gospel, Jesus teaches us to love our enemies. An enemy is someone who is hostile to us, or who harms or injures us. We will need to think about this difficult teaching.

✦ All make the Sign of the Cross.

**In the name of the Father and of the Son and of the Holy Spirit. Amen.**

## PSALM  (For a longer psalm, see page xiii.) Psalm 27:1b (1a)

The LORD is my light and my salvation;
   whom shall I fear?

**The LORD is my light and my salvation;
   whom shall I fear?**

The LORD is the stronghold of my life;
   of whom shall I be afraid?

**The LORD is my light and my salvation;
   whom shall I fear?**

◆ All stand and sing **Alleluia**.

## GOSPEL  Matthew 5:43–48

A reading from the holy Gospel according to Matthew

Jesus said: "You have heard that it was said, 'You shall love your neighbor and hate your enemy.' But I say to you, love your enemies and pray for those who persecute you, so that you may be children of your Father in heaven; for he makes his sun rise on the evil and on the good, and sends rain on the righteous and on the unrighteous. For if you love those who love you, what reward do you have? Do not even the tax-collectors do the same? And if you greet only your brothers and sisters, what more are you doing than others? Do not even the Gentiles do the same? Be perfect, therefore, as your heavenly Father is perfect."

The Gospel of the Lord.

◆ All sit and observe silence.

## FOR SILENT REFLECTION

Can you think of anyone who has hurt you, or who treats you badly? How can you love this person? Does love mean letting people hurt us?

## CLOSING PRAYER

Let us stand and bring our hopes and needs to God as we pray, "Lord, hear our prayer."

◆ All may add their own prayers here.

Let us pray: **Our Father . . . Amen.**

Loving God,
you forgive the wrongs we do,
welcoming us back to you.
Help us to forgive others.
How often we want to teach people a lesson
when they hurt us and treat us badly!
Grant us the grace to learn instead
the Gospel lesson of loving kindness.
We ask this through our Lord Jesus Christ,
   your Son, who lives and reigns with
   you in the unity of the Holy Spirit,
   one God, for ever and ever.
**Amen.**

✦ All make the Sign of the Cross.

# PRAYER FOR **MONDAY FEBRUARY 21, 2011**

## OPENING

In today's Gospel Jesus heals a boy with epilepsy [EP-ih-lep-see].

✚ All make the Sign of the Cross.

**In the name of the Father and of the Son and of the Holy Spirit. Amen.**

## PSALM  (For a longer psalm, see page xiii.) Psalm 27:1b (1a)

The LORD is my light and my salvation; whom shall I fear?

**The LORD is my light and my salvation; whom shall I fear?**

The LORD is the stronghold of my life; of whom shall I be afraid?

**The LORD is my light and my salvation; whom shall I fear?**

◆ All stand and sing **Alleluia.**

## GOSPEL  Mark 9:17b–18, 21, 22b–29

A reading from the holy Gospel according to Mark

A man said, "Teacher, I brought you my son; he has a spirit that makes him unable to speak; and whenever it seizes him, it dashes him down; and he foams and grinds his teeth and becomes rigid; and I asked your disciples to cast it out, but they could not do so." Jesus asked the father, "How long has this been happening to him?" And he said, "From childhood. If you are able to do anything, have pity on us and help us." Jesus said to him, "If you are able! All things can be done for the one who believes." Immediately the father of the child cried out, "I believe; help my unbelief!" When Jesus saw that a crowd came running together, he rebuked the unclean spirit, saying to it, "You spirit that keep this boy from speaking and hearing, I command you, come out of him, and never enter him again!" After crying out and convulsing him terribly, it came out, and the boy was like a corpse, so that most of them said, "He is dead." But Jesus took him by the hand and lifted him up, and he was able to stand. When he had entered the house, his disciples asked him privately, "Why could we not cast it out?" He said to them, "This kind can come out only through prayer."

The Gospel of the Lord.

◆ All sit and observe silence.

## FOR SILENT REFLECTION

What does this story tell us about the power of prayer?

## CLOSING PRAYER

Let us stand and bring our hopes and needs to God as we pray, "Lord, hear our prayer."

◆ All may add their own prayers here.

Let us pray: **Our Father . . . Amen.**

All-powerful God,
we believe; help our unbelief!
We ask this through Jesus Christ our Lord.
**Amen.**

✚ All make the Sign of the Cross.

**ALSO ON THIS DAY:** Presidents' Day (U.S.A.)

# PRAYER FOR TUESDAY FEBRUARY 22, 2011

## OPENING

Today's feast of the Chair of Saint Peter honors Saint Peter as the one Jesus chose to lead the community after he left the earth. Bishops taught the people as they sat in a special chair called a cathedra [ka-THEE-dra), in their cathedral. The chair became the symbol of the Bishop's office, and Saint Peter was the leader of all the Church, just as our Pope is today.

✚ All make the Sign of the Cross.

**In the name of the Father and of the Son and of the Holy Spirit. Amen.**

## PSALM (For a longer psalm, see page xiii.) Psalm 27:1b (1a)

The LORD is my light and my salvation;
　whom shall I fear?

**The LORD is my light and my salvation;
　whom shall I fear?**

The LORD is the stronghold of my life;
　of whom shall I be afraid?

**The LORD is my light and my salvation;
　whom shall I fear?**

◆ All stand and sing **Alleluia**.

## GOSPEL   Matthew 16:13–19

A reading from the holy Gospel according to Matthew

Now when Jesus came into the district of Caesarea [sez-uh-REE-uh] Philippi [fih-LIP-i], he asked his disciples, "Who do people say that the Son of Man is?" And they said, "Some say John the Baptist, but others Elijah, and still others Jeremiah or one of the prophets." He said to them, "But who do you say that I am?" Simon Peter answered, "You are the Messiah, the Son of the living God." And Jesus answered him, "Blessed are you, Simon son of Jonah! For flesh and blood has not revealed this to you, but my Father in heaven. And I tell you, you are Peter, and on this rock I will build my church, and the gates of Hades will not prevail against it. I will give you the keys of the kingdom of heaven, and whatever you bind on earth will be bound in heaven, and whatever you loose on earth will be loosed in heaven."

The Gospel of the Lord.

◆ All sit and observe silence.

## FOR SILENT REFLECTION

What do you think Jesus means when he says he will give Peter the "keys of the kingdom"?

## CLOSING PRAYER

Let us stand and bring our hopes and needs to God as we pray, "Lord, hear our prayer."

◆ All may add their own prayers here.

Let us pray: **Our Father . . . Amen.**

Lord God,
you made Peter fit to lead
the Church on earth.
Continue to guide our Pope,
giving him knowledge, courage, and strength.
We ask this through Jesus Christ our Lord.
**Amen.**

✚ All make the Sign of the Cross.

# PRAYER FOR **WEDNESDAY FEBRUARY 23, 2011**

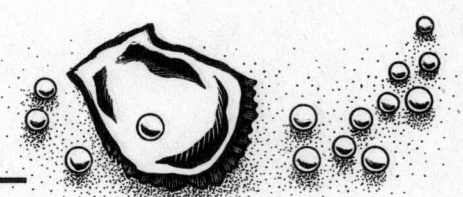

## OPENING

Today we remember Saint Polycarp [PAW-lee-karp], a Bishop of the second century who died for his faith. The day's reading comes from the book of Sirach [SEER-ak], a collection of wise sayings or advice. Remember that in one of the O Antiphons we sang during Advent, Jesus is called by the title "Wisdom."

✚ All make the Sign of the Cross.

**In the name of the Father and of the Son and of the Holy Spirit. Amen.**

## PSALM
(For a longer psalm, see page xiii.) Psalm 27:1b (1a)

The LORD is my light and my salvation;
 whom shall I fear?

**The LORD is my light and my salvation;
 whom shall I fear?**

The LORD is the stronghold of my life;
 of whom shall I be afraid?

**The LORD is my light and my salvation;
 whom shall I fear?**

## READING
Sirach 4:11–16

A reading from the Book of Sirach [SEER-ak]

Wisdom teaches her children
 and gives help to those who seek her.
Whoever loves her loves life,
 and those who seek her from early
  morning are filled with joy.
Whoever holds her fast inherits glory,
 and the Lord blesses the place she enters.
Those who serve her minister to
  the Holy One;
 the Lord loves those who love her.
Those who obey her will judge the nations,
 and all who listen to her will live secure.
If they remain faithful, they will inherit her;
 their descendants will also obtain her.

The word of the Lord.

◆ All observe silence.

## FOR SILENT REFLECTION

What can we do to obtain wisdom?

## CLOSING PRAYER

Let us stand and bring our hopes and needs to God as we pray, "Lord, hear our prayer."

◆ All may add their own prayers here.

Let us pray: **Our Father . . . Amen.**

O Divine Wisdom,
you who made us so wonderfully,
give us wise hearts.
Help us to recognize goodness,
to desire holiness,
and to pursue justice.
We ask this through our Lord Jesus Christ,
 your Son, who lives and reigns with
 you in the unity of the Holy Spirit,
 one God, for ever and ever.
**Amen.**

✚ All make the Sign of the Cross.

# PRAYER FOR THURSDAY FEBRUARY 24, 2011

## OPENING

Today we continue to read from the book of Sirach [SEER-ak]. We are reminded that, although we should trust in God's mercy, we must not use this as an excuse to keep on doing things that we know God would not like.

✢ All make the Sign of the Cross.

**In the name of the Father and of the Son and of the Holy Spirit. Amen.**

## PSALM (For a longer psalm, see page xiii.) Psalm 27:1b (1a)

The LORD is my light and my salvation;
 whom shall I fear?

**The LORD is my light and my salvation;
 whom shall I fear?**

The LORD is the stronghold of my life;
 of whom shall I be afraid?

**The LORD is my light and my salvation;
 whom shall I fear?**

## READING                           Sirach 5:4–8

A reading from the Book of Sirach [SEER-ak]

Do not say, "I sinned, yet what has
   happened to me?"
 for the Lord is slow to anger.
Do not be so confident of forgiveness
   that you add sin to sin.
Do not say, "His mercy is great,
 he will forgive the multitude of my sins",
for both mercy and wrath are with him,
 and his anger will rest on sinners.
Do not delay to turn back to the Lord,
 and do not postpone it from day to day;
for suddenly the wrath of the Lord will
   come upon you,
 and at the time of punishment you
   will perish.
Do not depend on dishonest wealth,
 for it will not benefit you on the day
   of calamity.

The word of the Lord.

◆ All observe silence.

## FOR SILENT REFLECTION

Why should we not delay returning to God when we have sinned?

## CLOSING PRAYER

Let us stand and bring our hopes and needs to God as we pray, "Lord, hear our prayer."

◆ All may add their own prayers here.

Let us pray: **Our Father . . . Amen.**

God our Father,
help us not to make excuses
for bad behavior,
but to desire your goodness
with all our hearts.
Only then can we become
all you have created us to be.
We ask this through Jesus Christ our Lord.
**Amen.**

✢ All make the Sign of the Cross.

# PRAYER FOR **FRIDAY FEBRUARY 25, 2011**

## OPENING

We continue to read today from the book of Sirach [SEER-ak]. Today's reading speaks of the importance of having true friends. Here the word testing means to examine carefully.

✚ All make the Sign of the Cross.

**In the name of the Father and of the Son and of the Holy Spirit. Amen.**

## PSALM     (For a longer psalm, see page xiii.) Psalm 27:1b (1a)

The LORD is my light and my salvation;
　whom shall I fear?

The LORD is my light and my salvation;
　whom shall I fear?

The LORD is the stronghold of my life;
　of whom shall I be afraid?

The LORD is my light and my salvation;
　whom shall I fear?

## READING     Sirach 6:7–10, 14–17

A reading from the Book of Sirach [SEER-ak]

When you gain friends, gain them
　　through testing,
　and do not trust them hastily.
For there are friends who are such when
　　it suits them,
　but they will not stand by you in time
　　of trouble.
And there are friends who change
　　into enemies,
　and tell of the quarrel to your disgrace.
And there are friends who sit at your table,
　but they will not stand by you in time
　　of trouble.
Faithful friends are a sturdy shelter:
　whoever finds one has found a treasure.
Faithful friends are beyond price;
　no amount can balance their worth.
Faithful friends are life-saving medicine;
　and those who fear the Lord will
　　find them.
Those who fear the Lord direct their
　　friendship aright,
　for as they are, so are their neighbors also.

The word of the Lord.

◆ All observe silence.

## FOR SILENT REFLECTION

How do you know when someone is a "faithful friend"?

## CLOSING PRAYER

Let us stand and bring our hopes and needs to God as we pray, "Lord, hear our prayer."

◆ All may add their own prayers here.

Let us pray: **Our Father . . . Amen.**

Loving God,
you give us family and friends
to console us in sad times,
help us through difficult times,
and rejoice with us in good times.
Help us to know who our true friends are,
and to be a faithful friend to others.
We ask this through Jesus Christ our Lord.
**Amen.**

✚ All make the Sign of the Cross.

# PRAYER FOR THE WEEK

WITH A READING FROM THE GOSPEL FOR **SUNDAY, FEBRUARY 27, 2011**

## OPENING

In today's Gospel, listen to what Jesus tells us about worrying.

✠ All make the Sign of the Cross.

**In the name of the Father and of the Son and of the Holy Spirit. Amen.**

## PSALM

(For a longer psalm, see page xiii.) Psalm 27:1b (1a)

The LORD is my light and my salvation; whom shall I fear?

**The LORD is my light and my salvation; whom shall I fear?**

The LORD is the stronghold of my life; of whom shall I be afraid?

**The LORD is my light and my salvation; whom shall I fear?**

◆ All stand and sing **Alleluia**.

## GOSPEL

Matthew 6:25–31, 33

A reading from the holy Gospel according to Matthew

"Therefore I tell you, do not worry about your life, what you will eat or what you will drink, or about your body, what you will wear. Is not life more than food, and the body more than clothing? Look at the birds of the air; they neither sow nor reap nor gather into barns, and yet your heavenly Father feeds them. Are you not of more value than they? And can any of you by worrying add a single hour to your span of life? And why do you worry about clothing? Consider the lilies of the field, how they grow; they neither toil nor spin, yet I tell you, even Solomon in all his glory was not clothed like one of these. But if God so clothes the grass of the field, which is alive today and tomorrow is thrown into the oven, will he not much more clothe you—you of little faith? Therefore do not worry, saying, 'What will we eat?' or 'What will we drink?' or 'What will we wear?' But strive first for the kingdom of God and his righteousness, and all these things will be given to you as well."

The Gospel of the Lord.

◆ All sit and observe silence.

## FOR SILENT REFLECTION

What do you think Jesus would say if you told him about your worries?

## CLOSING PRAYER

Let us stand and bring our hopes and needs to God as we pray, "Lord, hear our prayer."

◆ All may add their own prayers here.

Let us pray: **Our Father . . . Amen.**

God of peace,
we come to you with many worries.
We worry when people we love are ill
    or fighting.
We worry that people won't like us,
or when we have a test in school.
Help us not to worry,
but to trust that you are with us.
We ask this through Jesus Christ our Lord.
**Amen.**

✠ All make the Sign of the Cross.

# PRAYER FOR **MONDAY FEBRUARY 28, 2011**

## OPENING

Today's reading speaks of turning back to God when we have sinned. Iniquities [in-IH-kweh-tees] are actions that are wicked and unjust. To repent is to feel sorrow for doing what is wrong and to turn back to God.

✚ All make the Sign of the Cross.

**In the name of the Father and of the Son and of the Holy Spirit. Amen.**

## PSALM (For a longer psalm, see page xiii.) Psalm 27:1b (1a)

The LORD is my light and my salvation; whom shall I fear?

**The LORD is my light and my salvation; whom shall I fear?**

The LORD is the stronghold of my life; of whom shall I be afraid?

**The LORD is my light and my salvation; whom shall I fear?**

## READING Sirach 17:20, 24, 26, 29

A reading from the Book of Sirach [SEER-ak]

Their iniquities are not hidden from him, and all their sins are before the Lord.
Yet to those who repent he grants a return, and he encourages those who are losing hope.
Return to the Most High and turn away from iniquity, and hate intensely what he abhors [ub-HOHRS].
How great is the mercy of the Lord, and his forgiveness for those who return to him!
For not everything is within human capability [KAYP-uh-bil-ih-tee], since human beings are not immortal.

The word of the Lord.

◆ All observe silence.

## FOR SILENT REFLECTION

Why do you think God wants us to repent?

## CLOSING PRAYER

Let us stand and bring our hopes and needs to God as we pray, "Lord, hear our prayer."

◆ All may add their own prayers here.

Let us pray: **Our Father . . . Amen.**

Holy God,
when we have done something wrong we want to hide; but we cannot hide from you.
Give us a desire for what is good and holy, the grace to do your will,
and the willingness to return to you whenever we have chosen the wrong path.
We ask this through our Lord Jesus Christ, your Son, who lives and reigns with you in the unity of the Holy Spirit, one God, for ever and ever.
**Amen.**

✚ All make the Sign of the Cross.

# PRAYER FOR TUESDAY MARCH 1, 2011

## OPENING

Today's Gospel tells us what those who have given up everything to follow Jesus will receive.

✚ All make the Sign of the Cross.

**In the name of the Father and of the Son and of the Holy Spirit. Amen.**

## PSALM
(For a longer psalm, see page xiii.) Psalm 27:1b (1a)

The LORD is my light and my salvation; whom shall I fear?

**The LORD is my light and my salvation; whom shall I fear?**

The LORD is the stronghold of my life; of whom shall I be afraid?

**The LORD is my light and my salvation; whom shall I fear?**

◆ All stand and sing **Alleluia**.

## GOSPEL
Mark 10:28–31

A reading from the holy Gospel according to Mark

Peter began to say to Jesus, "Look, we have left everything and followed you." Jesus said, "Truly I tell you, there is no one who has left house or brothers or sisters or mother or father or children or fields, for my sake and for the sake of the good news, who will not receive a hundredfold now in this age—houses, brothers and sisters, mothers and children, and fields, with persecutions—and in the age to come eternal life. But many who are first will be last, and the last will be first."

The Gospel of the Lord.

◆ All sit and observe silence.

## FOR SILENT REFLECTION

Can you think of people who have left everything to follow Jesus? How do parents and families leave everything to follow Jesus?

## CLOSING PRAYER

Let us stand and bring our hopes and needs to God as we pray, "Lord, hear our prayer."

◆ All may add their own prayers here.

Let us pray: **Our Father . . . Amen.**

Lord God,
may we seek your will in all we do.
May our family be your family,
our friends, your friends,
our house, your home.
Help us to give our lives to you,
that we might share in the eternal life
you give to us.
We ask this through Jesus Christ our Lord.
**Amen.**

✚ All make the Sign of the Cross.

# PRAYER FOR **WEDNESDAY** MARCH 2, 2011

## OPENING

In today's Gospel we hear the apostles [uh-POS-lz], James and John, ask Jesus to give them special importance in the kingdom of heaven. Jesus' response tells us something about this kingdom.

✛ All make the Sign of the Cross.

**In the name of the Father and of the Son and of the Holy Spirit. Amen.**

## PSALM  (For a longer psalm, see page xiii.) Psalm 27:1b (1a)

The LORD is my light and my salvation;
 whom shall I fear?

**The LORD is my light and my salvation;
 whom shall I fear?**

The LORD is the stronghold of my life;
 of whom shall I be afraid?

**The Lord is my light and my salvation;
 whom shall I fear?**

◆ All stand and sing **Alleluia**.

## GOSPEL                                    Mark 10:35–40

A reading from the holy Gospel according to Mark

James and John, the sons of Zebedee [ZEB-uh-dee], came forward to him and said to him, "Teacher, we want you to do for us whatever we ask of you." And he said to them, "What is it you want me to do for you?" And they said to him, "Grant us to sit, one at your right hand and one at your left, in your glory." But Jesus said to them, "You do not know what you are asking. Are you able to drink the cup that I drink, or be baptized with the baptism that I am baptized with?" They replied, "We are able." Then Jesus said to them, "The cup that I drink you will drink; and with the baptism with which I am baptized, you will be baptized; but to sit at my right hand or at my left is not mine to grant, but it is for those for whom it has been prepared."

The Gospel of the Lord.

◆ All sit and observe silence.

## FOR SILENT REFLECTION

Why does Jesus say he is not the one to say who will have special importance in the kingdom of God?

## CLOSING PRAYER

Let us stand and bring our hopes and needs to God as we pray, "Lord, hear our prayer."

◆ All may add their own prayers here.

Let us pray: **Our Father . . . Amen.**

Almighty God,
help us to remember that you are God.
Your ways are not our ways,
your thoughts are not our thoughts.
Rid us of our foolish pride
so that we may approach you
with reverence and humility.
We ask this through Jesus Christ our Lord.
**Amen.**

✛ All make the Sign of the Cross.

# PRAYER FOR THURSDAY MARCH 3, 2011

## OPENING

Today we remember Saint Katharine Drexel [DREX-uhl] who founded an order of sisters to serve Native Americans and African Americans. The Gospel today tells of how Jesus healed a blind man.

✢ All make the Sign of the Cross.

**In the name of the Father and of the Son and of the Holy Spirit. Amen.**

## PSALM
(For a longer psalm, see page xiii.) Psalm 27:1b (1a)

The Lord is my light and my salvation;
  whom shall I fear?

**The Lord is my light and my salvation;
  whom shall I fear?**

The Lord is the stronghold of my life;
  of whom shall I be afraid?

**The Lord is my light and my salvation;
  whom shall I fear?**

◆ All stand and sing **Alleluia**.

## GOSPEL
Mark 10:46–52

A reading from the holy Gospel according to Mark

They came to Jericho (JAYR-ih-koh]. As he and his disciples and a large crowd were leaving Jericho (JAYR-ih-koh], Bartimaeus [bahr-tih-MAY-uhs] son of Timaeus [tim-AY-uhs], a blind beggar, was sitting by the roadside. When he heard that it was Jesus of Nazareth [NAZ-uh-reth], he began to shout out and say, "Jesus, Son of David, have mercy on me!" Many sternly ordered him to be quiet, but he cried out even more loudly, "Son of David, have mercy on me!" Jesus stood still and said, "Call him here." And they called the blind man, saying to him, "Take heart; get up, he is calling you." So throwing off his cloak, he sprang up and came to Jesus. Then Jesus said to him, "What do you want me to do for you?" The blind man said to him, "My teacher, let me see again." Jesus said to him, "Go; your faith has made you well." Immediately he regained his sight and followed him on the way.

The Gospel of the Lord.

◆ All sit and observe silence.

## FOR SILENT REFLECTION

Do you think this story is only about physical sight? What other kinds of seeing are there?

## CLOSING PRAYER

Let us stand and bring our hopes and needs to God as we pray, "Lord, hear our prayer."

◆ All may add their own prayers here.

Let us pray: **Our Father . . . Amen.**

Holy God,
sometimes we are blind.
We fail to see our need for you.
We don't notice the needs of others.
Give us the light of faith
so that we may see.
We ask this through Jesus Christ our Lord.
**Amen.**

✢ All make the Sign of the Cross.

# PRAYER FOR FRIDAY MARCH 4, 2011

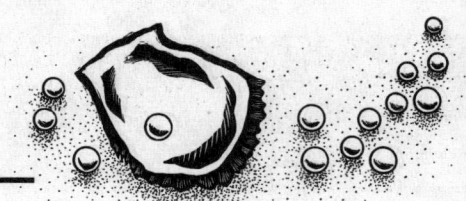

## OPENING

Today is the memorial of Saint Casimir [KAS-ih-meer], a royal prince who was devoted to God from childhood. He is the patron saint of Poland and Lithuania. In today's Gospel, Jesus quotes a passage from the prophet Jeremiah [jayr-uh-MI-uh], who warns the people that true worship of God demands just and holy living.

✛ All make the Sign of the Cross.

**In the name of the Father and of the Son and of the Holy Spirit. Amen.**

## PSALM
(For a longer psalm, see page xiii.) Psalm 27:1b (1a)

The LORD is my light and my salvation;
  whom shall I fear?

**The LORD is my light and my salvation;
  whom shall I fear?**

The LORD is the stronghold of my life;
  of whom shall I be afraid?

**The LORD is my light and my salvation;
  whom shall I fear?**

◆ All stand and sing **Alleluia**.

## GOSPEL
Mark 11:15–19

A reading from the holy Gospel according to Mark

Jesus and the disciples came to Jerusalem. And he entered the temple and began to drive out those who were selling and those who were buying in the temple, and he overturned the tables of the money-changers and the seats of those who sold doves; and he would not allow anyone to carry anything through the temple. He was teaching and saying, "Is it not written:
  'My house shall be called a house of prayer
    for all the nations'?
  But you have made it a den of robbers."
And when the chief priests and the scribes heard it, they kept looking for a way to kill him; for they were afraid of him, because the whole crowd was spellbound by his teaching. And when evening came, Jesus and his disciples went out of the city.

The Gospel of the Lord.

◆ All sit and observe silence.

## FOR SILENT REFLECTION

Why do we need a "house of prayer"?

## CLOSING PRAYER

Let us stand and bring our hopes and needs to God as we pray, "Lord, hear our prayer."

◆ All may add their own prayers here.

Let us pray: **Our Father . . . Amen.**

God of righteousness,
help us to be reverent and open to you
in our houses of prayer
so that we can come closer to you
and learn to do your will.
We ask this through Jesus Christ our Lord.
**Amen.**

✛ All make the Sign of the Cross.

**ALSO ON THIS DAY:** World Day of Prayer

# PRAYER FOR THE WEEK

WITH A READING FROM THE GOSPEL FOR **SUNDAY, MARCH 6, 2011**

## OPENING

Today's Gospel reading reminds us that there is more to being God's people than performing great works.

✠ All make the Sign of the Cross.

**In the name of the Father and of the Son and of the Holy Spirit. Amen.**

## PSALM (For a longer psalm, see page xiii.) Psalm 27:1b (1a)

The LORD is my light and my salvation;
 whom shall I fear?

**The LORD is my light and my salvation;
 whom shall I fear?**

The LORD is the stronghold of my life;
 of whom shall I be afraid?

**The LORD is my light and my salvation;
 whom shall I fear?**

◆ All stand and sing **Alleluia**.

## GOSPEL  Matthew 7:21–23

A reading from the holy Gospel according to Matthew

Jesus said, "Not everyone who says to me, 'Lord, Lord,' will enter the kingdom of heaven, but only one who does the will of my Father in heaven. On that day many will say to me, 'Lord, Lord, did we not prophesy in your name, and cast out demons in your name, and do many deeds of power in your name?' Then I will declare to them, 'I never knew you; go away from me, you evildoers.'"

The Gospel of the Lord.

◆ All sit and observe silence.

## FOR SILENT REFLECTION

How do we know that we are doing God's will?

## CLOSING PRAYER

Let us stand and bring our hopes and needs to God as we pray, "Lord, hear our prayer."

◆ All may add their own prayers here.

Let us pray: **Our Father . . . Amen.**

God our Father,
protect us from pretenders,
from people who say they are doing your will
but are really doing whatever they want.
The sheep know their shepherd's voice.
Help us to recognize your voice
and to follow where you lead us.
We ask this through our Lord Jesus Christ,
 your Son, who lives and reigns with
 you in the unity of the Holy Spirit,
 one God, for ever and ever.

**Amen.**

✠ All make the Sign of the Cross.

---

**ALSO ON THIS DAY:** Girl Scout Sunday (U.S.A.)

# PRAYER FOR MONDAY MARCH 7, 2011

## OPENING

In today's Gospel, Jesus tells a parable about wicked tenants [TEN-uhntz]. A tenant is a person who rents property from the owner.

✢ All make the Sign of the Cross.

**In the name of the Father and of the Son and of the Holy Spirit. Amen.**

## PSALM
(For a longer psalm, see page xiii.) Psalm 27:1b (1a)

The LORD is my light and my salvation;
  whom shall I fear?

**The LORD is my light and my salvation;
  whom shall I fear?**

The LORD is the stronghold of my life;
  of whom shall I be afraid?

**The LORD is my light and my salvation;
  whom shall I fear?**

◆ All stand and sing **Alleluia**.

## GOSPEL
Mark 12:1–5a, 6–11

A reading from the holy Gospel according to Mark

Then Jesus began to speak to them in parables. "A man planted a vineyard, put a fence around it, dug a pit for the wine press, and built a watchtower; then he leased it to tenants and went to another country. When the season came, he sent a slave to the tenants to collect from them his share of the produce of the vineyard. But they seized him, and beat him, and sent him away empty-handed. And again he sent another slave to them; this one they beat over the head and insulted. Then he sent another, and that one they killed. He had still one other, a beloved son. Finally he sent him to them, saying, 'They will respect my son.' But those tenants said to one another, 'This is the heir; come, let us kill him, and the inheritance will be ours.' So they seized him, killed him, and threw him out of the vineyard. What then will the owner of the vineyard do? He will come and destroy the tenants and give the vineyard to others. Have you not read this scripture:
  'The stone that the builders rejected
    has become the cornerstone;
  this was the Lord's doing,
    and it is amazing in our eyes'?"

The Gospel of the Lord.

◆ All sit and observe silence.

## FOR SILENT REFLECTION

Who is the beloved son in this parable?

## CLOSING PRAYER

Let us stand and bring our hopes and needs to God as we pray, "Lord, hear our prayer."

◆ All may add their own prayers here.

Let us pray: **Our Father . . . Amen.**

All-powerful God,
give us the gift of faith
so that we may welcome into our hearts
your beloved Son.
We ask this through the same Christ our Lord.
**Amen.**

✢ All make the Sign of the Cross.

# PRAYER FOR TUESDAY MARCH 8, 2011

## OPENING

In today's Gospel, some Pharisees [FAYR-uh-seez] and some Herodians [her-OH-dee-uhns] try to trap Jesus into saying something that would anger the Jews. The Jews resented the taxes of the powerful Roman government. A denarius [dih-NAHR-ee-uhs] is a coin. Caesar [SEE-zer] is the Roman emperor.

✚ All make the Sign of the Cross.

**In the name of the Father and of the Son and of the Holy Spirit. Amen.**

## PSALM  (For a longer psalm, see page xiii.) Psalm 27:1b (1a)

The LORD is my light and my salvation;
   whom shall I fear?

**The LORD is my light and my salvation;
   whom shall I fear?**

The LORD is the stronghold of my life;
   of whom shall I be afraid?

**The LORD is my light and my salvation;
   whom shall I fear?**

◆ All stand and sing **Alleluia.**

## GOSPEL                                   Mark 12:13–17

A reading from the holy Gospel according to Mark

Then they sent to him some Pharisees [FAYR-uh-seez] and some Herodians [her-OH-dee-uhns] to trap him in what he said. And they came and said to him, "Teacher, we know that you are sincere, and show deference to no one; for you do not regard people with partiality, but teach the way of God in accordance with truth. Is it lawful to pay taxes to the emperor, or not? Should we pay them, or should we not?" But knowing their hypocrisy, he said to them, "Why are you putting me to the test? Bring me a denarius [dih-NAHR-ee-us] and let me see it." And they brought one. Then he said to them, "Whose head is this, and whose title?" They answered, "The emperor's." Jesus said to them, "Give to the emperor the things that are the emperor's, and to God the things that are God's." And they were utterly amazed at him.

The Gospel of the Lord.

◆ All sit and observe silence.

## FOR SILENT REFLECTION

What belongs to God?

## CLOSING PRAYER

Let us stand and bring our hopes and needs to God as we pray, "Lord, hear our prayer."

◆ All may add their own prayers here.

Let us pray: **Our Father . . . Amen.**

Lord God,
you are the ruler of the universe.
and all of creation belongs to you.
Help us to live as your children
in humility and truth.
We ask this in the name of Jesus our Lord.
**Amen.**

✚ All make the Sign of the Cross.

---

**ALSO ON THIS DAY:** Mardi Gras

# HOME PRAYER
## KEEPING LENT

*Before you begin, place a candle, an empty bowl, and a jar with a slit cut into the lid (for coins to give to the poor) where the household will gather in prayer. Find the reading (Luke 10:25–37) in your Bible, ask for a volunteer to read it, and encourage the reader to practice reading it twice. You may wish to begin with a simple song, such as "Jesus, Remember Me," or "Amen" (but not "Alleluia" during Lent). An older child or adult reads the leader parts.*

**LEADER:**
Lent is a season of turning to God in simplicity and sincerity as we prepare to celebrate the joy of Easter. Our hearts feel heavy as we remember our sins, but we are also confident in God's mercy and forgiveness.

The three great Lenten practices are prayer, fasting, and almsgiving (almsgiving means giving money or other help to the needy). Doing these three things will help us to keep Lent as a holy season. In our prayer today, let's be open to God's kindness as we promise to pray with more love, avoid treats, and collect our coins to give to the poor.

✠ All make the Sign of the Cross.

**In the name of the Father and of the Son and of the Holy Spirit. Amen.**

**LEADER:** *Psalm 51: 1a and 6*
Please repeat the psalm response:
Have mercy on me, O God,
 according to your steadfast love.

**ALL: Have mercy on me, O God,
 according to your steadfast love.**

**LEADER:**
You desire truth in the inward being;
 therefore teach me wisdom in my
  secret heart.

**ALL: Have mercy on me, O God,
 according to your steadfast love.**

◆ All stand and sing **Praise to you, Lord Jesus Christ** . . .

**READER:** *Luke 10:25–37*
A reading from the holy Gospel according to Luke

◆ The reader reads the scripture passage from the Bible.

The Gospel of the Lord.

◆ All sit and observe silence. An adult lights the candle.

**LEADER:**
Merciful and loving Father,
just as the warmth from this candle rises
 up to heaven,
receive and bless our Lenten prayers.
In our Lenten fast,
may our hearts be as open and ready
to be filled with your love as this bowl.
And may the coins we gather for the poor
during this holy season
help us to love God and love our neighbor,
just as the Good Samaritan did.
We ask for this blessing through Jesus Christ
 our Lord.

**ALL: Amen.**

**LEADER:**
Let us pray as Jesus taught us: **Our Father** . . .
**Amen.**

✠ All make the Sign of the Cross.

# LENT AND TRIDUUM

## WEDNESDAY, MARCH 9 TO FRIDAY, APRIL 15

# LENT 2011

## THE MEANING OF LENT

Jesus said, "'You shall love the Lord your God with all your heart, and with all your soul, and with all your mind.' This is the greatest and first commandment. And a second is like it: 'You shall love your neighbor as yourself.' On these two commandments hang all the law and the prophets" (Matthew 22:37b–40).

We can't love someone we don't know. If we want to love God, we need to meet him and spend time with him. How do we do that? We can listen to God's words in the Holy Bible. We can speak to him in the freedom and quiet of our hearts. And we can come face to face with God in the Sacraments, particularly the Eucharist and the Sacrament of Reconciliation, where we can meet him in the person of Jesus Christ as often as we like.

We also meet Jesus Christ in each other. It is because God first loved us that we are able to love one another. Sometimes it is a challenge to see the face of Christ in our neighbor and to love our Lord Jesus in the person before us.

Coming to know our God more intimately through Jesus Christ is the work of our lives. That work began at our Baptism when we went down into the waters with Christ and rose to new life with him. Each year during Lent and Triduum we ponder this mystery and we pray for the people who are preparing for Baptism at the Easter Vigil.

It is easy to get distracted from our relationship with Jesus; Too often we turn away from God and do our will instead of God's will. Too often we turn away from God and do our will instead of God's will. This turning back is called repenting (turning again). After a time of distraction or willful turning away we feel great sorrow that we have neglected or damaged our relationship with God and we do penance. Repentance and penance are two important works of Lent. Also during Lent we come closer to God by spending more time praying, either with others or when we're alone, by fasting, which means eating less or giving up something that distracts us from knowing God, and by giving alms, which means giving money, time, or possessions to help people in need.

Will giving up candy for six weeks help us to love God more? Will putting a few coins aside help us to see and love Christ in the people who stand in front of us every day? Will eating fish on Fridays help us to meet God? Everything depends on our openness to God. God wants us to change the things we do so that our hearts, souls, and minds will overflow with divine love for God, our neighbors, and also for ourselves. Remember, we are to love others as we love ourselves. All of our work during Lent leads to Easter, when we will join in celebrating the Resurrection and the risen life that we receive in Baptism.

### TRIDUUM

Lent's purpose—to lead us to the Triduum—becomes more focused as we celebrate Palm Sunday of the Lord's Passion and enter into Holy Week. However, the Lenten season doesn't actually end until the Mass of the Lord's Supper on Holy Thursday evening. At that moment we enter the Triduum, the three holiest days of the Church year. These days are counted from sunset to sunset. So the first day of Triduum begins on Holy Thursday evening and includes Good Friday. The second day runs from Good Friday evening through Holy Saturday. And the third day runs from Holy Saturday evening through Easter Sunday evening. You will find a prayer service to be used on one of the school days of Holy Week (pages 244–245), and Home Prayer pages to copy and send home so that families can keep the Three Days of Triduum holy (pages 246–248).

## PREPARING TO CELEBRATE LENT IN THE CLASSROOM

Remember that you'll need to change your prayer tablecloth from green to purple!

For the first day of Lent that you meet with the children, place on the prayer table a small glass bowl, a finger towel, and a glass pitcher half-full of water. Copy this prayer on an index card:

# 2011 LENT

*Lord, wash away my iniquity, cleanse me from my sin.*

Gather the children around the empty glass bowl. Remind them of the moment during Mass when the priest washes his hands. Explain that this hand washing is silent prayer that the priest does with his hands. Ask a student volunteer to hold his or her fingertips over the bowl and pour a little water over them; dry them with the towel. When you are finished, ask the children what this prayer might mean. What is the priest asking God to do? Why would the priest wash his hands at this moment? After the children have had a chance to reflect on the meaning of the gesture, suggest that the priest is not only asking for clean hands and ask: What else would the priest like God to clean? Then bring out the index card with the prayer. Explain that this is the prayer the priest says as he washes his hands. How can the priest wash away his sins by having someone pour water on his fingers? Finish your reflection by going around the table and practicing the gesture with each other, taking turns being the one who pours the water and being the one whose hands are cleaned. Ask the children if they think that the priest is the only one who needs a clean heart to approach the altar of the Lord.

After you have explored the themes in The Meaning of Lent with the children, open the classroom Bible and read the parable of the Good Samaritan (Luke 10:25–37) together. Draw attention to Jesus' final words, "Go and do likewise." Ask the children what they can do that would be like the action of the Good Samaritan. Talk together about the needs of people in your area and think of how to respond to them. Perhaps the children could create cards for people in hospitals or nursing homes, collect pennies for disaster relief, or bring canned goods for the local food pantry. If the children are older, consider taking them to prepare and serve a meal at a local soup kitchen. Ask the children how they might "go and do likewise" in their own families as well.

Special prayer services and one Home Prayer are provided on page 196 and on pages pages 202–203, 209–210.

## SACRED SPACE

It's time to remove your living plant from the prayer table and put it near a window. For Lent you could decorate your prayer table with a stalk of dried wheat or some bare branches in a vase.

## SACRED MUSIC

Children love to sing "Jesus, Remember Me," and "What Wondrous Love Is This?" Other songs for Lent are "Amazing Grace," the American spiritual, "Somebody's Knockin' at Your Door" and the Latin hymn "Ubi Caritas." We don't sing "Alleluia" during Lent. Tell the children we are saving all our Alleluia joy for Easter. For the Prayer for the Week, where there is a Gospel, we sing an acclamation, such as "Praise to you, Lord Jesus Christ" to whatever tune the parish is using.

## PRAYERS FOR LENT

Lent is the perfect time to learn or to review an Act of Contrition. Psalm 51 is also a beautiful prayer for this season of penance and conversion.

## A NOTE TO CATECHISTS

If any children in your group are preparing to celebrate the sacraments of initiation at the Easter Vigil, gather them to read the following three great accounts from the Gospel of John: 1) Jesus and the woman at the well (John 4:5–15, 19b–26, 39a, 40–42); 2) Jesus and the man born blind (John 9:1, 6–9, 13–17, 34–38); and 3) Jesus raises Lazarus (John 11:3–7, 17, 20–27, 33b–45). These are long passages and may require some time to read and discuss with your students, but fight the temptation to rush through them! After you have read and meditated together, consider inviting the children to act out these highly dramatic accounts. All of us will benefit from these readings as we prepare to celebrate the joy of the Resurrection.

# GRACE BEFORE MEALS

## LENT

**LEADER:**
We adore you, O Christ, and we praise you

**ALL:** Because by your holy cross you have redeemed the world.

✜ All make the Sign of the Cross.

**In the name of the Father and of the Son and of the Holy Spirit. Amen.**

**LEADER:**
Generous God,
even when we don't love you as we should,
you give us food and water
to strengthen us and help us grow.
Today, may this food we are about to eat
remind us of your loving mercy
and inspire us to turn to you with all
 our hearts.
We ask this through Christ, our Lord.

**ALL: Amen.**

✜ All make the Sign of the Cross.

**In the name of the Father and of the Son and of the Holy Spirit. Amen.**

# PRAYER AT DAY'S END
## LENT

**LEADER:**
Father forgive us

**ALL:** For we don't always know what we do.

✚ All make the Sign of the Cross.

**In the name of the Father and of the Son and of the Holy Spirit. Amen.**

**LEADER:**
Merciful Lord,
we don't know why we forget that you
    love us
and that we depend on you for everything.
As our school day comes to an end,
help us to remember your compassion for us
so that we will turn back to you in gratitude,
in awe, and in love.
We ask this through Christ, our Lord.

✚ All make the Sign of the Cross.

**In the name of the Father and of the Son and of the Holy Spirit. Amen.**

# PRAYER SERVICE
## ASH WEDNESDAY

*Prepare eight leaders for this prayer service. Before you begin, have the children write the word, "Alleluia" on a large piece of paper. Have them decorate the word with beautiful pictures. Bring the "illuminated" word to the prayer service, and a box large enough to hold it. The fifth leader will need a Bible to read the Gospel passage (Matthew 6:1–2) and may need help locating it and practicing. You may wish to begin by singing, "I Want to Walk as a Child of the Light" and end with "Amazing Grace." If there will be singing, prepare a song leader.*

**FIRST LEADER:**

✚ All make the Sign of the Cross.

May the mercy of God surround us as we offer our hearts to the Lord.

**ALL: Amen.**

Today we begin the season of Lent, a period of 40 days we set aside for prayer, fasting, and doing good things for others. In this way we prepare for Easter, that greatest feast in the Church, when we celebrate Jesus' rising from the dead.

**SECOND LEADER:**

Every year on Ash Wednesday, all over the world, Catholics receive a cross of ashes on their foreheads. This is a sign of sorrow for sin. It is a public sign. It tells our friends and neighbors that we know we are not perfect. We sometimes do what is wrong. We break the law of God. We hurt other people. We act with selfishness. Today we tell God and each other that we are sorry for our sins. We are going to try, with God's help, to become better people. The cross of ashes we receive means all of these things.

# ASH WEDNESDAY

**THIRD LEADER:**

Let us pray:
O God, who is merciful and understands us:
God, you love us beyond any love we can
 understand!
May our prayer, fasting, and works of mercy
help us to follow your Son,
who is the Way, the Truth, and the Life.
We ask this through Jesus Christ, our Lord.

**ALL: Amen.**

**FOURTH LEADER:**

- ◆ Point to the word "Alleluia."

In Hebrew, this word means "Praise
the Lord."

During the season of Lent, we will not say
this joyous word; not in church, at school,
or at home. Instead, during Lent, before
we read the Gospel we will sing or say, "Praise
to you, Lord Jesus Christ, King of endless
glory." Now we will bury this word in
this box, to stay here for the next 40 days.
At Easter we'll say this beautiful word
once again.

- ◆ Put the word in the box and cover it. Put the box to the side. All stand and sing **Praise to you, Lord Jesus Christ** . . .

**FIFTH LEADER:**  Matthew 6:1–2

A reading from the holy Gospel according to
Matthew

- ◆ The fifth leader reads the passage from the Bible, adding the words "Jesus said" at the beginning.

The Gospel of the Lord.

- ◆ All sit and observe silence.

**SIXTH LEADER:**

Let us pray as Jesus taught us: **Our Father** . . .
**Amen.**

Lord God,
during this Lent, help us to remember
how great you are and how small we are.
Help us to turn to you often in prayer
 and awe.
When the Forty Days of Lent are finished,
let our hearts be so full of your greatness
that we will be ready to celebrate the joy
 of Easter.
May our Lenten promises teach us
 to thank you
for every moment that we breathe and live,
even when life brings pain.
We ask this through Christ our Lord.

**ALL: Amen.**

**SEVENTH LEADER:**

Let us offer to one another a sign of
Christ's peace:

**EIGHTH LEADER:**

May the Lord bless us,

- ✚ All make the Sign of the Cross.

protect us from all evil
and bring us to everlasting life.

**ALL: Amen.**

# PRAYER FOR **WEDNESDAY MARCH 9, 2011**

## OPENING

Today is Ash Wednesday, the first day of the holy season of Lent. The word "Lent" comes from *lencten,* the Anglo-Saxon word for spring. Like spring, Lent is a season of growth. Today's Gospel reading describes how to give to those in need. These gifts are called alms (ahmz). Giving helps us to grow spiritually.

✚ All make the Sign of the Cross.

**In the name of the Father and of the Son and of the Holy Spirit. Amen.**

## PSALM (For a longer psalm, see page xiv.) Psalm 51:10b, 1 (10a)

Create in me a clean heart, O God.

**Create in me a clean heart, O God.**

And put a new and right spirit within me.
Have mercy on me, O God,
   according to your steadfast love;
according to your abundant mercy
   blot out my transgressions.

**Create in me a clean heart, O God.**

◆ All stand and sing **Praise to you Lord Jesus Christ** . . .

## GOSPEL                                   Matthew 6:1–4

A reading from the holy Gospel according to Matthew

Jesus said to his disciples: "Beware of practicing your piety before others in order to be seen by them; for then you have no reward from your Father in heaven.

So whenever you give alms, do not sound a trumpet before you, as the hypocrites do in the synagogues and in the streets, so that they may be praised by others. Truly I tell you, they have received their reward. But when you give alms, do not let your left hand know what your right hand is doing, so that your alms may be done in secret; and your Father who sees in secret will reward you."

The Gospel of the Lord.

◆ All sit and observe silence.

## FOR SILENT REFLECTION

Why is it important not to show off when we give?

## CLOSING PRAYER

Let us stand and bring our hopes and needs to God as we pray, "Lord, hear our prayer."

◆ All may add their own prayers here.

Let us pray: **Our Father . . . Amen.**

Lord God,
in this Lenten season of growth
teach us humility
and help our love to grow.
May our faith grow stronger
and our selfishness weaker.
We ask this through Christ our Lord.
**Amen.**

✚ All make the Sign of the Cross.

# PRAYER FOR THURSDAY MARCH 10, 2011

## OPENING

In today's reading, God reminds the Jewish people that he has given us the freedom to choose between good and evil, between life and death.

✛ All make the Sign of the Cross.

**In the name of the Father and of the Son and of the Holy Spirit. Amen.**

## PSALM  (For a longer psalm, see page xiv.) Psalm 51:10b, 1 (10a)

Create in me a clean heart, O God.

**Create in me a clean heart, O God.**

And put a new and right spirit within me.
Have mercy on me, O God,
   according to your steadfast love;
according to your abundant mercy
   blot out my transgressions.

**Create in me a clean heart, O God.**

## READING  Deuteronomy 30:15–16; 19–20

A reading from the Book of Deuteronomy [doo-ter-AH-nuh-mee]

See, I have set before you life and prosperity, death and adversity. If you obey the commandments of the LORD your God that I am commanding you today, by loving the LORD your God, walking in his ways, and observing his commandments, decrees, and ordinances, then you shall live and become numerous, and the LORD your God will bless you in the land that you are entering to possess. I call heaven and earth to witness against you today that I have set before you life and death, blessings and curses. Choose life so that you and your descendents may live, loving the LORD your God, obeying him, and holding fast to him; for that means life to you and length of days, so that you may live in the land that the LORD swore to give to your ancestors, to Abraham, to Isaac, and to Jacob.

The word of the Lord.

◆ All observe silence.

## FOR SILENT REFLECTION

What are some of the ways in which we can choose life?

## CLOSING PRAYER

Let us stand and bring our hopes and needs to God as we pray, "Lord, hear our prayer."

◆ All may add their own prayers here.

Let us pray: **Our Father . . . Amen.**

Lord, Lover of Life,
you created us, you sustain us,
and you renew our lives every day.
Help us to choose life today
by doing your will, loving truth,
pursuing justice, and praising you.
We ask this through Jesus Christ our Lord.
**Amen.**

✛ All make the Sign of the Cross.

# PRAYER FOR **FRIDAY**
# MARCH 11, 2011

## OPENING

Today the reading teaches about fasting (not eating certain foods or eating less).

✚ All make the Sign of the Cross.

**In the name of the Father and of the Son and of the Holy Spirit. Amen.**

## PSALM  (For a longer psalm, see page xiv.) Psalm 51:10b, 1 (10a)

Create in me a clean heart, O God.

**Create in me a clean heart, O God.**

And put a new and right spirit within me.
Have mercy on me, O God,
    according to your steadfast love;
according to your abundant mercy
    blot out my transgressions.

**Create in me a clean heart, O God.**

## READING  Isaiah 58:4, 6–9a

A reading from the Book of the Prophet Isaiah [i-ZAY-uh]

Look, you fast only to quarrel and to fight
    and to strike with a wicked fist.
Such fasting as you do today
    will not make your voice heard on high.
Is not this the fast that I choose:
    to loose the bonds of injustice,
    to undo the thongs of the yoke,
to let the oppressed go free,
    and to break every yoke?
Is it not to share your bread with the hungry,
    and bring the homeless poor into
        your house;
when you see the naked, to cover them,
    and not to hide yourself from your
        own kin.
Then your light shall break forth like
        the dawn,
    and your healing shall spring up quickly;
your vindicator shall go before you,
    the glory of the LORD shall be your
        rear guard.
Then you shall call, and the LORD
        will answer;
    you shall cry for help, and he will say,
        Here I am.

The word of the Lord.

◆ All observe silence.

## FOR SILENT REFLECTION

How can our Lenten fasting help us learn how to "fast" from selfishness, injustice, and greed?

## CLOSING PRAYER

Let us stand and bring our hopes and needs to God as we pray, "Lord, hear our prayer."

◆ All may add their own prayers here.

Let us pray: **Our Father . . . Amen.**

Almighty God,
by our Lenten fasting
teach us to live justly and love sincerely.
We ask this through Jesus Christ the Lord.
**Amen.**

✚ All make the Sign of the Cross.

**ALSO ON THIS DAY:** Daylight saving time begins on Sunday. (Turn clocks forward.)

# PRAYER FOR THE WEEK

WITH A READING FROM THE GOSPEL FOR **SUNDAY, MARCH 13, 2011**

## OPENING

In the Gospel on this first Sunday of Lent, Jesus meets with three temptations when he goes into the desert to pray. We will hear about two of the temptations.

✠ All make the Sign of the Cross.

**In the name of the Father and of the Son and of the Holy Spirit. Amen.**

## PSALM (For a longer psalm, see page xiv.) Psalm 51:10b, 1 (10a)

Create in me a clean heart, O God.

**Create in me a clean heart, O God.**

And put a new and right spirit within me.
Have mercy on me, O God,
   according to your steadfast love;
according to your abundant mercy
   blot out my transgressions.

**Create in me a clean heart, O God.**

◆ All stand and sing **Praise to you Lord Jesus Christ** . . .

## GOSPEL Matthew 4:1–4, 8–11

A reading from the holy Gospel according to Matthew

Then Jesus was led up by the Spirit into the wilderness to be tempted by the devil. He fasted for forty days and forty nights, and afterwards he was famished. The tempter came and said to him, "If you are the Son of God, command these stones to become loaves of bread." But he answered, "It is written,

  'One does not live by bread alone,
    but by every word that comes from the mouth of God.'"

Again, the devil took him to a very high mountain and showed him all the kingdoms of the world and their splendor; and he said to him, "All these I will give you, if you will fall down and worship me." Jesus said to him, "Away with you, Satan! for it is written,

  'Worship the Lord your God, and serve only him.'"

Then the devil left him, and suddenly angels came and waited on him.

The Gospel of the Lord.

◆ All sit and observe silence.

## FOR SILENT REFLECTION

What does Jesus teach us about dealing with temptation?

## CLOSING PRAYER

Let us stand and bring our hopes and needs to God as we pray, "Lord, hear our prayer."

◆ All may add their own prayers here.

Let us pray: **Our Father . . . Amen.**

God our Father,
protect us from all temptation,
cleanse our hearts, and teach us to pray.
Grant this through Christ our Lord.
**Amen.**

✠ All make the Sign of the Cross.

**ALSO ON THIS DAY:** Daylight saving time begins. (Turn clocks forward.)

# PRAYER FOR **MONDAY MARCH 14, 2011**

## OPENING

Our Lenten practices of almsgiving, fasting, and prayer help us to grow in holiness. Today's reading talks about what it means to be holy. To profane [pro-FAYN] something is to show disrespect for it. To revile [rih-VYL] means to insult or abuse. To reprove [ree-PROOV] someone is to correct. To incur [in-CUR] something is to bring it upon yourself.

✢ All make the Sign of the Cross.

**In the name of the Father and of the Son and of the Holy Spirit. Amen.**

## PSALM  (For a longer psalm, see page xiv.) Psalm 51:10b, 1 (10a)

Create in me a clean heart, O God.

**Create in me a clean heart, O God.**

And put a new and right spirit within me.
Have mercy on me, O God,
   according to your steadfast love;
according to your abundant mercy
   blot out my transgressions.

**Create in me a clean heart, O God.**

## READING  Leviticus 19:1–2, 11–12, 14, 17–18

A reading from the Book of Leviticus [lih-VIT-ih-kuhs]

The Lord spoke to Moses, saying: "Speak to all the congregation of the people of Israel and say to them: You shall be holy, for I the Lord your God am holy.

You shall not steal; you shall not deal falsely; and you shall not lie to one another. And you shall not swear falsely by my name, profaning [pro-FAYN-ing] the name of your God: I am the Lord.

You shall not revile [rih-VYL] the deaf or put a stumbling-block before the blind; you shall fear your God: I am the Lord.

You shall not hate in your heart anyone of your kin; you shall reprove [ree-PROOV] your neighbor, or you will incur [in-CUR] guilt yourself. You shall not take vengeance or bear a grudge against any of your people, but you shall love your neighbor as yourself: I am the Lord."

The word of the Lord.

◆ All observe silence.

## FOR SILENT REFLECTION

What do you think it means to be holy as God is holy?

## CLOSING PRAYER

Let us stand and bring our hopes and needs to God as we pray, "Lord, hear our prayer."

◆ All may add their own prayers here.

Let us pray: **Our Father . . . Amen.**

Holy God,
grant us the grace
to stand on the firm ground of faith.
Give us hope to shelter us from every storm,
and feed us daily with your life-giving love.
We ask this through Jesus Christ our Lord.
**Amen.**

✢ All make the Sign of the Cross.

**ALSO ON THIS DAY:** Commonwealth Day (Canada)

# PRAYER SERVICE
## LENT

*Prepare eight leaders for this service. The fourth leader will need a Bible to read the Gospel passage (Romans 7:15–17) and may need help finding it and practicing. You may wish to begin by singing, "I Want to Walk as a Child of the Light" and end with "Lord, Who Throughout These Forty Days." If the group will sing, prepare a song leader.*

✙ All make the Sign of the Cross.

**In the name of the Father and of the Son and of the Holy Spirit. Amen.**

### FIRST LEADER:
Lent is a time of preparing our hearts for the joy of Easter. Why should we have to get ready for joy? The reason is that we can get distracted from God by many things—arguments, or the idea that life isn't fair, or wanting something so much that we forget what's really important. So during Lent we put God right before our eyes and stare in his direction. Our prayer, fasting, and acts of charity to others should all help us to see him more clearly and to hear his voice in our hearts.

When we keep our eyes fixed on God, we begin to see all the ways we fall short of his love and generosity. Then we turn to him in sadness, sharing our sorrow about having done what is wrong in his sight and asking for forgiveness. When we see all our own faults, then we are more able to forgive others for their unkindness to us or to those we love.

### SECOND LEADER:
Forgiveness is a mark of the followers of Jesus. It is our great strength! If we were unable to forgive, our anger and resentment would eat us alive. Being able to forgive makes our hearts lighter and leads to deeper

# LENT
## CONTINUED

understanding among people. It also leads to knowledge about ourselves. When we forgive others, we begin to recognize our great need to work for and with Christ to bring peace.

**THIRD LEADER:**
Let us pray:
God of infinite power,
grant us a little of your strength
so that we can forgive with joy,
our love for others may be sincere,
and our hearts may be full
of your loving kindness.
We ask this through your Son,
who forgave even those who made him
　　suffer and die,
Jesus Christ our Lord.

**ALL: Amen.**

**FOURTH LEADER:**　　　　　　　　Romans 7:15–17
A reading from the Letter of Saint Paul to the Romans

◆ Read the passage from the Bible.

The word of the Lord.

◆ All observe silence.

**FIFTH LEADER:**
Let us stand and pray the Act of Contrition together.

My God, I am sorry for my sins with all
　　my heart.
In choosing to do wrong and failing to
　　do good,
I have sinned against you
whom I should love above all things.
I firmly intend, with your help,
to do penance, to sin no more,
and to avoid whatever leads me to sin.
Our Savior Jesus Christ
suffered and died for us.
In his name, my God, have mercy.
Amen.

**SIXTH LEADER:**
Let us pray as Jesus taught us: **Our Father . . .**
Amen.

**SEVENTH LEADER:**
Let us offer each other a sign of Christ's peace.

◆ All offer each other a sign of peace.

Let us pray:
merciful Lord,
you call us to follow your wonderful ways,
and to live in the light of your peace.
May we always listen
for the sound of your voice,
and pay attention to the love you give.
All that you make and do is good!
May we live according to the nature
　　you gave us
and do the good you intend us to do.
We ask this through your Son, our Light and
　　Peace, Jesus Christ the Lord.

**ALL: Amen.**

**EIGHTH LEADER:**
May the Lord bless us,

✠ All make the Sign of the Cross.

protect us from all evil
and bring us to everlasting life.

**ALL: Amen.**

# PRAYER FOR TUESDAY
# MARCH 15, 2011

## OPENING

In today's reading, the prophet, Isaiah [ī-ZAY-uh], compares God's promise to save his people to the rain and snow that give new life to the earth.

✠ All make the Sign of the Cross.

**In the name of the Father and of the Son and of the Holy Spirit. Amen.**

## PSALM    (For a longer psalm, see page xiv.) Psalm 51:10b, 1 (10a)

Create in me a clean heart, O God.

**Create in me a clean heart, O God.**

And put a new and right spirit within me.
Have mercy on me, O God,
  according to your steadfast love;
according to your abundant mercy
  blot out my transgressions.

**Create in me a clean heart, O God.**

## READING                                    Isaiah 55:10–11

A reading from the Book of the Prophet Isaiah [ī-ZAY-uh]

> For as the rain and the snow come down
>     from heaven,
>   and do not return there until they have
>     watered the earth,
> making it bring forth and sprout,
>   giving seed to the sower and bread
>     to the eater,
> so shall my word be that goes out from
>     my mouth;
>   it shall not return to me empty,
> but it shall accomplish that which
>     I purpose,
>   and succeed in the thing for which
>     I sent it.

The word of the Lord.

◆ All observe silence.

## FOR SILENT REFLECTION

What helps us to grow during the springtime of Lent?

## CLOSING PRAYER

Let us stand and bring our hopes and needs to God as we pray, "Lord, hear our prayer."

◆ All may add their own prayers here.

Let us pray: **Our Father . . . Amen.**

Loving God,
you bless all of creation with new life.
Give us faith
that we can live with you for ever.
Lift up our hearts
through our prayer and care for others.
Teach us wisdom
as we read your word.
We ask this through our Lord Jesus Christ,
    your Son, who lives and reigns with
    you in the unity of the Holy Spirit,
    one God, for ever and ever.
**Amen.**

✠ All make the Sign of the Cross.

# PRAYER FOR **WEDNESDAY** MARCH 16, 2011

## OPENING

Today's Gospel speaks of the "sign of Jonah [JOH-nuh]." Jonah was a prophet, sent by God to the city of Nineveh [NIN-uh-vuh]. The people of Ninevah listened to Jonah and all the people in the city turned away from their sinful ways and returned to God.

✢ All make the Sign of the Cross.

**In the name of the Father and of the Son and of the Holy Spirit. Amen.**

## PSALM (For a longer psalm, see page xiv.) Psalm 51:10b, 1 (10a)

Create in me a clean heart, O God.

**Create in me a clean heart, O God.**

And put a new and right spirit within me.
Have mercy on me, O God,
 according to your steadfast love;
according to your abundant mercy
 blot out my transgressions.

**Create in me a clean heart, O God.**

◆ All stand and sing **Praise to you Lord Jesus Christ** . . .

## GOSPEL   Luke 11:29–30, 32

A reading from the holy Gospel according to Luke

When the crowds were increasing, Jesus began to say, "This generation is an evil generation; it asks for a sign, but no sign will be given to it except the sign of Jonah. For just as Jonah [JOH-nuh] became a sign to the people of Nineveh [NIN-uh-vuh], so the Son of Man will be to this generation. The people of Nineveh will rise up at the judgment with this generation and condemn it, because they repented at the proclamation of Jonah, and see, something greater than Jonah is here!

The Gospel of the Lord.

◆ All sit and observe silence.

## FOR SILENT REFLECTION

How is Jesus like the sign of Jonah?

## CLOSING PRAYER

Let us stand and bring our hopes and needs to God as we pray, "Lord, hear our prayer."

◆ All may add their own prayers here.

Let us pray: **Our Father . . . Amen.**

Merciful God,
when the people of Ninevah
turned away from sin and returned to you
you forgave and blessed them.
Jesus calls us to repent,
to turn away from sin,
and enter into eternal life.
Help us to return to you.
We ask this through our Lord Jesus Christ,
 your Son, who lives and reigns with
 you in the unity of the Holy Spirit,
 one God, for ever and ever.
**Amen.**

✢ All make the Sign of the Cross.

# PRAYER SERVICE
## MEMORIAL OF SAINT PATRICK

*Prepare six leaders for this service. The third reader will need a Bible for the Gospel passage and may need help finding it and practicing. After the story of Saint Patrick you may wish to begin by singing "Lord of All Hopefulness," and end with "Christ Be Beside Me" (to the tune of "Morning Has Broken") or "The Summons." If there will be singing, prepare a song leader.*

✢ All make the Sign of the Cross.

**In the name of the Father and of the Son and of the Holy Spirit. Amen.**

**FIRST LEADER:**
Praise be to God,
who in every age sends great missionaries
    like Saint Patrick
to preach the Good News of Jesus Christ!

**ALL: Amen.**

Listen now to the story of Saint Patrick, who lived in the fifth century: As a teen, Saint Patrick was kidnapped from Scotland and sold as a slave in Ireland. Several years later, with God's help, he escaped to Britain, where he studied to become a priest and later was ordained a bishop. Then he went back to Ireland and brought the faith of Jesus to all the Irish people. He helped them believe that God didn't live in the trees of the forest, but in the hearts of all people.

**SONG LEADER:**
Please join in singing our opening song.

continued on next page

# MEMORIAL FOR SAINT PATRICK
## CONTINUED

**SECOND LEADER:**
Let us pray:
Holy Trinity, one God in three persons,
we thank you for sending us holy men
    and women
who help people to understand you.
May we always look for guides who will give
    us a deeper knowledge of your
    mysteries.
We ask this through Christ our Lord.

**ALL: Amen.**

◆ All stand and sing **Praise to you, Lord Jesus Christ** . . .

**THIRD LEADER:**                 Matthew 28: 18–20
A reading from the holy Gospel according to Matthew

◆ The third leader reads the Gospel passage from the Bible.

The Gospel of the Lord.

◆ All observe silence.

**FOURTH LEADER:**
Let us bring our hopes and needs to God as we pray, "Lord, hear our prayer."

For all the children of the world, may we find good guides and models of faith. May we develop our talents and use them wisely, we pray to the Lord . . .

For our Irish ancestors and all those who came before us. May we live the faith they passed on to us and treasure the heritage they have given us, we pray to the Lord . . .

For the homeless, the hungry, for those who are sick or suffering in any way, and for those who have died, we pray to the Lord . . .

**FIFTH LEADER:**
Let us pray as Jesus taught us: **Our Father** . . . **Amen.**

◆ Pause and then say:

Let us offer one another a sign of Christ's peace.

**SIXTH LEADER:**
Let us pray:
God of our ancestors,
give us the strength and courage
    of Saint Patrick
so that we may bring the love and joy
    of your kingdom
to all the world.
We ask this through Christ our Lord.

**ALL: Amen.**

✚ All make the Sign of the Cross.

**In the name of the Father and of the Son and of the Holy Spirit. Amen.**

# PRAYER FOR THURSDAY MARCH 17, 2011

## OPENING

Today we remember Saint Patrick, who brought the Gospel to Ireland. The reading from the Gospel today encourages us to call on God with confidence, trusting that we will receive what we truly need.

✠ All make the Sign of the Cross.

**In the name of the Father and of the Son and of the Holy Spirit. Amen.**

## PSALM  (For a longer psalm, see page xiv.) Psalm 51:10b, 1 (10a)

Create in me a clean heart, O God.

**Create in me a clean heart, O God.**

And put a new and right spirit within me.
Have mercy on me, O God,
   according to your steadfast love;
according to your abundant mercy
   blot out my transgressions.

**Create in me a clean heart, O God.**

◆ All stand and sing **Praise to you Lord Jesus Christ** . . .

## GOSPEL                                    Matthew 7:7–11

A reading from the holy Gospel according to Matthew

"Ask, and it will be given you; search, and you will find; knock, and the door will be opened for you. For everyone who asks receives, and everyone who searches finds, and for everyone who knocks, the door will be opened. Is there anyone among you who, if your child asks for bread, will give a stone? Or if the child asks for a fish, will give a snake? If you then, who are evil, know how to give good gifts to your children, how much more will your Father in heaven give good things to those who ask him!"

The Gospel of the Lord.

◆ All sit and observe silence.

## FOR SILENT REFLECTION

What do you need to ask of God?

## CLOSING PRAYER

Let us stand and bring our hopes and needs to God as we pray, "Lord, hear our prayer."

◆ All may add their own prayers here.

Let us pray: **Our Father . . . Amen.**

Generous God,
our hearts are made for you.
With confidence we call on you
to satisfy our deepest needs.
Give us what we ask of you this day;
all that is good and helpful to our growth,
for we ask in the name of Jesus Christ,
   our Lord.
Amen.

✠ All make the Sign of the Cross.

# PRAYER SERVICE
## SOLEMNITY OF SAINT JOSEPH

*Prepare six leaders for this prayer service. The third leader will need a Bible for the Gospel passage (Luke 2:41–51) and may need help finding it and practicing. After the opening remarks, you may wish to begin by singing "You Are the Light of the World" or "Blest Are They" and end with "We Are Called." If there will be singing, prepare a song leader.*

**FIRST LEADER:**
Praise be to God for the faithfulness and humility of Saint Joseph!

**ALL: Amen.**

Saint Joseph was chosen by God to be Jesus' foster father. When the Bible describes Saint Joseph, we can see his love and devotion to God come shining through. God blessed Saint Joseph with the gift of openness to the angel of the Lord, who came to him in dreams. Joseph protected and raised Jesus as his own child, sharing his knowledge and wisdom with the boy. Together with Mary, he made a loving and reverent home for God's son, and Jesus grew in wisdom, age, and grace.

**SECOND LEADER:**

✚ All make the Sign of the Cross.

**In the name of the Father and of the Son and of the Holy Spirit. Amen.**

Let us pray:
Faithful God,
Saint Joseph showed courage
and unselfish love when he took Mary
    to be his wife,
when he brought Jesus and Mary to Egypt

# SOLEMNITY OF SAINT JOSEPH

to save them from the evil king Herod,
and when he helped Mary look for Jesus
 in Jerusalem.
Help us to imitate Saint Joseph
and to find strength in his example.
We ask this through the same Jesus Christ
 our Lord.

**ALL: Amen.**

- All stand and sing **Praise to you, Lord Jesus Christ** . . .

**THIRD LEADER:** Luke 2:41–51
A reading from the holy Gospel according to Luke

- The third reader reads the Gospel passage from the Bible.

The Gospel of the Lord.

- All remain standing and observe silence.

**FOURTH LEADER:**
Let us bring our hopes and needs to God as we pray, **Lord, hear our prayer.**

For children who need the care of someone like Saint Joseph, we pray to the Lord.

For all those who are preparing for the Sacrament of Marriage, may they take Mary and Joseph as their models, we pray to the Lord.

For all those who have been exiled from their native lands due to war, persecution, or political upheavals, we pray to the Lord.

For fathers and foster fathers, that they may find the patience, gentleness, and energy they need to be good parents, we pray to the Lord.

For all those who are sick or dying, may the prayers of Saint Joseph bring them comfort and solace, we pray to the Lord.

**FIFTH LEADER:**
Let us pray as Jesus taught us: **Our Father . . . Amen.**

- Pause and then say the following.

Let us offer one another a sign of Christ's peace.

**SIXTH LEADER:**
Let us pray:
Heavenly Father,
We rely on the prayers of Saint Joseph
as we face the challenges of our lives.
May we respond to your voice as
 Saint Joseph did
and may we one day come to enjoy
the splendor of your presence with Mary,
 Saint Joseph,
and all the saints who live with you
 in unending light.
We ask this through Christ, our Lord.

**ALL: Amen.**

✛ All make the Sign of the Cross.

**In the name of the Father and of the Son and of the Holy Spirit. Amen.**

# PRAYER FOR **FRIDAY** **MARCH 18, 2011**

## OPENING

Today's Gospel stresses that we should not keep hatred and resentment in our hearts. In order to come closer to God, we must be at peace with one another.

✜ All make the Sign of the Cross.

**In the name of the Father and of the Son and of the Holy Spirit. Amen.**

## PSALM  (For a longer psalm, see page xiv.) Psalm 51:10b, 1 (10a)

Create in me a clean heart, O God.

**Create in me a clean heart, O God.**

And put a new and right spirit within me.
Have mercy on me, O God,
   according to your steadfast love;
according to your abundant mercy
   blot out my transgressions.

**Create in me a clean heart, O God.**

◆ All stand and sing **Praise to you Lord Jesus Christ** . . .

## GOSPEL                         Matthew 5:21–24

A reading from the holy Gospel according to Matthew

Jesus said, "You have heard that it was said to those of ancient times, 'You shall not murder'; and 'whoever murders shall be liable to judgment.' But I say to you that if you are angry with a brother or sister, you will be liable to judgment; and if you insult a brother or sister, you will be liable to the council; and if you say, 'You fool,' you will be liable to the hell of fire. So when you are offering your gift at the altar, if you remember that your brother or sister has something against you, leave your gift there before the altar and go; first be reconciled to your brother or sister, and then come and offer your gift."

The Gospel of the Lord.

◆ All sit and observe silence.

## FOR SILENT REFLECTION

Are you holding onto resentments? Is there someone you need to forgive today?

## CLOSING PRAYER

Let us stand and bring our hopes and needs to God as we pray, "Lord, hear our prayer."

◆ All may add their own prayers here.

Let us pray: **Our Father . . . Amen.**

Lord our God,
help us to forgive those who hurt us
and to ask forgiveness from those
   we have hurt.
Cleanse [clenz] our hearts from all anger
and fill us with your peace.
We ask this through Jesus Christ, our Lord.
**Amen.**

✜ All make the Sign of the Cross.

---

**ALSO ON THIS DAY:** Tomorrow is the Solemnity of Saint Joseph.

Tomorrow Purim (Jewish Feast of Esther) begins at sunset.

Holi (Hindu spring festival of color and joy) begins tomorrow.

# PRAYER FOR THE WEEK

WITH A READING FROM THE GOSPEL FOR **SUNDAY, MARCH 20, 2011**

## OPENING

In today's Gospel Jesus is transfigured [tranz-FIG-yrd], or changed. He appears with Moses [MOH-suhs], who received the Ten Commandments from God, and Elijah [ee-LĪ-juh], who was to announce the Messiah [meh-SĪ-uh].

✠ All make the Sign of the Cross.

**In the name of the Father and of the Son and of the Holy Spirit. Amen.**

## PSALM
(For a longer psalm, see page xiv.) Psalm 51:10b, 1 (10a)

Create in me a clean heart, O God.

Create in me a clean heart, O God.

And put a new and right spirit within me.
Have mercy on me, O God,
   according to your steadfast love;
according to your abundant mercy
   blot out my transgressions.

Create in me a clean heart, O God.

◆ All stand and sing **Praise to you Lord Jesus Christ** . . .

## GOSPEL
Matthew 17:1b–9

A reading from the holy Gospel according to Matthew

Jesus took with him Peter and James and his brother John and led them up a high mountain, by themselves. And he was transfigured before them, and his face shone like the sun, and his clothes became dazzling white. Suddenly there appeared to them Moses and Elijah, talking with him. Then Peter said to Jesus, "Lord, it is good for us to be here; if you wish, I will make three dwellings here, one for you, one for Moses, and one for Elijah [ee-LI-juh]." While he was still speaking, suddenly a bright cloud overshadowed them, and from the cloud a voice said, "This is my Son, the Beloved; with him I am well pleased; listen to him!" When the disciples heard this, they fell to the ground and were overcome by fear. But Jesus came and touched them, saying, "Get up and do not be afraid." And when they looked up, they saw no one except Jesus himself alone.

The Gospel of the Lord.

◆ All sit and observe silence.

## FOR SILENT REFLECTION

Why do you think Moses and Elijah appeared with Jesus?

## CLOSING PRAYER

Let us stand and bring our hopes and needs to God as we pray, "Lord, hear our prayer."

◆ All may add their own prayers here.

Let us pray: **Our Father . . . Amen.**

Loving Father,
in this story we see your beloved Son.
Help us to also see him in our lives.
We ask this through Christ our Lord.
**Amen.**

✠ All make the Sign of the Cross.

**ALSO ON THIS DAY:** First day of spring
Purim (Jewish Feast of Esther)
Holi (Hindu spring festival of color and joy) ends today.

# PRAYER FOR **MONDAY MARCH 21, 2011**

## OPENING

Today's Gospel encourages us to focus on our own growth, rather than criticizing others. Lent is a good time to examine our lives, to forgive those who have hurt us, and give to those who have less than we do.

✢ All make the Sign of the Cross.

**In the name of the Father and of the Son and of the Holy Spirit. Amen.**

## PSALM    (For a longer psalm, see page xiv.) Psalm 51:10b, 1 (10a)

Create in me a clean heart, O God.

**Create in me a clean heart, O God.**

And put a new and right spirit within me.
Have mercy on me, O God,
   according to your steadfast love;
according to your abundant mercy
   blot out my transgressions.

**Create in me a clean heart, O God.**

◆ All stand and sing **Praise to you Lord Jesus Christ** . . .

## GOSPEL    Luke 6:36–38

A reading from the holy Gospel according to Luke

"Be merciful, just as your Father is merciful."
   "Do not judge, and you will not be judged; do not condemn, and you will not be condemned. Forgive and you will be forgiven, give, and it will be given to you. A good measure, pressed down, shaken together, running over, will be put into your lap; for the measure you give will be the measure you get back."
The Gospel of the Lord.

◆ All sit and observe silence.

## FOR SILENT REFLECTION

Do you find it easy to forgive? Are you quick to judge? Do you find it hard to share? Think about what you want God to help you change in yourself this Lent.

## CLOSING PRAYER

Let us stand and bring our hopes and needs to God as we pray, "Lord, hear our prayer."

◆ All may add their own prayers here.

Let us pray: **Our Father . . . Amen.**

Lord God,
you allowed Peter, James, and John
to see a glimpse of Christ in glory.
We too want to understand who Jesus is.
Draw us into to your holy light
so that we may share
in the divine life of Jesus.
We ask this through the same Jesus Christ
   our Lord.
**Amen.**

✢ All make the Sign of the Cross.

# PRAYER FOR TUESDAY MARCH 22, 2011

## OPENING

In today's Gospel, Jesus warns us that if we want to be close to him and his Father, we need to be servants, not show offs.

✚ All make the Sign of the Cross.

**In the name of the Father and of the Son and of the Holy Spirit. Amen.**

## PSALM  (For a longer psalm, see page xiv.) Psalm 51:10b, 1 (10a)

Create in me a clean heart, O God.

**Create in me a clean heart, O God.**

And put a new and right spirit within me.
Have mercy on me, O God,
   according to your steadfast love;
according to your abundant mercy
   blot out my transgressions.

**Create in me a clean heart, O God.**

◆ All stand and sing **Praise to you Lord Jesus Christ** . . .

## GOSPEL  Matthew 23:1–3, 5a, 6–12

A reading from the holy Gospel according to Matthew

Then Jesus said to the crowds and to his disciples, "The scribes and the Pharisees [FAIR-ih-seez] sit on Moses' seat; therefore, do whatever they teach you and follow it; but do not do as they do, for they do not practice what they teach. They do all their deeds to be seen by others. They love to have the place of honor at banquets and the best seats in the synagogues, and to be greeted with respect in the market places, and to have people call them rabbi. But you are not to be called rabbi, for you have one teacher, and you are all students. And call no one your father on earth, for you have one Father—the one in heaven. Nor are you to be called instructors, for you have one instructor, the Messiah. The greatest among you will be your servant. All who exalt themselves will be humbled, and all who humble themselves will be exalted."

The Gospel of the Lord.

◆ All sit and observe silence.

## FOR SILENT REFLECTION

What are some ways in which we can serve others?

## CLOSING PRAYER

Let us stand and bring our hopes and needs to God as we pray, "Lord, hear our prayer."

◆ All may add their own prayers here.

Let us pray: **Our Father . . . Amen.**

Almighty God,
your Son is worthy of praise and honor,
yet he came as a servant.
Help us to follow his example,
so that by praising God and serving others
we may know happiness and peace.
We ask this through Jesus Christ, our Lord.
**Amen.**

✚ All make the Sign of the Cross.

# PRAYER FOR **WEDNESDAY MARCH 23, 2011**

## OPENING

In today's Gospel, Jesus continues to teach about the difference between our idea of greatness and God's.

✚ All make the Sign of the Cross.

**In the name of the Father and of the Son and of the Holy Spirit. Amen.**

## PSALM  (For a longer psalm, see page xiv.) Psalm 51:10b, 1 (10a)

Create in me a clean heart, O God.

**Create in me a clean heart, O God.**

And put a new and right spirit within me.
Have mercy on me, O God,
   according to your steadfast love;
according to your abundant mercy
   blot out my transgressions.

**Create in me a clean heart, O God.**

◆ All stand and sing **Praise to you Lord Jesus Christ** . . .

## GOSPEL  Matthew 20:17a, 20–28

A reading from the holy Gospel according to Matthew

While Jesus was going up to Jerusalem, the mother of the sons of Zebedee [ZEH-beh-dee] came to Jesus with her sons, and kneeling before him, she asked a favor of him. And he said to her, "What do you want?" She said to him, "Declare that these two sons of mine will sit, one at your right hand and one at your left, in your kingdom." But Jesus answered, "You do not know what you are asking. Are you able to drink the cup that I am about to drink?" They said to him, "We are able." He said to them, "You will indeed drink my cup, but to sit at my right hand and at my left, this is not mine to grant, but it is for those for whom it has been prepared by my Father." When the ten heard it, they were angry with the two brothers. But Jesus called them to him and said, "You know that the rulers of the Gentiles lord it over them, and their great ones are tyrants over them. It will not be so among you; but whoever wishes to be great among you must be your servant, and whoever wishes to be first among you must be your slave; just as the Son of Man came not to be served but to serve, and to give his life as a ransom for many."

The Gospel of the Lord.

◆ All sit and observe silence.

## FOR SILENT REFLECTION

Who do you know who serves others?

## CLOSING PRAYER

Let us stand and bring our hopes and needs to God as we pray, "Lord, hear our prayer."

◆ All may add their own prayers here.

Let us pray: **Our Father . . . Amen.**

Loving and generous God,
lead us on the path of service.
Help us to use our gifts
for the well-being of others.
We ask this through Christ our Lord.
**Amen.**

✚ All make the Sign of the Cross.

# PRAYER FOR THURSDAY MARCH 24, 2011

## OPENING

In today's reading, the prophet Jeremiah paints a pretty grim picture of what life is like for people who rely only on human strength and wisdom. Listen to what he says about those who trust in God.

✟ *All make the Sign of the Cross.*

**In the name of the Father and of the Son and of the Holy Spirit. Amen.**

## PSALM        (For a longer psalm, see page xiv.) Psalm 51:10b, 1 (10a)

Create in me a clean heart, O God.

**Create in me a clean heart, O God.**

And put a new and right spirit within me.
Have mercy on me, O God,
   according to your steadfast love;
according to your abundant mercy
   blot out my transgressions.

**Create in me a clean heart, O God.**

## READING        Jeremiah 17:5–8

A reading from the Book of the Prophet Jeremiah

Thus says the LORD:
Cursed are those who trust in
      mere mortals
   and make mere flesh their strength,
      whose hearts turn away from the LORD.
They shall be like a shrub in the desert,
   and shall not see when relief comes.
They shall live in the parched places
      of the wilderness,
   in an uninhabited salt land.
Blessed are those who trust in the LORD,
   whose trust is the LORD.
They shall be like a tree planted by water,
   sending out its roots by the stream.
It shall not fear when heat comes,
   and its leaves shall stay green;
in the year of drought it is not anxious,
   and it does not cease to bear fruit.

The word of the Lord.

◆ *All observe silence.*

## FOR SILENT REFLECTION

Do you think Jeremiah is right? Are you happier when you trust in God?

## CLOSING PRAYER

Let us stand and bring our hopes and needs to God as we pray, "Lord, hear our prayer."

◆ *All may add their own prayers here.*

Let us pray: **Our Father . . . Amen.**

Holy God,
during this Lenten season
help us to become more trusting,
more prayerful,
and more open to your grace.
We ask this through your Son, Jesus Christ
      our Lord.
**Amen.**

✟ *All make the Sign of the Cross.*

# PRAYER FOR FRIDAY MARCH 25, 2011

## OPENING

Today is the solemnity of the Annunciation [uh-NUN-see-ay-shun] of the Lord, when God's messenger, the angel Gabriel, announced to Mary that she would give birth to the Messiah.

✛ All make the Sign of the Cross.

**In the name of the Father and of the Son and of the Holy Spirit. Amen.**

## PSALM  (For a longer psalm, see page xiv.) Psalm 51:10b, 1 (10a)

Create in me a clean heart, O God.

**Create in me a clean heart, O God.**

And put a new and right spirit within me.
Have mercy on me, O God,
  according to your steadfast love;
according to your abundant mercy
  blot out my transgressions.

**Create in me a clean heart, O God.**

◆ All stand and sing **Praise to you Lord Jesus Christ** . . .

## GOSPEL  Luke 1:26a, 26c–27a, 27c–35, 37–38

A reading from the holy Gospel according to Luke

In the sixth month the angel Gabriel was sent by God to a virgin. The virgin's name was Mary. And he came to her and said, "Greetings, favored one! The Lord is with you." But she was much perplexed by his words and pondered what sort of greeting this might be. The angel said to her, "Do not be afraid, Mary, for you have found favor with God. And now, you will conceive in your womb and bear a son, and you will name him Jesus. He will be great, and will be called the Son of the Most High, and the Lord God will give to him the throne of his ancestor David. He will reign over the house of Jacob forever, and of his kingdom there will be no end." Mary said to the angel, "How can this be, since I am a virgin?" The angel said to her, "The Holy Spirit will come upon you, and the power of the Most High will overshadow you; therefore the child to be born will be holy; he will be called Son of God. For nothing will be impossible with God." Then Mary said, "Here am I, the servant of the Lord; let it be with me according to your word." Then the angel departed from her.

The Gospel of the Lord.

◆ All sit and observe silence.

## FOR SILENT REFLECTION

Why do you think Mary said "yes" to the angel?

## CLOSING PRAYER

Let us stand and bring our hopes and needs to God as we pray, "Lord, hear our prayer."

◆ All may add their own prayers here.

Let us pray: **Our Father . . . Amen.**

Almighty God,
help us to trust you as Mary did
so that we can serve you well.
We ask this through Jesus Christ the Lord.
**Amen.**

✛ All make the Sign of the Cross.

# PRAYER FOR THE WEEK

WITH A READING FROM THE GOSPEL FOR **SUNDAY, MARCH 27, 2011**

## OPENING

Today Jesus has a surprising conversation.

✤ All make the Sign of the Cross.

**In the name of the Father and of the Son and of the Holy Spirit. Amen.**

## PSALM   (For a longer psalm, see page xiv.) Psalm 51:10b, 1 (10a)

Create in me a clean heart, O God.

**Create in me a clean heart, O God.**

And put a new and right spirit within me.
Have mercy on me, O God,
   according to your steadfast love;
according to your abundant mercy
   blot out my transgressions.

**Create in me a clean heart, O God.**

◆ All stand and sing **Praise to you Lord Jesus Christ** . . .

## GOSPEL                                    John 4:5a, 6–15

A reading from the holy Gospel according to John

So Jesus came to a Samaritan [suh-MAYR-uh-tuhn] city. Jacob's well was there, and Jesus, tired out by his journey, was sitting by the well. It was about noon.

   A Samaritan woman came to draw water, and Jesus said to her, "Give me a drink." (His disciples had gone to the city to buy food.) The Samaritan woman said to him, "How is it that you, a Jew, ask a drink of me, a woman of Samaria?" (Jews do not share things in common with Samaritans.) Jesus answered her, "If you knew the gift of God, and who it is that is saying to you, 'Give me a drink,' you would have asked him, and he would have given you living water." The woman said to him, "Sir, you have no bucket, and the well is deep. Where do you get that living water? Are you greater than our ancestor Jacob, who gave us the well, and with his sons and his flocks drank from it?" Jesus said to her, "Everyone who drinks of this water will be thirsty again, but those who drink of the water that I will give them will never be thirsty. The water that I will give will become in them a spring of water gushing up to eternal life." The woman said to him, "Sir, give me this water, so that I may never be thirsty or have to keep coming here to draw water."

The Gospel of the Lord.

◆ All sit and observe silence.

## FOR SILENT REFLECTION

What is this water that Jesus is talking about?

## CLOSING PRAYER

Let us stand and bring our hopes and needs to God as we pray, "Lord, hear our prayer."

◆ All may add their own prayers here.

Let us pray: **Our Father . . . Amen.**

Almighty God,
give us the water of everlasting life.
We ask this through Christ our Lord.
**Amen.**

✤ All make the Sign of the Cross.

**ALSO ON THIS DAY:** Girl Scout Sunday (U.S.A.)

# PRAYER FOR **MONDAY** MARCH 28, 2011

## OPENING

In today's Gospel, Jesus is in the synagogue in his hometown of Nazareth [NAZ-uh-reth]. He has just read the prophecy of Isaiah that says "The Spirit of the Lord is upon me . . ." and has told the people, "Today this scripture has been fulfilled in your hearing."

✚ All make the Sign of the Cross.

**In the name of the Father and of the Son and of the Holy Spirit. Amen.**

## PSALM  (For a longer psalm, see page xiv.) Psalm 33:20 (22)

Let your steadfast love, O Lord, be upon us,
 even as we hope in you.

**Let your steadfast love, O Lord, be upon us,
 even as we hope in you.**

Our soul waits for the Lord;
 he is our help and shield.

**Let your steadfast love, O Lord, be upon us,
 even as we hope in you.**

◆ All stand and sing **Praise to you Lord Jesus Christ** . . .

## GOSPEL  Luke 4:24–26, 28–30

A reading from the holy Gospel according to Luke

Jesus said, "Truly I tell you, no prophet is accepted in the prophet's hometown. But the truth is, there were many widows in Israel in the time of Elijah [ee-LĪ-juh], when the heaven was shut up three years and six months, and there was a severe famine over all the land; yet Elijah was sent to none of them except to a widow at Zarephath [ZAYR-uh-fath] in Sidon [SĪ-duhn]." When they heard this, all in the synagogue were filled with rage. They got up, drove him out of the town, and led him to the brow of the hill on which their town was built, so that they might hurl him off the cliff. But he passed through the midst of them and went on his way.

The Gospel of the Lord.

◆ All sit and observe silence.

## FOR SILENT REFLECTION

Why do you think people in Jesus' hometown find it hard to accept who he is?

## CLOSING PRAYER

Let us stand and bring our hopes and needs to God as we pray, "Lord, hear our prayer."

◆ All may add their own prayers here.

Let us pray: **Our Father . . . Amen.**
Lord God,
it is difficult for us to see your Son
when we don't expect to see him.
It is difficult to hear his voice
in the familiar voices of family and friends.
Yet he does speak to us in familiar places,
and through our friends and family,
for he has come to dwell with us.
Help us to expect him in our hometown.
We ask this through the same Christ our Lord.
**Amen.**

✚ All make the Sign of the Cross.

# PRAYER FOR TUESDAY MARCH 29, 2011

## OPENING

In today's Gospel Jesus teaches us about forgiveness and mercy.

✚ All make the Sign of the Cross.

**In the name of the Father and of the Son and of the Holy Spirit. Amen.**

## PSALM  (For a longer psalm, see page xiv.) Psalm 33:20 (22)

Let your steadfast love, O Lord, be upon us,
  even as we hope in you.

**Let your steadfast love, O Lord, be upon us,
  even as we hope in you.**

Our soul waits for the Lord;
  he is our help and shield.

**Let your steadfast love, O Lord, be upon us,
  even as we hope in you.**

◆ All stand and sing **Praise to you Lord Jesus Christ . . .**

## GOSPEL  Matthew 18:21–23, 26–29a, 30, 32–33

A reading from the holy Gospel according to Matthew

Then Peter came and said to him, "Lord, if another member of the church sins against me, how often should I forgive? As many as seven times?" Jesus said to him, "Not seven times, but, I tell you, seventy-seven times."

"For this reason the kingdom of heaven may be compared to a king who wished to settle accounts with his slaves. The slave who could not pay his debt fell on his knees before the king, saying, 'Have patience with me, and I will pay you everything.' And out of pity for him, the lord of that slave released him and forgave him the debt. But that same slave, as he went out, came upon one of his fellow slaves who owed him a hundred denarii [dih-NAHR-ee]; and seizing him by the throat, he said, 'Pay what you owe.' Then his fellow slave fell down and pleaded with him. But he refused; then he went and threw him into prison until he would pay the debt. Then his lord summoned him and said to him, 'You wicked slave! I forgave you all that debt because you pleaded with me. Should you not have had mercy on your fellow slave, as I had mercy on you?'"

The Gospel of the Lord.

◆ All sit and observe silence.

## FOR SILENT REFLECTION

How has God forgiven you? Does remembering this help you forgive others?

## CLOSING PRAYER

Let us stand and bring our hopes and needs to God as we pray, "Lord, hear our prayer."

◆ All may add their own prayers here.

Let us pray: **Our Father . . . Amen.**

God of Mercy,
how often you have forgiven us!
Help us to be more forgiving of others.
We ask this through Jesus Christ our Lord.
**Amen.**

✚ All make the Sign of the Cross.

# PRAYER FOR WEDNESDAY MARCH 30, 2011

## OPENING

God gave the Jewish people commandments, or laws, so that by living according to these commandments, they could be God's people. The first commandment is to believe in God.

✚ All make the Sign of the Cross.

**In the name of the Father and of the Son and of the Holy Spirit. Amen.**

## PSALM (For a longer psalm, see page xiv.) Psalm 33:20 (22)

Let your steadfast love, O Lord, be upon us,
 even as we hope in you.

**Let your steadfast love, O Lord, be upon us, even as we hope in you.**

Our soul waits for the Lord;
 he is our help and shield.

**Let your steadfast love, O Lord, be upon us, even as we hope in you.**

◆ All stand and sing **Praise to you Lord Jesus Christ** . . .

## GOSPEL  Matthew 5:17–19

A reading from the holy Gospel according to Matthew

Jesus said, "Do not think that I have come to abolish the law or the prophets; I have come not to abolish but to fulfill. For truly I tell you, until heaven and earth pass away, not one letter, not one stroke of a letter, will pass from the law until all is accomplished. Therefore, whoever breaks one of the least of these commandments, and teaches others to do the same, will be called least in the kingdom of heaven; but whoever does them and teaches them will be called great in the kingdom of heaven. For I tell you, unless your righteousness exceeds that of the scribes and Pharisees, you will never enter the kingdom of heaven."

The Gospel of the Lord.

◆ All sit and observe silence.

## FOR SILENT REFLECTION

Why do you think it is so important to keep the commandments?

## CLOSING PRAYER

Let us stand and bring our hopes and needs to God as we pray, "Lord, hear our prayer."

◆ All may add their own prayers here.

Let us pray: **Our Father . . . Amen.**

Lord God,
you come to us in love
to show us the way to you.
Help us to obey your commandments,
to love and serve you and one another.
We ask this through our Lord Jesus Christ,
 your Son, who lives and reigns with
 you in the unity of the Holy Spirit,
 one God, for ever and ever.
**Amen.**

✚ All make the Sign of the Cross.

# PRAYER FOR **THURSDAY MARCH 31, 2011**

## OPENING

In today's reading, the prophet Jeremiah [jayr-uh-MĪ-uh] delivers a message to the people from their God.

✚ All make the Sign of the Cross.

**In the name of the Father and of the Son and of the Holy Spirit. Amen.**

## PSALM   (For a longer psalm, see page xiv.) Psalm 33:20 (22)

Let your steadfast love, O Lord, be upon us,
  even as we hope in you.

**Let your steadfast love, O Lord, be upon us,
  even as we hope in you.**

Our soul waits for the Lord;
  he is our help and shield.

**Let your steadfast love, O Lord, be upon us,
  even as we hope in you.**

## READING   Jeremiah 7:23–26

A reading from the book of the prophet Jeremiah [jayr-uh-MĪ-uh]

But this command I gave them, "Obey my voice, and I will be your God, and you shall be my people; and walk only in the way that I command you, so that it may be well with you." Yet they did not obey or incline their ear, but, in the stubbornness of their evil will, they walked in their own counsels, and looked backwards rather than forwards. From the day that your ancestors came out of the land of Egypt until this day, I have persistently sent all my servants the prophets to them, day after day; yet they did not listen to me, or pay attention, but they stiffened their necks. They did worse than their ancestors did.

The word of the Lord.

◆ All observe silence.

## FOR SILENT REFLECTION

Are we, like the people in this passage, sometimes stubborn and not obeying God?

## CLOSING PRAYER

Let us stand and bring our hopes and needs to God as we pray, "Lord, hear our prayer."

◆ All may add their own prayers here.

Let us pray: **Our Father . . . Amen.**

Heavenly Father,
you teach us how to live;
but we do not listen.
We go our own way
and do our own thing
and then complain
that we aren't happy.
Help us to love you more,
that we might live in peace and joy.
We ask this through Christ our Lord.
**Amen.**

✚ All make the Sign of the Cross.

# PRAYER FOR FRIDAY APRIL 1, 2011

## OPENING

In today's Gospel Jesus reminds us of the two greatest commandments.

✢ All make the Sign of the Cross.

**In the name of the Father and of the Son and of the Holy Spirit. Amen.**

## PSALM
(For a longer psalm, see page xiv.) Psalm 33:20 (22)

Let your steadfast love, O Lord, be upon us,
even as we hope in you.

**Let your steadfast love, O Lord, be upon us,
even as we hope in you.**

Our soul waits for the Lord;
he is our help and shield.

**Let your steadfast love, O Lord, be upon us,
even as we hope in you.**

◆ All stand and sing **Praise to you Lord Jesus Christ . . .**

## GOSPEL
Mark 12:28–34

A reading from the holy Gospel according to Mark

One of the scribes came near and heard them disputing with one another, and seeing that Jesus answered them well, he asked him, "Which commandment is the first of all?" Jesus answered, "The first is, 'Hear, O Israel: the Lord our God, the Lord is one; you shall love the Lord your God with all your heart, and with all your soul, and with all your mind, and with all your strength.' The second is this, 'You shall love your neighbor as yourself.' There is no other commandment greater than these." Then the scribe said to him, "You are right, teacher; you have truly said that, 'He is One, and besides him there is no other'; and 'to love him with all the heart, and with all the understanding, and with all the strength, and to love one's neighbor as oneself;' this is much more important than all whole burnt offerings and sacrifices." When Jesus saw that he answered wisely, he said to him, "You are not far from the kingdom of God." After that no one dared to ask him any question.

The Gospel of the Lord.

◆ All sit and observe silence.

## FOR SILENT REFLECTION

Why do you think that loving God is the first commandment?

## CLOSING PRAYER

Let us stand and bring our hopes and needs to God as we pray, "Lord, hear our prayer."

◆ All may add their own prayers here.

Let us pray: **Our Father . . . Amen.**

God our Father,
send your love into our hearts
so that we may praise you
and be good sisters and brothers
to one another.
Grant this through Jesus Christ our Lord.
**Amen.**

✢ All make the Sign of the Cross.

# PRAYER FOR THE WEEK

WITH A READING FROM THE GOSPEL FOR **SUNDAY, APRIL 3, 2011**

## OPENING

In today's Gospel Jesus heals a blind man. As you listen, remember other stories we have read in which "seeing" means more than just physical sight.

✦ All make the Sign of the Cross.

**In the name of the Father and of the Son and of the Holy Spirit. Amen.**

## PSALM  (For a longer psalm, see page xiv.) Psalm 33:20 (22)

Let your steadfast love, O Lord, be upon us,
 even as we hope in you.

**Let your steadfast love, O Lord, be upon us,
 even as we hope in you.**

Our soul waits for the Lord;
 he is our help and shield.

**Let your steadfast love, O Lord, be upon us,
 even as we hope in you.**

◆ All stand and sing **Praise to you Lord Jesus Christ** . . .

## GOSPEL                                           John 9:1–7

A reading from the holy Gospel according to John

As he walked along, he saw a man blind from birth. His disciples asked him, "Rabbi [RAB-ī], who sinned, this man or his parents, that he was born blind?" Jesus answered, "Neither this man nor his parents sinned; he was born blind so that God's works might be revealed in him. We must work the works of him who sent me while it is day; night is coming when no one can work. As long as I am in the world, I am the light of the world." When he had said this, he spat on the ground and made mud with the saliva and spread the mud on the man's eyes, saying to him, "Go, wash in the Pool of Siloam" [sih-LOH-uhm] (which means Sent). Then he went and washed and came back able to see.

The Gospel of the Lord.

◆ All sit and observe silence.

## FOR SILENT REFLECTION

What do you think Jesus means when he says "I am the light of the world"? What does this light do?

## CLOSING PRAYER

Let us stand and bring our hopes and needs to God as we pray, "Lord, hear our prayer."

◆ All may add their own prayers here.

Let us pray: **Our Father . . . Amen.**

God of light,
even though we have eyes, often we do not see
that you are reaching out to heal us.
Through your healing
may the power of your love be seen.
We ask this in the name of Jesus Christ
 our Lord.
**Amen.**

✦ All make the Sign of the Cross.

# PRAYER FOR MONDAY
# APRIL 4, 2011

## OPENING

In today's reading, the prophet Isaiah [ī-ZAY-uh] tells of God's promise for creation.

✛ All make the Sign of the Cross.

**In the name of the Father and of the Son and of the Holy Spirit. Amen.**

## PSALM     (For a longer psalm, see page xiv.) Psalm 33:20 (22)

Let your steadfast love, O Lord, be upon us,
  even as we hope in you.

**Let your steadfast love, O Lord, be upon us,
  even as we hope in you.**

Our soul waits for the Lord;
  he is our help and shield.

**Let your steadfast love, O Lord, be upon us,
  even as we hope in you.**

## READING     Isaiah 65:17–20a, 21

A reading from the book of the prophet Isaiah [ī-ZAY-uh]

  For I am about to create new heavens
    and a new earth;
  the former things shall not be remembered
    or come to mind.
  But be glad and rejoice forever
    in what I am creating;
  for I am about to create Jerusalem as a joy,
    and its people as a delight.
  I will rejoice in Jerusalem
      [juh-ROO-suh-lem],
    and delight in my people;
  no more shall the sound of weeping be
      heard in it,
    or the cry of distress.
  No more shall there be in it
    an infant who lives but a few days,
    or an old person who does not live out
      a lifetime.
  They shall build houses and inhabit them;
    they shall plant vineyards and eat
      their fruit.

The word of the Lord.

◆ All observe silence.

## FOR SILENT REFLECTION

How do you think this promise will be fulfilled?

## CLOSING PRAYER

Let us stand and bring our hopes and needs to God as we pray, "Lord, hear our prayer."

◆ All may add their own prayers here.

Let us pray: **Our Father . . . Amen.**

God, our Creator,
we believe that the day will come
when all people will live in peace,
and all of creation will sing your praises.
Help us to prepare for that day.
We ask this through Jesus Christ our Lord.
**Amen.**

✛ All make the Sign of the Cross.

# PRAYER FOR TUESDAY APRIL 5, 2011

## OPENING

In today's Gospel Jesus heals a man who has been ill for a long time. As you listen, notice who begins this relationship, Jesus or the paralyzed [PAIR-uh-līzd] man.

✦ All make the Sign of the Cross.

**In the name of the Father and of the Son and of the Holy Spirit. Amen.**

## PSALM  (For a longer psalm, see page xiv.) Psalm 33:20 (22)

Let your steadfast love, O Lord, be upon us,
   even as we hope in you.

**Let your steadfast love, O Lord, be upon us,
   even as we hope in you.**

Our soul waits for the Lord;
   he is our help and shield.

**Let your steadfast love, O Lord, be upon us,
   even as we hope in you.**

◆ All stand and sing **Praise to you Lord Jesus Christ** . . .

## GOSPEL   John 5:1–9a

A reading from the holy Gospel according to John

After this there was a festival of the Jews, and Jesus went up to Jerusalem [juh-ROO-suh-lem].

Now in Jerusalem by the Sheep Gate there is a pool, called in Hebrew Bethzatha (Beth-ZAH-thuh), which has five porticoes. In these lay many invalids—blind, lame, and paralyzed. One man was there who had been ill for thirty-eight years. When Jesus saw him lying there and knew that he had been there a long time, he said to him, "Do you want to be made well?" The sick man answered him, "Sir, I have no one to put me into the pool when the water is stirred up; and while I am making my way, someone else steps down ahead of me." Jesus said to him, "Stand up, take your mat and walk." At once the man was made well, and he took up his mat and began to walk.

The Gospel of the Lord.

◆ All sit and observe silence.

## FOR SILENT REFLECTION

What did the paralyzed man say when Jesus asked if he wanted to be healed?

## CLOSING PRAYER

Let us stand and bring our hopes and needs to God as we pray, "Lord, hear our prayer."

◆ All may add their own prayers here.

Let us pray: **Our Father . . . Amen.**

God, our Healer,
your healing power is ever present;
but sometimes we get distracted
by our pains and worries
and don't ask for what we need.
Reach out to us, Lord.
Remind us of your love.
We ask this through your son, Jesus Christ
      our Lord.
**Amen.**

✦ All make the Sign of the Cross.

# PRAYER FOR WEDNESDAY APRIL 6, 2011

### OPENING

In today's Gospel Jesus describes his relationship with his heavenly Father.

✠ All make the Sign of the Cross.

**In the name of the Father and of the Son and of the Holy Spirit. Amen.**

### PSALM  (For a longer psalm, see page xiv.) Psalm 33:20 (22)

Let your steadfast love, O Lord, be upon us,
 even as we hope in you.

Let your steadfast love, O Lord, be upon us,
 even as we hope in you.

Our soul waits for the Lord;
 he is our help and shield.

Let your steadfast love, O Lord, be upon us,
 even as we hope in you.

◆ All stand and sing **Praise to you Lord Jesus Christ** . . .

### GOSPEL  John 5:19–24a

A reading of the holy Gospel according to John

Jesus said to them, "Very truly, I tell you, the Son can do nothing on his own, but only what he sees the Father doing; for whatever the Father does, the Son does likewise. The Father loves the Son and shows him all that he himself is doing; and he will show him greater works than these, so that you will be astonished. Indeed, just as the Father raises the dead and gives them life, so also the Son gives life to whomever he wishes. The Father judges no one but has given all judgment to the Son, so that all may honor the Son just as they honor the Father. Anyone who does not honor the Son does not honor the Father who sent him. Very truly, I tell you, anyone who hears my word and believes him who sent me has eternal life."

The Gospel of the Lord.

◆ All sit and observe silence.

### FOR SILENT REFLECTION

From this description, what do we learn about how the Father and the Son work together?

### CLOSING PRAYER

Let us stand and bring our hopes and needs to God as we pray, "Lord, hear our prayer."

◆ All may add their own prayers here.

Let us pray: **Our Father . . . Amen.**

Loving God,
as we read your holy word,
help us to know you better
through your beloved Son.
We ask this through our Lord Jesus Christ,
 your Son, who lives and reigns with
 you and the Holy Spirit, one God,
 for ever and ever.
**Amen.**

✠ All make the Sign of the Cross.

# PRAYER FOR **THURSDAY APRIL 7, 2011**

## OPENING

In today's Gospel, Jesus challenges people who claim to know scripture but are unwilling to listen to God with their hearts.

✢ All make the Sign of the Cross.

**In the name of the Father and of the Son and of the Holy Spirit. Amen.**

## PSALM  (For a longer psalm, see page xiv.) Psalm 33:20 (22)

Let your steadfast love, O Lord, be upon us,
  even as we hope in you.

Let your steadfast love, O Lord, be upon us,
  even as we hope in you.

Our soul waits for the Lord;
  he is our help and shield.

Let your steadfast love, O Lord, be upon us,
  even as we hope in you.

◆ All stand and sing **Praise to you Lord Jesus Christ** . . .

## GOSPEL  John 5:39–47

A reading from the holy Gospel according to John

Jesus said, "You search the scriptures because you think that in them you have eternal life; and it is they that testify on my behalf. Yet you refuse to come to me to have life. I do not accept glory from human beings. But I know that you do not have the love of God in you. I have come in my Father's name, and you do not accept me; if another comes in his own name, you will accept him. How can you believe when you accept glory from one another and do not seek the glory that comes from the one who alone is God? Do not think that I will accuse you before the Father; your accuser [uh-kyoo-ser] is Moses [MOH-suhs], on whom you have set your hope. If you believed Moses, you would believe me, for he wrote about me. But if you do not believe what he wrote, how will you believe what I say?"

The Gospel of the Lord.

◆ All sit and observe silence.

## FOR SILENT REFLECTION

What do you think this Gospel tell us about how we ought to read scripture?

## CLOSING PRAYER

Let us stand and bring our hopes and needs to God as we pray, "Lord, hear our prayer."

◆ All may add their own prayers here.

Let us pray: **Our Father . . . Amen.**

Holy God,
help us to listen to your word
with open hearts and minds.
May our study lead to prayer
and our prayer lead
to good works and praise.
We ask this through Jesus Christ our Lord.
**Amen.**

✢ All make the Sign of the Cross.

# PRAYER FOR **FRIDAY** **APRIL 8, 2011**

## OPENING

In today's Gospel we hear that people cannot seem to accept who Jesus is, in spite of all his teaching and healing. Listen to what Jesus says to them.

✛ All make the Sign of the Cross.

**In the name of the Father and of the Son and of the Holy Spirit. Amen.**

## PSALM (For a longer psalm, see page xiv.) Psalm 33:20 (22)

Let your steadfast love, O Lord, be upon us,
  even as we hope in you.

Let your steadfast love, O Lord, be upon us,
  even as we hope in you.

Our soul waits for the Lord;
  he is our help and shield.

Let your steadfast love, O Lord, be upon us,
  even as we hope in you.

◆ All stand and sing **Praise to you Lord Jesus Christ** . . .

## GOSPEL John 7:25–30

A reading from the holy Gospel according to John

Now some of the people of Jerusalem were saying, "Is not this the man whom they are trying to kill? And here he is, speaking openly, but they say nothing to him! Can it be that the authorities really know that this is the Messiah? Yet we know where this man is from; but when the Messiah comes, no one will know where he is from." Then Jesus cried out as he was teaching in the temple, "You know me, and you know where I am from. I have not come on my own. But the one who sent me is true, and you do not know him. I know him, because I am from him, and he sent me." Then they tried to arrest him, but no one laid hands on him, because his hour had not yet come.

The Gospel of the Lord.

◆ All sit and observe silence.

## FOR SILENT REFLECTION

Why does Jesus say the people know him?

## CLOSING PRAYER

Let us stand and bring our hopes and needs to God as we pray, "Lord, hear our prayer."

◆ All may add their own prayers here.

Let us pray: **Our Father . . . Amen.**

Lord God,
give us the eyes of faith
to see your truth in the words of scripture,
your love in the sacraments of the Church,
and your joy in the example of the saints.
We ask this through Christ our Lord.
**Amen.**

✛ All make the Sign of the Cross.

# PRAYER FOR THE WEEK

WITH A READING FROM THE GOSPEL FOR **SUNDAY, APRIL 10, 2011**

## OPENING

Today is the fifth Sunday of Lent. We will hear the story of Jesus raising his friend Lazarus [LAZ-uh-ruhs] from the dead. Listen to what Jesus tells Martha [MAHR-thuh], the sister of Lazarus.

✛ All make the Sign of the Cross.

**In the name of the Father and of the Son and of the Holy Spirit. Amen.**

## PSALM
(For a longer psalm, see page xiv.) Psalm 33:20 (22)

Let your steadfast love, O Lord, be upon us,
even as we hope in you.

**Let your steadfast love, O Lord, be upon us,
even as we hope in you.**

Our soul waits for the Lord;
he is our help and shield.

**Let your steadfast love, O Lord, be upon us,
even as we hope in you.**

◆ All stand and sing **Praise to you Lord Jesus Christ** . . .

## GOSPEL
John 11:5b–6, 17, 20–27

A reading from the holy Gospel according to John

Though Jesus loved Martha and her sister and Lazarus, after having heard that Lazarus was ill, he stayed two days longer in the place where he was. When Jesus arrived, he found that Lazarus had already been in the tomb for four days. When Martha heard that Jesus was coming, she went and met him, while Mary stayed at home. Martha said to Jesus, "Lord, if you had been here, my brother would not have died. But even now I know that God will give you whatever you ask of him." Jesus said to her, "Your brother will rise again." Martha said to him, "I know that he will rise again in the resurrection on the last day." Jesus said to her, "I am the resurrection and the life. Those who believe in me, even though they die, will live, and everyone who lives and believes in me will never die. Do you believe this?" She said to him, "Yes, Lord, I believe that you are the Messiah, the Son of God, the one who is coming into the world."

The Gospel of the Lord.

◆ All sit and observe silence.

## FOR SILENT REFLECTION

Jesus asks us to believe that he is the Resurrection and the life. How do we come to know and trust Jesus this well?

## CLOSING PRAYER

Let us stand and bring our hopes and needs to God as we pray, "Lord, hear our prayer."

◆ All may add their own prayers here.

Let us pray: **Our Father . . . Amen.**

Lord God, Lover of Life,
give us faith to believe in
and share in eternal life through your Son,
    Jesus Christ our Lord.
**Amen.**

✛ All make the Sign of the Cross.

# PRAYER FOR MONDAY APRIL 11, 2011

## OPENING

In today's Gospel, Jesus challenges people who are more willing to look at the sins of others than at their own sins.

◆ All make the Sign of the Cross.

**In the name of the Father and of the Son and of the Holy Spirit. Amen.**

## PSALM  (For a longer psalm, see page xiv.) Psalm 33:20 (22)

Let your steadfast love, O Lord, be upon us,
  even as we hope in you.

**Let your steadfast love, O Lord, be upon us,
  even as we hope in you.**

Our soul waits for the Lord;
  he is our help and shield.

**Let your steadfast love, O Lord, be upon us,
  even as we hope in you.**

◆ All stand and sing **Praise to you Lord Jesus Christ** . . .

## GOSPEL  John 8:2–7, 9–11

A reading from the holy Gospel according to John

Early in the morning Jesus came again to the temple. All the people came to him and he sat down and began to teach them. The scribes and the Pharisees brought a woman who had been caught in adultery; and making her stand before all of them, they said to him, "Teacher, this woman was caught in the very act of committing adultery. Now in the law, Moses commanded us to stone such women. Now what do you say?" They said this to test him, so that they might have some charge to bring against him. Jesus bent down and wrote with his finger on the ground. When they kept on questioning him, he straightened up and said to them, "Let anyone among you who is without sin be the first to throw a stone at her." When they heard it, they went away, one by one, beginning with the elders; and Jesus was left alone with the woman standing before him. Jesus straightened up and said to her, "Woman, where are they? Has no one condemned you?" She said, "No one, sir." And Jesus said, "Neither do I condemn you. Go your way, and from now on do not sin again."

The Gospel of the Lord.

◆ All sit and observe silence.

## FOR SILENT REFLECTION

What does this story tell us about Jesus?

## CLOSING PRAYER

Let us stand and bring our hopes and needs to God as we pray, "Lord, hear our prayer."

◆ All may add their own prayers here.

Let us pray: **Our Father** . . . **Amen.**

Merciful God,
help us to see our own faults
and to forgive others as you have forgiven us.
We ask this through Christ our Lord.
**Amen.**

✚ All make the Sign of the Cross.

# PRAYER FOR TUESDAY APRIL 12, 2011

## OPENING

In today's Gospel, Jesus speaks of his relationship with God, his heavenly Father.

✢ All make the Sign of the Cross.

**In the name of the Father and of the Son and of the Holy Spirit. Amen.**

## PSALM
(For a longer psalm, see page xiv.) Psalm 33:20 (22)

Let your steadfast love, O Lord, be upon us, even as we hope in you.

**Let your steadfast love, O Lord, be upon us, even as we hope in you.**

Our soul waits for the Lord; he is our help and shield.

**Let your steadfast love, O Lord, be upon us, even as we hope in you.**

◆ All stand and sing **Praise to you Lord Jesus Christ** . . .

## GOSPEL
John 8:25–30

A reading from the holy Gospel according to John

They said to Jesus, "Who are you?" Jesus said to them, "Why do I speak to you at all? I have much to say about you and much to condemn; but the one who sent me is true, and I declare to the world what I have heard from him." They did not understand that he was speaking to them about the Father. So Jesus said, "When you have lifted up the Son of Man, then you will realize that I am he, and that I do nothing on my own, but I speak these things as the Father instructed me. And the one who sent me is with me; he has not left me alone, for I always do what is pleasing to him." As he was saying these things, many believed in him.

The Gospel of the Lord.

◆ All sit and observe silence.

## FOR SILENT REFLECTION

Jesus says that his heavenly Father does not leave him alone because he does what is pleasing to the Father. What do you think pleases God?

## CLOSING PRAYER

Let us stand and bring our hopes and needs to God as we pray, "Lord, hear our prayer."

◆ All may add their own prayers here.

Let us pray: **Our Father . . . Amen.**

Heavenly Father,
you are never far
from those who love you
and do your will.
Help us to do what pleases you
so that we will always be close to you.
We ask this through our Lord Jesus Christ,
your Son, who lives and reigns with
you in the unity of the Holy Spirit,
one God, for ever and ever.
**Amen.**

✢ All make the Sign of the Cross.

# PRAYER FOR **WEDNESDAY** **APRIL 13, 2011**

### OPENING

God led the Jewish people out of slavery in Egypt. In today's Gospel, Jesus tells their descendents that in him they can know the truth that will make them truly free.

✢ All make the Sign of the Cross.

**In the name of the Father and of the Son and of the Holy Spirit. Amen.**

### PSALM  (For a longer psalm, see page xiv.) Psalm 33:20 (22)

Let your steadfast love, O Lord, be upon us,
  even as we hope in you.

**Let your steadfast love, O Lord, be upon us,
  even as we hope in you.**

Our soul waits for the Lord;
  he is our help and shield.

**Let your steadfast love, O Lord, be upon us,
  even as we hope in you.**

◆ All stand and sing **Praise to you Lord Jesus Christ** . . .

### GOSPEL  John 8:31–38

A reading from the holy Gospel according to John

Then Jesus said to the Jews who had believed in him, "If you continue in my word, you are truly my disciples; and you will know the truth, and the truth will make you free." They answered him, "We are descendants of Abraham and have never been slaves to anyone. What do you mean by saying, 'You will be made free'?"

Jesus answered them, "Very truly, I tell you, everyone who commits sin is a slave to sin. The slave does not have a permanent place in the household; the son has a place there forever. So if the Son makes you free, you will be free indeed. I know that you are descendants of Abraham; yet you look for an opportunity to kill me, because there is no place in you for my word. I declare what I have seen in the Father's presence; as for you, you should do what you have heard from the Father."

The Gospel of the Lord.

◆ All sit and observe silence.

### FOR SILENT REFLECTION

What is this freedom Jesus talks about? How can we be free?

### CLOSING PRAYER

Let us stand and bring our hopes and needs to God as we pray, "Lord, hear our prayer."

◆ All may add their own prayers here.

Let us pray: **Our Father . . . Amen.**

Lord God,
you are the source of all truth.
Lead us out of slavery to sin
and into the freedom
of your truth.
We ask this through Jesus Christ our Lord.
**Amen.**

✢ All make the Sign of the Cross.

# PRAYER FOR **THURSDAY APRIL 14, 2011**

## OPENING

In today's Gospel, people question Jesus about who he is, but become angry when he tells them. On Monday, we heard about people who wanted to condemn a woman who had sinned. Now people want to condemn Jesus who has not sinned.

✚ All make the Sign of the Cross.

**In the name of the Father and of the Son and of the Holy Spirit. Amen.**

## PSALM  (For a longer psalm, see page xiv.) Psalm 33:20 (22)

Let your steadfast love, O Lord, be upon us,
  even as we hope in you.

**Let your steadfast love, O Lord, be upon us,
  even as we hope in you.**

Our soul waits for the Lord;
  he is our help and shield.

**Let your steadfast love, O Lord, be upon us,
  even as we hope in you.**

◆ All stand and sing **Praise to you Lord Jesus Christ . . .**

## GOSPEL  John 8:51–59

A reading from the holy Gospel according to John

Jesus said to them: "Very truly, I tell you, whoever keeps my word will never see death." The Jews said to him, "Now we know that you have a demon. Abraham died, and so did the prophets; yet you say, 'Whoever keeps my word will never taste death.' Are you greater than our father Abraham, who died? The prophets also died. Who do you claim to be?" Jesus answered, "If I glorify myself, my glory is nothing. It is my Father who glorifies me, he of whom you say, 'He is our God,' though you do not know him. But I know him; if I were to say that I do not know him, I would be a liar like you. But I do know him and I keep his word. Your ancestor Abraham rejoiced that he would see my day; he saw it and was glad." Then the Jews said to him, "You are not yet fifty years old, and have you seen Abraham?" Jesus said to them, "Very truly, I tell you, before Abraham was, I am." So they picked up stones to throw at him, but Jesus hid himself and went out of the temple.

The Gospel of the Lord.

◆ All sit and observe silence.

## FOR SILENT REFLECTION

Do you remember who in the Jewish scriptures is called "I AM"? Why do they want to condemn Jesus?

## CLOSING PRAYER

Let us stand and bring our hopes and needs to God as we pray, "Lord, hear our prayer."

◆ All may add their own prayers here.

Let us pray: **Our Father . . . Amen.**

Merciful God,
help us to be compassionate and forgiving.
We ask this through our Lord Jesus Christ.
**Amen.**

✚ All make the Sign of the Cross.

# PRAYER FOR FRIDAY APRIL 15, 2011

### OPENING

In today's Gospel, people accuse Jesus of blasphemy. Blasphemy [BLAS-fuh-mee] is showing disrespect for God.

✛ All make the Sign of the Cross.

**In the name of the Father and of the Son and of the Holy Spirit. Amen.**

### PSALM (For a longer psalm, see page xiv.) Psalm 33:20 (22)

Let your steadfast love, O LORD, be upon us,
even as we hope in you.

Let your steadfast love, O LORD, be upon us,
even as we hope in you.

Our soul waits for the LORD;
he is our help and shield.

Let your steadfast love, O LORD, be upon us,
even as we hope in you.

◆ All stand and sing **Praise to you Lord Jesus Christ** . . .

### GOSPEL  John 10:31–39

A reading from the holy Gospel according to John

The Jews took up stones again to stone him. Jesus replied, "I have shown you many good works from the Father. For which of these are you going to stone me?" The Jews answered, "It is not for a good work that we are going to stone you, but for blasphemy, because you, though only a human being, are making yourself God."

Jesus answered, "Is it not written in your law, 'I said, you are gods'? If those to whom the word of God came were called 'gods'—and the scripture cannot be annulled—can you say that the one whom the Father has sanctified and sent into the world is blaspheming because I said, 'I am God's Son'? If I am not doing the works of my Father, then do not believe me. But if I do them, even though you do not believe me, believe the works, so that you may know and understand that the Father is in me and I am in the Father." Then they tried to arrest him again, but he escaped from their hands.

The Gospel of the Lord.

◆ All sit and observe silence.

### FOR SILENT REFLECTION

Why do you think it was so hard for the people to believe that Jesus is God's Son?

### CLOSING PRAYER

Let us stand and bring our hopes and needs to God as we pray, "Lord, hear our prayer."

◆ All may add their own prayers here.

Let us pray: **Our Father . . . Amen.**

Holy God,
as we prepare for Holy Week,
give us a spirit of devotion
and deep respect for all that is sacred.
Open our hearts and minds
to the mystery of your presence.
We ask this through the same Christ our Lord.
**Amen.**

✛ All make the Sign of the Cross.

# PRAYER FOR THE WEEK

WITH A READING FROM THE GOSPEL FOR **SUNDAY, APRIL 17, 2011**

## OPENING

Today is Palm Sunday of the Lord's Passion and the beginning of the most holy week of the year. We begin joyfully, singing "Hosanna" but enter into a solemn spirit as we begin to reflect on the deep meaning of this week's events.

✢ All make the Sign of the Cross.

**In the name of the Father and of the Son and of the Holy Spirit. Amen.**

## PSALM   (For a longer psalm, see page xv.) Psalm 116:2 (1)

I love the LORD, because he has heard
　my voice and my supplications.

**I love the LORD, because he has heard
　my voice and my supplications.**

Because he inclined his ear to me,
　therefore I will call on him as long as I live.

**I love the LORD, because he has heard
　my voice and my supplications.**

◆ All stand and sing **Praise to you Lord Jesus Christ** . . .

## GOSPEL   Matthew 21:1b–5a, 6–9

A reading from the holy Gospel according to Matthew

Jesus sent two disciples, saying to them, "Go into the village ahead of you, and immediately you will find a donkey tied, and a colt with her; untie them and bring them to me. If anyone says anything to you, just say this, 'The Lord needs them.'" This took place to fulfill what had been spoken through the prophet, saying,

"Tell the daughter of Zion,
'Look, your king is coming to you,
　humble and mounted on a donkey.'"

The disciples went and did as Jesus had directed them; they brought the donkey and the colt, and put their cloaks on them, and he sat on them. A very large crowd spread their cloaks on the road, and others cut branches from the trees and spread them on the road. The crowds that went ahead of him and those that followed were shouting, "Hosanna to the Son of David! Blessed is the one who comes in the name of the Lord! Hosanna in the highest heaven!"

The Gospel of the Lord.

◆ All sit and observe silence.

## FOR SILENT REFLECTION

Why is the crowd so excited to greet Jesus?

## CLOSING PRAYER

Let us stand and bring our hopes and needs to God as we pray, "Lord, hear our prayer."

◆ All may add their own prayers here.

Let us pray: **Our Father . . . Amen.**

Holy, holy, holy Lord, God of power
　and might.
Heaven and earth are full of your glory.
Hosanna in the highest.
Blessed is he who comes in the name
　of the Lord.
Hosanna in the highest.
**Amen.**

✢ All make the Sign of the Cross.

# PRAYER SERVICE
## HOLY WEEK

*This prayer service may be used on any day of Holy Week. Arrange a simple environment. On a table covered with a violet cloth, place a candle and a Bible. Prepare six leaders of prayer. The second and third leaders will need Bibles to read the scripture passages (John 13:3–5, 12–15 and John 19:16–18, 28–30) and may need help finding them and practicing. You may wish to sing "Jesus, Remember Me" throughout, as indicated, and end with "We Remember." If there will be singing, prepare a song leader. Use deliberate, unhurried movements and a quiet voice to set a reverent tone that will invite the children into this time of reflection and prayer.*

✛ All make the Sign of the Cross.

**In the name of the Father and of the Son and of the Holy Spirit. Amen.**

### FIRST LEADER:

We are about to enter into the Triduum, the holiest days of the year. The Triduum begins on the evening of Holy Thursday with the Mass of the Lord's Supper when we recall that Jesus gave his body and blood and taught us to care for others when he washed the disciples' feet. The Triduum continues on Good Friday with the celebration of the Lord's Passion as we remember Christ's sacrifice for us. On the night of Holy Saturday, we celebrate the great Easter Vigil, when our Savior bursts out of the tomb, and on Easter Sunday we continue to celebrate the Resurrection with great joy. On these days, together with Christians all over the world, we remember the final events in Jesus' earthly life: Jesus' Last Supper, his Passion, Crucifixion and death, and his Resurrection.

◆ All stand and sing **Praise to you Lord Jesus Christ . . .**

# HOLY WEEK

**SECOND LEADER:**           John 13:3–5, 12–15

A reading from the holy Gospel according to John

- ◆ Read the Gospel passage from a Bible. All observe silence. Then all sing "Jesus Remember Me."

**THIRD LEADER:**           John 19:16b–18, 28–30

- ◆ Read the Gospel passage from a Bible.

The Gospel of the Lord.

- ◆ All sit and observe silence. Then all sing "Jesus, Remember Me."

**FOURTH LEADER:**

Listen to these words from the introduction to the Easter Vigil:

*. . . on this most holy night,*
*when our Lord Jesus Christ passed from death to life,*
*the Church invites all people throughout the world*
*to come together in vigil and prayer.*
*This is the Passover of the Lord:*
*If we honor the memory of his death and Resurrection*
*by hearing his word and celebrating his mysteries,*
*then we shall be confident*
*that we shall share his victory over death,*
*and live with him forever in God.*

- ◆ All observe silence. Then all sing "Jesus, Remember Me."

**FIFTH LEADER:**

Let us stand and pray as Jesus taught us:

**Our Father . . . Amen.**

God our Father,
the suffering and death of our dear Jesus is very sad for us,
but his Resurrection fills us with joy!
So much sorrow and so much joy during these few days!
These mysteries are hard to understand.
But we know your love is at work in these things.
Help us to celebrate with open hearts,
even if we don't understand everything.
Draw us closer to you and your Son and to each other.
Grant this through the same Jesus Christ our Lord.

**ALL: Amen.**

**SIXTH LEADER:**

May the Lord bless us,

- ✢ All make the Sign of the Cross.

protect us from all evil
and bring us to everlasting life.

**ALL: Amen.**

# HOME PRAYER
## GOOD FRIDAY

*Before you begin, find the reading (John 18:17–20) in your Bible, ask for a volunteer to read it, and encourage the reader to practice reading it twice. You may wish to begin with a simple song, such as "Jesus, Remember Me," or "Amen." (Remember, we don't sing "Alleluia" until the Easter Vigil.) Then an older child or adult reads the leader parts:*

**LEADER:**
Good Friday is a day when we remember great love. Jesus loves us in a way we can hardly imagine. Because of his love, death is not an end but the beginning of Life without end. Because of his love, the cross has become the sign of a love that joins heaven to earth and brings all the ends of the earth together. And so we love the cross, we are grateful for the cross, and we make the Sign of the Cross on our bodies as a sign that we belong to Jesus.

✠ All make the Sign of the Cross.

**In the name of the Father and of the Son and of the Holy Spirit. Amen.**

**LEADER:** *Psalm 31:5*
Please repeat the psalm response:
Into your hand I commit my spirit.

**ALL:** Into your hand I commit my spirit.

**LEADER:**
You have redeemed me, O Lord, faithful God.

**ALL:** Into your hand I commit my spirit.

◆ All stand and sing **Praise to you Lord Jesus Christ, king of endless glory.**

**LEADER:** *John 18:17–20*
A reading from the holy Gospel according to John

◆ Read the Gospel passage from the Bible.

The Gospel of the Lord.

◆ All sit and observe silence

**LEADER:**
Let us think about this together in the silence of our hearts: How much Jesus loves us! Can we ever repay him?

◆ All observe silence.

**LEADER:**
Let us pray:

**ALL: Our Father . . . Amen.**

**LEADER:**
God, our Father,
let us never forget how much you love us!
Whenever we feel pain or sadness,
let us remember that you sent your Son to
      live among us.
So you are not a God far off in the heavens
who is too high to know
what suffering can be.
Help us to remember your unimaginable love.
We ask this through Jesus Christ our Lord.

**ALL: Amen.**

✠ All make the Sign of the Cross.

# HOME PRAYER
## HOLY SATURDAY

*Wait until later in the day to use this prayer service. Have a candle ready and, before you begin, find the reading (Luke 24:1–5) in your Bible, ask for a volunteer to read it, and encourage the reader to practice reading it twice. You may begin with a simple song, such as "Jesus, Remember Me," or "Amen." (We will wait to sing "Alleluia" tonight, during the Easter Vigil!) Then an older child or an adult reads the leader parts.*

**LEADER:**
On this most holy night, the Easter Vigil, we stand in awe and wonder and immense gratitude in front of Jesus' empty tomb. Though Jesus shared the Father's ways with his disciples, nothing could have prepared them for the beautiful thing God the Father did when he brought his only Son, Jesus, back to life. Finally, we cannot hide from the truth that our God is an awesome God!

◆ *An adult lights the candle.*

We begin our prayer with the Sign of the Cross:

✠ *All make the Sign of the Cross.*

**In the name of the Father and of the Son and of the Holy Spirit. Amen.**

**LEADER:** *Psalm 118:17a and 24*
Please repeat the psalm response:
I shall not die, but I shall live.

**ALL: I shall not die, but I shall live.**

**LEADER:**
This is the day that the LORD has made; let us rejoice and be glad in it.

**ALL: I shall not die, but I shall live.**

◆ *All stand and sing* **Praise to you Lord Jesus Christ, king of endless glory.**

**LEADER:** *Luke 24:1–5*
A reading from the holy Gospel according to Luke

◆ *The reader reads the Gospel passage from the Bible.*

The Gospel of the Lord.

◆ *All sit and observe silence.*

**LEADER:**
Let us think about these questions together in the silence of our hearts: Why did the women go to the tomb to look for Jesus' body? Didn't they think—after all the amazing miracles that Jesus did and all his words of wisdom—that God would bring him back to life?

**LEADER:**
Let us pray:

**ALL: Our Father . . . Amen.**

**LEADER:**
Eternal and ever-living God and Father, you raised your Son Jesus from the dead and now your love and forgiveness are known throughout the world. Make us worthy of the life you offer through the same risen Son, Jesus Christ our Lord.

**ALL: Amen.**

✠ *All make the Sign of the Cross.*

# PRAYER FOR **MONDAY** APRIL 18, 2011

## OPENING

Today is the first day of Holy Week. In today's Gospel, notice the difference between how Mary and Judas behave toward Jesus.

✚ All make the Sign of the Cross.

**In the name of the Father and of the Son and of the Holy Spirit. Amen.**

## PSALM (For a longer psalm, see page xv.) Psalm 116:2 (1)

I love the LORD, because he has heard
 my voice and my supplications.

**I love the LORD, because he has heard
 my voice and my supplications.**

Because he inclined his ear to me,
 therefore I will call on him as long as I live.

**I love the LORD, because he has heard
 my voice and my supplications.**

◆ All stand and sing **Praise to you Lord Jesus Christ** . . .

## GOSPEL                                               John 12:1–8

A reading from the holy Gospel according to John

Six days before the Passover Jesus came to Bethany, the home of Lazarus, whom he had raised from the dead. There they gave a dinner for him. Martha served, and Lazarus was one of those at the table with him. Mary took a pound of costly perfume made of pure nard, anointed Jesus' feet, and wiped them with her hair. The house was filled with the fragrance of the perfume. But Judas Iscariot (ih-SCARE-ee-ut), one of his disciples (the one who was about to betray him), said, "Why was this perfume not sold for three hundred denarii (dih-NAHR-ee) and the money given to the poor?" (He said this not because he cared about the poor, but because he was a thief; he kept the common purse and used to steal what was put into it.) Jesus said, "Leave her alone. She bought it so that she might keep it for the day of my burial. You always have the poor with you, but you do not always have me."

The Gospel of the Lord.

◆ All sit and observe silence.

## FOR SILENT REFLECTION

What do you think Mary meant by her action with the costly perfume?

## CLOSING PRAYER

Let us stand and bring our hopes and needs to God as we pray, "Lord, hear our prayer."

◆ All may add their own prayers here.

Let us pray: **Our Father . . . Amen.**

Heavenly Father,
as we begin these holy days,
turn our hearts and minds to Jesus.
Help us to enter more deeply
into your divine love.
We ask this through the same Jesus Christ
 our Lord.
**Amen.**

✚ All make the Sign of the Cross.

**ALSO ON THIS DAY:** Jewish Passover begins at sunset.

# PRAYER FOR TUESDAY
# APRIL 19, 2011

## OPENING

In today's Gospel, Jesus lets his followers know that he will be leaving them. He also says that he is being glorified—he is sharing in the fullness of God's light and love.

✣ All make the Sign of the Cross.

**In the name of the Father and of the Son and of the Holy Spirit. Amen.**

## PSALM  (For a longer psalm, see page xv.) Psalm 116:2 (1)

I love the LORD, because he has heard
  my voice and my supplications.

**I love the LORD, because he has heard
  my voice and my supplications.**

Because he inclined his ear to me,
  therefore I will call on him as long as I live.

**I love the LORD, because he has heard
  my voice and my supplications.**

◆ All stand and sing **Praise to you Lord Jesus Christ** . . .

## GOSPEL  John 13:31–33abd, 36–38

A reading from the holy Gospel according to John

When Judas had gone out, Jesus said, "Now the Son of Man has been glorified, and God has been glorified in him. If God has been glorified in him, God will also glorify him in himself and will glorify him at once. Little children, I am with you only a little longer. You will look for me; and I say to you 'Where I am going, you cannot come.'"

Simon Peter said to him, "Lord, where are you going?" Jesus answered, "Where I am going, you cannot follow me now; but you will follow afterward." Peter said to him, "Lord, why can I not follow you now? I will lay down my life for you." Jesus answered, "Will you lay down your life for me? Very truly, I tell you, before the cock crows, you will have denied me three times."

The Gospel of the Lord.

◆ All sit and observe silence.

## FOR SILENT REFLECTION

Jesus understands Peter's weakness better than Peter does. What do you think will give Peter the strength to become an important leader in the Church after the Resurrection of Jesus?

## CLOSING PRAYER

Let us stand and bring our hopes and needs to God as we pray, "Lord, hear our prayer."

◆ All may add their own prayers here.

Let us pray: **Our Father . . . Amen.**

God of Glory,
help us to understand the mysteries
of your Son's death and Resurrection.
May we someday share in the fullness
of your light and love
through the saving work of our Lord,
    Jesus Christ.
**Amen.**

✣ All make the Sign of the Cross.

# PRAYER FOR WEDNESDAY APRIL 20, 2011

In today's Gospel, Jesus' disciples prepare to celebrate Passover. Jewish people continue to celebrate this feast, recalling with thanksgiving how God brought them out of slavery in Egypt and into freedom. As they escaped quickly, there was no time for the bread to rise. Therefore this unleavened bread called matzah [MAH-zuh] is eaten during Passover.

✚ All make the Sign of the Cross.

**In the name of the Father and of the Son and of the Holy Spirit. Amen.**

## PSALM
(For a longer psalm, see page xv.) Psalm 116:2 (1)

I love the LORD, because he has heard
my voice and my supplications.

**I love the LORD, because he has heard
my voice and my supplications.**

Because he inclined his ear to me,
therefore I will call on him as long as I live.

**I love the LORD, because he has heard
my voice and my supplications.**

◆ All stand and sing **Praise to you Lord Jesus Christ . . .**

## GOSPEL
Matthew 26:17–20

A reading from the holy Gospel according to Matthew

On the first day of Unleavened Bread the disciples came to Jesus, saying, "Where do you want us to make the preparations for you to eat the Passover?" He said, "Go into the city to a certain man, and say to him, 'The Teacher says, "My time is near; I will keep the Passover at your house with my disciples."'" So the disciples did as Jesus had directed them, and they prepared the Passover meal.

When it was evening, he took his place with the twelve.

The Gospel of the Lord.

◆ All sit and observe silence.

## FOR SILENT REFLECTION

The Jewish people were willing to drop everything and leave in a hurry when God called them to follow him into freedom. How does Jesus call us into freedom? Are we ready to follow?

## CLOSING PRAYER

Let us stand and bring our hopes and needs to God as we pray, "Lord, hear our prayer."

◆ All may add their own prayers here.

Let us pray: **Our Father . . . Amen.**

Heavenly Father,
during these holy days
give us hearts eager for freedom.
May we prefer nothing
to the love of Christ.
We ask this through the same Christ our Lord.
**Amen.**

✚ All make the Sign of the Cross.

# PRAYER FOR **THURSDAY APRIL 21, 2011**

## OPENING

Today is Holy Thursday when we celebrate Jesus' gift of himself to us in the Holy Eucharist and remember the example of loving service Jesus set for us by washing the feet of his disciples.

✙ All make the Sign of the Cross.

**In the name of the Father and of the Son and of the Holy Spirit. Amen.**

## PSALM (For a longer psalm, see page xv.) Psalm 116:2 (1)

I love the LORD, because he has heard
 my voice and my supplications.

**I love the LORD, because he has heard
 my voice and my supplications.**

Because he inclined his ear to me,
 therefore I will call on him as long as I live.

**I love the LORD, because he has heard
 my voice and my supplications.**

◆ All stand and sing **Praise to you Lord Jesus Christ** . . .

## GOSPEL John 13:1, 3–5, 12–15

A reading from the holy Gospel according to John

Now before the festival of the Passover, Jesus knew that his hour had come to depart from this world and go to the Father. Having loved his own who were in the world, he loved them to the end. Jesus, knowing that the Father had given all things into his hands, and that he had come from God and was going to God, got up from the table, took off his outer robe, and tied a towel around himself. Then he poured water into a basin and began to wash the disciples' feet and to wipe them with the towel that was tied around him.

After he had washed their feet, had put on his robe, and had returned to the table, he said to them, "Do you know what I have done to you? You call me Teacher and Lord—and you are right, for that is what I am. So if I, your Lord and Teacher, have washed your feet, you also ought to wash one another's feet. For I have set you an example, that you also should do as I have done to you."

The Gospel of the Lord.

◆ All sit and observe silence.

## FOR SILENT REFLECTION

How does the Church continue the loving service of Jesus?

## CLOSING PRAYER

Let us stand and bring our hopes and needs to God as we pray, "Lord, hear our prayer."

◆ All may add their own prayers here.

Let us pray: **Our Father . . . Amen.**

Gracious God,
on this holy day, we pray for your Church.
Send your Spirit to make your Church holy.
Help us to follow the example of Jesus,
serving one another in love.
We ask this through Jesus Christ our Lord.
**Amen.**

✙ All make the Sign of the Cross.

# PRAYER FOR **GOOD FRIDAY**
# APRIL 22, 2011

### OPENING

Today's account of the death of Jesus is really about the triumph of love over death.

> ✣ All make the Sign of the Cross.
>
> **In the name of the Father and of the Son and of the Holy Spirit. Amen.**

### PSALM  (For a longer psalm, see page xv.) Psalm 116:2 (1)

I love the Lord, because he has heard
my voice and my supplications.

**I love the Lord, because he has heard
my voice and my supplications.**

Because he inclined his ear to me,
therefore I will call on him as long as I live.

**I love the Lord, because he has heard
my voice and my supplications.**

> ◆ All stand and sing **Praise to you Lord Jesus Christ . . .**

### GOSPEL  John 19:16b–18, 25b–30

A reading from the holy Gospel according to John

So they took Jesus; and carrying the cross by himself, he went out to what is called The Place of the Skull, which in Hebrew is called Golgotha (GAWL-guh-thuh). There they crucified him, and with him two others, one on either side, with Jesus between them. Meanwhile, standing near the cross of Jesus were his mother, and his mother's sister, Mary the wife of Clopas (KLOH-puhs), and Mary Magdalene (MAG-duh-lehn). When Jesus saw his mother and the disciple whom he loved standing beside her, he said to his mother, "Woman, here is your son." Then he said to the disciple, "Here is your mother." And from that hour the disciple took her into his own home.

After this, when Jesus knew that all was now finished, he said (in order to fulfill the scripture), "I am thirsty." A jar full of sour wine was standing there. So they put a sponge full of the wine on a branch of hyssop and held it to his mouth. When Jesus had received the wine, he said, "It is finished." Then he bowed his head and gave up his spirit.

The Gospel of the Lord.

> ◆ All sit and observe silence.

### FOR SILENT REFLECTION

If Jesus gives his mother to be our mother, who are we to one another?

### CLOSING PRAYER

Let us stand and bring our hopes and needs to God as we pray, "Lord, hear our prayer."

> ◆ All may add their own prayers here.

Let us pray: **Our Father . . . Amen.**

Loving God,
you are a God of life, not death.
Open our hearts to the fullness of eternal life
that your Son offers through his sacrifice.
We ask this through Jesus Christ the Lord.
**Amen.**

> ✣ All make the Sign of the Cross.

**ALSO ON THIS DAY:** Earth Day

# EASTER

## SUNDAY, APRIL 24 TO SUNDAY, JUNE 12

# EASTER 2011

## THE MEANING OF EASTER

Three days after his death on the cross, "Jesus himself stood among the disciples and said to them, 'Peace be with you.' They were startled and terrified, and thought that they were seeing a ghost. He said to them, 'Why are you frightened, and why do doubts arise in your hearts? Look at my hands and my feet; see that it is I myself. Touch me and see" (Luke 24:36b–39a).

God is love. Out of nothingness, the power of God's love, a divine spark of life, kindled the dawn of creation in an explosion of heat and light. Out of love, God created human beings in the divine image to share in God's life. At all times and among every people, God has welcomed those who do good and seek God in their hearts. Whenever we have turned away from God, God calls us back. When human wickedness might have prevailed, God cleansed creation, choosing Noah and his family to help preserve every species and forge a new life on a renewed earth. God called Abraham to enter into a covenant with God, promising what seemed impossible to make a great nation of Abraham and Sarah's descendents. When God's people were enslaved, God called Moses to lead them into freedom and when his people needed a king, God sent a shepherd boy named David to became a great king. God's people became a strong and prayerful people.

From the dawn of creation, God has shown the power of divine love. Out of emptiness, God creates a universe. God protects the earth from the wicked, and from a couple too old to have children, makes a great and holy people. He frees his people from slavery and gives a little boy the grace to become a great king. Out of death on a cross, God's Son now conquers death, and invites us to enter into eternal life. And in the midst of their confusion after Jesus' crucifixion, the Holy Spirit unites the followers of Christ, giving birth to a Church that will spread the news of God's love throughout the world.

After Jesus rose from the dead, the Bible tells us that he stayed with his friends for a little while to teach them: "Then Jesus said to them, 'These are my words that I spoke to you while I was still with you—that everything written about me in the law of Moses, the prophets, and the psalms must be fulfilled.' Then he opened their minds to understand the scriptures, and he said to them, 'Thus it is written, that the Messiah is to suffer and to rise from the dead on the third day, and that repentance and forgiveness of sins is to be proclaimed in his name to all nations, beginning from Jerusalem'" (Luke 24:44b–47).

Even with the help of Jesus, it was difficult for the disciples to understand what the Resurrection meant. Today, with the help of the Holy Spirit, we are still struggling to understand this amazing wonder: the God who loves us, is with us.

## PREPARING TO CELEBRATE EASTER IN THE CLASSROOM

The liturgical color for the Easter season is white, so your prayer table cloth will need to change once more. If you plan a procession to change the cloth, consider having the child second in line carry a large white pillar candle (the first child will carry the white cloth). You may use the same white pillar you used during Christmas. Make sure you dim the lights before you begin. Then after all the objects have been returned to the prayer table, light the white pillar and chant the following phrase and response three times:

**LEADER:** The Light of Christ!

**ALL: Thanks be to God!**

You may use a chant from your parish hymnal or sing both phrases on one note. When you are finished singing, read a Gospel account of the Resurrection (John 20:11–18, for example). Sing Alleluia and then announce the following: "Jesus has risen from the dead; Jesus, the light of the world, has destroyed death. The light of the risen Christ will never go out, for he shares his light and life with each of us. Not only that, but his light can spread and grow. Jesus shares his new life with each of us." Then call each child by name, one at a time, inviting them to come forward. For each child, light a small votive candle from the large pillar. As you give it to the child, say "The risen Christ shares his light with (child's name)." The child will then put the votive candle on the prayer table and sit down. Don't rush! Wait until the child is seated before you call the next child's name. If you are worried about fire, allow each child to hold his or her votive holder briefly, then you can place the candle on the table beside the lit pillar. Make sure you light a votive for yourself. When all the small candles are lit, sit in silence with the children and enjoy the beauty of the light. End your celebration by singing all the Alleluias that you know!

### SACRED SPACE

Place some fresh daisies or lilies in a vase on your prayer table. You might also like to put a small glass bowl with a little water in it on the prayer table. When you introduce the water to your students you may say, "Jesus said, 'Let anyone who is thirsty come to me, and let the one who believes in me drink'" (John 7:37b–38a). Perhaps one of your students, or someone they know, received the sacrament of Baptism at the Holy Saturday celebration of the Easter Vigil. If so, while standing before the water, you could explain that the water of Baptism recalls the great flood that Noah had to pass through to reach God's promise of peace, the Red Sea that Moses and the Israelites had to pass through to reach freedom, and the death that Jesus had to pass through to reach the life of the Resurrection. When we pass through (are baptized with) the water in the baptismal font, we enter into that same new life of the resurrected Christ.

The Easter Season ends with the solemnity of Pentecost. When you celebrate Pentecost as a group, make sure you exchange your white prayer table cloth for a red one.

### SACRED MUSIC

Here are some Easter songs that children love: "Jesus Christ Is Risen Today," "What Wondrous Love Is This," "Alleluia, Sing to Jesus," "Come Down, O Love Divine," and "O Sons and Daughters." For Pentecost you might enjoy singing "Come, Holy Ghost" or "Veni Sancte Spiritus."

### PRAYERS FOR EASTER

The following prayer is a beautiful psalm from the Easter Vigil:

Psalm 42:1–2, 43:3–4

As a deer longs for flowing streams,
    so my soul longs for you, O God.
My soul thirsts for God
    for the living God.
When shall I come and behold
    the face of God?
O send out your light and your truth;
    let them lead me;
let them bring me to your holy hill
    and to your dwelling.
Then I will go to the altar of God
    to God my exceeding joy;
and I will praise you with the harp,
    O God, my God.

## A NOTE TO CATECHISTS

You may wish to study the prayers of Baptism with your students. The prayer of Blessing the Waters of Baptism is particularly rich in symbolism. With older children you could move from the prayer to the account in the Bible that the prayer mentions, then back to the prayer again. You might want to wonder, along with the children, over the long sacred history of water.

# GRACE BEFORE MEALS
## EASTER

**LEADER:**
Jesus Christ is truly risen from the dead!

**ALL: Alleluia, Alleluia!**

✢ All make the Sign of the Cross.

**In the name of the Father and of the Son and of the Holy Spirit. Amen.**

**LEADER:**
God of the living,
in every moment of our lives,
you make us live and grow.
This food you have given us
is a sign of your constant care and attention.
Grant that we may treasure your gift of life
and be grateful for everything you do
    to sustain us.
We ask this through Jesus Christ the Lord.

**ALL: Amen.**

✢ All make the Sign of the Cross.

**In the name of the Father and of the Son and of the Holy Spirit. Amen.**

274

# PRAYER AT DAY'S END
## EASTER

**LEADER:**
Why do you look for the living among the dead?

**ALL:** Jesus is no longer in the tomb! He is risen!

✚ All make the Sign of the Cross.

**In the name of the Father and of the Son and of the Holy Spirit. Amen.**

**LEADER:**
Loving Father,
we turn our hearts to you
at the end of this school day.
Send your Holy Spirit to renew our hearts
so that we may live this new, eternal life
that is the promise of the Resurrection.
We ask this through your Son, who is your
living Word, Jesus Christ our Lord.
Alleluia!

**ALL:** Amen.

✚ All make the Sign of the Cross.

**In the name of the Father and of the Son and of the Holy Spirit. Amen.**

# PRAYER SERVICE
## EASTER

*Prepare seven leaders for this prayer service. The third and fourth leaders will need Bibles for the scripture passages and may need help finding them and practicing. You may wish to begin by singing "Jesus Christ Is Risen Today" and end with "Alleluia, Sing to Jesus." If there will be singing, prepare a song leader.*

**FIRST LEADER:**
The grace, peace, and light of the Risen Christ be with us all.

**ALL: Amen.**

**FIRST LEADER:**
Today we celebrate Easter, the holiest, most important feast of the Church, when we remember the Resurrection of Jesus Christ. Jesus won a great victory over death! He rose from death to new life and he will never die again! We can follow him and we, too, can rise from the dead and live forever with him. Easter is so important to us that one day could never contain all our joy; so we celebrate Easter for 50 days!

**SECOND LEADER:**

✠ All make the Sign of the Cross.

**In the name of the Father and of the Son and of the Holy Spirit. Amen.**

Let us pray:
Heavenly Father,
our hearts are filled with thankfulness
 and praise
as we think about Jesus' great love for us,
the sacrifice he made,
and the never-ending life he lives and shares
 with us now.

# EASTER

May we always thank you for the gift your
   Son has given to us.
We ask this through the same Jesus Christ
   our Lord.

**ALL: Amen.**

**THIRD LEADER:**          Isaiah 42:10–12

A reading from the Book of the Prophet
Isaiah

◆ Read the Isaiah passage from the Bible.

The word of the Lord.

◆ All observe silence. Then all stand and sing **Alleluia**.

**FOURTH LEADER:**          John 20:11–18

A reading from the holy Gospel according to
John

◆ Read the Gospel passage from the Bible.

The Gospel of the Lord.

◆ All sit and observe silence.

**FIFTH LEADER:**

Let us stand and bring our hopes and needs
to God as we pray, **Lord, hear our prayer.**

For all who live in fear or worry, may the
power of the Resurrection give them new
hope, we pray to the Lord.

For an end to hatred, divisions, and war,
we pray to the Lord.

For all who are unable to see the hand of
God at work in their lives, may God open
their eyes, we pray to the Lord.

For those who are sick and for those who
have died, we pray to the Lord.

**SIXTH LEADER:**

Let us pray as Jesus taught us.

**ALL: Our Father . . . Amen.**

◆ Pause and then say the following.

Let us offer one another a sign of
Christ's peace.

**SEVENTH LEADER:**

Let us pray:
Lord God almighty,
in the death and Resurrection of your Son,
   Jesus Christ,
you have created a new heaven and
   a new earth.
Bring the light and life of the Resurrection
into our hearts so that we, too, may be
   renewed in holiness.
We ask this through our Lord Jesus Christ,
   your Son, who lives and reigns with
   you in the unity of the Holy Spirit,
   one God, for ever and ever.

**ALL: Amen.**

✢ All make the Sign of the Cross.

# PRAYER FOR THE WEEK

WITH A READING FROM THE GOSPEL FOR **SUNDAY, APRIL 24, 2011**

## OPENING

Alleluia! Alleluia! Christ is risen! Light has overcome darkness, joy is born of sorrow, and life has destroyed death forever. Today we begin the great celebration that will continue for the next 50 days. Let us rejoice and sing Alleluia!

✦ All make the Sign of the Cross.

**In the name of the Father and of the Son and of the Holy Spirit. Amen.**

## PSALM  (For a longer psalm, see page xv.) Psalm 118:27a, (24)

This is the day that the LORD has made;
   let us rejoice and be glad in it.

**This is the day that the LORD has made;
   let us rejoice and be glad in it.**

The LORD is God,
   and he has given us light.

**This is the day that the LORD has made;
   let us rejoice and be glad in it.**

◆ All stand and sing **Alleluia**.

## GOSPEL  John 20:3–9

A reading from the holy Gospel according to John

Peter and the other disciple set out and went toward the tomb. The two were running together, but the other disciple outran Peter and reached the tomb first. He bent down to look in and saw the linen wrappings lying there, but he did not go in. Then Simon Peter came, following him, and went into the tomb. He saw the linen wrappings lying there, and the cloth that had been on Jesus' head, not lying with the linen wrappings but rolled up in a place by itself. Then the other disciple, who reached the tomb first, also went in, and he saw and believed; for as yet they did not understand the scripture, that he must rise from the dead.

The Gospel of the Lord.

◆ All sit and observe silence.

## FOR SILENT REFLECTION

What does the Gospel mean when it says, "he saw and believed"? What do you think he believed and what made him believe?

## CLOSING PRAYER

Let us stand and bring our hopes and needs to God as we pray, "Lord, hear our prayer."

◆ All may add their own prayers here.

Let us pray: **Our Father . . . Amen.**

Alleluia! Alleluia! Christ is risen!
With joy let us call on Christ, our Risen Lord:
Light of all people, be our light.
Breathe into us eternal life,
that our joy may be complete.
May we live with you, our risen Lord,
   forever and ever.
**Amen.**

✦ All make the Sign of the Cross.

**ALSO ON THIS DAY:** Orthodox Easter

# PRAYER FOR MONDAY
# APRIL 25, 2011

## OPENING

Today and throughout the Easter season, we will be reading from the Acts of the Apostles [uh-POS-uhlz]. Acts tells us what happened to Jesus' followers after his Resurrection. Through the preaching of the disciples, the Christian community grew. Today we hear Peter telling people in Jerusalem about the Resurrection.

✢ All make the Sign of the Cross.

**In the name of the Father and of the Son and of the Holy Spirit. Amen.**

## PSALM  (For a longer psalm, see page xv.) Psalm 118:27a, (24)

This is the day that the LORD has made;
    let us rejoice and be glad in it.

**This is the day that the LORD has made;
    let us rejoice and be glad in it.**

The LORD is God,
    and he has given us light.

**This is the day that the LORD has made;
    let us rejoice and be glad in it.**

## READING  Acts 2:14, 22b–24, 32

A reading from the Acts of the Apostles [uh-POS-uhlz]

But Peter, standing with the eleven, raised his voice and addressed them: "Men of Judea and all who live in Jerusalem, let this be known to you, and listen to what I say."

"Jesus of Nazareth, a man attested to you by God with deeds of power, wonders, and signs that God did through him among you, as you yourselves know—this man, handed over to you according to the definite plan and foreknowledge of God, you crucified and killed by the hands of those outside the law. But God raised him up, having freed him from death, because it was impossible for him to be held in its power."

"This Jesus God raised up, and of that all of us are witnesses."

The word of the Lord.

◆ All observe silence.

## FOR SILENT REFLECTION

Why was it impossible for Jesus to be held by the power of death?

## CLOSING PRAYER

Let us stand and bring our hopes and needs to God as we pray, "Lord, hear our prayer."

◆ All may add their own prayers here.

Let us pray: **Our Father . . . Amen.**

Alleluia! Alleluia! Christ is risen!
God our Father,
we rejoice and give thanks
for a world that is new again,
and a people who are free again.
Open our hearts to receive our risen Lord
in whose name we pray.
**Amen.**

✢ All make the Sign of the Cross.

# PRAYER FOR **TUESDAY APRIL 26, 2011**

### OPENING

Today we will hear how the disciples continued Jesus' ministry of preaching and teaching.

✚ All make the Sign of the Cross.

**In the name of the Father and of the Son and of the Holy Spirit. Amen.**

### PSALM  (For a longer psalm, see page xv.) Psalm 118:27a, (24)

This is the day that the LORD has made;
 let us rejoice and be glad in it.

**This is the day that the LORD has made;
 let us rejoice and be glad in it.**

The LORD is God,
 and he has given us light.

**This is the day that the LORD has made;
 let us rejoice and be glad in it.**

### READING  Acts 2:36–41

A reading from the Acts of the Apostles [uh-POS-uhlz]

Peter continued: "Therefore let the entire house of Israel know with certainty that God has made him both Lord and Messiah, this Jesus whom you crucified."

Now when they heard this, they were cut to the heart and said to Peter and to the other apostles, "Brothers, what should we do?" Peter said to them, "Repent, and be baptized every one of you in the name of Jesus Christ so that your sins may be forgiven; and you will receive the gift of the Holy Spirit. For the promise is for you, for your children, and for all who are far away, everyone whom the Lord our God" those who welcomed his message were baptized, and that day about three thousand persons were added.

The word of the Lord.

◆ All observe silence.

### FOR SILENT REFLECTION

Why do you think so many people were moved by Peter's preaching?

### CLOSING PRAYER

Let us stand and bring our hopes and needs to God as we pray, "Lord, hear our prayer."

◆ All may add their own prayers here.

Let us pray: **Our Father . . . Amen.**

Alleluia! Alleluia! Christ is risen!
God our Father,
we rejoice that the disciples
told the story of your Son,
who always remained with them,
 inspiring them.
May we also be good witnesses for Christ,
to our family, friends, and all we meet.
We ask this through the same Jesus Christ
 our Lord.
**Amen.**

✚ All make the Sign of the Cross.

---

**ALSO ON THIS DAY:** Jewish Passover ends at nightfall.

# PRAYER FOR **WEDNESDAY**
# APRIL 27, 2011

## OPENING

In today's reading, we hear how the apostles [uh-POS-uhlz] continued the healing work of Jesus.

✢ All make the Sign of the Cross.

**In the name of the Father and of the Son and of the Holy Spirit. Amen**

## PSALM  (For a longer psalm, see page xv.) Psalm 118:27a, (24)

This is the day that the Lord has made;
   let us rejoice and be glad in it.

**This is the day that the Lord has made;
   let us rejoice and be glad in it.**

The Lord is God,
   and he has given us light.

**This is the day that the Lord has made;
   let us rejoice and be glad in it.**

## READING  Acts 3:1–2a, 3–7, 9–10

A reading from the Acts of the Apostles [uh-POS-uhlz]

One day Peter and John were going up to the temple at the hour of prayer, at three o'clock in the afternoon. And a man lame from birth was being carried in. When he saw Peter and John about to go into the temple, he asked them for alms. Peter looked intently at him, as did John, and said, "Look at us." And he fixed his attention on them, expecting to receive something from them. But Peter said, "I have no silver or gold, but what I have I give you; in the name of Jesus Christ of Nazareth, stand up and walk." And he took him by the right hand and raised him up; and immediately his feet and ankles were made strong. All the people saw him walking and praising God, and they recognized him as the one who used to sit and ask for alms at the Beautiful Gate of the temple; and they were filled with wonder and amazement at what had happened to him.

The word of the Lord.

◆ All observe silence.

## FOR SILENT REFLECTION

What is it that Peter has to give? What do we have to give?

## CLOSING PRAYER

Let us stand and bring our hopes and needs to God as we pray, "Lord, hear our prayer."

◆ All may add their own prayers here.

Let us pray: **Our Father . . . Amen.**

Alleluia! Alleluia! Christ is risen!
Holy and loving God,
help us to ask for what we really need:
your healing love in our lives.
Strengthen us so we may walk
in the ways of truth and goodness.
We ask this through our Lord Jesus Christ,
    your Son, who lives and reigns with
    you in the unity of the Holy Spirit,
    one God, for ever and ever.
**Amen.**

✢ All make the Sign of the Cross.

# PRAYER FOR THURSDAY APRIL 28, 2011

## OPENING

Today's reading continues the story we heard yesterday, of the healing of the crippled man. Listen to the people's reaction to and what Peter has to say.

✚ All make the Sign of the Cross.

**In the name of the Father and of the Son and of the Holy Spirit. Amen.**

## PSALM
(For a longer psalm, see page xv.) Psalm 118:27a, (24)

This is the day that the LORD has made;
 let us rejoice and be glad in it.

**This is the day that the LORD has made;
 let us rejoice and be glad in it.**

The LORD is God,
 and he has given us light.

**This is the day that the LORD has made;
 let us rejoice and be glad in it.**

## READING
Acts 3:11–13a, 16

A reading from the Acts of the Apostles [uh-POS-uhlz]

While he clung to Peter and John, all the people ran together to them in the portico called Solomon's Portico, utterly astonished. When Peter saw it, he addressed the people, "You Israelites, why do you wonder at this, or why do you stare at us, as though by our own power or piety we had made him walk? The God of Abraham, the God of Isaac, and the God of Jacob, the God of our ancestors has glorified his servant Jesus. And by faith in his name, his name itself has made this man strong, whom you see and know; and the faith that is through Jesus has given him this perfect health in the presence of all of you."

The word of the Lord.

◆ All observe silence.

## FOR SILENT REFLECTION

When do we call on the power of the name of Jesus?

## CLOSING PRAYER

Let us stand and bring our hopes and needs to God as we pray, "Lord, hear our prayer."

◆ All may add their own prayers here.

Let us pray: **Our Father . . . Amen.**

Alleluia! Alleluia! Christ is risen!
Holy God,
may the name of Jesus
be in our minds and hearts,
ever reminding us of your great love.
Give us faith in your saving power
and help us to live as people of faith,
relying on your strength, wisdom, and love.
We ask this through your Son, the same Lord
 Jesus Christ, who lives and reigns with
 you in the unity of the Holy Spirit,
 one God, for ever and ever.
**Amen.**

✚ All make the Sign of the Cross.

# PRAYER FOR **FRIDAY**
# APRIL 29, 2011

## OPENING

For eight days after Easter Sunday (called an octave [AHK-tiv]) the Church celebrates as if it were still the very day of Resurrection. So each day of this past week has been part of "Easter week." In today's reading, Peter explains how Jesus' followers have the power to heal.

✢ All make the Sign of the Cross.

**In the name of the Father and of the Son and of the Holy Spirit. Amen.**

## PSALM
(For a longer psalm, see page xv.) Psalm 118:27a, (24)

This is the day that the LORD has made;
 let us rejoice and be glad in it.

**This is the day that the LORD has made;
 let us rejoice and be glad in it.**

The LORD is God,
 and he has given us light.

**This is the day that the LORD has made;
 let us rejoice and be glad in it.**

## READING
Acts 4:1–5a, 7–8, 10a

A reading from the Acts of the Apostles [uh-POS-uhlz]

While Peter and John were speaking to the people, the priests, the captain of the temple, and the Sadducees came to them, much annoyed because they were teaching the people and proclaiming that in Jesus there is the resurrection of the dead. So they arrested them and put them in custody until the next day, for it was already evening. But many of those who heard the word believed; and they numbered about five thousand.

The next day their rulers, elders, and scribes assembled in Jerusalem. When they had made the prisoners stand in their midst, they inquired, "By what power or by what name did you do this?" Then Peter, filled with the Holy Spirit, said to them, "Rulers of the people and elders, let it be known to all of you, and to all the people of Israel, that this man is standing before you in good health by the name of Jesus Christ of Nazareth."

The word of the Lord.

◆ All observe silence.

## FOR SILENT REFLECTION

Why do you think some people are annoyed while others believe when they see the disciples healing in Jesus' name?

## CLOSING PRAYER

Let us stand and bring our hopes and needs to God as we pray, "Lord, hear our prayer."

◆ All may add their own prayers here.

Let us pray: **Our Father . . . Amen.**

Alleluia! Alleluia! Christ is risen!
Lord God,
open our hearts to recognize your presence
in the good works and love of others.
We ask this through Christ our Lord.
**Amen.**

✢ All make the Sign of the Cross.

---

**ALSO ON THIS DAY:** Arbor Day (U.S.A.)

# PRAYER FOR THE WEEK

WITH A READING FROM THE GOSPEL FOR **SUNDAY, MAY 1, 2011**

## OPENING

Today is Divine Mercy Sunday when we remember God's great compassion. In today's Gospel, Jesus prepares his disciples to do his work in the world. Pay attention to what he gives them.

✢ All make the Sign of the Cross.

**In the name of the Father and of the Son and of the Holy Spirit. Amen.**

## PSALM    (For a longer psalm, see page xv.) Psalm 118:27a, (24)

This is the day that the LORD has made;
   let us rejoice and be glad in it.

**This is the day that the LORD has made;
   let us rejoice and be glad in it.**

The LORD is God,
   and he has given us light.

**This is the day that the LORD has made;
   let us rejoice and be glad in it.**

◆ All stand and sing **Alleluia**.

## GOSPEL    John 20:19–22

A reading from the holy Gospel according to John

When it was evening on that day, the first day of the week, and the doors of the house where the disciples had met were locked for fear of the Jews, Jesus came and stood among them and said, "Peace be with you." After he said this, he showed them his hands and his side. Then the disciples rejoiced when they saw the Lord. Jesus said to them again, "Peace be with you. As the Father has sent me, so I send you." When he had said this, he breathed on them and said to them "Receive the Holy Spirit."

The Gospel of the Lord.

◆ All sit and observe silence.

## FOR SILENT REFLECTION

What are the two gifts Jesus gives his disciples before sending them out into the world to continue his work? How does Jesus give these gifts to us?

## CLOSING PRAYER

Let us stand and bring our hopes and needs to God as we pray, "Lord, hear our prayer."

◆ All may add their own prayers here.

Let us pray: **Our Father . . . Amen.**

Loving God,
help us to receive your gift
of the Holy Spirit
and to share with one another
your gift of peace.
Make us one in the Spirit
and a source of peace
for the world.
We ask this through Jesus Christ our Lord.
**Amen.**

✢ All make the Sign of the Cross.

**ALSO ON THIS DAY:** Yom HaShoah (Holocaust Remembrance Day)
May Day

# PRAYER FOR MONDAY MAY 2, 2011

## OPENING

Today we continue to read about the disciples' work and experiences after Jesus' Resurrection. When we last read from Acts, Peter and John had been arrested by the authorities.

✦ All make the Sign of the Cross.

**In the name of the Father and of the Son and of the Holy Spirit. Amen.**

## PSALM     (For a longer psalm, see page xv.) Psalm 118:27a, (24)

This is the day that the LORD has made;
   let us rejoice and be glad in it.

**This is the day that the LORD has made;
   let us rejoice and be glad in it.**

The LORD is God,
   and he has given us light.

**This is the day that the LORD has made;
   let us rejoice and be glad in it.**

## READING     Acts 4:23–24a; 29–31

A reading from the Acts of the Apostles [uh-POS-uhlz]

After they were released, they went to their friends and reported what the chief priests and elders had said to them. When they had heard it, they raised their voices together to God and said, "And now, Lord, look at their threats and grant to your servants to speak your word with all boldness, while you stretch out your hand to heal, and signs and wonders are performed through the name of your holy servant Jesus." When they had prayed, the place in which they were gathered together was shaken; and they were all filled with the Holy Spirit and spoke the word of God with boldness.

The word of the Lord.

◆ All observe silence.

## FOR SILENT REFLECTION

How can we be bold as Christians?

## CLOSING PRAYER

Let us stand and bring our hopes and needs to God as we pray, "Lord, hear our prayer."

◆ All may add their own prayers here.

Let us pray: **Our Father . . . Amen.**

God our Father,
give us strength to proclaim your justice
in the face of injustice.
Grant us the courage to speak the truth
even when it is easier to lie.
Help us to be bold Christians,
willing to fight for the good
and to defend the powerless.
We ask this through the same Jesus Christ
   our Lord.
**Amen.**

✦ All make the Sign of the Cross.

# PRAYER SERVICE
## HONORING MARY IN MAY

*Prepare six leaders for this service. The third leader will need a Bible for the scripture passage and may need help finding it and practicing. On the prayer table place a picture or small statue of Mary and some fresh flowers. You may wish to end by singing "Immaculate Mary." If so, prepare a song leader.*

**FIRST LEADER:**
In the whole history of the world, nobody has ever been quite so brave as Mary, a teenager from a little, unknown town in Israel. Everything depended on what she would say when the angel Gabriel announced to her that she would become pregnant and give birth to the Son of God. It is sometimes easy for us to forget that Mary had a choice. After she heard what the angel had to say, she could have said, "No way!" She could have thought about all the things she'd rather be doing. But instead, Mary took a radical step. She said to Gabriel, "let it happen" according to God's plan. She didn't make any bargains. She didn't say, "Okay, but if I do this thing for you, then you've got to help me explain it to my mom and Joseph." Mary let God have her whole life, body and soul, with no ifs, ands, or buts. At this May crowning, let us pray that we can become as generous as Mary was with her life.

**SECOND LEADER:**

✦ All make the Sign of the Cross.

**In the name of the Father and of the Son and of the Holy Spirit. Amen.**

# HONORING MARY IN MAY

Let us pray:
Loving Father,
we rejoice that Mary said "yes" to you;
she opened her heart to the mysterious,
    unpredictable ways of Divine Love.
May her prayers help us to forget the silly
    quarrels, fads, and small goals we set
    for ourselves
so that we, too, may say "yes" to you.
We ask this through our Way to Life and
    holiness, Jesus Christ our Lord.

**ALL: Amen.**

**THIRD LEADER:**     Revelation 12:1–5
A reading from the Book of Revelation

◆ Read the passage from the Bible.

The word of the Lord.

**FOURTH LEADER:**
With Mary beside us, let us stand and bring our hopes and needs to God as we pray, **Lord, hear our prayer.**

Mary, you listened to God and trusted him to guide your life. May we be ready to listen to God in all situations, we pray to the Lord.

Mary, you are a courageous witness to Christ. May we be be brave witnesses also, in spite of pressure from others, we pray to the Lord.

Mary, you are the Queen of Peace. May God guard the human dignity of all those suffering in countries torn by war, and help us in our desire to bring an end to all violence and hatred, we pray to the Lord.

Mary, you cared for Jesus with so much love. May we be moved to help the needy and know the joy of generosity, we pray to the Lord.

Mary, you show the world a mother's love. May all those who are sick or who have died be comforted, we pray to the Lord.

**FIFTH LEADER:**
Let us pray the Hail Mary: **Hail Mary, full of grace . . .**

◆ Pause and then say the following.

Let us offer one another the sign of Christ's peace.

**SIXTH LEADER:**
Let us pray:
Generous and Eternal God,
as he was dying, Jesus gave his mother, Mary,
to all people everywhere to be our mother.
We know that she loves us and hopes
that we may find the true path
to a worthy, vivid, and beautiful Life.
Her son is that holy path to joy.
With the help of Mary's prayers,
may we step boldly and courageously onto
    this Path of Life
and place ourselves in your hands.
We ask this through our only Way and
    Truth, Jesus Christ our Lord.

**ALL: Amen.**

✚ All make the Sign of the Cross.

**In the name of the Father and of the Son and of the Holy Spirit. Amen.**

# PRAYER FOR TUESDAY MAY 3, 2011

### OPENING

Today we celebrate the feast of the apostles Saint Philip and Saint James, who were among the first to proclaim the good news. In the reading today, we hear Paul reminding the Corinthians [kohr-IN-thee-uhnz] of the Good News he first proclaimed to them. The name Cephas [SEE-fuhs], which we will hear in the reading, refers to the disciple, Peter. Jesus used it to replace Peter's original name, Simon.

✠ All make the Sign of the Cross.

**In the name of the Father and of the Son and of the Holy Spirit. Amen.**

### PSALM (For a longer psalm, see page xv.) Psalm 118:27a, (24)

This is the day that the LORD has made;
 let us rejoice and be glad in it.

**This is the day that the LORD has made;
 let us rejoice and be glad in it.**

The LORD is God,
 and he has given us light.

**This is the day that the LORD has made;
 let us rejoice and be glad in it.**

### READING 1 Corinthians 15:3–8

A reading from the First Letter of Saint Paul to the Corinthians [kohr-IN-thee-uhnz]

For I handed on to you as of first importance what I in turn had received: that Christ died for our sins in accordance with the scriptures, and that he was buried, and that he was raised on the third day in accordance with the scriptures, and that he appeared to Cephas [SEE-fuhs], then to the twelve. Then he appeared to more than five hundred brothers and sisters at one time, most of whom are still alive, though some have died. Then he appeared to James, then to all the apostles. Last of all, as to someone untimely born, he appeared also to me.

The word of the Lord.

◆ All observe silence.

### FOR SILENT REFLECTION

Paul is trying to help people believe in the Resurrection of Jesus. How does what he says help you to believe?

### CLOSING PRAYER

Let us stand and bring our hopes and needs to God as we pray, "Lord, hear our prayer."

◆ All may add their own prayers here.

Let us pray: **Our Father . . . Amen.**

God our Father,
even though we have not seen your
  Son ourselves,
we believe the people who did see him
and wrote stories that we could read
in the scriptures.
Help us to share our faith in you with others,
so that all may enjoy the fullness of life in you.
We ask this through our Lord Jesus Christ
**Amen.**

✠ All make the Sign of the Cross.

---

**ALSO ON THIS DAY:** National Teacher Day

# PRAYER FOR WEDNESDAY MAY 4, 2011

## OPENING

In today's reading we hear how God is with the early Christians.

✚ All make the Sign of the Cross.

**In the name of the Father and of the Son and of the Holy Spirit. Amen.**

## PSALM (For a longer psalm, see page xv.) Psalm 118:27a, (24)

This is the day that the LORD has made;
　let us rejoice and be glad in it.

**This is the day that the LORD has made;
　let us rejoice and be glad in it.**

The LORD is God,
　and he has given us light.

**This is the day that the LORD has made;
　let us rejoice and be glad in it.**

## READING Acts 5:17a, 18–20, 21ce–23, 25–26

A reading from the Acts of the Apostles [uh-POS-uhlz]

Then the high priest took action; he arrested the apostles and put them in the public prison. But during the night an angel of the Lord opened the prison doors, brought them out, and said, "Go, stand in the temple and tell the people the whole message about this life."

When the high priest and those with him arrived, they sent to the prison to have them brought. But when the temple police went there, they did not find them in the prison; so they returned and reported, "We found the prison securely locked and the guards standing at the doors, but when we opened them, we found no one inside." Then someone arrived and announced, "Look, the men whom you put in prison are standing in the temple and teaching the people!" Then the captain went with the temple police and brought them, but without violence, for they were afraid of being stoned by the people.

The word of the Lord.

◆ All observe silence.

## FOR SILENT REFLECTION

Who has the real power in this story?

## CLOSING PRAYER

Let us stand and bring our hopes and needs to God as we pray, "Lord, hear our prayer."

◆ All may add their own prayers here.

Let us pray: **Our Father . . . Amen.**

Holy God,
whenever we are afraid,
help us to remember
that you are with us in unexpected ways.
Be with us, Lord, in all we do.
We ask this through our Lord Jesus Christ,
　　your Son, who lives and reigns with
　　you in the unity of the Holy Spirit,
　　one God, for ever and ever.
**Amen.**

✚ All make the Sign of the Cross.

# PRAYER FOR THURSDAY MAY 5, 2011

## OPENING

Today we continue to read the story of the arrest of the apostles [uh-POS-uhlz]. Listen to the reason the apostles give for disobeying the high priest.

✛ All make the Sign of the Cross.

**In the name of the Father and of the Son and of the Holy Spirit. Amen.**

## PSALM  (For a longer psalm, see page xv.) Psalm 118:27a, (24)

This is the day that the LORD has made;
   let us rejoice and be glad in it.

**This is the day that the LORD has made;
   let us rejoice and be glad in it.**

The LORD is God,
   and he has given us light.

**This is the day that the LORD has made;
   let us rejoice and be glad in it.**

## READING  Acts 5:27–32

A reading from the Acts of the Apostles [uh-POS-uhlz]

When the temple police had brought the apostles, they had them stand before the council. The high priest questioned them, saying, "We gave you strict orders not to teach in this name, yet here you have filled Jerusalem with your teaching and you are determined to bring this man's blood upon us." But Peter and the apostles answered, "We must obey God rather than any human authority. The God of our ancestors raised up Jesus, whom you had killed by hanging him on a tree. God exalted him at his right hand as Leader and Savior that he might give repentance to Israel and forgiveness of sins. And we are witnesses to these things, and so is the Holy Spirit whom God has given to those who obey him."

The word of the Lord.

◆ All observe silence.

## FOR SILENT REFLECTION

Why didn't the high priest want the apostles to teach about Jesus?

## CLOSING PRAYER

Let us stand and bring our hopes and needs to God as we pray, "Lord, hear our prayer."

◆ All may add their own prayers here.

Let us pray: **Our Father . . . Amen.**

God of power and might,
teach us your ways
and help us to live,
not by self will,
but according to your will.
We ask this through your Son, the same Jesus
   Christ our Lord who lives and reigns
   with you in the unity of the Holy
   Spirit, one God, for ever and ever.
**Amen.**

✛ All make the Sign of the Cross.

---

**ALSO ON THIS DAY:** Cinco de Mayo (Mexico)
National Day of Prayer (U.S.A.)

# PRAYER FOR FRIDAY
# MAY 6, 2011

## OPENING

In today's reading from Acts we hear what a respected Jewish teacher named Gamaliel [ga-MAY-lee-ul] has to say about the apostles.

✠ All make the Sign of the Cross.

**In the name of the Father and of the Son and of the Holy Spirit. Amen.**

## PSALM
(For a longer psalm, see page xv.) Psalm 118:27a, (24)

This is the day that the LORD has made;
  let us rejoice and be glad in it.

**This is the day that the LORD has made;
  let us rejoice and be glad in it.**

The LORD is God,
  and he has given us light.

**This is the day that the LORD has made;
  let us rejoice and be glad in it.**

## READING
Acts 5:34–35, 38b–42

A reading from the Acts of the Apostles [uh-POS-uhlz]

A Pharisee [FAIR-uh-see] in the council named Gamaliel [ga-MAY-lee-ul], a teacher of the law, respected by all the people, stood up and ordered the men to be put outside for a short time. Then he said to them, "Fellow Israelites [IZ-ree-uh-lītz], consider carefully what you propose to do to these men. I tell you, keep away from these men and let them alone; because if this plan or this undertaking is of human origin, it will fail; but if it is of God, you will not be able to overthrow them—in that case you may even be found fighting against God!"

They were convinced by him, and when they had called in the apostles, they had them flogged. Then they ordered them not to speak in the name of Jesus and let them go. As the apostles left the council, they rejoiced that they were considered worthy to suffer dishonor for the sake of the name. And every day in the temple and at home they did not cease to teach and to proclaim Jesus as the Messiah [meh-SI-uh].

The word of the Lord.

◆ All observe silence.

## FOR SILENT REFLECTION

Why can something that is "of God" not be overthrown?

## CLOSING PRAYER

Let us stand and bring our hopes and needs to God as we pray, "Lord, hear our prayer."

◆ All may add their own prayers here.

Let us pray: **Our Father . . . Amen.**

God of power and wisdom,
may your truth bring us peace
and your goodness fill us with joy,
so that we may know how to recognize
your presence in our lives.
We ask this through Christ our Lord.
**Amen.**

✠ All make the Sign of the Cross.

# PRAYER FOR THE WEEK

WITH A READING FROM THE GOSPEL FOR **SUNDAY, MAY 8, 2011**

## OPENING

In today's Gospel, Jesus appears to two of his followers as they are going to the town of Emmaus (eh-MAY-uhs).

✚ All make the Sign of the Cross.

**In the name of the Father and of the Son and of the Holy Spirit. Amen.**

## PSALM  (For a longer psalm, see page xv.) Psalm 118:27a, (24)

This is the day that the LORD has made;
  let us rejoice and be glad in it.

**This is the day that the LORD has made;
  let us rejoice and be glad in it.**

The LORD is God,
  and he has given us light.

**This is the day that the LORD has made;
  let us rejoice and be glad in it.**

◆ All stand and sing **Alleluia.**

## GOSPEL  Luke 24:13–17, 18a, 18c, 19b, 20–21a, 22, 23, 25

A reading from the holy Gospel according to Luke

Now on that same day two of them were going to a village called Emmaus, about seven miles from Jerusalem, and talking with each other about all these things that had happened. While they were talking and discussing, Jesus himself came near and went with them, but their eyes were kept from recognizing him. And he said to them, "What are you discussing with each other while you walk along?" They stood still, looking sad. Then one of them answered him, "Are you the only stranger in Jerusalem who does not know about Jesus of Nazareth, and how our chief priests and leaders handed him over to be condemned to death and crucified him. But we had hoped that he was the one to redeem Israel. Moreover, some women of our group astounded us. They were at the tomb early this morning, and when they did not find his body there, they came back and told us that they had indeed seen a vision of angels who said that he was alive." Then he said to them, "Oh, how foolish you are, and how slow of heart to believe all that the prophets have declared!"

The Gospel of the Lord.

◆ All sit and observe silence.

## FOR SILENT REFLECTION

What do you imagine the disciples were feeling after Jesus' death?

## CLOSING PRAYER

Let us stand and bring our hopes and needs to God as we pray, "Lord, hear our prayer."

◆ All may add their own prayers here.

Let us pray: **Our Father . . . Amen.**

God of wonder,
we cannot imagine the heights of your power
or the depths of your love.
Be ever with us on the way,
when we feel confused, lost, and afraid.
We ask this through our Lord Jesus Christ.
  **Amen.**

---

**ALSO ON THIS DAY:** Mother's Day (U.S.A.) (Canada)

# PRAYER FOR MONDAY MAY 9, 2011

## OPENING

Just as the work of Jesus continued in the work of the disciples, so their work also continued in those whom they chose to help them. In today's reading we hear of Stephen [STEE-vuhn], one of the first people chosen by the disciples to help teach and preach.

✢ All make the Sign of the Cross.

**In the name of the Father and of the Son and of the Holy Spirit. Amen.**

## PSALM  (For a longer psalm, see page xv.) Psalm 118:27a, (24)

This is the day that the LORD has made;
   let us rejoice and be glad in it.

**This is the day that the LORD has made;
   let us rejoice and be glad in it.**

The LORD is God,
   and he has given us light.

**This is the day that the LORD has made;
   let us rejoice and be glad in it.**

## READING  Acts 6:8–9a, 9c–12, 15

A reading from the Acts of the Apostles [uh-POS-uhlz]

Stephen [STEE-vuhn], full of grace and power, did great wonders and signs among the people. Then some of those who belonged to the synagogue of the Freedman (as it was called) stood up and argued with Stephen. But they could not withstand the wisdom and the Spirit with which he spoke. They stirred up the people as well as the elders and the scribes; then they suddenly confronted him, seized him, and brought him before the council. And all who sat in the council looked intently at him, and they saw that his face was like the face of an angel.

The word of the Lord.

◆ All observe silence.

## FOR SILENT REFLECTION

How was Stephen able to do "great wonders and signs"?

## CLOSING PRAYER

Let us stand and bring our hopes and needs to God as we pray, "Lord, hear our prayer."

◆ All may add their own prayers here.

Let us pray: **Our Father . . . Amen.**

Holy God,
You called the disciples to follow you.
You also called Stephen to continue
      the holy work
of teaching, preaching, and caring
      for your people.
Help us to listen for your call to service
and to respond with courage and love.
We ask this through your Son, Jesus Christ
      our Lord, who lives and reigns with
      you, in the unity of the Holy Spirit,
      forever and ever.
**Amen.**

✢ All make the Sign of the Cross.

# PRAYER FOR TUESDAY MAY 10, 2011

## OPENING

Today we hear of the stoning of Stephen [STEE-vuhn], the first Christian to die for his faith.

✢ All make the Sign of the Cross.

**In the name of the Father and of the Son and of the Holy Spirit. Amen.**

## PSALM   (For a longer psalm, see page xv.) Psalm 118:27a, (24)

This is the day that the LORD has made;
  let us rejoice and be glad in it.

**This is the day that the LORD has made;
  let us rejoice and be glad in it.**

The LORD is God,
  and he has given us light.

**This is the day that the LORD has made;
  let us rejoice and be glad in it.**

## READING   Acts 7:51ac–52a, 54a, 55–58a, 59–60

A reading from the Acts of the Apostles [uh-POS-uhlz]

Stephen replied, "You stiff-necked people, you are forever opposing the Holy Spirit, just as your ancestors used to do. Which of the prophets did your ancestors not persecute?"

When they heard these things, they became enraged. But filled with the Holy Spirit, he gazed into heaven and saw the glory of God and Jesus standing at the right hand of God. "Look," he said, "I see the heavens opened and the Son of Man standing at the right hand of God!" But they covered their ears, and with a loud shout all rushed together against him. Then they dragged him out of the city and began to stone him. While they were stoning Stephen, he prayed, "Lord Jesus, receive my spirit." Then he knelt down and cried out in a loud voice, "Lord, do not hold this sin against them." When he said this, he died.

The word of the Lord.

◆ All observe silence.

## FOR SILENT REFLECTION

Like Jesus, Stephen forgave the people who were killing him. Can we be more like Jesus this week by forgiving someone who has hurt us?

## CLOSING PRAYER

Let us stand and bring our hopes and needs to God as we pray, "Lord, hear our prayer."

◆ All may add their own prayers here.

Let us pray: **Our Father . . . Amen.**

God, our Creator,
you made us in your image
and sent your Son to show us how to live.
Help us to imitate Jesus
so that we can be all we are meant to be.
We ask this through Jesus Christ our Lord.
**Amen.**

✢ All make the Sign of the Cross.

# PRAYER FOR WEDNESDAY MAY 11, 2011

## OPENING

As we read Acts, we learn that people reacted differently to the news about Jesus. Today's reading picks up just after the death of Stephen, which we heard about yesterday. The word persecution [per-suh-KYOO-shun] means the cruel treatment of a group of people. We learn that a man named Saul persecutes [per-suh-KYOOTZ] Christians. This man would later became Paul. We also hear how the Samaritans (suh-MAYR-uh-tuhns) respond when the apostle Philip brings the good news to them.

✢ All make the Sign of the Cross.

**In the name of the Father and of the Son and of the Holy Spirit. Amen.**

## PSALM (For a longer psalm, see page xv.) Psalm 118:27a, (24)

This is the day that the LORD has made;
 let us rejoice and be glad in it.

**This is the day that the LORD has made;
 let us rejoice and be glad in it.**

The LORD is God,
 and he has given us light.

**This is the day that the LORD has made;
 let us rejoice and be glad in it.**

## READING Acts 8:1b–3, 5–8

A reading from the Acts of the Apostles [uh-POS-uhlz]

That day a severe persecution began against the church in Jerusalem, and all except the apostles were scattered throughout the countryside of Judea and Samaria. Devout men buried Stephen and made loud lamentation over him. But Saul was ravaging the church by entering house after house; dragging off both men and women, he committed them to prison.

 Philip went down to the city of Samaria (suh-MAYR-ee-uh) and proclaimed the Messiah to them. The crowds with one accord listened eagerly to what was said by Philip, hearing and seeing the signs that he did, for unclean spirits, crying with loud shrieks, came out of many who were possessed; and many others who were paralyzed or lame were cured. So there was great joy in that city.

The word of the Lord.

◆ All observe silence.

## FOR SILENT REFLECTION

Why do you think some people are more eager to receive the good news than others?

## CLOSING PRAYER

Let us stand and bring our hopes and needs to God as we pray, "Lord, hear our prayer."

◆ All may add their own prayers here.

Let us pray: **Our Father . . . Amen.**

All-powerful God,
give us open hearts
that are eager to hear your word
so that we may have life.
We ask this through Christ our Lord.
**Amen.**

✢ All make the Sign of the Cross.

# PRAYER FOR THURSDAY MAY 12, 2011

## OPENING

Today's Gospel tells us what we will receive if we listen with eager hearts to the Word of God.

✚ All make the Sign of the Cross.

**In the name of the Father and of the Son and of the Holy Spirit. Amen.**

## PSALM
(For a longer psalm, see page xv.) Psalm 118:27a, (24)

This is the day that the LORD has made;
  let us rejoice and be glad in it.

**This is the day that the LORD has made;
  let us rejoice and be glad in it.**

The LORD is God,
  and he has given us light.

**This is the day that the LORD has made;
  let us rejoice and be glad in it.**

◆ All stand and sing **Alleluia**.

## GOSPEL
John 6:44–51

A reading from the holy Gospel according to John

Jesus said, "No one can come to me unless drawn by the Father who sent me; and I will raise that person up on the last day. It is written in the prophets, 'And they shall all be taught by God.' Everyone who has heard and learned from the Father comes to me. Not that anyone has seen the Father except the one who is from God; he has seen the Father. Very truly, I tell you, whoever believes has eternal life. I am the bread of life. Your ancestors ate the manna in the wilderness, and they died. This is the bread that comes down from heaven, so that one may eat of it and not die. I am the living bread that came down from heaven. Whoever eats of this bread will live forever; and the bread that I will give for the life of the world is my flesh."

The Gospel of the Lord.

◆ All sit and observe silence.

## FOR SILENT REFLECTION

How is Jesus the bread of life for you?

## CLOSING PRAYER

Let us stand and bring our hopes and needs to God as we pray, "Lord, hear our prayer."

◆ All may add their own prayers here.

Let us pray: **Our Father . . . Amen.**

God our Father,
you sent your Son Jesus into the world
so that through him we might come to you.
Give us a holy hunger
for this living bread.
We ask this through the same Lord Jesus
  Christ you Son, who lives and reigns
  with you in the unity of the Holy
  Spirit, one God, for ever and ever.
**Amen.**

✚ All make the Sign of the Cross.

# PRAYER FOR FRIDAY
# MAY 13, 2011

## OPENING

Today we hear about the conversion of Saint Paul, who was called Saul before his conversion. Once he had persecuted [PER-suh-kyoo-tuhd] the Christians, but would soon become a leader in the early Christian Church.

✚ All make the Sign of the Cross.

**In the name of the Father and of the Son and of the Holy Spirit. Amen.**

## PSALM  (For a longer psalm, see page xv.) Psalm 118:27a, (24)

This is the day that the LORD has made;
 let us rejoice and be glad in it.

**This is the day that the LORD has made;
 let us rejoice and be glad in it.**

The LORD is God,
 and he has given us light.

**This is the day that the LORD has made;
 let us rejoice and be glad in it.**

## READING  Acts Acts 9:1–9

A reading from the Acts of the Apostles [uh-POS-uhlz]

Meanwhile Saul, still breathing threats and murder against the disciples of the Lord, went to the high priest and asked him for letters to the synagogues at Damascus, so that if he found any who belonged to the Way, men or women, he might bring them bound to Jerusalem. Now as he was going along and approaching Damascus, suddenly a light from heaven flashed around him. He fell to the ground and heard a voice saying to him, "Saul, Saul, why do you persecute me?" He asked, "Who are you, Lord?" The reply came, "I am Jesus, whom you are persecuting. But get up and enter the city, and you will be told what you are to do." The men who were traveling with him stood speechless because they heard the voice but saw no one. Saul got up from the ground, and though his eyes were open, he could see nothing; so they led him by the hand and brought him into Damascus [duh-MAS-kus]. For three days he was without sight, and neither ate nor drank.

The word of the Lord.

◆ All observe silence.

## FOR SILENT REFLECTION

What does Jesus mean when he says that Paul is persecuting him?

## CLOSING PRAYER

Let us stand and bring our hopes and needs to God as we pray, "Lord, hear our prayer."

◆ All may add their own prayers here.

Let us pray: **Our Father . . . Amen.**

God of Light,
our prejudice, hatred, and pride
blind us to your presence.
Sometimes we need to see in new ways.
Restore our soul's sight,
and enlighten our minds.
We ask this through Jesus Christ our Lord.
**Amen.**

✚ All make the Sign of the Cross.

# PRAYER FOR THE WEEK

WITH A READING FROM THE GOSPEL FOR **SUNDAY, MAY 15, 2011**

## OPENING

Today is called Good Shepherd Sunday—named for the Gospel reading that we are about to hear. Jesus calls himself the Good Shepherd because he protects and cares for his flock.

✚ All make the Sign of the Cross.

**In the name of the Father and of the Son and of the Holy Spirit. Amen.**

## PSALM     (For a longer psalm, see page xv.) Psalm 118:27a, (24)

This is the day that the Lord has made;
  let us rejoice and be glad in it.

**This is the day that the Lord has made;
  let us rejoice and be glad in it.**

The Lord is God,
  and he has given us light.

**This is the day that the Lord has made;
  let us rejoice and be glad in it.**

◆ All stand and sing **Alleluia.**

## GOSPEL     John 10:1–5, 7b, 9b, 10b

A reading from the holy Gospel according to John

"Very truly, I tell you, anyone who does not enter the sheepfold by the gate but climbs in by another way is a thief and a bandit. The one who enters by the gate is the shepherd of the sheep. The gatekeeper opens the gate for him, and the sheep hear his voice. He calls his own sheep by name and leads them out. When he has brought out all his own, he goes ahead of them, and the sheep follow him because they know his voice. They will not follow a stranger, but they will run from him because they do not know the voice of strangers." Jesus said to them, "Very truly, I tell you, I am the gate for the sheep. Whoever enters by me will be saved, and will come in and go out and find pasture. I came that they may have life, and have it abundantly."

The Gospel of the Lord.

◆ All sit and observe silence.

## FOR SILENT REFLECTION

Why do the sheep recognize the shepherd's voice? How can we recognize the voice of Jesus in our lives?

## CLOSING PRAYER

Let us stand and bring our hopes and needs to God as we pray, "Lord, hear our prayer."

◆ All may add their own prayers here.

Let us pray: **Our Father . . . Amen.**

Lord God,
how tenderly your Son cares for your sheep,
leading us together into life.
Help us to recognize his voice
and to follow wherever he leads us.
We ask this through the same Jesus Christ.
**Amen.**

✚ All make the Sign of the Cross.

# PRAYER FOR MONDAY MAY 16, 2011

## OPENING

In today's Gospel, Jesus continues to describe himself as a shepherd. Listen to see why he says he is the "good shepherd."

✣ All make the Sign of the Cross.

**In the name of the Father and of the Son and of the Holy Spirit. Amen.**

## PSALM   (For a longer psalm, see page xv.) Psalm 118:27a, (24)

This is the day that the LORD has made;
 let us rejoice and be glad in it.

**This is the day that the LORD has made;
 let us rejoice and be glad in it.**

The LORD is God,
 and he has given us light.

**This is the day that the LORD has made;
 let us rejoice and be glad in it.**

◆ All stand and sing **Alleluia**.

## GOSPEL   John 10:11–18

A reading from the holy Gospel according to John

"I am the good shepherd. The good shepherd lays down his life for the sheep. The hired hand, who is not the shepherd and does not own the sheep, sees the wolf coming and leaves the sheep and runs away—and the wolf snatches them and scatters them. The hired hand runs away because a hired hand does not care for the sheep. I am the good shepherd. I know my own and my own know me, just as the Father knows me and I know the Father. And I lay down my life for the sheep. I have other sheep that do not belong to this fold. I must bring them also, and they will listen to my voice. So there will be one flock, one shepherd. For this reason the Father loves me, because I lay down my life in order to take it up again. No one takes it from me, but I lay it down of my own accord. I have power to lay it down, and I have power to take it up again. I have received this command from my Father."

The Gospel of the Lord.

◆ All sit and observe silence.

## FOR SILENT REFLECTION

How is Jesus the good shepherd?

## CLOSING PRAYER

Let us stand and bring our hopes and needs to God as we pray, "Lord, hear our prayer."

◆ All may add their own prayers here.

Let us pray: **Our Father . . . Amen.**

Loving God,
you long to bring all your people
under your protection and care.
You want us to be one flock.
We pray today for unity.
May all people know your loving care.
We ask this through Jesus Christ our Lord.
**Amen.**

✣ All make the Sign of the Cross.

# PRAYER FOR TUESDAY MAY 17, 2011

### OPENING

Today's reading from the Acts of the Apostles [uh-POS-uhlz] tells us of when the followers of Jesus were first called Christians. To exhort [ex-HORT] means to urge someone very seriously.

✠ All make the Sign of the Cross.

**In the name of the Father and of the Son and of the Holy Spirit. Amen.**

### PSALM   (For a longer psalm, see page xv.) Psalm 118:27a, (24)

This is the day that the LORD has made;
    let us rejoice and be glad in it.

**This is the day that the LORD has made;
    let us rejoice and be glad in it.**

The LORD is God,
    and he has given us light.

**This is the day that the LORD has made;
    let us rejoice and be glad in it.**

### READING                              Acts 11:22b–26

A reading from the Acts of the Apostles [uh-POS-uhlz]

The church in Jerusalem sent Barnabas to Antioch [AN-tee-awk]. When he came and saw the grace of God, he rejoiced, and he exhorted [ex-HORT-d] them all to remain faithful to the Lord with steadfast devotion; for he was a good man, full of the Holy Spirit and of faith. And a great many people were brought to the Lord. Then Barnabas went to Tarsus [TAR-sus] to look for Saul, and when he had found him, he brought him to Antioch [AN-tee-awk]. So it was that for an entire year they met with the church, and taught a great many people, and it was in Antioch that the disciples were first called "Christians."

The word of the Lord.

◆ All observe silence.

### FOR SILENT REFLECTION

Imagine that you had never heard of Jesus. What would it be like to have strangers come into your town teaching you the story and all that it means?

### CLOSING PRAYER

Let us stand and bring our hopes and needs to God as we pray, "Lord, hear our prayer."

◆ All may add their own prayers here.

Let us pray: **Our Father . . . Amen.**

Lord God,
the name of your Son
has power to heal and save.
May we remember this power
whenever we call ourselves Christian.
We ask this through your Son, our Lord
    Jesus Christ, who lives and reigns with
    you in the unity of the Holy Spirit,
    one God, for ever and ever.
**Amen.**

✠ All make the Sign of the Cross.

---

**ALSO ON THIS DAY:** Vesak (Buddhist celebration of the Birth of the Buddha)

# PRAYER FOR WEDNESDAY MAY 18, 2011

## OPENING

Jesus uses different images to describe himself. In Monday's Gospel reading, he called himself the Good Shepherd. In today's Gospel, he calls himself light.

✢ All make the Sign of the Cross.

**In the name of the Father and of the Son and of the Holy Spirit. Amen.**

## PSALM (For a longer psalm, see page xv.) Psalm 118:27a, (24)

This is the day that the LORD has made;
   let us rejoice and be glad in it.

**This is the day that the LORD has made;
   let us rejoice and be glad in it.**

The LORD is God,
   and he has given us light.

**This is the day that the LORD has made;
   let us rejoice and be glad in it.**

◆ All stand and sing **Alleluia.**

## GOSPEL John 12:44–46, 49–50

A reading from the holy Gospel according to John

Then Jesus cried aloud: "Whoever believes in me believes not in me but in him who sent me. And whoever sees me sees him who sent me. I have come as light into the world, so that everyone who believes in me should not remain in darkness. I have not spoken on my own, but the Father who sent me has himself given me a commandment about what to say and what to speak. And I know that his commandment is eternal life. What I speak, therefore, I speak just as the Father has told me."

The Gospel of the Lord.

◆ All sit and observe silence.

## FOR SILENT REFLECTION

Can you think of ways in which the "light" of Jesus makes a difference in your life?

## CLOSING PRAYER

Let us stand and bring our hopes and needs to God as we pray, "Lord, hear our prayer."

◆ All may add their own prayers here.

Let us pray: **Our Father . . . Amen.**

Generous God,
in your great love
you sent your only Son into the world
to be the world's light.
Shine in our hearts,
fill us with your radiant presence,
and teach us to walk as children of light.
We ask this through your Son, our Lord
   Jesus Christ, who lives and reigns with
   you in the unity of the Holy Spirit,
   one God, for ever and ever.
**Amen.**

✢ All make the Sign of the Cross.

# PRAYER FOR **THURSDAY MAY 19, 2011**

## OPENING

In today's Gospel, Jesus has just washed the feet of his disciples. Now he will explain how he wants them to serve people in the future. He will also say what it means to be a servant and what it means to be a messenger. As you listen, think about what Jesus is teaching us by his example and by what he says.

✚ All make the Sign of the Cross.

**In the name of the Father and of the Son and of the Holy Spirit. Amen.**

## PSALM     (For a longer psalm, see page xv.) Psalm 118:27a, (24)

This is the day that the Lord has made;
  let us rejoice and be glad in it.

**This is the day that the Lord has made;
  let us rejoice and be glad in it.**

The Lord is God,
  and he has given us light.

**This is the day that the Lord has made;
  let us rejoice and be glad in it.**

◆ All stand and sing **Alleluia**.

## GOSPEL     John 13:12–17

A reading from the holy Gospel according to John

After Jesus had washed their feet, had put on his robe, and had returned to the table, he said to them, "Do you know what I have done to you? You call me Teacher and Lord—and you are right for that is what I am. So if I, your Lord and Teacher, have washed your feet, you also ought to wash one another's feet. For I have set you an example, that you also should do as I have done to you. Very truly, I tell you, servants are not greater than their master, nor are messengers greater than the one who sent them. If you know these things, you are blessed if you do them."

The Gospel of the Lord.

◆ All sit and observe silence.

## FOR SILENT REFLECTION

How can we serve one another? How does a servant or a messenger act?

## CLOSING PRAYER

Let us stand and bring our hopes and needs to God as we pray, "Lord, hear our prayer."

◆ All may add their own prayers here.

Let us pray: **Our Father . . . Amen.**

Holy God,
help us to follow the example of Jesus
and serve one another
through good works and acts of kindness.
We ask this through our Lord Jesus Christ.
**Amen.**

✚ All make the Sign of the Cross.

# PRAYER FOR FRIDAY MAY 20, 2011

## OPENING

In today's Gospel, Jesus tells us that he is the way. Listen closely and see if you can understand what this means.

✚ All make the Sign of the Cross.

**In the name of the Father and of the Son and of the Holy Spirit. Amen.**

## PSALM     (For a longer psalm, see page xv.) Psalm 118:27a, (24)

This is the day that the LORD has made;
  let us rejoice and be glad in it.

**This is the day that the LORD has made;
  let us rejoice and be glad in it.**

The LORD is God,
  and he has given us light.

**This is the day that the LORD has made;
  let us rejoice and be glad in it.**

◆ All stand and sing **Alleluia**.

## GOSPEL     John 14:1–6

A reading from the holy Gospel according to John

Jesus said to his disciples, "Do not let your hearts be troubled. Believe in God, believe also in me. In my Father's house there are many dwelling places. If it were not so, would I have told you that I go to prepare a place for you? And if I go and prepare a place for you, I will come again and will take you to myself, so that where I am, there you may be also. And you know the way to the place where I am going." Thomas said to him, "Lord, we do not know where you are going. How can we know the way?" Jesus said to him, "I am the way, the truth and the life."

The Gospel of the Lord.

◆ All sit and observe silence.

## FOR SILENT REFLECTION

Where is Jesus going? How is he the "way" for us?

## CLOSING PRAYER

Let us stand and bring our hopes and needs to God as we pray, "Lord, hear our prayer."

◆ All may add their own prayers here.

Let us pray: **Our Father . . . Amen.**

God of life and truth,
you show us the way
to the fullness of eternal life.
Help us to come to you
by following the example of your Son.
We ask this through the same Jesus Christ
    our Lord who lives and reigns with
    you, in the unity of the Holy Spirit,
    forever and ever.
**Amen.**

✚ All make the Sign of the Cross.

# PRAYER FOR THE WEEK

WITH A READING FROM THE GOSPEL FOR **SUNDAY, MAY 22, 2011**

## OPENING

In today's Gospel, Jesus helps Philip [FIL-ip] understand who he is. Listen closely to what Jesus says.

✚ All make the Sign of the Cross.

**In the name of the Father and of the Son and of the Holy Spirit. Amen.**

## PSALM (For a longer psalm, see page xvi.) Psalm 23:2 (1)

The LORD is my shepherd, I shall not want.

**The LORD is my shepherd, I shall not want.**

He makes me lie down in green pastures;
he leads me beside still waters;

**The LORD is my shepherd, I shall not want.**

◆ All stand and sing **Alleluia**.

## GOSPEL John 14:8–12

A reading from the holy Gospel according to John

Philip said to him, "Lord, show us the Father, and we will be satisfied." Jesus said to him, "Have I been with you all this time, Philip, and you still do not know me? Whoever has seen me has seen the Father. How can you say, 'Show us the Father?' Do you not believe that I am in the Father and the Father is in me? The words that I say to you I do not speak on my own; but the Father who dwells in me does his works. Believe me that I am in the Father and the Father is in me; but if you do not, then believe me because of the works themselves. Very truly, I tell you, the one who believes in me will also do the works that I do and, in fact, will do greater works than these, because I am going to the Father."

The Gospel of the Lord.

◆ All sit and observe silence.

## FOR SILENT REFLECTION

What works did Jesus do that his followers can also do? Why are Jesus' followers able to do what Jesus has done?

## CLOSING PRAYER

Let us stand and bring our hopes and needs to God as we pray, "Lord, hear our prayer."

◆ All may add their own prayers here.

Let us pray: **Our Father . . . Amen.**

God our Father,
like Philip, we struggle to understand
　　just who Jesus is.
Give us faith when we do not understand.
Help us to grow in faith by listening to your
　　holy word,
doing good works, and turning to you
　　in prayer.
We ask this through the same Jesus Christ
　　our Lord.
**Amen.**

✚ All make the Sign of the Cross.

# PRAYER FOR MONDAY
# MAY 23, 2011

## OPENING

In today's reading we hear about the ministry of Paul after his conversion. Notice how Paul and Barnabas [BAHR-nuh-buhs], another convert, carry on the healing work of Jesus and the first apostles. Also notice the reaction of the crowd.

✢ All make the Sign of the Cross.

**In the name of the Father and of the Son and of the Holy Spirit. Amen.**

## PSALM
(For a longer psalm, see page xvi.) Psalm 23:2 (1)

The Lord is my shepherd, I shall not want.

**The Lord is my shepherd, I shall not want.**

He makes me lie down in green pastures;
he leads me beside still waters;

**The Lord is my shepherd, I shall not want.**

## READING
Acts 14:8–11a, 11c, 13–15

A reading from the Acts of the Apostles [uh-POS-uhlz]

In Lystra (LIS-truh) there was a man sitting who could not use his feet and had never walked, for he had been crippled from birth. He listened to Paul as he was speaking. And Paul, looking at him intently and seeing that he had faith to be healed, said in a loud voice, "Stand upright on your feet." And the man sprang up and began to walk. When the crowds saw what Paul had done, they shouted, "The gods have come down to us in human form!" The priest of Zeus, whose temple was just outside the city, brought oxen and garlands to the gates; he and the crowds wanted to offer sacrifice. When the apostles Barnabas and Paul heard of it, they tore their clothes and rushed out into the crowd, shouting, "Friends, why are you doing this? We are mortals just like you, and we bring you good news, that you should turn from these worthless things to the living God, who made the heaven and the earth and the sea and all that is in them."

The word of the Lord.

◆ All observe silence.

## FOR SILENT REFLECTION

Why is Paul upset when the people think that he and Barnabas are gods?

## CLOSING PRAYER

Let us stand and bring our hopes and needs to God as we pray, "Lord, hear our prayer."

◆ All may add their own prayers here.

Let us pray: **Our Father . . . Amen.**

Holy and eternal God,
open our hearts to your healing power
for you alone are the source of all good.
We ask this through Jesus Christ our Lord.
**Amen.**

✢ All make the Sign of the Cross.

---

**ALSO ON THIS DAY:** Victoria Day (Canada)

# PRAYER FOR TUESDAY MAY 24, 2011

### OPENING

In today's Gospel, we look back at Jesus' farewell to his followers. Knowing the hour of his Passion is near, he tells them what he wants for them, and what he wants them to remember about him.

✚ All make the Sign of the Cross.

**In the name of the Father and of the Son and of the Holy Spirit. Amen.**

### PSALM  (For a longer psalm, see page xvi.) Psalm 23:2 (1)

The LORD is my shepherd, I shall not want.

**The LORD is my shepherd, I shall not want.**

He makes me lie down in green pastures;
he leads me beside still waters;

**The LORD is my shepherd, I shall not want.**

◆ All stand and sing **Alleluia**.

### GOSPEL   John 14:27–31a

A reading from the holy Gospel according to John

Jesus said to his disciples, "Peace I leave with you; my peace I give to you. I do not give to you as the world gives. Do not let your hearts be troubled, and do not let them be afraid. You heard me say to you, 'I am going away, and I am coming to you.' If you loved me, you would rejoice that I am going to the Father, because the Father is greater than I. And now I have told you this before it occurs, so that when it does occur, you may believe. I will no longer talk much with you, for the ruler of this world is coming. He has no power over me; but I do as the Father has commanded me, so that the world may know that I love the Father."

The Gospel of the Lord.

◆ All sit and observe silence.

### FOR SILENT REFLECTION

In what way do you think the peace that the world gives is different from the peace that Jesus gives?

### CLOSING PRAYER

Let us stand and bring our hopes and needs to God as we pray, "Lord, hear our prayer."

◆ All may add their own prayers here.

Let us pray: **Our Father . . . Amen.**

Loving God,
bless us with your peace.
Change our sorrows into joy,
our worries into trust,
and our anger into patience.
Help us to remember that you are with us.
We ask this through Jesus Christ our Lord,
**Amen.**

✚ All make the Sign of the Cross.

# PRAYER FOR WEDNESDAY MAY 25, 2011

## OPENING

In today's Gospel, Jesus tells us to "abide" in him, meaning that we are to dwell or live in him. He uses the image of a vine to explain how we can live in him.

✢ All make the Sign of the Cross.

**In the name of the Father and of the Son and of the Holy Spirit. Amen.**

## PSALM  (For a longer psalm, see page xvi.) Psalm 23:2 (1)

The Lord is my shepherd, I shall not want.

**The Lord is my shepherd, I shall not want.**

He makes me lie down in green pastures; he leads me beside still waters;

**The Lord is my shepherd, I shall not want.**

◆ All stand and sing **Alleluia**.

## GOSPEL  John 15:1, 4–5, 7–8

A reading from the holy Gospel according to John

Jesus said to his disciples, "I am the true vine, and my Father is the vinegrower. Abide in me as I abide in you. Just as the branch cannot bear fruit by itself unless it abides in the vine, neither can you unless you abide in me. I am the vine, you are the branches. Those who abide in me and I in them bear much fruit, because apart from me you can do nothing. If you abide in me, and my words abide in you, ask for whatever you wish, and it will be done for you. My Father is glorified by this, that you bear much fruit and become my disciples."

The Gospel of the Lord.

◆ All sit and observe silence.

## FOR SILENT REFLECTION

What sort of fruit do you think we might produce when we abide in Jesus?

## CLOSING PRAYER

Let us stand and bring our hopes and needs to God as we pray, "Lord, hear our prayer."

◆ All may add their own prayers here.

Let us pray: **Our Father . . . Amen.**

God our Creator,
Christ is the vine and we, your people
are like branches growing from this vine.
Like a good gardener, you tend this vine
watering and pruning.
Help us to grow in love and goodness,
bringing forth the fruits of good works
 and holiness.
We ask this through Jesus Christ, our Lord.
**Amen.**

✢ All make the Sign of the Cross.

# PRAYER FOR **THURSDAY** MAY 26, 2011

### OPENING

Today we remember Saint Philip Neri [NEER-ī], an Italian priest known for his service to the sick, pilgrims, and penitents. In today's Gospel Jesus continues to talk about how we can "abide" or live in him.

✢ All make the Sign of the Cross.

**In the name of the Father and of the Son and of the Holy Spirit. Amen.**

### PSALM   (For a longer psalm, see page xvi.) Psalm 23:2 (1)

The LORD is my shepherd, I shall not want.

**The LORD is my shepherd, I shall not want.**

He makes me lie down in green pastures;
he leads me beside still waters;

**The LORD is my shepherd, I shall not want.**

◆ All stand and sing **Alleluia**.

### GOSPEL   John 15:9–11

A reading from the holy Gospel according to John

Jesus said to his disciples, "As the Father has loved me, so I have loved you; abide in my love. If you keep my commandments, you will abide in my love, just as I have kept my Father's commandments and abide in his love. I have said these things to you so that my joy may be in you, and that your joy may be complete.

The Gospel of the Lord.

◆ All sit and observe silence.

### FOR SILENT REFLECTION

When have you experienced joy from following Christ's commandments and feeling close to him?

### CLOSING PRAYER

Let us stand and bring our hopes and needs to God as we pray, "Lord, hear our prayer."

◆ All may add their own prayers here.

Let us pray: **Our Father . . . Amen.**

Holy God,
you sent your Son to show us the way to you.
When we learn to love you,
and our neighbors as ourselves,
we will be full and overflowing
with the joy only you can give.
Teach us to love,
that our joy may be complete.
We ask this through your Son, the same Jesus Christ our Lord, who lives and reigns with you in the unity of the Holy Spirit, one God, forever and ever.
**Amen.**

✢ All make the Sign of the Cross.

# PRAYER FOR FRIDAY MAY 27, 2011

## OPENING

In today's Gospel Jesus calls his followers his friends. Listen to what Jesus says about friendship.

✝ All make the Sign of the Cross.

**In the name of the Father and of the Son and of the Holy Spirit. Amen.**

## PSALM
(For a longer psalm, see page xvi.) Psalm 23:2 (1)

The LORD is my shepherd, I shall not want.

**The LORD is my shepherd, I shall not want.**

He makes me lie down in green pastures; he leads me beside still waters;

**The LORD is my shepherd, I shall not want.**

◆ All stand and sing **Alleluia**.

## GOSPEL
John 15:12–17

A reading from the holy Gospel according to John

Jesus said to his disciples, "This is my commandment, that you love one another as I have loved you. No one has greater love than this, to lay down one's life for one's friends. You are my friends if you do what I command you. I do not call you servants any longer, because the servant does not know what the master is doing; but I have called you friends, because I have made known to you everything I have heard from my Father. You did not choose me but I chose you. And I appointed you to go and bear fruit, fruit that will last, so that the Father will give you whatever you ask him in my name. I am giving you these commands so that you may love one another."

The Gospel of the Lord.

◆ All sit and observe silence.

## FOR SILENT REFLECTION

How do we know when we are being Jesus' friends?

## CLOSING PRAYER

Let us stand and bring our hopes and needs to God as we pray, "Lord, hear our prayer."

◆ All may add their own prayers here.

Let us pray: **Our Father . . . Amen.**

All powerful and loving God,
your Son has shown us
how to be friends of yours
and good friends to one another.
May holy love, not selfishness,
guide us in all we do.
We ask this through your Son, the same Jesus Christ, our Lord, who lives and reigns with you in the unity of the Holy Spirit, one God, forever and ever.
**Amen.**

✝ All make the Sign of the Cross.

# PRAYER FOR THE WEEK

WITH A READING FROM THE GOSPEL FOR **SUNDAY, MAY 29, 2011**

## OPENING

Today, we continue to read from the Gospel of John. An advocate [AD-voh-kuht] is a helper who supports or works for someone. Jesus is referring to the Holy Spirit.

✦ All make the Sign of the Cross.

**In the name of the Father and of the Son and of the Holy Spirit. Amen.**

## PSALM   (For a longer psalm, see page xvi.) Psalm 23:2 (1)

The LORD is my shepherd, I shall not want.

**The LORD is my shepherd, I shall not want.**

He makes me lie down in green pastures; he leads me beside still waters;

**The LORD is my shepherd, I shall not want.**

◆ All stand and sing **Alleluia**.

## GOSPEL   John 14:15–21

A reading from the holy Gospel according to John

Jesus answered, "If you love me, you will keep my commandments. And I will ask the Father, and he will give you another Advocate [AD-voh-kuht], to be with you forever. This is the Spirit of truth, whom the world cannot receive, because it neither sees him nor knows him. You know him, because he abides with you, and he will be in you. I will not leave you orphaned; I am coming to you. In a little while the world will no longer see me, but you will see me; because I live, you also will live. On that day you will know that I am in my Father, and you in me, and I in you. They who have my commandments and keep them are those who love me; and those who love me will be loved by my Father, and I will love them and reveal myself to them."

The Gospel of the Lord.

◆ All sit and observe silence.

## FOR SILENT REFLECTION

Do you know the Spirit? How?

## CLOSING PRAYER

Let us stand and bring our hopes and needs to God as we pray, "Lord, hear our prayer."

◆ All may add their own prayers here.

Let us pray: **Our Father . . . Amen.**

Lord God,
send the Spirit of truth
into our minds,
and the Spirit of love
into our hearts,
so that we may know you.
We ask this through Jesus Christ our Lord. **Amen.**

✦ All make the Sign of the Cross.

# PRAYER FOR MONDAY
# MAY 30, 2011

## OPENING

In today's Gospel, Jesus continues to talk about the Holy Spirit. To "testify" [TES-tih-fī] is to witness to or show.

✚ All make the Sign of the Cross.

**In the name of the Father and of the Son and of the Holy Spirit. Amen.**

## PSALM  (For a longer psalm, see page xvi.) Psalm 23:2 (1)

The LORD is my shepherd, I shall not want.

**The LORD is my shepherd, I shall not want.**

He makes me lie down in green pastures; he leads me beside still waters;

**The LORD is my shepherd, I shall not want.**

◆ All stand and sing **Alleluia.**

## GOSPEL  John 15:26—16:4a

A reading from the holy Gospel according to John

Jesus said to his disciples, "When the Advocate comes, whom I will send to you from the Father, the Spirit of truth who comes from the Father, he will testify on my behalf. You are also to testify because you have been with me from the beginning.

I have said these things to you to keep you from stumbling. They will put you out of the synagogues. Indeed, an hour is coming when those who kill you will think that by doing so they are offering worship to God. And they will do this because they have not known the Father or me. But I have said these things to you so that when their hour comes you may remember that I told you about them."

The Gospel of the Lord.

◆ All sit and observe silence.

## FOR SILENT REFLECTION

What does the Holy Spirit show us?

## CLOSING PRAYER

Let us stand and bring our hopes and needs to God as we pray, "Lord, hear our prayer."

◆ All may add their own prayers here.

Let us pray: **Our Father . . . Amen.**

Loving God,
send your Holy Spirit
into our hearts
as our helper and guide.
Through the Spirit,
may we know your truth.
In the Spirit,
may we live in unity.
With the Holy Spirit,
may we walk with you.
We ask this through Jesus Christ our Lord.
**Amen.**

✚ All make the Sign of the Cross.

**ALSO ON THIS DAY:** Memorial Day (U.S.A.)

# PRAYER FOR TUESDAY MAY 31, 2011

## OPENING

Today we celebrate the feast of the Visitation. The Gospel today helps us think about the visit that Mary paid to her elderly cousin Elizabeth. Both women were pregnant and both were overflowing with gratitude for the special children they were expecting.

✢ All make the Sign of the Cross.

**In the name of the Father and of the Son and of the Holy Spirit. Amen.**

## PSALM
(For a longer psalm, see page xvi.) Psalm 23:2 (1)

The LORD is my shepherd, I shall not want.

**The LORD is my shepherd, I shall not want.**

He makes me lie down in green pastures;
he leads me beside still waters;

**The LORD is my shepherd, I shall not want.**

◆ All stand and sing **Alleluia**.

## GOSPEL
Luke 1:39–44, 46–49, 56

A reading from the holy Gospel according to Luke

In those days Mary set out and went with haste to a Judean town in the hill country, where she entered the house of Zechariah and greeted Elizabeth. When Elizabeth heard Mary's greeting, the child leaped in her womb. And Elizabeth was filled with the Holy Spirit and exclaimed with a loud cry, "Blessed are you among women, and blessed is the fruit of your womb. And why has this happened to me, that the mother of my Lord comes to me? For as soon as I heard the sound of your greeting, the child in my womb leaped for joy."
And Mary said,
"My soul magnifies the Lord,
  and my spirit rejoices in God my Savior,
for he has looked with favor on the
    lowliness of his servant.
  Surely, from now on all generations will
    call me blessed;
for the Mighty One has done great things
    for me,
  and holy is his name."
And Mary remained with her about three months and then returned to her home.
The Gospel of the Lord.

◆ All sit and observe silence.

## FOR SILENT REFLECTION

Why do you think Elizabeth's child leaped in her body at the sound of Mary's voice?

## CLOSING PRAYER

Let us stand and bring our hopes and needs to God as we pray, "Lord, hear our prayer."

◆ All may add their own prayers here.

Let us pray: **Our Father . . . Amen.**

God of life,
we thank you for the gift of Jesus
and John the Baptist.
May we be a good spiritual friend to someone
and may we find the spiritual friends we need.
Grant this through Christ our Lord.
**Amen.**

✢ All make the Sign of the Cross.

# PRAYER FOR WEDNESDAY JUNE 1, 2011

## OPENING

In today's reading Saint Paul preaches to the people of Athens, Greece [ATH-uhnz GREES]. He has noticed many temples around the city that are full of idols. The people he is speaking to have never heard of God the Father, or of Jesus. Listen to what Paul says to them.

✝ All make the Sign of the Cross.

**In the name of the Father and of the Son and of the Holy Spirit. Amen.**

## PSALM

(For a longer psalm, see page xvi.) Psalm 23:2 (1)

The Lord is my shepherd, I shall not want.

**The Lord is my shepherd, I shall not want.**

He makes me lie down in green pastures;
he leads me beside still waters;

**The Lord is my shepherd, I shall not want.**

## READING

Acts 17:22–24c, 26–28a

A reading from the Acts of the Apostles [uh-POS-uhlz]

Paul proclaimed, "Athenians, I see how extremely religious you are in every way. For as I went through the city and looked carefully at the objects of your worship, I found among them an altar with the inscription, 'To an unknown god.' What therefore you worship as unknown, this I proclaim to you. The God who made the world and everything in it, he who is Lord of heaven and earth, does not live in shrines made by human hands. From one ancestor he made all nations to inhabit the whole earth, and he allotted the times of their existence and the boundaries of the places where they would live, so that they would search for God and perhaps grope for him and find him—though indeed he is not far from each one of us. For 'In him, we live and move and have our being.'"

The word of the Lord.

◆ All observe silence.

## FOR SILENT REFLECTION

What do you think Paul means when he says that people search for God although he is not far from each one of us?

## CLOSING PRAYER

Let us stand and bring our hopes and needs to God as we pray, "Lord, hear our prayer."

◆ All may add their own prayers here.

Let us pray: **Our Father . . . Amen.**

God of creation,
you are near to all who seek you
in their hearts.
May those who long for you, find you.
Bless all our teachers, preachers,
missionaries, parents, grandparents,
and all who help others to know you.
We ask this through Jesus Christ our Lord.
**Amen.**

✝ All make the Sign of the Cross.

# PRAYER SERVICE
## ASCENSION

*Prepare seven leaders for this service. The third and fourth leaders will need a Bible from which to read the scripture passages and may need help finding them and practicing. You may wish to begin by singing "Alleluia! Sing to Jesus" and end with "Sing Out, Earth and Skies." If so, prepare a song leader.*

**FIRST LEADER:**
Praise be to our Lord Jesus Christ
who has been taken up to heaven!

**ALL:** Amen.

**FIRST LEADER:**
Today we celebrate the Ascension of the Lord—40 days after Easter—when Jesus returned to his Father in heaven, so he could be with all people everywhere, forever and ever!

**SECOND LEADER:**

✛ All make the Sign of the Cross.

**In the name of the Father and of the Son and of the Holy Spirit. Amen.**

Let us pray:
Heavenly Father,
just before your Son Jesus Christ ascended
    into heaven
to sit at your right hand,
he promised that he would be with us always.
Help us to feel his strong, living presence in
    our lives,
especially today as we pray together.
We ask this through Jesus Christ, our Lord.

**ALL:** Amen.

# ASCENSION

**THIRD LEADER:**  Ephesians 3:5, 8b–10

A reading from the Letter of Saint Paul to the Ephesians

◆ Read the passage from the Bible.

The word of the Lord.

◆ All stand and sing **Alleluia**.

**FOURTH LEADER:**  Matthew 28:16–20

A reading from the holy Gospel according to Matthew

◆ Read the passage from the Bible.

The Gospel of the Lord.

◆ All sit and observe silence.

**FIFTH LEADER:**

Let us stand and bring our hopes and needs to God as we pray, **"Lord, hear our prayer."**

For our teachers and catechists, and everyone who teaches us about God, we pray to the Lord.

For our mothers and fathers, and everyone who takes care of us, we pray to the Lord.

For all the children in the world, may they learn to be peacemakers for the world, we pray to the Lord.

For all those in the world who suffer from violence or hunger, we pray to the Lord.

For those who are sick and for those who have died, we pray to the Lord.

**SIXTH LEADER:**

Let us pray the prayer that Jesus taught us: **Our Father . . . Amen.**

◆ Pause and then say the following:

Let us offer one another the sign of Christ's peace.

**SEVENTH LEADER:**

Let us pray:
Lord our God,
your Son now sits at your right hand in glory,
and yet we know that he is also here with us.
Even though we cannot see him,
Jesus Christ lives in us and through us.
May his care and protection bring us peace
    and joy.
We ask this through the same Jesus Christ,
    our Lord.

**ALL: Amen.**

✚ All make the Sign of the Cross.

**In the name of the Father and of the Son and of the Holy Spirit. Amen.**

# PRAYER FOR THURSDAY JUNE 2, 2011

## OPENING

In some places, the solemnity [so-LEM-ni-tee] of the Ascension [uh-SEN-shuhn] of our Lord is celebrated on this traditional Ascension Thursday. In other areas it will be celebrated this Sunday. The Gospel for today tells the story of that important event—Jesus' last instructions to the disciples and his ascension into heaven. Let's pay attention to those last moments that the disciples spend with Jesus.

✦ All make the Sign of the Cross.

**In the name of the Father and of the Son and of the Holy Spirit. Amen.**

## PSALM (For a longer psalm, see page xvi.) Psalm 23:2 (1)

The LORD is my shepherd, I shall not want.

**The LORD is my shepherd, I shall not want.**

He makes me lie down in green pastures;
he leads me beside still waters;

**The LORD is my shepherd, I shall not want.**

◆ All stand and sing **Alleluia**.

## GOSPEL          Matthew 28:16–20

A reading from the holy Gospel according to Matthew

Now the eleven disciples went to Galilee, to the mountain to which Jesus had directed them. When they saw him, they worshiped him; but some doubted. And Jesus came and said to them, "All authority in heaven and on earth has been given to me. Go therefore and make disciples of all nations, baptizing them in the name of the Father, and of the Son, and of the Holy Spirit, and teaching them to obey everything that I have commanded you. And remember, I am with you always, to the end of the age."

The Gospel of the Lord.

◆ All sit and observe silence.

## FOR SILENT REFLECTION

How do we see Jesus even though he has ascended into heaven?

## CLOSING PRAYER

Let us stand and bring our hopes and needs to God as we pray, "Lord, hear our prayer."

◆ All may add their own prayers here.

Let us pray: **Our Father . . . Amen.**

God our Father,
help us to remember
that you and your Son are always with us,
even when we feel lonely and afraid.
Let your light shine in our hearts
so that we can see
your love and goodness in our lives.
We ask this through the same Jesus Christ
    our Lord.
**Amen.**

✦ All make the Sign of the Cross.

# PRAYER FOR FRIDAY JUNE 3, 2011

## OPENING

In today's Gospel, Jesus knows his followers will experience pain and worry after his Ascension [uh-SEN-shuhn]. The word "labor [LAY-buhr]" is used in this reading for the work a mother does when she is giving birth. "Anguish" is anxiety. Listen to what Jesus tells his followers about the anxiety they will experience.

✦ All make the Sign of the Cross.

**In the name of the Father and of the Son and of the Holy Spirit. Amen.**

## PSALM
(For a longer psalm, see page xvi.) Psalm 23:2 (1)

The LORD is my shepherd, I shall not want.

**The LORD is my shepherd, I shall not want.**

He makes me lie down in green pastures;
he leads me beside still waters;

**The LORD is my shepherd, I shall not want.**

◆ All stand and sing **Alleluia**.

## GOSPEL
John 16:20–23

A reading from the holy Gospel according to John

Jesus said to his disciples, "Very truly, I tell you, you will weep and mourn, but the world will rejoice; you will have pain, but your pain will turn into joy. When a woman is in labor, she has pain, because her hour has come. But when her child is born, she no longer remembers the anguish because of the joy of having brought a human being into the world. So you have pain now; but I will see you again, and your hearts will rejoice, and no one will take your joy from you. On that day you will ask nothing of me. Very truly, I tell you, if you ask anything of the Father in my name, he will give it to you."

The Gospel of the Lord.

◆ All sit and observe silence.

## FOR SILENT REFLECTION

According to Jesus, which will be more powerful, joy or pain? When do you feel joyful?

## CLOSING PRAYER

Let us stand and bring our hopes and needs to God as we pray, "Lord, hear our prayer."

◆ All may add their own prayers here.

Let us pray: **Our Father . . . Amen.**

Loving God,
the life that flows from you
is more powerful than death;
thank you for giving us eternal life.
The joy you give is greater than our
    deepest sorrow;
give us the joy of your presence.
The peace you offer is deeper than our
    worries and fears;
grant us the gift of your peace.
We ask this through our Lord Jesus Christ.
**Amen.**

✦ All make the Sign of the Cross.

# PRAYER FOR THE WEEK

WITH A READING FROM THE GOSPEL FOR **SUNDAY, JUNE 5, 2011**

## OPENING

Today some parishes will celebrate the Seventh Sunday of Easter. (If you are celebrating the Ascension of the Lord, see the order of prayer for Thursday, June 2.) This moment, when Jesus ascended into heaven to return to his Father, marks the end of Jesus' time on earth with his disciples. In today's Gospel, to "glorify" means to praise.

✝ All make the Sign of the Cross.

**In the name of the Father and of the Son and of the Holy Spirit. Amen.**

## PSALM
(For a longer psalm, see page xvi.) Psalm 23:2 (1)

The LORD is my shepherd, I shall not want.

**The LORD is my shepherd, I shall not want.**

He makes me lie down in green pastures;
he leads me beside still waters;

**The LORD is my shepherd, I shall not want.**

◆ All stand and sing **Alleluia**.

## GOSPEL
John 17:1–6a, 11

A reading from the holy Gospel according to John

After Jesus had spoken these words, he looked up to heaven and said, "Father, the hour has come; glorify your Son so that the Son may glorify you, since you have given him authority over all people, to give eternal life to all whom you have given him. And this is eternal life, that they may know you, the only true God, and Jesus Christ whom you have sent. I glorified you on earth by finishing the work that you gave me to do. So now, Father, glorify me in your own presence with the glory that I had in your presence before the world existed.

"I have made your name known to those whom you gave me from the world. And now I am no longer in the world, but they are in the world, and I am coming to you. Holy Father, protect them in your name that you have given me, so that they may be one, as we are one."

The Gospel of the Lord.

◆ All sit and observe silence.

## FOR SILENT REFLECTION

How did Jesus glorify the Father?

## CLOSING PRAYER

Let us stand and bring our hopes and needs to God as we pray, "Lord, hear our prayer."

◆ All may add their own prayers here.

Let us pray: **Our Father . . . Amen.**

Lord God,
we praise you for your great goodness;
we give thanks to you for your
    marvelous love.
We praise you who heal the wounded;
and befriend all those in need.
We sing to you and give thanks.
We glorify your holy name
through Christ our Lord.
**Amen.**

✝ All make the Sign of the Cross.

# PRAYER FOR MONDAY JUNE 6, 2011

## OPENING

In today's Gospel, the disciples are confident, but Jesus knows their confidence will be shaken when he is crucified. Listen to what he tells them.

✚ All make the Sign of the Cross.

**In the name of the Father and of the Son and of the Holy Spirit. Amen.**

## PSALM          (For a longer psalm, see page xvi.) Psalm 23:2 (1)

The LORD is my shepherd, I shall not want.

**The LORD is my shepherd, I shall not want.**

He makes me lie down in green pastures; he leads me beside still waters;

**The LORD is my shepherd, I shall not want.**

◆ All stand and sing **Alleluia**.

## GOSPEL                              John 16:29–33

A reading from the holy Gospel according to John

Jesus' disciples said, "Yes, now you are speaking plainly, not in any figure of speech! Now we know that you know all things, and do not need to have anyone question you; by this we believe that you came from God." Jesus answered them, "Do you now believe? The hour is coming, indeed it has come, when you will be scattered, each one to his home, and you will leave me alone. Yet I am not alone because the Father is with me. I have said this to you, so that in me you may have peace. In the world you face persecution. But take courage; I have conquered the world!"

The Gospel of the Lord.

◆ All sit and observe silence.

## FOR SILENT REFLECTION

What do you think Jesus wants us to do if our faith is shaken?

## CLOSING PRAYER

Let us stand and bring our hopes and needs to God as we pray, "Lord, hear our prayer."

◆ All may add their own prayers here.

Let us pray: **Our Father . . . Amen.**

Loving God,
although many of his friends abandoned him,
Jesus was never alone because you were
   with him.
May we never forget that you are with us.
Give us faith in your saving love
and grant us your peace.
We ask this through the same Jesus Christ
   our Lord.
**Amen.**

✚ All make the Sign of the Cross.

# PRAYER FOR TUESDAY JUNE 7, 2011

### OPENING

In today's reading, Paul is speaking to people to whom he has preached the Gospel. He knows he may not see them again. Listen to what he says to them.

✝ All make the Sign of the Cross.

**In the name of the Father and of the Son and of the Holy Spirit. Amen.**

### PSALM
*(For a longer psalm, see page xvi.) Psalm 23:2 (1)*

The LORD is my shepherd, I shall not want.

**The LORD is my shepherd, I shall not want.**

He makes me lie down in green pastures; he leads me beside still waters;

**The LORD is my shepherd, I shall not want.**

### READING
*Acts 20:18b, 20–24*

A reading from the Acts of the Apostles [uh-POS-uhls]

Paul said to them: "You yourselves know how I lived among you the entire time from the first day that I set foot in Asia. I did not shrink from doing anything helpful, proclaiming the message to you and teaching you publicly and from house to house, as I testified to both Jews and Greeks about repentance toward God and faith toward our Lord Jesus. And now, as a captive to the Spirit, I am on my way to Jerusalem, not knowing what will happen to me there, except that the Holy Spirit testifies to me in every city that imprisonment and persecutions are waiting for me. But I do not count my life of any value to myself, if only I may finish my course and the ministry that I received from the Lord Jesus, to testify to the good news of God's grace."

The word of the Lord.

◆ All observe silence.

### FOR SILENT REFLECTION

What is most important to Paul? What is most important to you?

### CLOSING PRAYER

Let us stand and bring our hopes and needs to God as we pray, "Lord, hear our prayer."

◆ All may add their own prayers here.

Let us pray: **Our Father . . . Amen.**

Lord God,
help us to remember what is important.
We are so easily distracted.
We worry about things that never happen,
and spend our time trying to get things
that don't make us happy.
Teach us what to value.
We ask this through Jesus Christ, our Lord.
**Amen.**

✝ All make the Sign of the Cross.

---

**ALSO ON THIS DAY:** Shavuot (Jewish celebration of God's gift of the Torah) begins at sunset.

# PRAYER FOR WEDNESDAY JUNE 8, 2011

## OPENING

In today's Gospel, Jesus prays for his disciples on the night before he will die. Listen to what Jesus wants for his followers. To "sanctify [SANK-tih-fī]" is to bless and make holy.

✚ All make the Sign of the Cross.

**In the name of the Father and of the Son and of the Holy Spirit. Amen.**

## PSALM  (For a longer psalm, see page xvi.) Psalm 23:2 (1)

The Lord is my shepherd, I shall not want.

**The Lord is my shepherd, I shall not want.**

He makes me lie down in green pastures; he leads me beside still waters;

**The Lord is my shepherd, I shall not want.**

◆ All stand and sing **Alleluia**.

## GOSPEL  John 17:11b–13, 17–19

A reading from the holy Gospel according to John

Jesus prayed, "Holy Father, protect them in your name that you have given me, so that they may be one, as we are one. While I was with them, I protected them in your name that you have given me. I guarded them, and not one of them was lost except the one destined to be lost, so that the scripture might be fulfilled. But now I am coming to you, and I speak these things in the world so that they may have my joy made complete in themselves. Sanctify them in the truth; your word is truth. As you have sent me into the world, so I have sent them into the world. And for their sakes I sanctify myself, so that they also may be sanctified in truth."

The Gospel of the Lord.

◆ All sit and observe silence.

## FOR SILENT REFLECTION

What do you think the Gospel might mean when it says, "so that they may be one, as we are one"?

## CLOSING PRAYER

Let us stand and bring our hopes and needs to God as we pray, "Lord, hear our prayer."

◆ All may add their own prayers here.

Let us pray: **Our Father . . . Amen.**

God, our Father,
bless us as we study your word,
and teach us how to live
by following Jesus' example.
Send your Spirit of Truth
into our hearts
and make us holy.
We ask this through Jesus Christ our Lord.
**Amen.**

✚ All make the Sign of the Cross.

---

**ALSO ON THIS DAY:** Shavuot (Jewish celebration of God's gift of the Torah)

# PRAYER FOR THURSDAY JUNE 9, 2011

## OPENING

Today's Gospel continues Jesus' prayer on the night before he died. Jesus didn't pray for his disciples only. Listen to find out for whom Jesus is praying.

✢ All make the Sign of the Cross.

**In the name of the Father and of the Son and of the Holy Spirit. Amen.**

## PSALM         (For a longer psalm, see page xvi.) Psalm 23:2 (1)

The LORD is my shepherd, I shall not want.

**The LORD is my shepherd, I shall not want.**

He makes me lie down in green pastures;
he leads me beside still waters;

**The LORD is my shepherd, I shall not want.**

◆ All stand and sing **Alleluia**.

## GOSPEL                                John 17:20–24

A reading from the holy Gospel according to John

Jesus prayed, "I ask not only on behalf of these, but also on behalf of those who will believe in me through their word, that they may all be one. As you, Father, are in me and I am in you, may they also be in us, so that the world may believe that you have sent me. The glory that you have given me I have given them, so that they may be one, as we are one, I in them and you in me, that they may be completely one, so that the world may know that you have sent me and have loved them even as you have loved me. Father, I desire that those also, whom you have given me, may be one with me where I am, to see my glory, which you have given me because you loved me before the foundation of the world."

The Gospel of the Lord.

◆ All sit and observe silence.

## FOR SILENT REFLECTION

Who do you think "those who will believe in me" through the disciples' word might be? Does Jesus continue to pray for his followers?

## CLOSING PRAYER

Let us stand and bring our hopes and needs to God as we pray, "Lord, hear our prayer."

◆ All may add their own prayers here.

Let us pray: **Our Father . . . Amen.**

Loving Father,
we know that you will do
all Jesus asks of you,
for Jesus asks nothing you do not desire.
Therefore, with confidence, we pray
     for unity
in our families, our Church, our world.
We ask this through Jesus Christ our Lord.
**Amen.**

✢ All make the Sign of the Cross.

**ALSO ON THIS DAY:** Shavuot (Jewish celebration of God's gift of the Torah) ends at nightfall.

# PRAYER SERVICE
## PENTECOST

*Prepare six leaders for this service. The third leader will need a Bible for the Gospel passage and may need help finding it and practicing. You may wish to begin by singing "Come, Holy Ghost" and end with "Lord, Send Out Your Spirit." If there will be singing prepare a song leader.*

**FIRST LEADER:**

May the power, comfort, and healing of the Holy Spirit come to us!

**ALL: Amen.**

Fifty days after Jesus rose from the dead, the Holy Spirit descended upon the disciples and Mary. The Holy Spirit has been called the Advocate, or Helper. With the help of the Holy Spirit, we can do things that we could never accomplish on our own. The Holy Spirit has also been called, "the Giver of Life." From the beginning, the Holy Spirit moved over the waters of Creation and brought life from them. Now, when the Holy Spirit moves in our own lives, we are enlivened, encouraged, and revitalized for his creative work of love in the world.

**SECOND LEADER:**

✛ All make the Sign of the Cross.

**In the name of the Father and of the Son and of the Holy Spirit. Amen.**

Let us pray:
Holy Spirit,
just as you were present at the beginning
  of the world,
create our minds and bodies anew.

*continued on next page*

# PENTECOST
## CONTINUED

Open our eyes to the hidden threads of love
that connect us to one another,
even to those we call our "enemies."
We ask this through Christ our Lord. **Amen.**

◆ All stand and sing Alleluia

**THIRD LEADER:**  John 7:37–39
A reading from the holy Gospel according to John

◆ Read the passage from the Bible.

The Gospel of the Lord.

◆ All sit and observe silence.

**FOURTH LEADER:**
Let us bring our hopes and needs to God as we pray, "Lord, hear our prayer."

Holy Spirit, may your flame come to rest on all peoples so that they may live in peace, we pray to the Lord.

Holy Spirit, may your light shine in all minds so that we may behold the full truth of Christ, we pray to the Lord.

Holy Spirit, you shower your people with gifts; may we always ask for your assistance, we pray to the Lord.

Holy Spirit, heal and comfort those who are sick and bring those who have died into the light of your presence, we pray to the Lord.

**FIFTH LEADER:**
Let us pray as Jesus taught us:

**ALL: Our Father . . . Amen.**

◆ Pause and then say the following:

Let us offer one another the sign of Christ's peace.

◆ All exchange the sign of peace.

**SIXTH LEADER:**
Let us pray:
Holy Spirit,
we ask you to strengthen us with your
    sevenfold gifts.
May your gift of wisdom help us to live
    according to your divine plan;
may holy understanding open for us the
    mysteries of the kingdom of heaven;
may our growing knowledge of you help us
    to love you more deeply;
may your counsel unify us with all Creation;
may we grow in strength for doing your will;
may reverence for all that is holy help us to
    recognize how great you are;
and may wonder and awe for you
help us to enter more deeply
into the mysterious life of the holy Trinity.
We ask this through Jesus Christ, our Lord.

**ALL: Amen.**

✠ All make the Sign of the Cross.

# PRAYER FOR FRIDAY
# JUNE 10, 2011

## OPENING

In some passages we have read, Jesus describes himself as a shepherd. In today's Gospel, he tells Peter to care for his sheep. Remember that Peter was named Simon before Jesus gave him the new name, Peter, which means "rock".

✚ All make the Sign of the Cross.

**In the name of the Father and of the Son and of the Holy Spirit. Amen.**

## PSALM   (For a longer psalm, see page xvi.) Psalm 23:2 (1)

The LORD is my shepherd, I shall not want.

**The LORD is my shepherd, I shall not want.**

He makes me lie down in green pastures;
he leads me beside still waters;

**The LORD is my shepherd, I shall not want.**

◆ All stand and sing **Alleluia**.

## GOSPEL READING   John 21:15–17ac, 19b

A reading from the holy Gospel according to John

When they had finished breakfast, Jesus said to Simon Peter, "Simon son of John, do you love me more than these?" He said to him, "Yes, Lord; you know that I love you." Jesus said to him, "Feed my lambs." A second time he said to him, "Simon, son of John, do you love me?" He said to him, "Yes, Lord; you know that I love you. Jesus said to him, "Tend my sheep." He said to him a third time, "Simon son of John, do you love me?" And he said to him, "Lord, you know everything; you know that I love you." Jesus said to him, "Feed my sheep." After this he said to him, "Follow me."

The Gospel of the Lord.

◆ All sit and observe silence.

## FOR SILENT REFLECTION

Why is it so important for Peter to love Jesus? Who are the sheep he is to feed, and what will Peter feed them?

## CLOSING PRAYER

Let us stand and bring our hopes and needs to God as we pray, "Lord, hear our prayer."

◆ All may add their own prayers here.

Let us pray: **Our Father . . . Amen.**

Lord God,
send us holy men and women,
filled with your love,
goodness, and truth
to care for your flock.
We ask this through Jesus Christ, your Son,
and our Good Shepherd, who lives
and reigns with you in the unity of the
Holy Spirit, one God, for ever and
ever.

**Amen.**

✚ All make the Sign of the Cross.

# PRAYER FOR THE WEEK

WITH A READING FROM THE GOSPEL FOR **SUNDAY, JUNE 12, 2011**

## OPENING

Today, fifty days after Easter, we celebrate the great solemnity [so-LEM-ni-tee] of Pentecost, when Jesus' promise to send the Holy Spirit is fulfilled. Listen to how Jesus gives the Spirit to the disciples.

✠ All make the Sign of the Cross.

**In the name of the Father and of the Son and of the Holy Spirit. Amen.**

## PSALM
(For a longer psalm, see page xvi.) Psalm 23:2 (1)

The Lord is my shepherd, I shall not want.

**The Lord is my shepherd, I shall not want.**

He makes me lie down in green pastures;
he leads me beside still waters;

**The Lord is my shepherd, I shall not want.**

◆ All stand and sing **Alleluia**.

## GOSPEL
John 20:19–23

A reading from the holy Gospel according to John

When it was evening on that day, the first day of the week, and the doors of the house where the disciples had met were locked for fear of the Jews, Jesus came and stood among them and said, "Peace be with you." After he said this, he showed them his hands and his side. Then the disciples rejoiced when they saw the Lord. Jesus said to them again, "Peace be with you. As the Father has sent me, so I send you." When he had said this, he breathed on them and said to them, "Receive the Holy Spirit. If you forgive the sins of any, they are forgiven them; if you retain the sins of any, they are retained."

The Gospel of the Lord.

◆ All sit and observe silence.

## FOR SILENT REFLECTION

When Jesus breathes on the disciples he tells them to receive the Holy Spirit. How is receiving the Spirit like breathing?

## CLOSING PRAYER

Let us stand and bring our hopes and needs to God as we pray, "Lord, hear our prayer."

◆ All may add their own prayers here.

Let us pray: **Our Father . . . Amen.**

Come, Holy Spirit, Come!
fill our souls with holy light;
feed our hearts with your love;
renew our bodies with health and strength.
Help us to receive you,
to take in the wonder and joy of your presence
that we may proclaim the good news to others.
Grant this through Jesus Christ our Lord.
**Amen.**

✠ All make the Sign of the Cross.

# ORDINARY TIME SUMMER

## MONDAY, JUNE 13 TO FRIDAY, JUNE 24

# SUMMER ORDINARY TIME

## THE MEANING OF ORDINARY TIME

Jesus said, "I am the vine, you are the branches. Those who abide in me and I in them bear much fruit, because apart from me you can do nothing" (John 15:5).

A vine begins as a single branch. As it grows new branches begin to grow from the first one. Then more branches form. The whole vine is made up of many branches that spread and grow. A vine must have roots. Jesus is the vine rooted in the eternal love of the Father. The Holy Spirit helps the branches to grow strong and beautiful. The whole vine is made up of many branches that spread and grow as God's love grows in them.

In the parable of the True Vine, Jesus tells us that he is the whole vine while each of us is a branch on that one plant. Although it may seem as though each of us is separate and alone, Jesus says that we need each other just as each branch of the vine depends on all the others.

During Lent we studied the Great Commandment (see The Meaning of Lent, page 198). When we love God and love our neighbor the way that Jesus taught, that love draws us closer to the ones we love. Through our love for one another, we begin to share in a life that is stronger and bigger than we are by ourselves.

Did you know that right after people are baptized, we call them *neophytes* (NEE-oh-fites), a word that means "new, young plants"? People who have just been baptized are brand-new branches sprouting on the True Vine that is the body of Christ. When a new branch sprouts on a vine, we can see that the vine is growing.

Remember that Ordinary Time is a season of precious growth and change. Each of us grows in holiness during Ordinary Time, but we do not just grow by ourselves apart from other people. Because God's love is the source of our growth, as we grow in holiness, we also grow closer together.

Jesus tells us to "abide" in him. To abide means to stay or to remain. When the branches remain attached to the vine, they continue to receive God's life and love. There are many ways we can stay in Jesus. For example, how does Holy Communion help us to stay part of Christ's Body, the Vine of Life? What do we receive from God at Mass? And what do we offer back to God? When we pray, we turn to God and open our hearts to him. When we lift our thoughts and hopes to God, our souls rest in him. We also come closer to God by doing loving acts. Whenever we open our hearts to God in prayer, and make room in our hearts for others, God's love abides in us.

Jesus promises that when we *abide* in his love, we will "bear fruit." What is this marvelous fruit that grows from us, the branches of the True Vine? Can it be sweet, life-giving, and satisfying like fruit from a tree? Or is it something even more wonderful?

People have been thinking and praying over the words of Jesus for hundreds of years. When we ponder these words in our study, turn to them in our prayer, and celebrate them in our worship, we will discover something wonderful. Our study, prayer, and worship will bear fruit. Jesus himself tells us, "I have said these things to you so that my joy may be in you, and that your joy may be complete" (John 15:11).

## PREPARING TO CELEBRATE ORDINARY TIME IN THE CLASSROOM

This will be your last time changing the prayer table cloth this year! Even if you haven't had a procession each time the cloth changes, try to have one now. As the school year winds down, it is good to bring the students' focus squarely on the prayer life of your classroom community. You may wish to invite the students to choose something to carry in the procession that has helped their spiritual growth this year. Clear an area near the prayer table, spread it with a green cloth, and let the children place their objects there. As a final project, ask them to write a short essay or poem about the significance of the object they chose. Suggest that they illustrate their work. Invite them

# SUMMER ORDINARY TIME

to share their writings aloud during one of your final prayer times together. (Not every student will feel comfortable sharing private thoughts in front of a group. Don't force them to participate in this aspect of your celebration.) You might even consider collecting all the papers into a booklet, which you can photocopy for each student to keep as a memento of the year.

## SACRED SPACE

Bring your potted plant back to the prayer table. You may want to discuss how it might be different from how it looked when you first placed it on the prayer table. Some plants, such as spider plants, send out shoots with new plants on them. If your spider plant is sufficiently mature, you may even have enough "spider babies" to clip them and give one to each of your students in a paper cup with a little soil in it.

## SACRED MUSIC

If you have been singing with your students all year, they will probably be quite comfortable with at least one or two of their favorite hymns. Consider scheduling a visit to one of the other classrooms to offer a small concert or sing-along (an older classroom could visit a younger grade, smaller children could sing for the "big kids"). If your students are particularly confident, you may even suggest that they volunteer to sing for an all-school Mass or end-of-the-year prayer service. If you invite parents to the class for one of your final sessions, please do not be shy about including them in your prayer! And by all means, sing for them!

Some songs that work well in this season are "Christ for the World We Sing", "Lord, I Want to Be a Christian", and "The King of Love My Shepherd Is."

## PRAYERS FOR ORDINARY TIME

There are only a few precious places in the Gospel where we have the chance to listen to Jesus as he prays to his Father in heaven. In these moments, we can see clearly what it is Jesus wants for the world. The following prayer taken from the Gospel according to John shows how much Jesus wants us to abide in his love and to live with each other in the love and peace shared by the Father, Son, and Holy Spirit. Now after meditating with the children on Christ's parable of the True Vine, this would be an ideal time to introduce this prayer for unity and love.

"As you, Father, are in me and I am in you, may my followers also be in us, so that the world may believe that you have sent me. The glory that you have given me I have given them, so that they may be one, as we are one, I in them and you in me, that they may become completely one, so that the world may know that you have sent me and have loved them even as you have loved me" (John 17:21b–23).

## A NOTE TO CATECHISTS

You may wish to write the names of your students into your personal calendar during the summer months so that you will remember to pray for them even when your group is no longer meeting. Prayer is the most useful and effective way we have to be of service to those about whom we care.

# GRACE BEFORE MEALS
## ORDINARY TIME • Summer

**LEADER:**
Lord, you feed the hungry heart.

**ALL: Our heart longs for you.**

✙ All make the Sign of the Cross.

**In the name of the Father and of the Son and of the Holy Spirit. Amen.**

**LEADER:**
Mighty God,
you fill the hungry with good things
and send the rich away empty.
Make us poor in spirit before this food
 you give
so that we may receive it in gratitude
 and wonder.
We ask this through your Son, Jesus Christ
 our Lord.

**ALL: Amen.**

✙ All make the Sign of the Cross.

**In the name of the Father and of the Son and of the Holy Spirit. Amen.**

# PRAYER AT DAY'S END
## ORDINARY TIME • Summer

**LEADER:**
All creation, bless the Lord!

**ALL: Bless his holy name!**

✢ All make the Sign of the Cross.

**In the name of the Father and of the Son and of the Holy Spirit. Amen.**

**LEADER:**
God of Love,
you are the source of our peace and unity.
May this day of work,
which we offer to you in joy,
allow peace to grow in our hearts,
in our friendships, our school,
    our community,
and in our world.
We ask this through our Lord Jesus Christ,
    your Son, who lives and reigns with
    you in the unity of the Holy Spirit,
    one God, forever and ever.

**ALL: Amen.**

✢ All make the Sign of the Cross.

**In the name of the Father and of the Son and of the Holy Spirit. Amen.**

# PRAYER FOR MONDAY JUNE 13, 2011

## OPENING

After Pentecost, the young church, guided by the Holy Spirit, spread the good news of the Gospel throughout many countries. This week we will read some of the teachings of Jesus that the disciples would have been sharing with people. Today's reading is a famous and difficult lesson. Also today, we remember Saint Anthony [AN-thuh-nee] of Padua [PAD-yoo-uh], a well-loved preacher of medieval times.

✜ All make the Sign of the Cross.

**In the name of the Father and of the Son and of the Holy Spirit. Amen.**

## PSALM (For a longer psalm, see page xvii.) Psalm 104:1b–2a (1a)

Bless the LORD, O my soul.

**Bless the LORD, O my soul.**

O LORD my God, you are very great.
You are clothed with honor and majesty,
   wrapped in light as with a garment.

**Bless the LORD, O my soul.**

◆ All stand and sing **Alleluia.**

## GOSPEL  Matthew 5:38–42

A reading from the holy Gospel according to Matthew

Jesus said to the crowds, "You have heard that it was said, 'An eye for an eye and a tooth for a tooth.' But I say to you, do not resist [ree-ZIST] an evildoer. But if anyone strikes you on the right cheek, turn the other also; and if anyone wants to sue [soo] you and take your coat, give your cloak as well; and if anyone forces you to go one mile, go also the second mile. Give to everyone who begs from you, and do not refuse anyone who wants to borrow from you."

The Gospel of the Lord.

◆ All sit and observe silence.

## FOR SILENT REFLECTION

How difficult is it to keep from hitting back when we are hit? Why do you think Jesus asks us to do these things?

## CLOSING PRAYER

Let us stand and bring our hopes and needs to God as we pray, "Lord, hear our prayer."

◆ All may add their own prayers here.

Let us pray: **Our Father . . . Amen.**

Loving God,
your Son has told us not to strike back when we are struck
and to be generous with everyone.
Help us to learn this new way of acting
and to understand how it serves you and
   our neighbor.
We ask this through the same Jesus Christ
   our Lord.
**Amen.**

✜ All make the Sign of the Cross.

# PRAYER FOR **TUESDAY JUNE 14, 2011**

## OPENING

Today we continue to read from the teachings of Jesus written in the Gospel according to Matthew. These may seem puzzling to us because they are the opposite of what we would naturally do. We have to think deeply about these ideas, pray about them, and practice them until they become comfortable.

✢ All make the Sign of the Cross.

**In the name of the Father and of the Son and of the Holy Spirit. Amen.**

## PSALM  (For a longer psalm, see page xvii.) Psalm 104:1b–2a (1a)

Bless the LORD, O my soul.

**Bless the LORD, O my soul.**

O LORD my God, you are very great.
You are clothed with honor and majesty,
  wrapped in light as with a garment.

**Bless the LORD, O my soul.**

◆ All stand and sing **Alleluia**.

## GOSPEL                           Matthew 5:43–48

A reading from the holy Gospel according to Matthew

Jesus said, "You have heard that it was said, 'You shall love your neighbor and hate your enemy.' But I say to you, love your enemies and pray for those who persecute you, so that you may be children of your Father in heaven; for he makes his sun rise on the evil and on the good, and sends rain on the righteous and on the unrighteous. For if you love those who love you, what reward do you have? Do not even the tax collectors do the same? And if you greet only your brothers and sisters, what more are you doing than others? Do not even the Gentiles do the same? Be perfect, therefore, as your heavenly Father is perfect."

The Gospel of the Lord.

◆ All sit and observe silence.

## FOR SILENT REFLECTION

Can you think of someone who has done wrong to you, for whom you could pray today?

## CLOSING PRAYER

Let us stand and bring our hopes and needs to God as we pray, "Lord, hear our prayer."

◆ All may add their own prayers here.

Let us pray: **Our Father . . . Amen.**

Loving and generous God,
give us the grace to understand
those who do wrong to us
and to pray for those
we do not like.
Change our hearts so that we can help
to bring your kingdom to this world.
Grant this through Christ our Lord.
**Amen.**

✢ All make the Sign of the Cross.

---

**ALSO ON THIS DAY:** Flag Day (U.S.A.)

# PRAYER FOR **WEDNESDAY** JUNE 15, 2011

## OPENING

Today we read from Saint Paul's letter to the Christians in the town of Corinth [KOR-inth] in Greece. He is teaching the people about generosity, and he compares giving to sowing seed in the ground so that it will grow into an abundant [uh-BUHN-duhnt] harvest. To reap is to cut and gather in the harvest.

✚ All make the Sign of the Cross.

**In the name of the Father and of the Son and of the Holy Spirit. Amen.**

## PSALM   (For a longer psalm, see page xvii.) Psalm 104:1b–2a (1a)

Bless the LORD, O my soul.

**Bless the LORD, O my soul.**

O LORD my God, you are very great.
You are clothed with honor and majesty,
  wrapped in light as with a garment.

**Bless the LORD, O my soul.**

## READING   2 Corinthians 9:6–11

A reading from the Second Letter of Saint Paul to the Corinthians [kor-IN-thee-unz]

The point is this: the one who sows sparingly will also reap sparingly, and the one who sows bountifully will also reap bountifully. Each of you must give as you have made up your mind, not reluctantly or under compulsion, for God loves a cheerful giver. And God is able to provide you with every blessing in abundance, so that by always having enough of everything, you may share abundantly in every good work. As it is written,

"He scatters abroad, he gives to the poor;
  his righteousness endures for ever."

He who supplies seed to the sower and bread for food will supply and multiply your seed for sowing and increase the harvest of your righteousness. You will be enriched in every way for your great generosity, which will produce thanksgiving to God through us.

The word of the Lord.

◆ All observe silence.

## FOR SILENT REFLECTION

What do you think grows abundantly when we are cheerful givers? What harvest could Paul be talking about?

## CLOSING PRAYER

Let us stand and bring our hopes and needs to God as we pray, "Lord, hear our prayer."

◆ All may add their own prayers here.

Let us pray: **Our Father . . . Amen.**

Lord God,
you bless those who are generous.
Protect us from the fear
of not having enough for ourselves
and give us the grace to be cheerful givers.
We ask this through Christ our Lord.
**Amen.**

✚ All make the Sign of the Cross.

# PRAYER FOR **THURSDAY JUNE 16, 2011**

## OPENING

In today's Gospel, Jesus teaches us how to pray. Listen and see if you recognize his prayer.

✛ All make the Sign of the Cross.

**In the name of the Father and of the Son and of the Holy Spirit. Amen.**

## PSALM   (For a longer psalm, see page xvii.) Psalm 104:1b–2a (1a)

Bless the LORD, O my soul.

**Bless the LORD, O my soul.**

O LORD my God, you are very great.
You are clothed with honor and majesty,
   wrapped in light as with a garment.

**Bless the LORD, O my soul.**

◆ All stand and sing **Alleluia**.

## GOSPEL   Matthew 6:7–15

A reading from the holy Gospel according to Matthew

Jesus said to the crowds, "When you are praying, do not heap up empty phrases as the Gentiles [JEN-tilz] do; for they think that they will be heard because of their many words. Do not be like them, for your Father knows what you need before you ask him."

   "Pray then in this way:
   Our Father in heaven,
      hallowed be your name.
      Your kingdom come.
      Your will be done,
         on earth as it is in heaven.
      Give us this day our daily bread.
      And forgive us our debts,
         as we also have forgiven our debtors.
      And do not bring us to the time of trial,
         but rescue us from the evil one.
For if you forgive others their trespasses, your heavenly Father will also forgive you; but if you do not forgive others, neither will your Father forgive your trespasses."

The Gospel of the Lord.

◆ All sit and observe silence.

## FOR SILENT REFLECTION

What do you think Jesus' prayer teaches us about how to pray?

## CLOSING PRAYER

Let us stand and bring our hopes and needs to God as we pray, "Lord, hear our prayer."

◆ All may add their own prayers here.

Let us pray: **Our Father . . . Amen.**

Our Father,
teach us to pray.
Help us to be humble and reverent
in your presence,
yet confident of your love for us.
We ask this through Christ our Lord.
**Amen.**

✛ All make the Sign of the Cross.

# PRAYER FOR **FRIDAY** JUNE 17, 2011

### OPENING

In today's Gospel, Jesus uses two images, the image of treasure and the image of light. Listen to see if you can understand the lessons Jesus is teaching.

✢ All make the Sign of the Cross.

**In the name of the Father and of the Son and of the Holy Spirit. Amen.**

### PSALM  (For a longer psalm, see page xvii.) Psalm 104:1b–2a (1a)

Bless the LORD, O my soul.

**Bless the LORD, O my soul.**

O LORD my God, you are very great.
You are clothed with honor and majesty,
  wrapped in light as with a garment.

**Bless the LORD, O my soul.**

◆ All stand and sing **Alleluia**.

### GOSPEL                                     Matthew 6:19–23

A reading from the holy Gospel according to Matthew

Jesus said: "Do not store up for yourselves treasures on earth, where moth and rust consume and where thieves break in and steal; but store up for yourselves treasures in heaven, where neither moth nor rust consumes and where thieves do not break in and steal. For where your treasure is, there your heart will be also."

"The eye is the lamp of the body. So, if your eye is healthy, your whole body will be full of light; but if your eye is unhealthy, your whole body will be full of darkness. If then the light in you is darkness, how great is the darkness!"

The Gospel of the Lord.

◆ All sit and observe silence.

### FOR SILENT REFLECTION

What do you treasure? How can our eyes help us to see by God's light?

### CLOSING PRAYER

Let us stand and bring our hopes and needs to God as we pray, "Lord, hear our prayer."

◆ All may add their own prayers here.

Let us pray: **Our Father . . . Amen.**

God of Light,
you are the treasure we seek,
help us to find you.
Your word is light.
As we study your word,
enlighten our minds and hearts
with your wisdom.
We ask this through Jesus Christ our Lord.
**Amen.**

✢ All make the Sign of the Cross.

# PRAYER FOR THE WEEK

WITH A READING FROM THE GOSPEL FOR **SUNDAY, JUNE 19, 2011**

## OPENING

In our readings this year we have seen how God the Father, out of his great love for us, sent his Son, and how Jesus promised to send the Holy Spirit to help and guide us. Last week, we read how this promise was fulfilled. Today we celebrate the solemnity (suh-LEM-nuh-tee) of the Most Holy Trinity, the great mystery of the unity of the Father, Son, and Holy Spirit. Their love is the source of our love for one another.

✢ All make the Sign of the Cross.

**In the name of the Father and of the Son and of the Holy Spirit. Amen.**

## PSALM (For a longer psalm, see page xvii.) Psalm 104:1b–2a (1a)

Bless the LORD, O my soul.

**Bless the LORD, O my soul.**

O LORD my God, you are very great.
You are clothed with honor and majesty,
　wrapped in light as with a garment.

**Bless the LORD, O my soul.**

◆ All stand and sing **Alleluia**.

## GOSPEL John 3:16–18

A reading from the holy Gospel according to John

Jesus said, "For God so loved the world that he gave his only Son, so that everyone who believes in him may not perish but may have eternal life."

"Indeed, God did not send the Son into the world to condemn the world, but in order that the world might be saved through him. Those who believe in him are not condemned; but those who do not believe are condemned already, because they have not believed in the name of the only Son of God."

The Gospel of the Lord.

◆ All sit and observe silence.

## FOR SILENT REFLECTION

How do you know that God loves you?

## CLOSING PRAYER

Let us stand and bring our hopes and needs to God as we pray, "Lord, hear our prayer."

◆ All may add their own prayers here.

Let us pray: **Our Father . . . Amen.**

Most holy God,
how can we understand
the mystery of your great love
that binds Father, Son, and Holy Spirit?
On this holy day, we ask
that you open our hearts
to receive this love.
Make us one with you as you are one.
We ask this through Christ our Lord.
**Amen.**

✢ All make the Sign of the Cross.

---

**ALSO ON THIS DAY:** Father's Day (U.S.A.) (Canada)

# PRAYER FOR MONDAY
# JUNE 20, 2011

### OPENING

In today's Gospel, Jesus teaches a lesson about judging others. He is speaking of judging as in a court of law, where someone is condemned or punished for a crime.

✢ All make the Sign of the Cross.

**In the name of the Father and of the Son and of the Holy Spirit. Amen.**

### PSALM   (For a longer psalm, see page xvii.) Psalm 104:1b–2a (1a)

Bless the L{\sc ord}, O my soul.

**Bless the L{\sc ord}, O my soul.**

O L{\sc ord} my God, you are very great.
You are clothed with honor and majesty,
   wrapped in light as with a garment.

**Bless the L{\sc ord}, O my soul.**

◆ All stand and sing **Alleluia.**

### GOSPEL                                    Matthew 7:1–5

A reading from the holy Gospel according to Matthew

Jesus said, "Do not judge, so that you may not be judged. For with the judgment you make you will be judged, and the measure you give will be the measure you get. Why do you see the speck in your neighbor's eye, but do not notice the log in your own eye? Or how can you say to your neighbor, 'Let me take the speck out of your eye', while the log is in your own eye? You hypocrite, first take the log out of your own eye, and then you will see clearly to take the speck out of your neighbor's eye."

The Gospel of the Lord.

◆ All sit and observe silence.

### FOR SILENT REFLECTION

Which is easier—seeing our own faults or the faults of others? Why should we not blame others for small faults when we are guilty of a greater fault?

### CLOSING PRAYER

Let us stand and bring our hopes and needs to God as we pray, "Lord, hear our prayer."

◆ All may add their own prayers here.

Let us pray: **Our Father . . . Amen.**

Merciful God,
you graciously forgive us;
help us to be forgiving of others.
You call us to live in your truth;
help us to be honest with ourselves,
neither hiding nor making too much
   of our faults.
We ask this through Christ our Lord. Amen.

✢ All make the Sign of the Cross.

# PRAYER FOR TUESDAY JUNE 21, 2011

## OPENING

Today we remember Saint Aloysius Gonzaga [al-oh-WISH-uhs gon-ZAH-guh], the patron saint of Catholic youth. When he was only sixteen, he decided to become a Jesuit [JEZH-oo-iht] priest. He cared for the sick until his death at age twenty-three. As you listen to today's Gospel, ask yourself if Saint Aloysius Gonzaga obeyed the commandment Jesus speaks of.

✢ All make the Sign of the Cross.

**In the name of the Father and of the Son and of the Holy Spirit. Amen.**

## PSALM  (For a longer psalm, see page xvii.) Psalm 104:1b–2a (1a)

Bless the Lord, O my soul.

**Bless the Lord, O my soul.**

O Lord my God, you are very great.
You are clothed with honor and majesty,
  wrapped in light as with a garment.

**Bless the Lord, O my soul.**

◆ All stand and sing **Alleluia**.

## GOSPEL  Matthew 7:12–14

A reading from the holy Gospel according to Matthew

Jesus said, "In everything do to others as you would have them do to you; for this is the law and the prophets."

"Enter through the narrow gate; for the gate is wide and the road is easy that leads to destruction, and there are many who take it. For the gate is narrow and the road is hard that leads to life, and there are few who find it."

The Gospel of the Lord.

◆ All sit and observe silence.

## FOR SILENT REFLECTION

Can you remember a time when you treated someone as you would wish to be treated? Was it difficult or easy? How did it make you feel?

## CLOSING PRAYER

Let us stand and bring our hopes and needs to God as we pray, "Lord, hear our prayer."

◆ All may add their own prayers here.

Let us pray: **Our Father . . . Amen.**

Loving God,
it is difficult for us
to let go of our selfishness
and really love others as we want to be loved.
Grant us the grace to come to you
by following the example of Jesus.
Help us to learn from him
the way of selfless love
and humble service.
We ask this through the same Jesus Christ
  our Lord.
**Amen.**

✢ All make the Sign of the Cross.

---

**ALSO ON THIS DAY:** First day of summer

# PRAYER FOR WEDNESDAY JUNE 22, 2011

## OPENING

Today we remember Saint Thomas More, a great lawyer, writer, and Lord Chancellor [CHAN-sih-ler] of England, and his friend, Saint John Fisher, a bishop and teacher. Both remained faithful to the Church and God's will even when to do so cost them their lives.

✦ All make the Sign of the Cross.

**In the name of the Father and of the Son and of the Holy Spirit. Amen.**

## PSALM (For a longer psalm, see page xvii.) Psalm 104:1b–2a (1a)

Bless the LORD, O my soul.

**Bless the LORD, O my soul.**

O LORD my God, you are very great.
You are clothed with honor and majesty,
    wrapped in light as with a garment.

**Bless the LORD, O my soul.**

◆ All stand and sing **Alleluia**.

## GOSPEL READING  Matthew 7:15–20

A reading from the holy Gospel according to Matthew

Jesus said, "Beware of false prophets, who come to you in sheep's clothing but inwardly are ravenous wolves. You will know them by their fruits. Are grapes gathered from thorns, or figs from thistles? In the same way, every good tree bears good fruit, but the bad tree bears bad fruit. A good tree cannot bear bad fruit, nor can a bad tree bear good fruit. Every tree that does not bear good fruit is cut down and thrown into the fire. Thus you will know them by their fruits."

The Gospel of the Lord.

◆ All sit and observe silence.

## FOR SILENT REFLECTION

What "good fruits" have you noticed that have led you to trustworthy people?

## CLOSING PRAYER

Let us stand and bring our hopes and needs to God as we pray, "Lord, hear our prayer."

◆ All may add their own prayers here.

Let us pray: **Our Father . . . Amen.**

God our Father,
help us to choose carefully
the good fruit that will lead us
to helpful companions in the Christian life.
We ask this through Jesus Christ our Lord.
**Amen.**

✦ All make the Sign of the Cross.

# PRAYER FOR **THURSDAY** JUNE 23, 2011

## OPENING

Today's Gospel teaches us how to be wise instead of foolish.

✙ All make the Sign of the Cross.

**In the name of the Father and of the Son and of the Holy Spirit. Amen.**

## PSALM  (For a longer psalm, see page xvii.) Psalm 104:1b–2a (1a)

Bless the Lord, O my soul.

**Bless the Lord, O my soul.**

O Lord my God, you are very great.
You are clothed with honor and majesty,
    wrapped in light as with a garment.

**Bless the Lord, O my soul.**

◆ All stand and sing **Alleluia.**

## GOSPEL READING  Matthew 7:24–29

A reading from the holy Gospel according to Matthew

Jesus said: "Everyone then who hears these words of mine and acts on them will be like a wise man who built his house on rock. The rain fell, the floods came, and the winds blew and beat on that house, but it did not fall, because it had been founded on rock. And everyone who hears these words of mine and does not act on them will be like a foolish man who built his house on sand. The rain fell, and the floods came, and the winds blew and beat against that house, and it fell—and great was its fall!"

Now when Jesus had finished saying these things, the crowds were astounded at his teaching, for he taught them as one having authority, and not as their scribes.

The Gospel of the Lord.

◆ All sit and observe silence.

## FOR SILENT REFLECTION

What is the "house" Jesus speaks of? When you study scripture and do good works, what kind of house are you building?

## CLOSING PRAYER

Let us stand and bring our hopes and needs to God as we pray, "Lord, hear our prayer."

◆ All may add their own prayers here.

Let us pray: **Our Father . . . Amen.**

Lord God,
help us to build faithful lives
that will stand strong
in the face of temptations, suffering,
and life's many challenges.
May our hearts be a place
where you are welcome.
We ask this through your Son,
    our Lord Jesus Christ.
**Amen.**

✙ All make the Sign of the Cross.

# PRAYER FOR FRIDAY
# JUNE 24, 2011

## OPENING

Today we celebrate the solemnity (suh-LEM-nuh-tee) of the Nativity of Saint John the Baptist, who had a special calling to prepare the way for the coming of the Messiah. Circumcision (ser-kuhm-SIH-zhuhn) is the ritual by which boys enter into the covenant [KUV-uh-nuhnt] between God and the Jewish people.

✚ All make the Sign of the Cross.

**In the name of the Father and of the Son and of the Holy Spirit. Amen.**

## PSALM (For a longer psalm, see page xvii.) Psalm 104:1b–2a (1a)

Bless the LORD, O my soul.

**Bless the LORD, O my soul.**

O LORD my God, you are very great.
You are clothed with honor and majesty,
    wrapped in light as with a garment.

**Bless the LORD, O my soul.**

◆ All stand and sing **Alleluia**.

## GOSPEL                Luke 1:57–63, 80

A reading from the holy Gospel according to Luke

Now the time came for Elizabeth to give birth, and she bore a son. Her neighbors and relatives heard that the Lord had shown his great mercy to her, and they rejoiced with her.

On the eighth day they came to circumcise (SER-kuhm-siz) the child, and they were going to name him Zechariah after his father. But his mother said, "No; he is to be called John." They said to her, "None of your relatives has this name." Then they began motioning to his father to find out what name he wanted to give him. He asked for a writing-tablet and wrote, "His name is John." And all of them were amazed. The child grew and became strong in spirit, and he was in the wilderness until the day he appeared publicly to Israel.

The Gospel of the Lord.

◆ All sit and observe silence.

## FOR SILENT REFLECTION

Who has prepared the way for you to receive Jesus?

## CLOSING PRAYER

Let us stand and bring our hopes and needs to God as we pray, "Lord, hear our prayer."

◆ All may add their own prayers here.

Let us pray: **Our Father . . . Amen.**

We thank you, O God,
for sending into our lives holy men
    and women
to prepare us to receive you.
Help us to listen and learn from them.
You call each of us to do your work of love.
Help us, by your grace, to fulfill our calling.
We ask this through Jesus Christ our Lord.
**Amen.**

✚ All make the Sign of the Cross.

# PRAYER SERVICE
## LAST DAY OF SCHOOL

*You may involve up to seven leaders for this service. The third leader will need a Bible for the Gospel passage (Matthew 28:16–20) and may need help finding it and practicing. You may wish to begin by singing "All You Works of God" and end with "All the Ends of the Earth." If so, prepare a song leader.*

**FIRST LEADER:**

What a blessing this school year has been! We have memories of joy and pain, of great achievements and maybe disappointments. But our school community has pulled through this year together, praying, studying, laughing, caring about each other, and sharing all the ups and downs of our time together.

**SECOND LEADER:**

✚ All make the Sign of the Cross.

**In the name of the Father and of the Son and of the Holy Spirit. Amen.**

Let us pray:
God of all times and seasons,
as this school year ends,
we turn to you with hearts
filled with grateful amazement
at all you've helped us to learn and be.
Every time one of us extended a helping hand to another,
every time we forgave each other,
every time we put our trust in you,
your Son, Jesus Christ, was present among us.
We have grown in our love for you
and in our desire to walk in your ways.
May we never forget all you have done for us.
We ask this through the same Christ, our Lord.

**ALL: Amen.**

**THIRD LEADER:** *Psalm 145:2–7*

Please repeat the Psalm response:
Every day I will bless you.

**ALL: Every day I will bless you.**

**THIRD LEADER:**

Great is the LORD, and greatly to be praised;
 his greatness is unsearchable.

**ALL: Every day I will bless you.**

**THIRD LEADER:**

One generation shall laud your works
  to another
 and shall declare your mighty acts.
On the glorious splendor of your majesty,
 and on your wondrous works,
  I will meditate.

**ALL: Every day I will bless you.**

**THIRD LEADER:**

The might of your awesome deeds shall
  be proclaimed,
 and I will declare your greatness.
They shall celebrate the fame of your
  abundant goodness
 and shall sing aloud of your righteousness.

**ALL: Every day I will bless you.**

◆ All stand and sing **Alleluia**.

*continued on next page*

# LAST DAY OF SCHOOL
## CONTINUED

**FOURTH LEADER:**                      Matthew 28:16–20
A reading from the holy Gospel according to Matthew

◆ Read the passage from the Bible.

The Gospel of the Lord.

◆ All sit and observe silence.

**FIFTH LEADER:**
Let us bring our hopes and needs to God as we pray, "Lord, hear our prayer."

In thanksgiving for our administrators, teachers, and school staff, and for all the large and small sacrifices they make out of love for us, we pray to the Lord.

That the gifts of this school year, like seeds planted in our hearts, will continue to grow, we pray to the Lord.

That all our difficulties will only serve to strengthen us in the knowledge of Christ's love and make us more compassionate toward others, we pray to the Lord.

That all the sick and suffering of our community can find healing and peace in our attention and care, we pray to the Lord.

**SIXTH LEADER:**
Lord Jesus Christ,
we have spent this year listening closely to
    your words
and to the words of your prophets and saints.
May your law of love sink into us and rule us
so that in joy we will give our thankful hearts
    to you completely.
Grant this through Jesus Christ our Lord.

**ALL:** Amen.

**SIXTH LEADER:**
Let us offer to one another a sign of
Christ's peace:

◆ All offer one another a sign of peace

**SEVENTH LEADER:**
Let us pray,
Lord God and Father Almighty,
    you know everything
and you know that we love you!
We will follow you in the quiet of our hearts
and in our love for one another.
You have promised to be with us always:
We count on your words
and bless you forever for your beautiful
    promises.
May we carry the love we've experienced
    this year
out into the world this summer and always.
We ask this through your Son, Jesus Christ
    our Lord.

**ALL:** Amen.

✚ All make the Sign of the Cross.

# PSALMS

## PSALM 23

*This psalm is appropriate during all liturgical seasons. It may be prayed in times of difficulty or stress, when comfort is needed, or to meditate on Christ's presence in the Sacraments.*

The LORD is my shepherd, I shall not want.
    He makes me lie down in green pastures;
he leads me beside still waters;
    he restores my soul.
He leads me in right paths
    for his name's sake.

Even though I walk through the darkest valley,
    I fear no evil;
for you are with me;
    your rod and your staff—
    they comfort me.

You prepare a table before me
    in the presence of my enemies;
you anoint my head with oil;
    my cup overflows.
Surely goodness and mercy shall follow me
    all the days of my life,
and I shall dwell in the house of the LORD
    my whole life long.

# PSALMS

## PSALM 27

Psalm 27:1, 4–5, 7–9, 13–14

*Use this psalm during times of darkness, anxiety, or uncertainty. This psalm is also an affirmation of God's goodness at any moment in life.*

The Lord is my light and my salvation;
   whom shall I fear?
The Lord is the stronghold of my life;
   of whom shall I be afraid?

One thing I asked of the Lord,
   that will I seek after:
to live in the house of the Lord
   all the days of my life,
to behold the beauty of the Lord,
   and to inquire in his temple.

For he will hide me in his shelter
   in the day of trouble;
he will conceal me under the cover of his tent;
   he will set me high on a rock.

Hear, O Lord, when I cry aloud,
   be gracious to me and answer me!
"Come," my heart says, "seek his face!"
   Your face, Lord do I seek.
   Do not hide your face from me.

I believe that I shall see the goodness of the Lord
   in the land of the living.
Wait for the Lord;
   be strong, and let your heart take courage;
   wait for the Lord!

# PSALM 51

Psalm 51:1–2, 6, 10, 12, 15

*This is a penitential psalm that is especially appropriate during a communal celebration of the sacrament of Reconciliation. It can also be incorporated into any Lenten prayer service.*

Have mercy on me, O God,
    according to your steadfast love;
according to your abundant mercy
    blot out my transgressions.
Wash me thoroughly from my iniquity,
    and cleanse me from my sin.

You desire truth in the inward being;
    therefore teach me wisdom in my secret heart.

Create in me a clean heart, O God,
    and put a new and right spirit within me.
Restore to me the joy of your salvation,
    and sustain in me a willing spirit.

O Lord, open my lips,
    and my mouth will declare your praise.

# PSALMS

## PSALM 103

Psalm 103:1–5, 19–22

*This is a deeply meditative psalm of grateful acknowledgment of God's gifts and mercy.*

Bless the L<small>ORD</small>, O my soul,
    and all that is within me,
    bless his holy name.
Bless the L<small>ORD</small>, O my soul,
    and do not forget all his benefits—
who forgives all your iniquity,
    who heals all your diseases,
who redeems your life from the Pit,
    who crowns you with steadfast love and mercy,
who satisfies you with good as long as you live
    so that your youth is renewed like the eagle's.

The L<small>ORD</small> has established his throne in the heavens,
    and his kingdom rules over all.
Bless the L<small>ORD</small>, O you his angels,
    you mighty ones who do his bidding,
    obedient to his spoken word.
Bless the L<small>ORD</small>, all his works,
    in all places of his dominion.
Bless the L<small>ORD</small>, O my soul.

# PSALM 139

Psalm 139:1–6, 13–16

*This psalm expresses the wonder and awe of our mysterious relationship to the God who knows us intimately and loves us completely.*

O Lord, you have searched me and known me.
You know when I sit down and when I rise up;
  you discern my thoughts from far away.
You search out my path and my lying down,
  and are acquainted with all my ways.
Even before a word is on my tongue,
  O Lord, you know it completely.
You hem me in, behind and before,
  and lay your hand upon me.
Such knowledge is too wonderful for me;
  it is so high that I cannot attain it.

For it was you who formed my inward parts;
  you knit me together in my mother's womb.
I praise you, for I am fearfully and wonderfully made.
  Wonderful are your works;
that I know very well.
  My frame was not hidden from you,
when I was being made in secret,
  intricately woven in the depths of the earth.
Your eyes beheld my unformed substance.
In your book were written
all the days that were formed for me,
  when none of them as yet existed.

PSALMS

# CANTICLES

## THE MAGNIFICAT OF MARY
Luke 1:46–55

*Mary prayed with these words when she visited her relative, Elizabeth, after Elizabeth declared, "Blessed are you among women and blessed is the fruit of your womb!" For centuries, this beautiful song of praise and trust has been the Church's evening prayer.*

And Mary said,
"My soul magnifies the Lord,
    and my spirit rejoices in God my savior,
for he has looked with favor on the lowliness of his servant.
    Surely, from now on all generations will call me blessed;
for the Mighty One has done great things for me,
    and holy is his name.
His mercy is for those who fear him
    from generation to generation.
He has shown strength with his arm;
    he has scattered the proud in the thoughts of their hearts.
He has brought down the powerful from their thrones,
    and lifted up the lowly;
he has filled the hungry with good things,
    and sent the rich away empty.
He has helped his servant Israel,
    in remembrance of his mercy,
according to the promise he made to our ancestors,
    to Abraham and to his descendants forever."

# CANTICLES

## THE BENEDICTUS OF ZECHARIAH  Luke 1:68–79

*Zechariah had been struck mute during the pregnancy of his wife, Elizabeth. After their baby was born, on the day when they gave him his name, Zechariah's voice was restored and he spoke these prophetic words over his child, John the Baptist. His prophecy is part of the Church's traditional morning prayer.*

"Blessed be the Lord God of Israel,
    for he has looked favorably on his people and redeemed them.
He has raised up a mighty savior for us
    in the house of his servant David,
as he spoke through the mouth of his holy prophets from of old,
    that we would be saved from our enemies and from the hand
        of all who hate us.
Thus he has shown the mercy promised to our ancestors,
    and has remembered his holy covenant,
the oath that he swore to our ancestor Abraham,
    to grant us that we, being rescued from the hands
        of our enemies,
might serve him without fear, in holiness and righteousness,
    before him all our days.
And you, child, will be called the prophet of the Most High;
    for you will go before the Lord to prepare his ways,
to give knowledge of salvation to his people
    by the forgiveness of their sins.
By the tender mercy of our God,
    the dawn from on high will break upon us,
to give light to those who sit in darkness and in the shadow
        of death,
    to guide our feet into the way of peace."

# BLESSING
## FOR BIRTHDAYS

✢ All make the Sign of the Cross.

**ALL:** In the name of the Father and of the Son and of the Holy Spirit. Amen.

**LEADER:**
Loving God,
you created all the people of the world,
and you know each of us by name.
We thank you for N.,
who today celebrates his/her birthday.
Bless him/her with your love and friendship
that he/she may grow in wisdom,
knowledge, and grace.
May he/she love his/her family always
and be faithful to his/her friends.
Grant this through Christ our Lord.

**ALL: Amen.**

**LEADER:**
Let us bow our heads and pray for N.

◆ All observe silence.

**LEADER:**
May God, in whose presence our ancestors walked, bless you.

**ALL: Amen.**

**LEADER:**
May God, who has been your shepherd from birth until now, keep you.

**ALL: Amen.**

**LEADER:**
May God, who saves you from all harm, give you peace.

**ALL: Amen.**

✢ All make the Sign of the Cross.

**In the name of the Father and of the Son and of the Holy Spirit. Amen.**